SOCIAL DIMENSIONS
OF SOVIET
INDUSTRIALIZATION

SOCIAL DIMENSIONS OF SOVIET INDUSTRIALIZATION

EDITED BY

WILLIAM G. ROSENBERG

AND

LEWIS H. SIEGELBAUM

INDIANA UNIVERSITY PRESS
Bloomington and Indianapolis

Publication of this book was assisted by a grant from the Joint Committee on Soviet Studies of the American Council of Learned Societies and the Social Science Research Council.

The paper used in this publication meets the minimum requirements of American National Standard for Information Sciences—Permanence of Paper for Printed Library Materials, ANSI Z39.48=1984.

Manufactured in the United States of America

Library of Congress Cataloging-in-Publication Data

Social dimensions of Soviet industrialization / edited by William G. Rosenberg and Lewis H. Siegelbaum.
    p. cm. — (Indiana-Michigan series in Russian and Eastern European studies)
Includes bibliographical references and index.
ISBN 0-253-34993-1 (cloth). — ISBN 0-253-20772-X (paper)
    1. Soviet Union—Industries—History. 2. Soviet Union—Economic policy—1928–1932. I. Rosenberg, William G. II. Siegelbaum, Lewis H. III. Series.
HC335.3.S63   1993
338.0947—dc20   92-19627

1 2 3 4 5 97 96 95 94 93

For Kendall E. Bailes
Admired Scholar, Courageous Friend

CONTENTS

INTRODUCTION

William G. Rosenberg and Lewis H. Siegelbaum

In April 1988 the fifth and final seminar in the series sponsored by the Social Science Research Council (SSRC) on Twentieth-Century Russian and Soviet Social History was held at the University of Michigan in Ann Arbor. Conceived and organized by Moshe Lewin in the late 1970s to stimulate new and systematic inquiry into unexplored or understudied aspects of Soviet social history, the seminars brought together small groups of scholars for two or three days of freewheeling discussion and analysis. Papers presented at these sessions largely reflected work in progress. Emphasis was on exploration rather than polished argument, and on working through new conceptualizations (or reworking old ones) that might assist in the development of new research. In this the seminars attempted to create a forum quite different from the usual scholarly conference. A number of valuable papers and communications were offered essentially for purposes of discussion, without much thought of subsequent publication; others were presented with obvious and deliberate gaps in the expectation that the seminar itself might facilitate their eventual closure.

Initially, there was little thought that the seminars would result in published books. The aim instead was to minimize inhibitions and encourage new thinking. However, the excitement generated at the sessions and the participants' belief that the research and ideas presented there were of value to scholars and students in the field led to a decision to rework the conference contributions for publication. Two volumes growing out of the seminars on the Civil War and New Economic Policy (NEP) have been well received: *Party, State, and Society in the Russian Civil War: Explorations in Social History,* edited by Diane P. Koenker, William G. Rosenberg, and Ronald Grigor Suny (Bloomington, 1989), and *Russia in the Era of NEP: Explorations in Soviet Society and Culture,* edited by Sheila Fitzpatrick, Alexander Rabinowitch, and Richard Stites (Bloomington, 1991).

The 1988 seminar on social dimensions of Soviet industrialization was largely organized by Kendall Bailes, whose tragic and untimely death occurred less than a month before the seminar convened. Despite his illness, Ken had hoped to serve as moderator. As with his own work on technology and society under Lenin and Stalin and particularly his study of science and Russian culture, Ken took a broad view of "social process" as it related to industrialization. He helped structure the seminar to bring into relief the variegated dimensions of what he rightly thought was a far more complex phenomenon than has generally been assumed. The concept of "industrialization" itself, in fact, proved to be much less tidy a focus for discussion than the Civil War or NEP. A good deal of effort was expended simply on the problem of conceptual coherence, and not everyone at the sessions went away convinced that much progress had been made.[1] Nonetheless, just as with earlier seminars, it was clear that a book developed from conference contributions could serve well in advancing the seminar's basic goals, particularly since the overall conclusion of the seminar raised an important challenge to conventional wisdom and especially to interpretations of this period now popular in Russia. The generous help of the SSRC made it possible for us to publish the present volume.

The essays presented here essentially touch on four general themes: the nature and role of social mobility in its various dimensions during the 1930s; the evolving relationships between "new" and "old" workers and related changes in worker "identity"; the management of industrialization, both in the broad (central) and narrow (shop-floor) sense; and the deeper (in the sense of structurally embedded) question of culture and its impact on the course of events. It should be emphasized that the essays do not discuss in any sustained way the economic dimensions of Soviet industrialization, which are amply treated in the literature. (See Guide to Further Reading at the end of the volume.) Nor is specific attention paid to politics or the purges as phenomena independent of the industrialization process. Here, too, we believe the literature is ample to provide most readers with the necessary background. Our emphasis instead is on the themes of mobility, social identity, management, and culture as aspects of the social dimensions of Soviet industrialization that are only now beginning to be systematically explored. Together, however, they implicitly raise the central (and currently vital) question of exactly what constituted the "administrative-command" basis of the Soviet industrial system as a whole, and whether, in fact, the administrative command conception itself accurately represents the process of Soviet industrialization, matters to which we shall return.

Sheila Fitzpatrick's important analysis of the nature of peasant migration during this period, for example, shows clearly the contradictory tensions this mobility involved and suggests it had much to do with the institutionalization of lasting urban-rural conflict, a core element of the Soviet industrialization process that continues to cause problems to this day. At a time of "forced draft" development in both agriculture and industry—which, given inadequate technology, was necessarily translated into the intensification of labor—it was clearly not in the interests of those responsible for collectivizing agriculture to facilitate unequivocally the out-migration of able workers. Yet such workers were precisely those most in demand by industry. Collectivization itself, moreover, involved both the forced recruitment into and the forced expulsion from newly organized state and collective farms. Industry, both in familiar and established urban centers and in the remote areas of gigantic new construction such as Magnitogorsk, reflected both an "upward" opportunity for some and desolation for others, especially the three out of every ten peasants whom Fitzpatrick estimates entered the wage labor force involuntarily between 1928 and 1932 in connection with "dekulakization."

The implications of this combination of rural workers both "pulled" by the relative attractions of industry and "pushed" in horribly repressive ways out of the patrimonial villages, as well as its effect on the tasks of recruitment *into* the rural labor force, were at a minimum horrendously destabilizing to both industrial and agrarian production. Fitzpatrick argues convincingly that the great majority of entrants into industry in this period bore some degree of grievance and that hundreds of thousands of former kulaks working in industry were, in fact, deeply embittered and hostile to the regime. Stephan Merl shows additionally that thousands of "upwardly mobile" tractor drivers and mechanics who voluntarily left the countryside failed to pass muster in industrial enterprises for one reason or another and soon brought their disappointment back to the village. In addition to creating on one hand what might be thought of as an oppositional "fifth column" at the very core of the industrialization effort, therefore, these migration patterns clearly created on the other a comparably alienated core of rural workers, many of whom, as Merl shows, subsequently "advanced" themselves further by rising in the ranks of collective and state farm administration.

Although our understanding of the psychological and social consequences of this extraordinary dispersal still lacks regional and chronological specificity, it is certainly sufficient to emphasize not only the centrality of social process to Soviet industrialization but also the very uniqueness of the Soviet experience as a whole. As Robert Johnson pointed out at the seminar, what occurred was not the *otkhodnichestvo* (out-migration) common elsewhere but *vykhodnichestvo* (an exodus), *zakhodnichestvo* (the coming to a new place), *perekhodnichestvo* (a resettlement), and especially *razkhodnichestvo*, a dispersion, the prefix in each case carrying with it additional nuances suggesting phenomena which were at once very powerful and uncertain. What is striking here is that the term *industrialization* itself usually connotes something very different. In addition to the teleology of *modernization*, which serves, as we know, to rationalize a variety of deprivations associated with industrial development everywhere, *industrialization* also implies fundamental similarities between societies in its throes. Additionally, it usually connotes equally fundamental elements of social integration rather than fracturing, with the corresponding creation of broad-based collective social identities.

Yet so great was the degree of social dislocation associated with Soviet industrialization and so mind-boggling the sought-after rate of growth that, as Reginald Zelnik argued in his commentary at the seminar, Stalin and others managed to create an industrial order that made even conditions at the turn of the century attractive by comparison. At least then, in Russia as elsewhere, the village could if necessary provide for a large portion of the work force some modicum of respite against the perduring offenses of factory life. Family ties persisted with those left behind, as did the corresponding emotional bonds and the opportunities, especially at harvest time, to come "home." In contrast, Soviet industrialization in the 1930s joined emotional desolation to an unprecedented level of physical destitution, wrought almost entirely by the regime's failure to anticipate the material consequences of explosive population growth in industrial areas and its abject refusal to divert investment resources to human welfare needs. In his important contribution to the seminar, John Barber suggested in some detail how overcrowding and inadequate nutrition probably produced serious epidemics of contagious diseases during these years and how migrants themselves probably carried diseases endemic in rural areas with them to the new industrial construction sites. Thus the "peasantization" of Soviet industry, as it has sometimes been labeled, was by no means a process whereby rural Russians (and others) were simply "integrated" into industrial life or even industrial environments.

But as Barber further pointed out during our discussions, neither can it adequately be described, as Soviet historians have been inclined to do, as a process of "dilution." This notion makes sense only if one accepts the parallel idea that there was a broad-based "proletarian" social identity in the 1930s that could, in fact, be diluted, a matter Barber and others believed was open to question. It may well have been the case that the pervasive mobility accompanying Soviet industrialization drastically undermined the meaning of established social categories. Collectivization and especially the horrors of dekulakization almost certainly reconstructed the social and cultural meanings of *peasant* as they reconstituted social, cultural, and political relations in the village, even if the full extent of this process, and especially the question of what ultimately remained of traditional peasant society and culture, remains unclear.[2] That mobility and consequent changes in social status were quite rarely associated with material betterment for those entering the industrial work force, as Merl and Fitzpatrick both indicate, suggests industrialization could not readily be perceived by the overwhelming majority of the population as associated with personal (as opposed to societal) "advancement," one of its principal ideological rationalizations in the West. Indeed, for many, "better" positions were soon defined as those with less rather than more responsibility and a greater feeling of personal security. Even within the industrial labor force, as Stephen Kotkin illustrates so well in his essay on Magnitogorsk, repression created a deep and dysfunctional disorder. In a society whose populace was now in nearly constant motion, "moving on" for many was a relatively easy way of escaping a variety of problems, especially if one's talents were in demand and one moved quickly enough.

There is substantial evidence that Soviet industrialization did indeed create something resembling a new working class, or at least a category of industrial wage earners with social and cultural attributes quite different from their predecessors. New workers entering the industrial labor force from the countryside brought much of the village with them. Drinking patterns, a renewed emphasis on kinship relations, patriarchal attitudes on the part of men toward women and the complex mix of submissiveness and domination of women toward men, even aspects of peasant religiosity—all undoubtedly found their way into the social relations and culture of the new industrial work force, even if, again, much additional research is needed before we understand the full dimensions of this process. In contrast to the prerevolutionary period in Russia, moreover, the 1930s may also have altered profoundly the traditional relationship between industrial labor and family life, although this, too, is an issue that remains to be explored. A characteristic feature of the social mobility accompanying late imperial Russian industrialization, at least, was that men moved from the village into a largely male industrial community and women stayed behind. In the 1930s, industrial construction sites and the burgeoning labor camps were flooded with deported families, all of whose members were soon necessarily involved in strife-riven processes of assimilation.

In this social maelstrom, better paid and more highly skilled "hereditary proletarians"—long idealized in party ideology—themselves often became isolated or estranged because of cultural differences and were frequently assaulted for their very ability to follow routines or meet production norms that others could not. Mechanization, as Hiroaki Kuromiya shows in his study of the Donbass miners, hardly meant an increase in output when those assigned to the machines had little training in their use and even less incentive to use them efficiently. Since "class" is essentially a relational identity and since it became increasingly unclear in the course of Soviet industrialization against whom or in relation to which other social groups "workers" could now be defined, the very nature of proletarian identity necessarily began to shift. The culture of the industrial workplace itself almost certainly superseded traditional patterns of labor-management struggle as determinants of identity (although this question, too, needs further study), and since the interactions which took place here were often highly collusive and designed to thwart rather than to advance productionist goals, workers in the 1930s undoubtedly acquired attitudes and behaviors deeply resistant to the "socialist workers' state" they were also struggling to create.

In these circumstances, the regime's perceptions of its work force, as Diane Koenker suggested at the seminar, also had to change. What had been its strongest social base of support—and indeed, a "class" whose enlistment in the offensive against the countryside had been thought to be crucial to the success of the whole industrialization project—now became a highly variegated and politically uncertain social formation. Here one might find at least part of the explanation for Stalin's deliberate efforts beginning in 1932 to create a particular "socialist" rather than "proletarian" identity for Soviet workers, an effort which was logically accompanied by stronger and more pervasive means of repression; here too the source of transformations in the criminal justice system, as Peter Solomon, Jr., discusses in his essay, and one of the reasons for the superficially quite different but fundamentally related phenomenon of Stakhanovism.

All of this, of course, affected the management of industrialization both on the shop floor and at the commanding heights, and raised issues that have presented a particularly fascinating challenge to the class analysis of industrial societies. The burgeoning of managerial personnel and the expansion of other technical and administrative occupations in the course of industrialization in both capitalist and state socialist societies have engendered frequent, sometimes radical, revisions in particular of classical Marxist assumptions about the increasingly polarized character of class relations in the former and their eventual supersession in the latter.[3] And the essays by Don K. Rowney, R. W. Davies, and David Shearer, as well as, in more focused ways, those of Lewis H. Siegelbaum, Kuromiya, and Solomon, treat this and related questions in a variety of contexts.

Rowney's survey of the institutional continuities between the tsarist and Soviet regimes and his cross-national comparisons of the social and educational backgrounds of managerial personnel are particularly valuable for establishing relative frameworks for analysis and evaluation. His paper at the seminar was nicely complemented by a valuable brief communication from William Chase and J. Arch Getty, which drew from the Soviet Data Bank at the University of Pittsburgh to show the emergence of some consistency in Soviet management personnel patterns after the cataclysmic upheavals of the early thirties, when more than 80 percent of those in major economic organizations had worked in their posts for two years or less.[4] Davies' essay interweaves recently published memoirs and fictional accounts drawn from real-life models with his own vast knowledge of Soviet economic history to show the very real limits to our understanding of management as "command." Kuromiya and Solomon add greatly to our understanding of what "management" actually meant with the onset of the industrialization drive by showing respectively the ambiguities and dangers of managers' positions in the volatile coal-mining sector and the use by managers and other administrators of a criminal justice system largely reoriented to "industrial" crimes. Comparative perspectives are also suggested—with other branches of Soviet industry in the case of Kuromiya's contribution, with the prosecution of agricultural crimes in the USSR and the British government's use of criminal sanctions in Solomon's. In a related contribution, Shearer looks closely at the structure of both work and management in Soviet machine-building plants and suggests that what emerged there during industrialization was a curious blend of modern technologies and more traditional methods, a "gigantic small shop," to use the characterization of German observers. And Siegelbaum's treatment of foremen shows the very ambiguity of management, especially its tensions, at the level of the "men in the middle," at once the leadership of the work force and the agents of those above.

In treating these "managerial" issues, too, the seminar raised important questions for further research. The use of quote marks around managerial, for one, reflects a judgment that the very conception of industrial management in the Soviet 1930s deserves additional work. It is clearly the case, as Berliner and Granick suggested many years ago, that we must continue to go beyond the prescriptive statements of leading party officials and legal definitions of responsibility to examine the concrete experiences of managers as they confronted tasks for which few had adequate training. It is not that such statements and laws were irrelevant, for correctly anticipating and interpreting signals from the top was vital to the success and indeed the survival of plant administrators. But because managers and foremen were everywhere and always subject to a variety of intense pressures in the 1930s, not only from above but from below as well, they were compelled to resort to practices that bore little relation to their prescribed authority. In this sense, managing meant at least two things: directing and controlling labor, monetary, physical, and organizational assets and coping with often sudden and unpredictable interventions, most commonly from political authorities. It would be interesting to try to determine, in fact, which set of pressures and interventions—those from above or below—had the strongest effect in shaping the patterns of industrial work in the 1930s and how they might have varied geographically and by industrial branch. Certainly as the Stalinist system is currently being disassembled, the related question of where leverage might best be applied toward this end depends to some extent on the nature of its origins.

It is also clear from the essays collected here, however, that no one system of management or administration prevailed during the industrialization drive. Rather, there was a succession of models, some influenced by Western technocratic thinking, others more beholden to tsarist antecedents, and still others deriving from mass participatory practices pioneered by the Bolsheviks during the early years of the regime and rekindled as the First Five-Year Plan got under way. The rise and fall of such models suggests not only the continual search among political authorities (Stalin certainly included) for a fomula conducive to the fulfillment of their objectives but also that management itself was too important simply to be left in the hands of the managers.

One hopes for additional research, consequently, that might reveal whether managers in the coal-mining industry, for example, might have suffered disproportionately during the Great Purge in 1936–38 compared with those in other industries because of the particular form and nature of labor-management relations.[5] Examining this question might go a long way toward evaluating the broader issue of worker-management tensions generally in that cataclysmic process. Similarly, it would be interesting to know whether the proliferation of ministries after World War II was essentially an extension of a process begun in 1932 with the breakup of the Supreme Economic Council (VSNKh) and continued with the division of the Commissariat of Heavy Industry five years later. What was behind this process? Was it a matter of administrative convenience (efficiency?) or was its essence political? In the light of previous and subsequent experience, it might also be asked whether Stalin's practice of intervening in deliberations among leading designers and senior industrial officials was a function of his hubris or stemmed from imperatives of the system. Finally there is the issue of the developing culture of the *nachal'stvo* itself: the expanding and increasingly powerful coterie of bosses. We know a great deal about the relationship between education and social mobility in the 1920s and early 1930s from the work of Fitzpatrick and about the upward mobility of workers in the late 1930s from Siegelbaum's book on Stakhanovism.[6] We need now a more comprehensive picture of how the changing social composition and circumstances of increasingly collusive industrial managers and party elites may have contributed to redefining not only the ways political power was exercised in relation to industrialization but also the places and forms in which power in the Stalinist system was most effectively realized. Certainly it is most interesting that the explanatory or symbolic function of criminal prosecutions had an importance equal to that of deterrence (Solomon), that the campaign against absenteeism died a quiet death in 1933 (Siegelbaum), and that the coal-mining industry became a hotbed of political violence which came to characterize the essence of Stalin's industrialization drive there (Kuromiya). In what ways, then, was the industrial system of the 1930s actually a keystone of Stalinist politics? And how did it impose its own limits there, as elsewhere, on what is thought of as totalitarian control?

This latter question might be said in the broadest sense to touch the political culture of Soviet industrialization, the last general theme of the seminar and one that was taken up by a number of participants, including Katerina Clark, Geoff Eley, an Moshe Lewin, whose essays round out this volume. Clark shows us how important the past became for writers during the early 1930s, something she labels "retrospectivist obsessions," not so much as part of the regime's need to establish legitimizing myths in these turbulent years as a response to the dehumanizing dislocations of industrial "modernization." Industrialization, she suggests, may well have served culturally as an "overarching metaphor for a historical event much broader in its implications than the introduction of modern machinery or the construction of giant hydroelectric plants, important as such activities indubitably were." Eley emphasized during the seminar how the "event" of industrialization itself should encourage Soviet historians to consider a more deinstitutionalized conception of politics than has been the rule and to explore much more carefully how the state, as a specifically constituted set of relations, was actually part of society, themes he also takes up in his essay. Much more attention needs to be paid to questions of gender and language—two aspects of Western European historical analysis without apparent impact, in Eley's view, on our understanding of the Soviet experience—and to the feature of "compression," which uniquely distinguishes Soviet industrialization from comparable processes elsewhere and necessarily affected Soviet political culture in ways that could not have been anticipated nor readily comprehended.

Again, the seminar did not reach for closure on these complex matters. The essays included in this volume, like the discussion itself, largely point in new research directions rather than offering new syntheses. Yet as Lewin implies with characteristic insight in the concluding contribution, one reason why synthesis has tended to elude us has to do with the very chaos of Soviet industrialization as a whole—a chaos belied by the metaphors of planning and a discourse of order, camouflaged by the misleading regularity of statistics, and obscured by Western conceptions of "totalitarian" control (now pervasively employed by Soviet scholars) which leave precious little room for the role of autonomous or irregular behavior. Like other approaches to historical understanding, those which emphasize social process have their limits. But one undeniable merit of the efforts reflected in this volume is their exposure of the ways in which even a limited understanding of the multiple social contexts in which Soviet industrialization occurred encourages a reconsideration of its overall systemic coherence, and hence the coherence of Stalinism itself. As Lewin suggested at the seminar, we might begin to think of a "system of incoherencies" rather than one of order and control, containing within it a series of incompatible logics. The shop and workplace clearly had its own ways of absorbing the contradictory pressures of industrialization. So did groups of managers and other administrators and officials, the enterprise as a whole, the ministries, even the state, which spoke in Stalin's voice. Each of these collectivities and each of the arterial social processes that kept them functioning may have operated according to some set of internal regularities. But nothing intrinsic or essential to "industrialization" necessarily forced these patterns to mesh together into anything resembling an orderly or logical pattern. The more powerful these internal contradictions, in fact, the more pressing may have been the need for those ostensibly in charge to create a discourse of order and control.

This does not mean, of course, that Soviet industrialization was not also state guided in essential and significant ways or, as Lewin again suggested, "state administered," drawing an important distinction between the politics of directing industrialization and administering a set of contradictory processes that the industrialization drive had set in motion. Yet the essays here suggest that the processes of guiding or administering had little in common with the usual connotations of "plan," even if the actual plans on which industrialization came to be framed still had both symbolic and actual importance. As Daniel Orlovsky pointed out to us, "implicit in the idea of this 'planned' economy was most certainly its exact opposite, the un-dreamed-of social problems and dynamics that acted as both cause and effect."

In this sense, one might conceive of Soviet industrialization in the way many of its leading protagonists did—as a gigantic military operation whose very ambitiousness and scale inevitably involved a great deal of pushing and shoving and tactical maneuvering on the ground. The great irony here is that the ostensible enemy, "backwardness," came to constitute the very means by which it supposedly was overcome. By 1941 there was a lot more industry in the Soviet Union and something in the way of a system of resource allocation, production, and distribution. But both the pushing and shoving and the tactical maneuvering which had gotten the country to that point and would see it through the Nazi onslaught became enmeshed in the "system."

The planners themselves, meanwhile, including the Great Planner, di-rectly commanded the heights, but the "administrative command system" we now trace to their efforts may have been as much a product of their failure at control as it was of their attempts to invoke it. This in turn may help explain why it is proving so difficult to reform.

These and other analytical issues, in any event, remain to be worked through. In the meantime, we are pleased this volume can extend the contentions and some of the conversations of the seminar to a broader audience.

NOTES

1. In addition to the contributors to this volume, participants included Reginald Zelnik, John Barber, William Chase, Laura Engelstein, Robert Johnson, Blair Ruble, Heather Hogan, Diane Koenker, Roberta Manning, Lynne Viola, Michael Gelb, Neil Weissman, Susan Solomon, Leopold Haimson, Jutta Scherrer, Miriam Desert, Patrick Dale, Daniel Orlovsky, and William McCagg.

2. An interesting intervention at the seminar by Lynne Viola suggested impor-tant residual characteristics of peasant culture and social relations in the aftermath of collectivization, an argument she has also made with exceptional skill in her recent published work. See esp. "Bab'i Bunty and Peasant Women's Protest during Collectivization," *Russian Review*, 1986, no. 1, pp. 28–31, and "The Peasant Night-mare: Visions of Apocalypse in the Soviet Countryside," *Journal of Modern History*, 1990, no. 4, pp. 747–70.

3. In the forefront of such revisions have been sociologists working within either the Marxist or the Weberian tradition, and occasionally both, whose conceptual and theoretical innovations have greatly enriched our understanding of the critical role played by management in widely differing political and economic systems. Among the most influential have been Ralf Dahrendorf, *Class and Class Conflict in Industrial Society* (Stanford, 1959); Reinhard Bendix, *Work and Authority in Industry: Ideologies of Management in the Course of Industrailization* (New York, 1963); John K. Galbraith, *The New Industrial State*, 2d ed. (Harmondsworth, 1972); Anthony Giddens, *The*

Class Structure of Advanced Societies (New York, 1973); and Erik Olin Wright, *Classes* (London, 1985).

4. William Chase and J. Arch Getty, "Industrial and Economic Personnel in the 1930s: A Communication."

5. On the repression of coal industry officials, see Hiroaki Kuromiya, "Stalinist Terror in the Donbass: A Note," *Slavic Review*, 1991, no. 1, pp. 157–62.

6. See Sheila Fitzpatrick, *Education and Social Mobility in the Soviet Union, 1921–34* (Cambridge, 1979), and Lewis H. Siegelbaum, *Stakhanovism and the Politics of Productivity in the USSR, 1935–1941* (Cambridge, 1988), esp. pp. 247–77.

SOCIAL DIMENSIONS
OF SOVIET
INDUSTRIALIZATION

I

CONCEPTUALIZING THE COMMAND ECONOMY

WESTERN HISTORIANS ON SOVIET INDUSTRIALIZATION

Lewis H. Siegelbaum and Ronald G. Suny

Like other aspects of Stalinism, Soviet industrialization has seldom been viewed neutrally; rather, it has been treated normatively either as a superior form of transition from agrarian to industrial society or as a disastrous and misguided alternative to the proven path of "free enterprise." In the West various theoretical conceptualizations have replaced or overlapped one another as popular and political attitudes toward the USSR shifted. Until recently, Soviet commentators viewed the industrial revolution carried out by the Stalinist party state as an enormous achievement *(dostizhenie)*, essential to both the economic and the social modernization of the USSR and indispensable for its survival in face of aggressive enemies to the west and east. Such a perspective was offered by Mikhail Gorbachev in his speech on Soviet history on the eve of the seventieth anniversary of the October Revolution, when he referred to the Stalinist policy of industrialization—rapid, forced, and disproportionately investing in heavy industry—as "the only possible path in those conditions, even though it was inconceivably difficult for the country and the people." "In those conditions," he went on, "when the feeling of the threat of imperialist aggression was growing rapidly, the party strengthened its conviction that it was necessary not just to cover but to literally race across, in the shortest possible historical span, the distance from the sledgehammer and the peasant's wooden plow to developed industry, without which the entire cause of the Revolution would have inevitably perished."[1] Not only was industrialization necessary for self-defense but, in the view of Marxist-Leninists, a socialist society was impossible to achieve except on the basis of industrialization. Since both ideology and reality compelled the choice for industrialism, the only legitimate grounds for debate concerned the form in which it was carried out—through the direction of what is now being referred to as the administrative-command system.

Non-Soviet Marxists, from the Mensheviks to Herbert Marcuse, have elaborated alternative analyses that, while accepting the need for industrialization, have highlighted the antagonistic relationship between the directors of the industrialization process and the primary producers. Much of the appeal of the literature inspired by Trotsky came from its identification of an alien stratum (or class) of bureaucrats that exploited the Soviet workers. Here the essentially manipulative and exploitative nature of Stalinist industrialization has been challenged as excessively repressive, unnecessary, and fundamentally anti-Marxist. "In the USSR, in our view," wrote Bruno Rizzi in his particular formulation of the problem, "it is the bureaucrats who are the owners, for it is they who hold power in their hands. It is they who manage the economy, just as was normal with the bourgeoisie. It is they who take the profits, just as do all exploiting classes, who fix wages and prices. I repeat—it is the bureaucrats. The workers count for nothing in the governing of society."[2] The long and rich debates in the Mensheviks' emigré journal, Sotsialisticheskii vestnik, among various Trotskyist groups and between independent Marxists and their liberal and conservative critics were largely carried on without much basic empirical research on the Soviet economy and society, relying on deductions made from underlying theoretical and moral principles. But they were exceptionally influential on those leftist intellectuals who stood precariously between the confident vision of Communist parties and the pessimism of the totalitarian school.

For theorists of totalitarianism such as Carl J. Friedrich, Zbigniew K. Brzezinski, and W. W. Rostow, who saw political dominance of all spheres of life as the key to understanding Soviet society, the ruling elite was not only exploitative but also malevolently committed to the goal of total control of society. Whatever the specific social makeup of the regime or economic structure, industrialization was an important part of the expansionist state's relentless takeover of all autonomous space within society and the destruction of the individual. As Friedrich and Brzezinski wrote, "Soviet industrial expansion . . . destroys traditional bonds, creates a situation of great social mobility, and results in population shifts and the weakening of nationality lines."[3] Here the draconian labor legislation and the support of the principle of one-man management (edinonachalie), the state integration of the trade unions, and the breakup of autonomous forms of worker organization such as the artel (in which workers pooled resources and wages) were all part of a single unified drive to eliminate all aspects of social independence. Even the directors of industry were controlled by fear. "In its combination of autocratic control from above, party stimulation and police informers, acclamatory participation and popular ritual," Friedrich and Brzezinski stated, "the factory in a sense is a small-scale replica of the pattern of controls and of the hierarchy of decision making characteristic of the Soviet Union in general."[4] In Rostow's collectively drafted synthesis, *The Dynamics of Soviet Society* (1953), each economic decision was predicated on a careful calculation of how it would contribute to the expansion of the power of the dictator internally and of the USSR internationally: "What is distinctive about the Soviet regime [in contrast to such authoritarian regimes as Ataturk's Turkey] is the extreme priority it accords to the pursuit of the goal of its own power, as opposed to a national program reflecting the aspirations of its citizens."[5]

For the totalitarian school, now enjoying a revival among post-Soviet Russian intellectuals, state socialism was equivalent to fascism, and the different levels of economic development or the noncapitalist nature of one and the capitalist essence of the other were largely irrelevant, as were the questions of who ruled and who benefited that divided the Marxists. Rostow noted that "such questions as who holds formal title to property, how 'profits,' that is to say, rewards, are determined, and whether former owners and decision makers continue to hold positions, provided they conform to the regimes's commands, are of relatively minor significance. What is decisive is the overpowering reality of totalitarian central control by the dictator and his party."[6]

The long reign of the totalitarian model coincided with the years of the Cold War and its slow thaw, and its emphasis on the similarity between fascism and communism and the radical difference between capitalist democracies and totalitarianism was ideologically employed in the postwar reconstruction of alliances. The decades of coexistence and détente (1960s–70s), however, saw the rise of theories that emphasized the similarity in the overall patterns of development in both East and West. The modernization school and its first cousin, convergence theory, argued that objective determinants such as technology and expertise would lead the Soviet Union toward a future not unlike that of the United States. The optimism of this view was expressed by one of its foremost proponents, Clark Kerr: "The empire of industrialism will embrace the whole world; and such similarities as it decrees will penetrate the outermost points of its sphere of influence and its sphere comes to be universal."[7] Here technology and the commonality of industrial structures were as determinant as politics in the totalitarian model. Fruitfully, however, the move away from the abstractions of totalitarianism opened the way for important observation and empirical work.

A telling example of the work of the late 1950s–early 1960s was David Granick's study of Soviet managers.[8] In stark contrast to the politics-dominated totalitarian view, Granick wrote about a much more open system in which bargaining and negotiation took place. Interest-group conflicts exploded the monolithic exercise of power by a single authority from above. Rather than emphasizing the differences between East and West, Granick argued that under the skin American and Soviet managers were brothers.

When one thinks of the underlying constraints common to both the American and Russian industrial systems, it is not really so surprising to find
similarities between management practices and environments. In both
countries, a rapidly growing, modern industrial structure has been built.
Both nations have been dominated by frontier aspirations, with a worship of
size, speed, and material success. Both share the common traditions of a
European-dominated culture. . . . The list of fundamental differences between the American and Russian ways of life is a long one, . . . but there are
also similarities, and one finds them in particular when looking at the ways of
administration and business management.[9]

Granick concluded that the managers in Russian industry did not constitute a separate class but were closely allied to Communist Party officials,
and together they ran the USSR. "The Red Executive is very much an
independent business man," he claimed, and neither the organization man
nor the party boss was any longer revolutionary. The thrust of the argument is clearly détentist.

Instead of democracy or dictatorship by an autocratic party boss, the
ultimate fate of both East and West was likely to be technocracy, a sharing
of power between experts and politicians. Once again, as in totalitarianism,
the historical specifics of the Soviet experience were blurred for comparative purposes, and the role of ideology and culture largely eliminated.
Moreover, the overly optimistic notion that industrialism would more or
less inevitably and globally lead to greater equality and democracy was
belied by observable trends in many countries where dictatorship, repression, and industrial growth were found to cohabit comfortably. Both the
totalitarian model and the convergence model can be seen as conceptual
alternatives to Marxism (though, in Marcuse, totalitarianism, convergence,
and Marxism all happily coexisted). But all these theoretical schemes, as
suggestive as they are in many aspects, failed to explain the peculiarities
and anomalies of the Soviet industrial experience. They tended to rush
ahead into generalization and theory before the necessary digging into the
complexities and contradictions of Soviet actuality had been undertaken.

Yet all along economists, sociologists, journalists, some eyewitnesses, and
a few historians were supplementing the abstract and flat pictures of
theorists and distant analysts. At the time of the Stalinist industrialization
drive, for example, a few observers and participants reported to Western
readers on the chaos and enthusiasm that attended the First and Second
Five-Year Plans. The American engineer Walter Arnold Rukeyser and the
worker John Scott provided a texture and detail of the events that would
soon be lost in more general accounts.[10] In a series of books based on his
personal experiences and talks with Soviet citizens, the journalist Maurice
Hindus articulated in revealing detail the pain and achievement of the
Stalinist revolution.[11]

Until the late 1960s, however, no fundamental research in the field of
Soviet industrialization was carried out by professional historians—with the

notable exception of E. H. Carr. Written over a span of a quarter century and buttressed by a massive bibliographic apparatus (which, perforce, did not include Soviet archives), Carr's ten volumes were essentially an account in the grand narrative tradition of how the Communist Party transformed itself from a revolutionary movement to a complex administrative structure, simultaneously replacing its chiliastic ambitions for world revolution with a program of national industrial modernization. Since almost everything could be linked in one way or another to these processes, Carr left nothing out. He refracted Soviet economic development, however, through the deliberations, debates, and decrees of the central organs of the party and state. For this reason he referred in the penultimate volume to the spring of 1929 as "a terminal landmark for the historian of the Soviet Union." From that time on, he continued, "we know little of the discussions in the inner counsels of the party . . . or of the view taken by any leading Soviet politician other than Stalin. . . . Later, the fog becomes thicker still, and, in spite of a few piecemeal revelations, envelops all Soviet policy in the nineteen-thirties."[12]

Given his state-centered, policy-oriented approach and the limitations of his sources, Carr's cutoff in 1929 made sense. But in the past two decades, historians have ventured beyond the landmark of 1929, beginning with the work of R. W. Davies, Carr's collaborator in his last years. Professor of economic studies at the University of Birmingham, Davies more than anyone else put Soviet industrialization on the historical agenda. He has now completed three volumes of his own monumental project, *The Industrialization of Soviet Russia,* which take the story to the end of 1930.[13]

Davies revises a basic impression left by the Carr volumes. Whereas Carr's *History of Soviet Russia* concluded that the foundations of a planned economy had been laid by the end of the 1920s, Davies demonstrates how in the course of 1929–30 the acceleration of the pace of industrialization undermined those basic structures. Acceleration was a function of the "great leap forward" mentality of the political elite, which remained oblivious to objective constraints. "[A]stonishing expansion in industrial investment" was thus accompanied by severe disorder in the supply and planning system. Enthusiasm and achievement were paradoxically combined with "vicious repression and waste." Progress proceeded along with growing turmoil.

Davies shows that despite the crisis in the countryside connected with collectivization and peasant resistance, Soviet planners managed to expand enormously investment in industry. Huge construction projects—the Stalingrad tractor factory, the Rostov-on-Don agricultural machinery plant, the Turksib railroad—were brought to completion in the first years of the Five-Year Plan, while still others, such as the Dneprostroi hydroelectric plant, were well on their way. A start had been made, however hesitantly, toward the rearmament of the Soviet Union, and several campaigns to raise worker productivity had been launched. Yet real wages were falling for workers, and the economy was in serious trouble. Existing industrial capacity was fully employed, and the decline in agricultural output and the peasants' slaughter of livestock led to a general fall in the standard of living. The huge investments in producer-goods industries led to acute shortages of labor, capital, and material in other crucial sectors. Quantities did not meet expected targets, and quality was low. The fabled Stalingrad tractor factory rolled out its first tractor with much fanfare in June 1930, but instead of the projected 2,000 tractors expected by September a mere forty-three were produced. And these began to fall apart after seventy-two hours of operation!

Davies ranges across a vast canvas, discussing at one time the political infighting within the Stalinist faction about the tempo of industrialization, at another the intricacies of financing and budgeting in a system that was abolishing the market and questioning the future use of money. He underscores the fantasies and willfulness of the Stalinists who pushed for high rates of industrial growth to the detriment of balances in the economy. But he refuses to romanticize the mixed-market economy of the New Economic Policy (NEP) that other historians, including Stephen F. Cohen and Moshe Lewin, believe offered a viable alternative to the excesses of Stalinism. He notes growing problems within NEP—mass urban unemployment, the need for replacement of prerevolutionary capital stock, the refusal of peasants to give up their grain in the absence of favorable terms of trade and available industrial goods.

The picture that Davies draws of the second "spinal" year of the Five-Year Plan is scrupulously balanced between positive achievement and excessive cost. His key tropic device is that "in spite of X, Y was achieved," where X connotes unanticipated complications and "confusions" and Y represents some advance measured in increased output or the near fulfillment of some planned task, albeit by applying drastic measures. For example: "In spite of the deficiencies in the norm campaign, the relation between wages and productivity achieved in the first eight months of 1929/30 was reasonably satisfactory," meaning that "monthly output per workers increased by 16.3 per cent, and the average wage by only 7.9 per cent."[14]

Though the text is often dense with information and broad lines of argument are sometimes lost in the forest of detail, Davies's volumes add up to economic history at its encyclopedic best. This recovery and integration of scattered and disaggregated data, however, does not adequately treat some topics of interest to social historians, most notably the relationship of state and society and the positions and actions of social classes and groups. Workers in general are treated as factors of production, and their agency is situated on the X rather than the Y axis.

In addition to his own prodigious research, Davies fostered a new generation of scholars through his directorship of the University of Birmingham's Centre for Russian and East European Studies (CREES). Beginning in the mid-1970s, CREES sponsored the Soviet Industrialisation Project Seminar (SIPS), which produced an impressive series of informal discussion papers and afforded Davies and younger scholars, many of them graduate students, the opportunity to examine discrete issues based on close readings of Soviet newspapers, journals, and statistical compendia. Though sometimes narrowly focused and highly technical, these analyses of working-class composition and standards of living, price policy, and industrial relations and performance were first forays into an unknown landscape. In June 1981 SIPS went international, convening the West European Conference on Soviet Industry and the Working Class in the Inter-War Years. As with the seminar papers, the contributions at the West European conference fell into two distinct genres. One was what Charles Maier has called "historical political economy," that is, interrogations of power relations underlying economic outcomes and the ways "classes or interests use political and ideological resources to bring about contested economic policies."[15] The other was essentially labor history, that subgenre of social history newly respectable among academics from the 1960s on, which investigated social processes and "outcomes" as they affected and were affected by industrial workers.[16] Both inquiries were informed by a Marxist appreciation of relations of production and an emphasis on the labor process. In these papers, the standpoint is almost exclusively within the factory gates, where rationalization, the functional division of management, the scientific organization of labor, the assembly line, and other capitalist-derived techniques are introduced and contested.

Meanwhile, on the other side of the Atlantic, the post-totalitarian investigations of Stalinist politics and culture were followed by a revived interest in Soviet industrialization. Although now scarcely believable, until the mid-1970s American academic mentors discouraged their graduate students in history from writing dissertations on the Stalin period. Partly a function of the lock that political science had on the field, this judgment was also based on the assessment that Soviet restrictions on source material did not permit scholarship of depth and quality that could match that of the history of earlier periods. This lamentable situation changed as new approaches broadened the understanding of sources, thanks to the seminal and enduring contributions of three innovative historians: Kendall Bailes, Sheila Fitzpatrick, and Moshe Lewin.

Bailes's study of the technical intelligentsia was an inspirational and exemplary model of empirical research shaped and argued through a clear conceptual framework that sought to integrate elements of the totalitarian model, primarily the element of coercion as a means of enforcing social cohesion, with the emerging group-conflict model. In addition to the more familiar bureaucratic and elite conflicts, Bailes included cultural as well as class conflict. By the end of his account of the rise-fall-and-rise of the technical intelligentsia, there is not much left of a conventional totalitarianism, but rather a very rich picture of mobility, integration, and politics of a

particularly violent kind, all in an environment of repressive state power
and social conflict.

To a historiography still obsessed with the brutalities of Stalin's personal
rule, Fitzpatrick brought a unique focus on the importance of upward
social mobility, especially of workers, during the First Five-Year Plan.
Analyzing the phenomenon of *vydvizhenstvo*, the systematic campaign to
promote workers from the bench into administrative positions via crash
courses in adult education, Fitzpatrick argued that Stalinism was a revolution that combined the regime's perceived need for its own technical
intelligentsia with workers' and rank-and-file Communists' desires to rise
within the social hierarchy. For Fitzpatrick's *vydvizhentsy*, "industrialization
was an heroic achievement—their own, Stalin's and that of Soviet power."[17]
Promoted workers proved to be the social bulwark of the Stalin regime and
its long-term beneficiaries, the "new class" in Djilas's term, or what Fitzpatrick called the "Brezhnev generation."[18]

Lewin's perspectives on industrialization have a character all their own.
As in his studies of the peasantry, so with workers and bosses, Lewin
integrates economic, social, and political history into a rich portrait of
contradictory processes. Typically he concludes one of his pioneering articles with this complex summation:

> The crudity of social relations and social policies, the despotic traits of the
> system and of the management, their control and stimulation by manipulat-
> ing hunger or by administering overdoses of privileges, favors, and perks in
> an overt or covert manner, the exaggerated material benefits for the power-
> ful coupled with terror against them or others, and in general the direct
> correlation and proximity of the carrot and the stick marked Soviet in-
> dustrialization and the style of the regime deeply.[19]

The author of books on Russian peasants and the state in the 1920s,
Soviet economic debates in the 1960s, and, most recently, the impact of
urbanization and professionalization on recent Soviet politics, Lewin
brought to the study of Soviet industrialization a rich appreciation of the
ironies of its "telescoping of stages," remarkable conceptual creativity, a
linguistic playfulness, and merciless criticism of the depradations of Stalinism. He ranges widely from discussions of "the ruralization of the cities"
(Lewin's characterization of the massive influx of peasants into town in the
early 1930s), to the "economization of the party" (part of the transformation of the Communist Party into an administrative and managerial elite),
to "the 'archaization' of the socio-economic system."

The context of a backward society rushing pell-mell into modernity only
to arrive at an "accentuation of backwardness" is always foregrounded in
Lewin's work, so that personalities and politics, hardly neglected in his
essays, are never liberated from the real social constraints in which they
operated. In seeking to explain the bacchanalia of experimentation and
campaigns, the "jolts and tilts" that punctuated industrial and social policy

in the 1930s, Lewin looks at both high politics and the social flux at all levels of society. He emphasizes the narrowing at the apex of political authority that occurred in the 1920s and the "pathologies" associated with Stalin's dictatorial rule. He illuminates the intricate hierarchies within industry, the frequent reshuffling of personnel, the *grubost'* (crudeness) that reflected the new political style of the bosses, workers' distrust of the *nachal'stvo* (management), and their withdrawal of initiative. He also refines the picture of mobility by reminding us that

> the 1930s was an era of great mobility, but for too many the direction was down, not up. . . . Professional training was impressive, but the majority of the working class were still working with their bare hands. . . . Acceding to a "position" of a *chernorabochii* [unskilled laborer] and living in overcrowded barracks (not to mention *zemlianki,* simple holes dug in the soil and covered with makeshift roofs) could not have looked like "upward" mobility to peasants who had previously had a farm of their own, however poor.[20]

Lewin would be the first to admit that much of the terrain covered in his essays needs to be sketched in and that a good deal of fog persists. Indeed, the essays might have been titled, in good Russian fashion, "Toward a History of the Making of the Soviet System," for they explicitly invite elaboration and debate.

Several historians have taken up that challenge and have pushed the study of Soviet industrialization in a new direction, namely, toward analyzing the nature of the work process and the informal organization of the shop floor. Donald Filtzer's book on workers during the 1930s represented the first overview of the "formation of modern Soviet production relations" since Solomon Schwarz's pioneering study published in 1951.[21] In contrast to Schwarz, whose chief concern was to demonstrate, via an exhaustive survey of labor legislation, the state's ever-tightening grip on workers, Filtzer insists that the state and workers fought each other to a standstill. While the former succeeded in "atomizing" the working class, it did not— and, given competition among enterprises for skilled labor and other resources, could not—wrest control of the labor process. Neither coercion in the form of decrees punishing violations of "labor discipline" nor incentive systems borrowed from the capitalist West broke the stalemate.

Filtzer's argument, reminiscent of the Trotskyist critique of Stalinism, contrasts the privileged conditions of the "exploiting class" of bureaucrats with the abysmal circumstances in which most Soviet workers labored and lived. Yet he is able to demonstrate through impressive empirical detail how workers confounded the regime's campaigns to increase productivity by engaging in both covert and overt acts of indiscipline and how managers, desperate to hold on to scarce labor resources, colluded with them.

Vladimir Andrle, an industrial sociologist at the University of York, added subtle refinements to the picture drawn by Filtzer.[22] Though he does not agree with Filtzer that atomization of the working class by the

Stalinist state left only individualist responses available, Andrle reinforces Filtzer's general point that older forms of collective working-class resistance were supplanted by the appropriation of considerable control over the labor process. Despite the loss of their institutional forms of representation and actual means of collective bargaining, the workers of the workers' state managed to gain a degree of relative protection and privilege.

Andrle elaborated the ways in which the abolition of markets and the party's commitment to "taut planning" (ambitious target setting) mitigated against stable relations between policymaking and policy implementation and gave rise to bureaucratism and "an almost anarchic competition for scarce resources within the state system of administration."[23] The party leaders believed that mass mobilization of labor and material resources alone could overcome Russia's backwardness and that that mobilization required their firm control over the industrialization drive. Ironically, their very efforts to legislate scrutiny and control not only failed to thwart bureaucratism and anarchy but also promoted new associations of managers and workers that at least made it possible to work, though at levels far below the exaggerated targets proposed by the regime.

Following Michael Burawoy's ethnographic study of workers "making out" in a Chicago engineering plant, Andrle argues that the shop-floor culture in Soviet plants of the 1930s operated similarly "to promote stability in work relations by upholding performance standards which fell short of the expectations generated by technological investment."[24] Not workers but outsiders provided the stimulus for raising performance standards, which in the absence of market conditions arrived in the form of political campaigns. Even as Soviet industrializers attempted to create a new Soviet "man," they were convinced that the only way to achieve prosperity was to borrow Western technology and the industrial culture that emphasized cleanliness, self-discipline, and a rational, methodical approach to work. Taylorism seemed the appropriate scientific solution to the problem of production efficiency. Yet even in its years of dominance, up to the mid-1930s, the regular rhythms of Taylorism were constantly upset by speed-up campaigns, *sturmovshchina* (storming), "shock work," and the fiddling of accounts by shop-floor managers and workers. "Taylorism," Andrle concludes, "may have been in theoretical harmony with the idea of industrialization under the auspices of a planned economy, but it was severely at odds with the realities of taut planning," which prevented long, stable, uninterrupted production runs and predictable output requirements and input supplies.[25] When scientific management as a strategy for creating a new industrial culture and improving efficiency was compromised, political leaders turned to other campaigns: socialist competition and, eventually, Stakhanovism.

Together with more recent contributions to Soviet social history, Andrle's study undermines the overly simple political interpretation of the totalitarian model in which an all-powerful state renders completely impotent an atomized population. Historians such as Hiroaki Kuromiya and Lewis Siegelbaum further enriched our understanding of labor relations in two monographs that linked high politics to the shop floor.[26] Both revealed the strategies by which workers and managers cooperated to limit the party state's direct involvement with production within the factory and preserve a sphere of autonomy. Kuromiya's study of the First Five-Year Plan period argued that the Stalin regime used the theme of "class war" to mobilize the support of primarily young male workers for assaults ("offenses") against "bourgeois specialists," political opponents, and trade unionists, not to mention kulaks and "unconscious" peasants opposed to collectivization. Staggering in its human and material costs, the prosecution of class struggle nonetheless "ideologically integrated" tens of thousands of cadres, the "new class" that came into its own in the post-Stalin era.

Siegelbaum's analysis of Stakhanovism focuses on the second half of the 1930s, by which time industrialization strategy had shifted from reliance on ever-increasing inputs of labor and mechanical power to their intensification. To break through bureaucratic inertia and return to the mass mobilization that had characterized the "great breakthrough" of the First Five-Year Plan, political leaders in 1935 launched an appeal to the ex-peasant majority in the industrial work force, with the appropriate xenophobic, antielitist, and populist overtones, to initiate new, more efficient productive practices. The Stakhanovite campaign was many things at once: a return to the policy of taut planning after a few years of more moderate target setting; a struggle against bureaucratic managers, cautious engineers, and unresponsive trade unions; an emphasis on personnel rather than technology (Stalin's famous phrase: "Cadres decide everything!"); and an exercise in cultural prescriptiveness designed to instruct workers in how to behave on the job, in other public arenas, and in their family lives. Although the campaign did shake up industrial relations, it left more images and symbols than concrete results. The Soviet industrial culture that remained was fraught with conflict and confusion, political intervention to raise production and enforce labor discipline, and the pervasive collusion of workers, foremen, and managers to protect themselves from an often unforgiving political environment. Stakhanovism was thus "something less but also something more than was originally foreseen or officially sanctioned."[27] Maneuvering and accommodation were at least as evident as enthusiasm and resistance.[28]

Studies of the factory floor and the labor process have now become possible thanks to the unprecedented access made available to Soviet archives and factory newspapers since the Gorbachev revolution. In current studies and monographs now in production the factory emerges not simply as a place of work but a minisociety. To be sure, Magnitogorsk and Dneprostroi, the subjects of two recent studies, were chaotic, even "idiotic," places.[29] But they did have their rules, norms of behavior, and hierarchies that needed to be learned if only to know which could be violated and negotiated. Just as engineers and other "commanders of production" learned about their authority and its limits, so there developed a certain folk wisdom among rural migrants about where to find work and, perhaps more important, shelter and food. Kinship, cultural identity, skill acquisition, and social mobility thus take on enhanced importance in understanding how millions of new workers made their way through and around the bureaucratically imposed structures.

The making (and unmaking) of the Soviet working class, not only in the simple demographic sense of creating a mammoth new work force but also in the retention, undermining, and reinterpretation of labor's traditions and vocabulary, has only begun to be explored. The discursive as well as the sociological dimensions of labor and management's experiences are only now beginning to be mapped out. At a conference called "The Making of the Soviet Working Class," held at Michigan State University in November 1990, older conceptions of class were subjected to vigorous interrogation, and discussants criticized the inadequate attention to the relationship between gender and class, class and ethnicity, and the influence of cultural representations in general.[30] How workers saw themselves was understood to be central to the formation of class. But in the context of Stalinist repression, expression or communication was impossible beyond very restricted limits. Soviet workers articulated their sense of self, defended their actual victories ("they pretend to pay us and we pretend to work"), and protected themselves against further erosion more often passively than in open resistance—at least until another revolutionary breakthrough at the end of the 1980s offered an unprecedented political opening.

The story of industrialization under noncapitalist conditions in the Soviet Union is now beginning to be told, and the 1930s are becoming part of the long history of the "modernization" of "Russia." The essays contained in this volume represent a broad cross-section of the new research we have discussed here. Organized around the four themes of rural-urban migration, social identity, management, and cultures of industrialization, they examine the Soviet industrial world-in-the-making from top to bottom via analyses of demographic data, the rhetoric of official decrees, speeches by prominent party figures and newspapers, and revelations contained in recently published memoirs. Composed as the industrial system they probe is being dismantled, they are as much products of their own time as the pioneering works of earlier decades were of theirs. Yet if the fatal flaws in that system now stand more clearly exposed than in the past, so do the historically specific conditions of the system's initial dynamism. In the sense that these essays reflect this double awareness, they make a valuable contribution to Western historiography.

NOTES

1. *Pravda* and *Izvestiia*, November 3, 1987; *Current Digest of the Soviet Press* 39, no. 44, December 2, 1987, p. 6.

2. Bruno Rizzi, *The Bureaucratization of the World: The USSR: Bureaucratic Collectivism*, trans. and with an intro. by Adam Westoby (London and New York: Tavistock, 1985; originally published in Paris, 1939). For an interesting account of the debates on the USSR among Marxists, see Antonio Carlo, "The Socio-Economic Nature of the USSR," *Telos*, no. 21, Fall 1974, pp. 2–86.

3. Carl J. Friedrich and Zbigniew K. Brzezinski, *Totalitarian Dictatorship and Autocracy*, 2d ed. (New York: Praeger, 1966), p. 233.

4. Ibid., p. 237.

5. W. W. Rostow, *The Dynamics of Soviet Society* (New York: New American Library, 1954), p. 133.

6. Ibid., p. 244.

7. Clark Kerr, J. T. Dunlop, F. H. Harbison, and C. A. Mayers, *Industrialism and Industrial Man: The Problems of Labour and Management in Economic Growth* (London: Heinemann, 1966), p. 46. The totalitarian and modernization-convergence schools are discussed and criticized in David Lane, *The Socialist Industrial State: Towards a Political Sociology of State Socialism* (London: George Allen & Unwin, 1976), pp. 44–62.

8. David Granick, *The Red Executive: A Study of the Organization Man in Russian Industry* (London: Macmillan, 1960).

9. Ibid., pp. 18–19.

10. Walter Arnold Rukeyser, *Working for the Soviets: An American Engineer in Russia* (New York: Covici-Friede, 1932); John Scott, *Behind the Urals: An American Worker in Russia's City of Steel* (New York: Houghton Mifflin, 1942; Bloomington: Indiana University Press, 1973).

11. See, for example, Maurice Hindus, *The Great Offensive* (London: Victor Gollancz, 1933).

12. E. H. Carr and R. W. Davies, *Foundations of a Planned Economy, 1926–1929*, I (London: Macmillan, 1969), pp. v–vi. Carr used the same metaphor in an interview, "The Russian Revolution and the West," *New Left Review*, no. 111, September–October 1978, p. 27.

13. The titles thus far published are *The Socialist Offensive: The Collectivisation of Soviet Agriculture, 1929–1930; The Soviet Collective Farm, 1929–1930;* and *The Soviet Economy in Turmoil, 1929–1930* (London: Macmillan, 1980–89; Cambridge, Mass.: Harvard University Press, 1980–89). More are in preparation. Davies had earlier published *The Development of the Soviet Budgetary System* (Cambridge: Cambridge University Press, 1958).

14. Davies, *The Soviet Economy in Turmoil, 1929–1930*, p. 270.

15. Charles Maier, *In Search of Stability: Explorations in Historical Political Economy* (Cambridge: Cambridge University Press, 1987), p. 5.

16. A parallel interest in Soviet industrialization developed on the European continent, most notably in West German, promoted by the Deutsche Forschungsgemeinschaft and the University of Bremen's project on "Sozialgeschichte der UdSSR 1917–1941." For some representative texts, see Tatjana Kirstein, *Sowjetische Industrialisierung-geplanter oder spontaner Prozess? Eine Strukturanalyse des wirtschaftspolitishcen Enscheidungsprozesses beim Aufbau des Ural-Kuzneck-Kombinats 1918–1930* (Baden-Baden, 1979); Walter Süss, *Der Betrieb in der UdSSR: Stellung, Organisation und Management, 1917–1932* (Frankfurt and Bern, 1980); Melanie Tatur, *"Wissenschaftliche Arbeitsorganisation": Arbeitswissenschaften und Arbeitsorganisation in der Sowjetunion, 1921–1935* (Wiesbaden, 1979). See also Charles Bettelheim (ed.), *L'industrialisation de l'URSS dans les années trentes: Actes de la Table Rond organisée par le*

Centre d'Etudes des Modes d'Industrialisation de l'Ecole des Hautes Etudes en Sciences Sociales (10 et ll decembre 1981) (Paris, 1982).

17. Sheila Fitzpatrick, *Education and Social Mobility in the Soviet Union, 1921–1934* (Cambridge: Cambridge University Press, 1979), p. 254. See also "Cultural Revolution as Class War," in Fitzpatrick (ed.), *Cultural Revolution in Russia, 1928–1931* (Bloomington: Indiana University Press, 1979), and "The Russian Revolution and Social Mobility: A Re-examination of the Question of Social Support for the Soviet Regime in the 1920s and 1930s," *Politics and Society* 13, no. 2, 1984, pp. 119–41.

18. While Fitzpatrick added an important dimension to our understanding of Soviet industrialization, her work to date does not deal directly with industrial production. The struggles and accomplishments that she analyzes occur not so much on the shop floor as in the makeshift classrooms where promotees received their training and in the conference halls where militant Communists confronted and denounced "bourgeois specialists" and insufficiently militant party members.

19. Moshe Lewin, *The Making of the Soviet System: Essays in the Social History of Interwar Russia* (New York: Pantheon, 1985), p. 257.

20. Ibid., p. 34.

21. Donald Filtzer, *Soviet Workers and Stalinist Industrialisation: The Formation of Modern Soviet Production Relations, 1928–1941* (London: Pluto Press, 1986).

22. Vladimir Andrle, *Workers in Stalin's Russia: Industrialization and Change in a Planned Economy* (Hemel Hempstead, Hartfordshire: Harvester-Wheatsheaf, 1988; New York: St. Martin's Press, 1988).

23. Ibid., p. 71.

24. Ibid., p. 154; Michael Burawoy, *Manufacturing Consent: Changes in the Labor Process Under Monopoly Capitalism* (Chicago: University of Chicago Press, 1979).

25. Andrle, *Workers in Stalin's Russia*, p. 99.

26. Hiroaki Kuromiya, *Stalin's Industrial Revolution: Politics and Workers, 1928–1932* (Cambridge: Cambridge University Press, 1988); Lewis Siegelbaum, *Stakhanovism and the Politics of Productivity in the USSR, 1935–1941* (Cambridge: Cambridge University Press, 1988).

27. Siegelbaum, *Stakhanovism and the Politics of Productivity in the USSR*, p. 7.

28. On Stakhanovism and particularly its connection with the Great Purges in industry, see Francesco Benvenuti, *Fuoco sui Sabotatori! Stachanovismo e Organizazione industriale in URSS, 1934–1938* (Rome: Valerio Levi, 1988), and Robert Maier, *Die Stachanov-Bewegung, 1935–1938* (Stuttgart: Franz Steiner Verlag, 1990). Andrle suggests in his concluding chapter that workers were not among the principal victims of the purges, though they had lost the collective capacity to combat the repression of the police and party. The regime understood that appeals to workers expressed in terms of class interests and antagonism to elites retained their power.

29. Anne Rassweiler, *The Generation of Power: The History of Dneprostroi* (Oxford: Oxford University Press, 1988); Stephen Kotkin, "Magnetic Mountain: City Building and City Life in the Soviet Union in the 1930s: A Study of Magnitogorsk," Ph.D. dissertation, University of California, Berkeley, 1988. Kotkin has published *Steeltown, USSR* (Berkeley and Los Angeles: University of California Press, 1991), a study of contemporary Magnitogorsk. Among other studies with a local or sectoral focus are David Shearer, "Rationalization and Reconstruction in the Soviet Machine-Building Industry, 1926–1934," Ph.D. dissertation, University of Pennsylvania, 1988; Kenneth Strauss, "The Transformation of the Soviet Working Class, 1929–1935," Ph.D. dissertation, University of Pennsylvania, 1990 (a study of the Serp i Molot factory in Moscow); and David Lloyd Hoffmann, "Urbanization and Social Change during Soviet Industrialization: In-Migration to Moscow, 1929–1937," Ph.D. dissertation, Columbia University, 1990.

30. The papers from this conference are being revised for publication in a volume edited by Lewis Siegelbaum and R. G. Suny.

II

THE GREAT DEPARTURE
RURAL-URBAN MIGRATION IN THE SOVIET UNION, 1929–33

Sheila Fitzpatrick

> In the history of primitive accumulation,
> all revolutions are epoch-making that act
> as levers for the capitalist class in course
> of formation; but, above all, those mo-
> ments when great masses of men are sud-
> denly and forcibly torn from their means
> of subsistence, and hurled as free and
> "unattached" proletarians on the labor
> market. The expropriation of the agri-
> cultural producer, of the peasant, from
> the soil, is the basis of the whole process.
>
> Karl Marx, *Capital*[1]

Marx's dramatic analysis of the expropriation of small landowners in late eighteenth-century England, though not in vogue among present-day economic historians, was known and accepted by all Soviet Marxists in the 1920s. Marx was, of course, writing about a capitalist industrial revolution, not a socialist one. But something very similar to the process he imagined, whereby millions of peasants were "suddenly and forcibly torn" from the land, really did occur in the Soviet Union at the beginning of the 1930s as a by-product of collectivization and industrialization.

During the First Five-Year Plan, millions of peasants were "hurled as free and 'unattached' proletarians on the labor market." A significant proportion, however, left the village as unfree laborers under various degrees of compulsion and restriction. The labor power of both the free and the unfree constituted a large part of the "capital" invested in Soviet industrialization, and the process of "primitive socialist accumulation" turned out to be every bit as painful as Marx had described capitalist

15

accumulation to be. Perhaps, ironically, the Soviet "socialist" experience fit Marx's analysis better than its Marxist leaders intended.

The mass exodus from the village in the years 1930 to 1932 is a remarkable episode in Soviet social history to which Western and Soviet scholars have paid surprisingly little attention.[2] Urban and labor historians, to be sure, recognize peasant influx into the towns and industrial labor force as a major theme of the First Five-Year Plan period. But historians of the peasantry and collectivization largely ignore it and thus miss one of the great paradoxes of Soviet collectivization, that it not only drove peasants into the kolkhoz but also drove them out of the countryside. According to the calculations of two Soviet labor historians, ten peasants quit peasant agriculture and entered the wage-earning labor force during the First Five-Year Plan for every thirty peasants who became kolkhoz members in the same period.[3]

Peasant departure is always an ambiguous phenomenon, as Marx acknowledged. The peasant is forced off the land and resents it. Yet, as a result of his departure from the land, he is likely to become an urban proletarian—a social status that Marx considered superior to that of peasant and that peasants may also in some contexts consider desirable and superior to their own. The "push" and "pull" factors in the peasant's decision to leave are never easy to separate. In the case of Soviet collectivization, moreover, two kinds of "push" have to be distinguished. There were peasants who, though "pushed" by adverse circumstances in the village ranging from collectivization to impending famine, still departed voluntarily. But there were other peasants who were "pushed" into completely involuntary departure when the OGPU, the Soviet secret police, deported them from their villages as kulaks.

This essay addresses three major issues relating to peasant departure during the First Five-Year Plan. The first is the issue of state policy, with particular reference to bureaucratic conflicts over industrial recruitment of peasants in the first phase of collectivization, the question of convict labor, and the introduction of the 1932 passport law restricting peasant migration to towns. The second issue concerns the quantitative dimensions of peasant departure during the First Five-Year Plan and the share in that process of Gulag and the administrative deportation and resettlement of kulaks. The third is the qualitative issue of the peasants' experience of departure and the impact of "push" and "pull" factors on different groups of departing peasants.

The Labor Recruitment Issue

During the period of the New Economic Policy (NEP), when industrial jobs were in short supply and unemployment was high, the concern of the party leadership, the trade unions, and the labor authorities was to keep jobs as far as possible for "real proletarians"—urban dwellers preferably of working-class origin, trade union members, party members, Civil War veterans. Peasants were not viewed as desirable recruits to the industrial labor force, and their efforts to enter it were often impeded. Kulaks, needless to say, were considered particularly undesirable, but for most of the NEP period they were less likely than poor peasants to seek employment as wage laborers in the towns.

This situation began to change at the end of the 1920s, presumably as a result of confrontation between the regime and the peasants over procurements. The first signs of abnormally high peasant departure were noted in the spring of 1929, and the labor authorities and trade unions found them disquieting. It was recognized, of course, that rapid industrialization would mean large-scale recruitment of peasants into the urban working class. But in the first half of 1929, the industrialization drive was only just getting started, and large-scale creation of new jobs had scarcely begun. The influx of peasants pushed registered unemployment in the towns to a record high in April 1929. Alarm about "peasantization" of the industrial labor force on the part of the Central Council of Trade Unions (VTsSPS) appears to have been the main motive behind its instruction to A. G. Rashin, head of the council's bureau of labor statistics, to conduct a selective trade union census.[4] According to Rashin's preliminary findings, reported to the Presidium of VTsSPS in October 1929 and based on a census of workers in the mining, metallurgical, and textile industries, 25 percent of all workers were "linked with agriculture," and in some enterprises, more than 50 percent.[5]

According to the formal rules governing industrial labor recruitment, kulaks were supposed to have last priority, if indeed they should be recruited at all. But data collected by the State Planning Commission, Gosplan, and circulated within the party leadership indicated that those leaving the village and taking industrial jobs were not poor peasants, as in the past, but prosperous peasants and kulaks who saw no future for themselves in agriculture.[6] The issue of kulak penetration of the working class was anxiously discussed in the trade unions' Central Council in the spring of 1929[7] and remained a concern throughout the year.[8]

In the countryside, meanwhile, conflict over procurements and collectivization intensified. Some district and regional party committees started to "dekulakize," that is, confiscate kulaks' property. But there was considerable confusion about what should be done with kulaks.[9] They were not welcome in the industrial labor force, or indeed in any branch of urban employment. The emerging consensus of authorities in the countryside was that they were not suitable for kolkhoz membership either. And yet, as one commentator on the question put it in mid-1929 (showing a low degree of foresight), they could hardly be sent away "to remote areas or a desert island."[10]

Perhaps, however, a more utilitarian variant of the "desert island" policy had already occurred to some members of the political leadership. As early as January 1928, Stalin had recommended using article 107 of the Criminal Code against kulak "hoarders," and many were in fact subject to criminal prosecution and conviction in 1928 and 1929. In July 1929 a secret edict was passed instructing the OGPU to create a labor camp network.[11] In December 1929, Stalin announced the policy of liquidating kulaks "as a class." In the first months of 1930, mass arrests of "first-category" kulaks and deportation of "second-category" kulaks began, both operations being conducted by the OGPU. At the same time, the drive to collectivize nonkulak peasants went into high gear. From mid-1929 the collectivizers were no longer trying to sign up individual households but whole villages and communes. Thus the objective was to collectivize the whole peasantry in as short a time as possible while removing the "kulak" elements from the villages.

These two policies, all-out collectivization and dekulakization, were to stimulate an enormous voluntary and involuntary outflow of peasants into the industrial labor force over the next three years. But their immediate impact was to disrupt the processes of peasant *otkhod* (temporary or seasonal departure for wage work) and industrial labor recruitment. Many rural authorities were unwilling to let newly signed-up kolkhoz members depart on otkhod, Labor Commissariat speakers reported: "When we tell them it's wrong, that they are disrupting construction [of socialist industry], they reply that they have their own construction to do." If the *otkhodniki* were allowed to depart, the *kolkhozy* often demanded monetary compensation, or a percentage of their wages earned outside. "The recruiter goes in . . . to recruit carpenters, and the kolkhoz administration says: 'Give us twelve rubles and we will give you carpenters.' The recruiter starts bargaining, and then the kolkhoz asks seven rubles a day. If the recruiter refuses to make a deal, he goes away without getting anyone."[12]

Furthermore, a trade unionist reported, full-time workers living in the village were being asked to give half or three-quarters of their wages to the kolhkoz: there was a "pitched battle" going on between workers and peasants on this account. There were also reports that workers with ties to the land were returning to the village,[13] a painful reminder of the Civil War exodus of workers from the towns to their native villages. What if life on the kolkhoz proved so attractive that no one ever wanted to leave? "Life in the countryside is beginning to improve," one speaker gloomily informed his colleagues in the Labor Commissariat in January 1930, "and there will no longer be the incentive to go and earn money in the town that existed up to now. There won't be that overwhelming need that drove many to go to the town for wages."[14] The industrialization drive, he feared, might founder on the contentment of a happy collectivized peasantry.

Industry was beginning its rapid expansion of the First Five-Year Plan period and already experiencing acute labor shortages in the first half of 1930. The Commissariat of Labor was supposed to organize labor recruitment for industry. This had previously been done by the labor exchanges, drawing on the pool of urban unemployed. But by the beginning of 1930, despite the continued registration of large numbers of unemployed[15] and the First Five-Year Plan projection that there would still be half a million unemployed even in 1932,[16] the labor exchanges were already having difficulty producing enough actual bodies to satisfy industrial demands. In any case, the enormous expansion of the construction industry called for the kind of unskilled labor that the villages (rather than the labor exchanges) would normally supply. Thus the labor organs were forced into the business of large-scale peasant recruitment just as the collectivization drive got under way.

All the new construction projects had chronic difficulties in attracting and retaining free workers; neither industry nor the Labor Commissariat's recruitment apparatus were equal to the task. Recruiters might, for example, spend weeks persuading fifty skilled fitters from Moscow and Leningrad to volunteer to go out to Magnitogorsk or the Stalingrad tractor works, only to have half of them return almost immediately because promised accommodation was not available or the plant had just received a contingent from Kharkov and was no longer interested in fitters. They might recruit central Russian peasants for work in the Donbass mines who were mistakenly dispatched to Moscow instead of the Ukraine and turned up on the doorstep of the trade union headquarters in the Palace of Labor.[17] Or the peasants might arrive at the mines and decide that they did not want to work there; as one mining official complained,

> We have to recruit thousands of people, and since July we have been recruiting them and bringing them down to the enterprises in batches. They come in rags and we clothe them, we issue work clothes, and they work for two or three days and go away in the same batches they came in. We are not recruiting kulaks but kolkhozniks, batraks, and poor peasants, but all the same they don't want to work and they go away, and on top of that they often take the work clothes with them.[18]

If we look at the data presented later in table 2.1, it is obvious that the industrial labor force was in fact growing very rapidly in 1930. The problem was that it was trying to grow more rapidly still, and there were problems of getting the labor to the places where it was most needed. In the late summer of 1930 the Commissariat of Labor faced a total industrial demand for one million additional workers, which it was unable to supply.[19] By this time, coercive solutions were beginning to be contemplated even by "rightists." At the Commissariat of Labor, led by the rightist Uglanov, it is clear that panic and demoralization had set in. A series of panicstricken discussions about possible inducements and forms of mobilization and coercion took place, and the commissariat's leaders, distraught under intense pressure for action from the party Central Committee, debated the practical pros and cons of drafting peasants as corvée labor.[20]

Possibly those who took part in the Labor Commissariat's discussions in 1930 were not even aware that deported kulaks were being put to work in industry (see below). They did know, however, about the use of convict labor in industry, for one speaker referred to it during a discussion of labor shortages in the timber industry at the commissariat's meeting on 21 June 1930. His suggestion was that convicts could be substituted for peasant otkhodniki in some regions, while the otkhodniki should be directed "to regions where one cannot use convict labor."[21]

Despite the new possibilities of unfree and semi-free labor being used in the industrialization drive, the recruitment of (free) labor for industry remained a great and preoccupying problem in 1930 and 1931. An institutional battle was involved between industrial and labor authorities, on one hand, and kolkhoz authorities, on the other.[22] Industry needed peasants to fill the expanding labor force, and the industrial leaders did not care if they were kolkhoz members or not. The central kolkhoz administration (Kolkhoztsentr), however, was anxious to keep peasants on the kolkhoz, or at least, if they insisted on going on otkhod, to see that the kolkhoz profited from it.[23] Behind this was an issue of principle: what collectivization meant in terms of the rights and obligations of members and the kolkhoz itself. Were kolkhoz members bound to the kolkhoz, or could they make individual decisions to leave, temporarily or permanently, in order to earn money in the towns or state farms? Also at stake was a question of priorities: whether industry's needs or those of collectivization stood higher.

In June 1931, after a year and a half of struggle over this question, the party Central Committee called a meeting of Soviet industrial leaders. The industrialists regarded the continuing labor shortages as a problem of the utmost seriousness, threatening a real breakdown of the industrialization drive. They wanted a clear decision that the collective farms not only lacked any right to prevent the departure of their members but also had the obligation to facilitate it. The meeting accordingly decided that it was necessary to get the peasant—any peasant who could work, regardless of kolkhoz membership, and for that matter regardless of class status within the peasantry—out of the village and into the labor force, using whatever incentives would produce the desired result.

The main mechanism was to be "organized recruitment" (*orgnabor*) of peasants to industry on the basis of contracts negotiated between the industrial enterprise and the kolkhoz. These contracts, as detailed in a government resolution of 30 June 1930,[24] were extremely disadvantageous to the kolkhoz, offering kolkhozniks all possible incentives to go to work as otkhodniki and no penalties if they chose to remain as permanent workers in industry. Returning before the expiration of a contract meant giving up benefits, but failing to return after the contract expired did not. The kolkhoz could take no cut at all from the industrial wages of its members. The otkhodnik was entitled to an equal share in the harvest with the kolkhoz members who actually did the harvesting, and the kolkhoz was forbidden to penalize his family in any way for his absence.

The 1931 decision on orgnabor, announced by Stalin in his famous "Six Conditions" speech on 23 June 1931, was remarkable for its absolute encouragement of peasant departure, regardless of kolkhoz interests. It was essentially a capitulation to pressure from the industrial leaders—and probably an unnecessary capitulation. As Stalin explained the rationale behind the new policy, it had become necessary to give industry some help in recruiting peasant labor because, with the elimination of rural poverty and discontent via collectivization, "there is no longer any 'flight of the muzhik from countryside to town' or spontaneous movement of labor."[25] In fact, however, peasant departure and industrial recruitment of labor were both running at unprecedentedly high levels by 1931. This was the year in which rural-urban migration was to reach an all-time high of over four million persons (see table 2.1). Moreover, as it turned out, famine in the Ukraine and other agricultural regions of the country would soon create a panicstricken exodus from the villages that had to be stopped by an abrupt reversal of policy at the end of 1932 and the introduction of internal passports.

The new orgnabor policy was also remarkable for its implicit rejection of any role for central planning or even centralized accounting in the recruitment and allocation of peasant labor. It gave individual industrial enterprises virtually a free hand in recruiting, which in a climate of labor shortages inevitably meant fierce competition between different enterprises and industries, as well as a return to some of the more dubious and corrupt recruitment practices of capitalist industry in the late tsarist era. Furthermore, the 1931 decision on orgnabor was the beginning of the end for the Commissariat of Labor, whose demise in 1933 was to leave a vacuum in the sphere of national organization of recruitment, allocation, and distribution of free labor that was to remain essentially unfilled throughout the Stalin era. From the early 1930s there was no serious attempt at central planning in the field of labor—with, perhaps, one significant exception, the OGPU (later the NKVD). The OGPU seems to have acquired its importance in this area more or less accidentally, as a result of the coincidence of dekulakization-related arrests and deportations and urgent industrial labor needs.[26] With the disappearance of the Commissariat of Labor and the decentralization of industry's labor recruitment, however, the OGPU became the only central authority with the ability to organize distribution of labor—that is, the labor of convicts and deportees—on a national scale.

Rates of Voluntary and Involuntary Departure

As can be seen in Table 2.1, 1931 was the peak in a four-year period of extraordinarily high urban in-migration, resulting in a total surplus of arrivals over departures for the period 1928–32 of 11.9 million.

Table 2.1. Growth of Urban Population and Wage Labor Force
in the Soviet Union, 1928–32 (in Millions)

	A. Rural-Urban Migration		B. Wage-Earning Population[27]	
Year	Total Arrivals in Towns	Surplus of Arrivals over Departures	Total Employed	Contingent of New Wage Earners[28]
1928	6.5	1.1	11.4	1.1— 1.2
1929	7.0	1.4	12.4	1.5— 1.6
1930	9.5	2.6	15.4	3.5— 3.6
1931	10.8	4.1	20.2	5.4— 5.6
1932	10.6	2.7	24.2	4.8— 5.0
Total		11.9		16.3—17.0

The peasants who left the village for the town—four out of five of them in the working-age group (16–59)[29]—had no trouble finding work, given the abundance of unskilled jobs in industry, construction, state trade, and food preparation.[30] During the First Five-Year Plan, the number of wage and salary earners in the Soviet Union doubled, from 11.4 to 24.2 million. At least ten million[31] of the new wage earners were peasants.[32]

The urban areas with the most spectacular growth in these years were new industrial towns, such as Magnitogorsk, and established cities receiving major capital investment for industrial growth under the First Five-Year Plan, such as Moscow, Stalingrad, and Sverdlovsk.[33] This suggests the importance of the "pull" factor in migration, namely, availability of unskilled jobs in industry for peasant migrants. At the same time, however, the changing geographical pattern of peasant departure—with sharp proportional increases in departure from regions with the highest levels of collectivization[34]—underlines the importance of collectivization as a "push" factor as well.

This "push," moreover, had a very special quality. It was not just a question of peasants leaving because they disliked collectivization but also of peasants being forcibly uprooted by the state and the OGPU. The policy of "liquidation of the kulaks as a class," formally introduced at the end of 1929, meant that peasants identified as kulaks were to be expropriated, that is, suffer confiscation of property and eviction with family from their homes in the village. According to Soviet statisticians' estimates of the late 1920s, there were almost a million peasant households (a total of over six million peasants) in the kulak category,[35] so the presumed target group of this campaign was huge.

Under the Central Committee's guidelines on dekulakization issued on 30 January 1930, kulaks were to be divided into three categories. Persons in all three categories were to be expropriated and evicted from their dwellings. In addition, kulaks in the first and second categories were to be physically removed from the region, in the case of first-category kulaks by being sentenced to labor camp (or, in some cases, executed) and in the case of second-category kulaks, together with their families and the families of first-category kulaks, by deportation and resettlement in distant parts of the USSR. The deportations of second-category kulaks, as well as the arrest of those in the first category, was the business of the OGPU.[36]

Much has been written on the question of whether the victims of dekulakization were really kulaks. But for our present purpose—estimation of the proportional share of dekulakization victims in the cohort of peasant entrants to the labor force during the First Five-Year Plan—that question is not important. What matters is how many peasants, regardless of their actual class status in the village, entered the labor force involuntarily as a result of being subject to dekulakization and associated administrative and punitive measures.

This has been a controversial topic in Western and Soviet scholarship. Some Western scholars have suggested that the apparently very rapid growth of urban population and the wage-earning labor force during the First Five-Year Plan was fraudulent, since the majority of rural-urban "migrants" were actually peasant convicts and deportees.[37] This argument rests on the assumption that labor camps of over 3,000 population were classified, like other settlements of this size, as urban. A few Soviet scholars have also spoken of the outflow from the village as a phenomenon primarily associated with repression rather than industrialization.[38]

Although this line of argument always seemed somewhat implausible, it was only recently that data on the Gulag labor camps have emerged from the OGPU archives, making it possible for the first time to attempt a serious calculation of the share of "involuntary" departures in the total outflow from the village. There were two routes of wholly involuntary departures, the first via prison and labor camp sentences, the second via deportation.

According to the new data, shown in table 2.2, the Gulag labor camp system was still relatively small in 1930–33, albeit growing steadily. At this period most convicts were in prisons, not camps, although the prisons periodically disgorged batches of long-sentence inhabitants into the camps.[39] If peasants were represented approximately according to their share in total population, e.g., at 75–80 percent of all convicts,[40] the total number of peasants in confinement at the beginning of 1933 would be in the range of 850,000 to 900,000. Presumably few members of this group would be included in table 2.1's "B" category of new wage earners.[43] But members of the the group could theoretically be included in table 2.1's "A" category of new urban inhabitants, even though, as prisoners, their urban status was only temporary. In the unlikely event that the entire group was included, it would have comprised 7–8 percent of the migration-related increase of urban population in the years 1928–32.

Table 2.2. Convicts in Soviet Prisons and Labor Camps, 1930–33
(Figures for 1 January)

	1930	1931	1932	1933
Labor camps[41]	179,000	212,000	268,700	334,300
Prisons[42]				800,000
Total				1,134,300

With regard to the second route of involuntary departure, deportation, it appears that the statistics published in the 1970s[44] are basically standing up to the scrutiny of glasnost. As of the beginning of 1935 there were 1,185,000 deported kulaks and their families living in the areas of resettlement (Urals, Siberia, Kazakhstan, etc.).[45] The number actually deported was obviously larger—probably over a million and a half persons[46]—but it was reduced by death[47] and illegal flight.[48] About 40 percent of the deported kulaks were resettled on the land in Siberia and other outlying regions, while the rest were put to work in industry.[49] They lived in special settlements *(spetsposelki)* and were forbidden to leave the area, but they were paid wages and their work situation was in many respects similar to that of free labor in the same enterprises.

At the beginning of 1935, 640,000 deported kulaks and family members were living in industrial spetsposelki (see table 2.3). That meant that the deported group contributed about 5 percent of the twelve million peasants who became urban dwellers in the years 1928–32, as shown in Table 2.1, "A" category. If half were wage earners,[50] that amounted to around 3 percent of the ten million peasants who became wage earners in the same period.

Summarizing our findings so far, it appears that the share of wholly involuntary departures (via imprisonment or deportation) among total peasant departures in the years 1928–32 was around 5–7 percent. Wholly

Table 2.3. Dekulakization, Deportation, and Resettlement of Kulaks, 1930–31

	Households	Persons
Expropriated	600,000[51]	3—3.5 million
Deported		
All	(350—450,000)	1,803,000
Outside oblast	241,000	1,160,000
Resettled[52]		
On land		445,000
In industry		640,000

involuntary departures, however, are not the only relevant category in our inquiry. There was clearly a range of possibilities between wholly voluntary and wholly involuntary departure. Specifically, the manner in which de-kulakization was conducted left a large group of peasants—the so-called third-category kulaks—in a situation in which "spontaneous" departure from the countryside might seem the only viable course of action.

Third-category kulaks were those slated for expropriation and eviction under the dekulakization drive but not for arrest and imprisonment or deportation outside the oblast. Provincial authorities were instructed to resettle the third-category kulaks, if possible, on inferior land in the same district, but few had the time or competence to accomplish this. Meanwhile the expropriated kulaks found themselves in limbo, cast out of the village community but not forcibly transported elsewhere. Understandably, many of these peasants "melted away" before a worse fate could befall them. In most cases they fled to the towns, where they found work, concealed their "kulak" past, and merged into the wage-earning labor force.[53]

An estimate of the total number of third-category kulaks can be obtained by subtracting the number deported outside the oblast from the total number of peasants dekulakized. For 1930–31 (see table 2.3), this number would be over 350,000 households, or approximately two million persons. Adding in dekulakizations for the years 1929 and 1932, the number might rise to perhaps 500,000 households, or 2.5–3 million persons.[54] It is likely that the great majority of these people, along with the large number of individual members of deported kulak families who managed to avoid deportation, ended up in the urban labor force but were essentially involuntary entrants to it.

Thus, allowing for some double counting of "wholly involuntary" and "essentially involuntary" departures,[55] we may conclude that as many as three out of every ten peasants migrating to town or entering the wage labor force in the years 1928–32 were probably departing wholly or essentially involuntarily from the villages in connection with dekulakization. This calculation, however, covers only peasants who were formerly dekulakized and does not include those who were "self-dekulakized" in the same period (that is, they left on their own initiative out of fear of being expropriated by the authorities).[56] We cannot know how many peasants left "voluntarily" because of their expectation or fear of dekulakization, but departures of this type may have been at least as numerous as those classified above as wholly and essentially involuntary.[57]

Modes of Departure

My analysis so far has focused on quantifiable data about voluntary and involuntary peasant departure. But it is also important to consider the variety (and often the ambiguity) of the experiences associated with departure from peasant life and the village, and the specificity of the experiences of this particular historical period. I will suggest a series of possible modes of departure involving different proportions of "push" and "pull" factors and different degrees of coercion in the "push" factor.

At the "pull" end of the continuum, there was straightforward voluntary departure of the type familiar from traditional Soviet memoirs and historical accounts: the eager young peasant leaving the village in response to the call of opportunity in industry and town. Such a path is described, for example, in the memoir of N. P. Sapozhnikov, a peasant from a poor Cossack family in the Urals who graduated from the sixth grade of the local school at the end of the 1920s.

> At that point, my education finished: the eight-year school was in the city, there was no money to go there. At that time rumors reached our stanitsa that an iron foundry would be built on Magnitnaia mountain. . . . The rumor that the biggest plant in the world [i.e., Magnitogorsk] would be built at Magnitnaia mountain excited everyone, old and young. It was said that huge numbers of people were going there. We, my cousin and I, decided to go too. . . .[58]

In a second mode of peasant departure, "push" predominated over "pull," but the push did not involve overt external force and was not directly associated with dekulakization. There were many well-to-do peasants who had contacts in the towns,[59] smelled trouble coming in 1929 or 1930, and decided to leave the village while the going was good. For example, in Kimry, famous as a center of bootmaking, peasant craftsmen in 1929 "sensed a change in Party policy," as the son of one of them later recalled.

> They hastily closed their workshops, dismissed their hired help, and turned to farming, so as to transform themselves from artisans and Nep-men into ordinary peasants. My father was one of the first to shut down his workshop. He . . . went off to work on the timber rafts. My eldest brother left for Moscow, where he became a stevedore.[60]

Others left when dekulakization became a strong possibility but before it actually occurred. In the Western Oblast, for example, a peasant-worker named Balashev, who had worked in industry before 1921 but had returned to the land in the 1920s, left again for a job in industry in 1931 after he had been given the "set quota" for individual grain delivery that marked him as a prosperous peasant;[61] and a miller's widow and leaseholder, Lokshina, departed to work in a Moscow leather plant in 1932 after being deprived of voting rights.[62]

A third mode of departure was flight from the village after being expropriated as a kulak but before suffering further consequences. This is the group that was regularly reported in official documents of 1930–31 as having "disappeared" or "melted away" before officials got around to resettling it, as they were supposed to do, on inferior land. Some left after obtaining false documents attesting to their status as "middle" or "poor" peasants, e.g., one Petro Shcherbakov of the village of Vertnoe, who bribed the rural soviet chairman with a sowing machine to get identification as a "middle" peasant. Others left without documents, like the *zemliachestvo* of dekulakized peasants from Mordovia that congregated in the construction workers' barracks of the TsIAM plant in Moscow in the early 1930s.[63]

The fourth mode of departure was the OGPU "push" to labor camps or deportation and resettlement, which involved no degree of choice on the peasant part. Recollections of individual experiences of dekulakization and deportation or prison and labor camp are now, for the first time, regularly appearing in the Soviet press.[64] The most remarkable such account is that of Ivan Tvardovskii, brother of the poet and son of a village blacksmith, who vividly describes his family's dekulakization and deportation in 1931, their unsettled wanderings around the Urals, their unsuccessful attempts to escape from exile and to return home, their later struggles to obtain passports and urban residence permits, and their final, grudging acceptance of a new existence as workers and urban dwellers.[65]

Yet it must be remembered that there was ambiguity in all modes of departure except the last. Individual departures were liable to retrospective reinterpretation, especially those that fell in the middle range of the continuum between free choice and compulsion. Even the son of a dekulakized kulak might choose to forget his father's fate, focus on his own life and prospects as an urban wage earner, and accept Soviet values.[66] Young peasants who became industrial workers and were then rewarded and praised as Stakhanovites were likely to put a positive gloss on the motives for joining the proletariat, whatever the actual circumstances of their departure from the village. They were likely to tell the Sapozhnikov story to themselves and others. (After all, for all we know, Sapozhnikov himself was a pseudo-Sapozhnikov, with skeletons hidden in the village cupboard.)

For such individuals, the real "meaning" of their move from village to town was something that was always subject to revaluation. Take the case of N. G. Parnikhin, the son of a prosperous peasant family who left his village in the Western Oblast as an adolescent in the early 1930s and went to work in Leningrad. He became a Stakhanovite at the carburetor plant and joined the Komsomol; and at age twenty, in 1936, he surely saw himself as a young peasant Sapozhnikov who had seen the way to a better life. But then came the day in 1937 when it was revealed that his departure from the village had followed the dekulakization of one of his aunts and he was expelled from the Komsomol for concealment of social origins.[67] Was Parnikhin a future Stakhanovite who was "pulled" or a kulak relative who was "pushed"? He was both (that is, he was potentially either), and so were a large number of his contemporaries involved in the Great Departure of the early 1930s.

The Passport Law of December 1932

Although industry needed the peasants' labor, nobody had expected an influx of peasants into town of the magnitude of the one that actually occurred during the First Five-Year Plan. The results were enormous overcrowding and poor living conditions, high labor turnover and indiscipline in the work force, and great pressure in the urban ratio system. The nation's economic problems were compounded in 1931 and 1932 by a shortfall in procurements and, in the latter part of 1932, the onset of famine in a number of major grain-producing regions, including the Ukraine, the Northern Caucasus, and the Volga.

Mass departures of peasants from famine-stricken areas were reported. In Western Siberia at the beginning of 1932, many raions noted "a mass departure of kolkhozniki to the city in connection with food difficulties"[68] and in May the West Siberian kraikom described this outmigration, in contrast to the steady flow of peasant departures that had preceded it, as becoming "completely abnormal" by virtue of its suddenness, scale, and the fact that many of the departing peasants were kolkhozniki who had already adjusted to the kolkhoz.[69] In the Northern Caucasus, as many as 100,000 persons left the kolkhozy on unauthorized otkhod in 1932, leading to the collapse and liquidation of seven kolkhozy,[70] and Sheboldaev reported that there was an influx of hungry peasants into Rostov and other major cities in the winter of 1932–33.[71]

In addition to provoking more peasant departures, the famine was threatening the state's ability to supply food to the towns and the army, not to mention its ability to export grain. Moreover, in a striking reversal of normal patterns, food obtained on urban ration cards was being sent back to the villages in the winter of 1932. Sheboldaev, secretary of the Northern Caucasus kraikom, recalled this ruefully a year later:

> Whereas before the village had given the town [and] the workers additional food supplies through the market, even if it was for a higher price, last year it was the opposite—part of the food intended for workers was being diverted in various ways (family ties, speculation, and so on) to the village.[72]

As is well known, Stalin denied the existence of a famine and attributed the procurement problems of 1932 to sabotage by kulaks and kulak-influenced peasants. A strongly antipeasant as well as antikulak mood was developing in the party leadership.[73]

The outcome of the crisis was a concerted effort in the winter of 1932–33 to close the towns to further peasant influx and reduce the urban population by expelling "alien class elements." On 27 December 1932, a new law mandated the introduction of internal passports. The new passports were to be issued to "all citizens of the USSR aged sixteen years and over, permanently living in towns and workers' settlements, working on transport, in the sovkhozy and at new construction sites"—that is, they were not to be issued to peasants.[74] To obtain a passport, citizens must be registered *(propisany)* under a new, stricter system as urban residents. The new passports would show the bearer's full name, age, nationality, social position, permanent place of residence, and place of employment.

Their introduction was to be accompanied by expulsion from the towns of "persons not linked with production or work in institutions or schools and not engaged in socially useful labor (with the exception of invalids and pensioners)" and the purging of towns, workers' settlements, new construction sites, etc. of "kulaks, criminals, and other antisocial elements hiding there." Persons refused passports had to leave the cities within ten days.[75]

This was accompanied by a reorganization of the rationing system to prevent double-dipping and to link access to rations directly to employment,[76] and by a labor discipline decree[77] intended inter alia to reduce the number of workers receiving rations and ease the pressure on housing.

Finally, to complete the series of decrees, the government issued a law on 17 March 1933 that revoked the earlier decree of 29 June 1931 and required kolkhoz peasants to have the permission of the kolkhoz administration to leave on otkhod. Kolkhozniki who left without permission would be expelled from the kolkhoz and not paid for the labor-days they had worked. The new law specifically warned "flitters who leave before the sowing and return for the harvest" that they would not share in the annual distribution of grain after the harvest.[78] In addition, as starving and desperate peasants tried to flee from the villages, the state set up cordons and sent out security detachments to prevent them; according to a recent Soviet source, 220,000 fleeing peasants were caught and returned to their villages in the spring of 1933.[79]

The reintroduction of internal passports, long vilified as instruments of tsarist repression, was a dramatic and (in Old Bolshevik perspective) disconcerting step. Enukidze, one of those who clearly found it embarrassing, tried to explain that this measure was not as regressive and repressive as it seemed. The government, he said, had no choice but to take measures to reduce "this great, senseless, wasteful flow of people from village to town, and from city to city" of the past eighteen months. He admitted, in an oblique way, that the measure was antipeasant, saying that it aimed to protect the towns not only from urban idlers and criminals but also from "the touring artist *(gastroler)* from the village, who doesn't take kindly to the collectivization of agriculture."[80]

Peasant bashing—sometimes in the guise of kulak bashing, sometimes overt—was prominent in the commentaries on the new laws. One newspaper's editorial, in its commentary on the law against worker absenteeism, quoted Lenin's dictum that the peasant worker aspires to give the Soviet state "as little and as poor work as possible and drag from 'it' as much money as possible."[81] *Pravda* went further in its editorial on the passport law a month later. While grudgingly conceding that there were some admirable new recruits to the labor force, especially "working-class youngsters and kolkhozniki," *Pravda* emphasized that the new construction sites were crawling with "hundreds of persons [who are] declassed and alien in a class sense to the proletariat, who sense the possibility of easy profits and try to corrupt and weaken the iron discipline of socialist labor." In *Pravda's* picture, the arrival of new peasant workers became a malevolent invasion of kulaks, determined "to live as [they are] accustomed, that is, parasitically, without working." "Exposed in their 'native' villages and raions by progressive kolkhozniki, party and Komsomol members, hundreds and thousands of kulaks and their henchmen . . . strive towards and penetrate the vital centers of our country—the cities, the new construction sites, the workers' settlements."[82]

The close connection between the new passport law and the law against absenteeism was stressed in the newspaper commentaries. Once the law against absenteeism had struck at "pseudo-workers who are disorganizing labor discipline and ruining production," and the "next logical step" was "to toss out *(vytriakhnut')* this social trash from the overcrowded cities, to unburden our industrial centers of people who are not essential to any socially useful labor." Removal of the "scum" would "preserve the housing fund of Soviet industrial centers for the accommodation of the cadres of workers and specialists which the country really needs."[83] It would get rid of kulaks, thieves, speculators, and swindlers and deal with the problems created by an influx of expropriated peasants, some of whom had become professional speculators in ration cards. "The task of purging, unburdening our cities and new construction sites and workers' settlements of . . . parasitical elements is very important," *Pravda* emphasized. Indeed, it was so important as "a *political* task" that it would be undertaken by the OGPU.[84]

Passportization was begun in Moscow on 5 January, with workers at the ninety leading industrial enterprises being issued passports first.[85] Persons not issued passports had to leave the city and were not allowed to settle in any of the other cities where the passport system had been introduced.

The *New York Times* reported in January that "an exodus on a small scale has already begun from Moscow" in connection with the imminent passportization; it cited "a recent inspection at the Moscow electric factory, one of the city's largest plants, showing that of about 5,000 employees 800 were not allowed to receive passports because they were classified as former White Guards, kulaks, disfranchised persons and criminals.[86] A few weeks later, the same paper carried a report from Finland of "wholesale exodus" from Leningrad of persons refused passports: "huge crowds of people are wandering along roads out of the city searching for food and shelter. It is reported that 10,000 persons have been thus deprived of their homes [in Leningrad]. . . . Some of the deported persons were taken by railway to rural districts a minimum of 60 miles from Leningrad."[87]

According to an apparently well-informed *Sotsialisticheskii vestnik* correspondent, the original target for deportations from Moscow alone was half a million, but "the unfortunates doomed to ruin put in motion such forces and raised such a moan that the number of persons being deported is now reduced: from Moscow, for example, they are deporting only 300,000 (!) and they are proposing to deport 800,000 altogether from the big cities! Those deported are doomed to outright hunger and homelessness, since food cards are taken from them, they are not allowed to take their furniture with them and even the amount of clothes that can be taken is limited."[88] In addition to those officially refused registration and required to leave, many people at risk (former kulaks and Nepmen and others deprived of voting rights) apparently left voluntarily once passportization was announced.[89]

Simultaneously, the law against absenteeism was going into effect, and new ration cards were being issued at the enterprises. The three processes comb ned in a drive to identify and remove "class enemies" from industry and reduce the work force that had to be paid and supplied with rations. In Baku, where many dekulakized peasants had found work, "a tense struggle for purity of the workers' ranks" began with the passportization process and continued through the first half of 1933, with large-scale arrests of "kulaks" and hints of strikes and "intentional disorganization of production" by workers.[90]

The draconian measures taken in the winter of 1932–33 halted peasant departure from the kolkhozy and migration to the cities—for a while. By 1934, however, the indices were already moving upward, though never again in the prewar period did they reach the dizzying heights of 1930–32. Urban arrivals were back at almost twelve million in 1934, after the temporary lull of 1933, and the surplus of arrivals over departures was between two and three million in both 1934 and 1935.[91] Employment figures were up correspondingly. According to a Soviet calculation, the net increase in the size of the employed labor force in the years 1934 to 1937 (allowing for natural attrition) was consistently above two million a year.[92]

A proportion of the new industrial recruits were urban residents not previously in employment, particularly women; and noncollectivized *edinolichniki* provided a significant part of the total peasant recruitment until their numbers dwindled sharply toward the end of the decade. Nevertheless, in the period 1935–37 a total of about 3.6 million kolkhozniki left for work in towns, according to annual reports submitted by the kolkhozy.[93] This was not counting the more than four million kolkhozniki in the sixteen to fifty-nine age group listed as being on otkhod each year in the second half of the 1930s[94] or the almost equal number of kolkhozniki who were not on otkhod but worked no more than fifty labor-days (less than a month) a year in the kolkhoz.[95]

Industrial enterprises were regularly threatened with dire penalties if they hired peasants without passports or kolkhozniki lacking kolkhoz permission to leave. But the very repetition of this injunction indicates that it was often being honored in the breach rather than the observance.[96] Orgnabor[97] played a part in industrial recruitment from the peasantry, particularly from the kolkhozy, but its role seems to have been largely limited to recruitment (or drafting) of peasants in groups for short-term employment in the remote and otherwise undesirable industrial industries such as logging in the north and mining in Siberia. Most industrial enterprises in accessible locations apparently recruited peasants from the surrounding region on an individual basis and without orgnabor formalities.[98] Otkhod, with or without kolkhoz permission, coexisted with orgnabor; and many otkhodniki, as well as some orgnaborshchiki, chose not to return to the kolkhoz.

We should not, therefore, exaggerate the degree to which the internal passport system and urban registration "bound peasants to the kolhkoz." Kolkhozniki could leave legally if they were sent on orgnabor (when they had the option of staying on after their term was up) or if the kolkhoz gave them permission. But many kolkhozniki clearly left illegally as well, obtaining passports and urban registration by informal means after being hired at the gate by industrial enterprises or obtaining other urban employment; and young kolkhozniki and children of kolkhoz members had little difficulty staying in towns after leaving the kolkhoz for further education or, in the case of males, for compulsory military training. The passport law notwithstanding, the state regarded kolkhozy as labor reserves for industry. If these reserves were tapped in an "organized" manner, so much the better. If not, industry still needed the labor, and its needs were paramount..

Nevertheless, the peasant departures of the Second Five-Year Plan belong in a very different category from those of the first. In the mid-1930s, despite the barriers erected against departure from the kolkhoz and rural-urban migration, a steady stream of kolkhozniki and edinolichniki left villages that had been impoverished and embittered by collectivization to seek a better life in the towns.

At the beginning of the 1930s, by contrast, out-migration had been a flood rather than a stream. In that era, moreover, mass peasant departure from the villages was inextricably linked to the fear and coercion associated with collectivization and, in particular, dekulakization. In only a minority of cases can "pull" factors have clearly predominated over "push." The majority of departing peasants left because the regime had given them a mighty shove, discouraging them from remaining in the village, or because it had actually uprooted them, transported them for long distances, and dumped them in unfamiliar and generally inhospitable conditions to make what they could of an unsought "new life."

The great exodus from the village at the beginning of the 1930s must be considered one of the formative experiences of Soviet society, a crucial determinant in the making of the Stalinist state and the defining of its relationship to society. The arrests and deportations of kulaks produced a major expansion of the OGPU's size and influence, and its empire of convict labor—mainly peasant—became a significant factor in Soviet industrialization. With the mass deportation of kulaks, the state explored for the first time the possibilities of forcible resettlement of large groups of people, a policy that was to be practiced more than once in the 1940s with regard to nationalities. Control of population movement became a state function, and the passport system, set up to cope with the famine-related crisis of 1932–33, became a permanent part of the administrative structure.

In the village, the residual impact on the peasant community of the mass departures and dekulakization of the early 1930s was arguably scarcely less important than that of collectivization itself. The First Five-Year Plan departures left the village weakened, its demographic structure already distorted by the shortages of young people and working-age men that were to become so acute after World War II. The kulak deportations were traumatic in themselves, and moreover left the village with a demoralizing legacy of ill-feeling, an entrenched habit of mutual denunciation for "kulak ties," and (on the part of those in possession of kulak property or occupying kulaks' houses) a lingering fear that the deported kulaks might be allowed to return. The introduction of the passport system made peasants second-class citizens, even though it was only a partial restriction on mobility in practice.

The towns, meanwhile, were swamped by the influx of raw newcomers. Given the dimensions of the total influx of peasants at this time, it would have been hard enough for the urban working class to absorb them under the best of circumstances. But these circumstances were almost the worst possible, for the great majority of peasant entrants must have had some degree of grievance about collectivization, and many were actually victims or potential victims of dekulakization. In the late 1920s the Communist Party and the trade unions had done their utmost to prevent kulaks entering the industrial working class, fearing ideological contamination and erosion of class consciousness. In the early 1930s, however, hundreds of thousands of former kulaks entered the working class, and their mood was surely infinitely more embittered and hostile to the regime than it had been before dekulakization.

It has been calculated in this essay that up to a third of all peasants migrating to town and entering the labor force in the First Five-Year Plan period—that is, three to four million persons—did so involuntarily as a result of dekulakization. While there are no doubt other reasons for the regime's waning enthusiasm for the "leading role of the proletariat" in the 1930s, the knowledge that many of today's workers were yesterday's kulaks, bitterly resentful of their dekulakization, was undoubtedly a contributing factor.

Worse still from the standpoint of an embattled and perpetually suspicious Communist Party, only a relatively small proportion of these "socially harmful elements" were clearly labeled as former kulaks by virtue of their known status as deportees, convicts, or ex-convicts with a Gulag sentence on their records. The majority of former kulaks and their families were undoubtedly doing their best to hide their resentment and the stain of their social origins and to pass as ordinary, loyal Soviet workers and employees— in short, they had become a new class of hidden enemies of Soviet power. For the party leaders, the great peasant exodus to town that laid the foundations for Soviet prewar industrial growth was also a paranoid nightmare come true.

NOTES

1. Vol. 1, (Moscow, 1958), p. 716.
2. An exception is Iu. V. Arutiunian, "Kollektivizatsiia sel'skogo khoziaistva i vysvobozhdenie rabochei sily dlia promyshlennosti," in *Formirovanie i razvitie sovetskogo rabochego klassa (1917–1961 gg.)* (Moscow, 1964).
3. A. I. Vdovin and V. A. Drobizhev, *Rost rabochego klassa SSSR 1917–1940 gg.* (Moscow, 1976), p. 127. While most of the departing peasants went into urban and industrial work, this calculation includes the smaller group that became agricultural wage earners working on state farms.
4. Tsentral'nyi Gosudarstvennyi Arkhiv Oktiabr'skoi Revoliutsii i Sotsialisticheskogo Stroitel'stva SSSR (TsGAOR), fond 5451, opis' 13, ed. khr. 14, 1. 37–40: meeting of Presidium of VTsSPS, 11 January 1929.
5. TsGAOR, f. 5451, op. 13, ed. khr. 15, 1. 136–37. Note that this figure is higher than the figure of under 21 percent that can be extrapolated from the published version of Rashin's findings (A. G. Rashin, *Sostav fabrichno-zavodskogo proletariata SSSR* [Moscow, 1930], pp. 3 and 25). The lower figure has usually been cited by Soviet scholars (e.g., O. I. Shkaratan, *Problemy sotsial'noi struktury rabochego klassa SSSR* [Moscow, 1970], p. 264), but it may well be that the unpublished higher figure more accurately represents Rashin's data.
6. V. P. Danilov, "Krest'ianskii otkhod na promysly v 1920-kh godakh," *Istoricheskie zapiski* 94 (1974), p. 112.
7. TsGAOR, f. 5515, op. 13, ed. khr. 14, 1. 122–23, 163, and passim: meetings of Presidium of Central Council of Trade Unions, 22 March and 12 April 1929. N. M. Antselovich, head of the union of agricultural and timber workers (the batraks' union), was particularly vehement in his denunciation of kulaks working in the mining and metallurgical industries.
8. In August the Labor Commissariat deplored "the penetration of considerable numbers of prosperous peasants" into the timber and construction industries, and in December it categorically forbade recruitment of kulaks for timber floating. TsGAOR, f. 5515, op. 1, ed. khr. 146, 1. 11 and 102. The prohibition, of course, applied to the use of kulaks as *free* labor.
9. Here as elsewhere, I use *kulak* to describe those persons who were labeled kulaks by Soviet authorities.
10. Quoted (from an article by Karpinskii of mid-1929) in R. W. Davies, *The Socialist Offensive: The Collectivisation of Soviet Agriculture, 1929–1930* (Cambridge, Mass., 1980), p. 138.
11. On the establishment of the Gulag labor camp system, see Peter H. Solomon,

Jr., "Soviet Penal Policy, 1917–1934: A Reinterpretation," *Slavic Review* 39, 1980, no. 2.

12. TsGAOR, f. 5515, op. 1, ed. khr. 235, l. 22–23.

13. In the summer, workers left the mines of the Ukrainian Donbass and Siberian Kuzbass in unprecedented numbers. The Donbass alone lost 55,000 workers, including 12,000 skilled coal hewers: TsGAOR, f. 5451, op. 14, ed. khr. 12, l. 141 and 173 (All-Union Central Council of Trade Unions, 1930). Although living conditions, food shortages, and bad accidents in the mines were part of the reason, it appears that collectivization was also a factor: workers and *otkhodniki* with ties to the village were returning, probably to find out what was happening to their land and their families.

14. TsGAOR, f. 5515, op. 1, ed. khr. 235, l. 21–32 (People's Commissariat of Labor, 24 January 1930).

15. On 1 August 1930 the labor exchanges still had 633,000 unemployed on the books and were apparently paying benefits to 200,000: TsGAOR, f. 5515, op. 1, ed. khr. 224, l. 112–13 (People's Commissariat of Labor, 1930). However, it was clear to the Commissariat of Labor by late July that something was wrong with these statistics, since the exchanges could no longer produce "real live people" for the jobs that were now available in abundance. A scandal followed, resulting in a change of leadership for the commissariat and the denunciation and probable arrest of the man held responsible for the erroneous statistical projections (L. E. Mints, a well-known economist and specialist on peasant *otkhod*).

16. *Itogi vypolneniia pervogo piatiletnego plana razvitiia narodnogo khoziaistva SSSR* (Moscow, 1933), p. 174.

17. TsGAOR, f. 5515, op. 1, ed. khr. 235, l. 506 (People's Commissariat of Labor, 1930).

18. *Sessiia TsIK Soiuza SSSR 6 sozyva: Stenograficheskii otchet i postanovleniia, 22–28 dekabria 1931 g.* (Moscow, 1931), Bulletin 17, p. 5.

19. TsGAOR, f. 5515, op. 1, ed. khr. 235, l. 278–91, 472–79, and passim (People's Commissariat of Labor, 1930).

20. TsGAOR, f. 5515, op. 1, ed. khr. 235, l. 278–91, 472–79, and passim (People's Commissariat of Labor, 1930).

21. TsGAOR, f. 5515, op. 1, ed. khr. 235, l. 283.

22. These conflicts are described in A. M. Panfilova, *Formirovanie rabochego klassa SSSR v gody pervoi piatiletki* (Moscow, 1964).

23. At a Narkomtrud meeting on this question in January, Kolkhoztsentr representatives argued that the kolkhozy should be allowed to take a 30–40 percent cut from the otkhod earnings of kolkhozniki. But the Narkomtrud collegium voted for a maximum of 15 percent. TsGAOR, f. 5515, op. 1, ed. khr. 235: meeting of 24 January 1930.

24. Panfilova, pp. 46–49.

25. Stalin, *Sochineniia* 13 (Moscow, 1951), p. 53.

26. See Solomon, "Soviet Penal Policy."

27. Data for "A" from *Trud v SSSR (Statisticheskii spravochnik)* (Moscow, 1936), p. 7. Data for "B" from Vdovin and Drobizhev, p. 109.

28. Allowing for natural attrition.

29. Data (for 1932 only) in *Trud v SSSR* (1936), p. 8.

30. See table in *Sotsialisticheskoe stroitel'stvo SSSR. Statisticheskii ezhegodnik* (Moscow, 1935), pp. 474–75.

31. The figure usually cited, 8.6 million new wage earners from the peasantry (68 percent of all new wage earners), calculates growth without allowing for natural attrition (*Itogi vypolneniia*, p. 174). My figure is recalculated on the basis of the Vdovin and Drobizhev figures, which factor in natural attrition. That the peasant

share of the total increase was in the 65–70 percent range is suggested not only by the *Itogi vyponeniia* figures but also by other contemporary data, for example, those of the 1932–33 trade union census.

32. Most of these people were working in the urban sector, although there was also an increase of about two million rural wage earners (sovkhoz workers, etc.) in the First Five-Year Plan period (*Sotsialisticheskoe stroitel'stvo SSSR* [1935], pp. 474–75). Note that the new urban wage earners from the peasantry were, in many cases, unaccompanied by their families, as is shown by the fact that the table 2.1 "A" figures are only slightly higher than the "B" figures. Wives and children often remained in the village, sometimes joining the kolkhoz and sometimes not.

33. For data on urban growth, see *Sotsialisticheskoe stroitel'stvo SSSR: Statisticheskii ezhegodnik* (Moscow, 1934), pp. 356–57, and *Statisticheskii sbornik* (Moscow-Leningrad, 1939), pp. 12–15.

34. See S. Klivanskii's table on *otkhodnichestvo*, broken down by region, in *Voprosy truda*, 1932, no. 10, p. 73. For ten major regions of the USSR, the rank ordering for rate of increase in peasant departure in the period 1928/9-1931 was exactly the same as the rank ordering for degree of collectivization (i.e., percentage of peasant households collectivized) as of 1 July 1931. The greatest increase in peasant departure was from agricultural regions, such as the Northern Caucasus and the Lower and Central Volga, not from the traditional regions of heavy industrial recruitment, such as the Moscow, Leningrad, and Western oblasts.

35. The kulak group constituted 3.9 percent of all peasant households and (since the kulak households tended to be larger than average) 5.2 percent of peasants (V. P. Danilov, *Sovetskaia dokolkhoznaia derevnia: Sotsial'naia struktura, sotsial'nye otnosheniia* [Moscow, 1979], pp. 310–11 and 316). There were twenty-five million peasant households with an average of five persons per household in the USSR at the end of the 1920s (*Narodnoe khoziaistvo SSSR: Statisticheskii spravochnik 1932* [Moscow, 1932], pp. 122 and 130).

36. For detailed discussion of the guidelines, see Davies, *Socialist Offensive*, pp. 232–37. Third-category kulaks were also liable to resettlement on inferior land outside the village but not to deportation outside the okrug or raion.

37. See, for example, David J. Dallin and Boris I. Nicolaevsky, *Forced Labour in the Soviet Union* (London, 1948), pp. 50–51, and Steven Rosefielde, "An Assessment of the Sources and Uses of Gulag Forced Labour 1928–1956,' *Soviet Studies* 33, 1981, no. 1, p. 68.

38. For example, Academician V. Tikhonov, one of the harshest critics of collectivization, denies that industrialization was a significant factor in rural-urban migration during the First Five-Year Plan and asserts that of the fifteen million peasants "disappearing" from the villages during this period, only a few million were genuinely entering the urban work force, the rest being deported or sent to labor camps or dying in the famine; see his "Chtoby narod prokormil sebia," *Literaturnaia gazeta*, 3 August 1988, p. 10, and his contribution to a roundtable on collectivation, in *Istoriia SSSR*, 1989, no. 3, pp. 30–31.

39. E. g., in the fall of 1929, when 64,000 convicts were transferred (Solomon, "Soviet Penal Policy," p. 208), and in the second half of 1933, after a secret instruction of the Central Committee on 8 May to transfer 400,000 from prison to camps (Smolensk Archive, WKP 178, 11. 135).

40. From the content of the circular, it is clear that widespread and arbitrary arrest of peasants was a major reason for prison overcrowding. "Kulaks sentenced to three to five years" are specifically mentioned as a category to be released from prison and sent (together with their dependents) to OGPU "labor settlements" and camps (Smolensk Archive, WKP 178, 1. 135).

41. Data given by V. Zemskov (Institute of History of the USSR, Academy of Sciences) in interview in *Argumenty i fakty*, 1989, no. 45, p. 6. More detailed data on

Gulag population are given by another historian, Dulgin, in his "Gulag: Otkryvaia arkhivy," published in the MVD newspaper *Na boevom postu*, 1989, no. 146 (27 December), pp. 3–4. The two data sets are basically the same, except that from the mid-1930s Dulgin adds statistics for Gulag's labor colonies to those on the labor camps.

42. Figure for May. From a secret instruction of 8 May 1933 to all party and soviets workers and all organs of OGPU, courts, and procuracy, signed Stalin (general secretary of the party Central Committee) and Molotov (chairman of Sovnarkom). Smolensk Archive, WKP 178, 11. 134–35.

43. Convict laborers in camps did not receive wages after March 1928 (Solomon, "Soviet Penal Policy," p. 210). Those in labor colonies were evidently paid wages not much below the average for free labor (see report in Smolensk Archive, WKP 351, 1. 45), but the number in labor colonies in the early 1930s seems to have been small.

44. Notably N. A. Ivnitskii, *Klassovaia bor'ba v derevne i likvidatsiia kulachestva kak klassa (1929–1932 gg.)* (Moscow, 1972), p. 326; N. I. Platunov, *Pereselencheskaia politika sovetskogo gosudarstva i ee osushchestvlenie v SSSR (1917–iiun' 1941 gg.)* (Tomsk, 1976), p. 220; and *Izmeneniia sotsial'noi struktury sovetskogo obshchestva 1921–seredina 30-kh godov* (Moscow, 1979), pp. 251–53.

45. Ivnitskii, *Klassovaia bor'ba*, p. 326.

46. In January 1932, Iagoda, head of the OGPU, reported to Stalin that 1.4 million kulaks had been deported and resettled since 1929 (Ivnitskii, contribution to roundtable on collectivization, *Istoriia SSSR*, 1989, no. 3, p. 44). This was undoubtedly not the final total, since the secret Central Committee resolution of May 1933 refers to requests from provincial authorities for permission to deport an additional 100,000 kulak households (i.e., probably more than 400,000 persons), which implies a continuing process through 1932 and the first months of 1933. The Central Committee did, however, place an upper limit of 12,000 on further deportations (Smolensk Archive, WKP 178, 11. 134–35).

47. See N. L. Rogalina, *Kollektivizatsiia: Uroki proidennogo puti* (Moscow, 1989), pp. 178–79, for a report of high death rates among deported kulaks resettled in Narym in 1931.

48. Although the deported kulaks allegedly recovered their civil rights with the new Constitution of 1936, they were in fact still deprived of the right to move out of their area of resettlement (although the grown children of deported kulaks recovered it in 1938), and remained so until 1947 (I. Ia. Trifonov, *Likvidatsiia ekspluatatorskikh klassov v SSSR* [Moscow, 1975], pp. 389–91).

49. The original intention may have been to settle all the deported kulaks on the land, but that was expensive and difficult to organize and made it harder for the OGPU to supervise them. For a discussion in fictional form of the issue of rural versus urban resettlement, see N. Skromnyi, "Perelom," *Sever*, 1986, no. 10, pp. 52–64.

50. No data are available on the breakdown between wage earners and dependents. This assumes that adult women among the deportees normally worked for wages and that average household size was smaller than it had been before dekulakization and deportation (see n. 55 below).

51. Figures in this table (rounded to nearest thousand) are taken from Ivnitskii, *Istoriia SSSR*, 1989 no. 3, p. 44 (1a, 2b); Dulgin, "Gulag: Otkryvaia arkhivy," *Na boevom postu*, 27 December 1989, p. 3 (2a); Trifonov, *Likvidatsiia*, p. 379 (3a and 3b).

52. Figures for 1 January 1935.

53. In the Northern Caucasus in 1930, for example, krai authorities first decided to try to resettle 11,000 households of third-category kulaks within the krai, then reduced the number to 8,000, and finally resettled "only 5,000 families . . . , since the rest turned out to have disappeared from the locality." A. N. Oskolkov, *Pobeda kolkhoznogo stroia v zernovykh raionakh Severnogo Kavkaza (Ocherki istorii par-*

tiinogo rukovodstva kollektivizatsiei krest'ianskikh i kazach'ikh khoziaistv) (Rostov-on-Don, 1973), p. 201.

54. There is no good basis for estimating dekulakizations in 1932, though it is evident from the Smolensk Archive document cited in n. 41 that they continued. I have worked from Ivnitskii's estimate of one million households with five million members dekulakized over the period 1929–33 (*Istoriia SSSR*, 1989, no. 3, p. 44), adjusting for the shorter time period. It will be noted that throughout this section I have focused on the period 1929–32, excluding 1933 because of the distorting effects of the famine and the repression associated with it on demographic and social processes in that year.

55. A dekulakized peasant who remained in the village or district was at high risk for subsequent arrest or deportation, even if he had been classified initially as a third-category kulak.

56. Rykov remarked that "the kulaks are fleeing from the raions not yet affected by total collectivization, anticipating that even if there is not total collectivization in their region today, there will be tomorrow." *Desiataia Ural'skaia oblastnaia konferentsiia Vsesoiuznoi Kommunisticheskoi Partii (bol'shevikov)* (Sverdlovsk, 1930), Bulletin 7, p. 19.

57. In 1927, 975,000 peasant households containing 6.4 million adults and children were classified as kulak. *Narodnoe khoziaistvo SSSR* (1932), pp. 122 and 130.

58. N. P. Sapozhnikov, "Kak ia stal domenshchikom," in *Byli industrial'nye* (Moscow, 1973), p. 280.

59. A report on collectivization in Uzbekistan, dated 27 March 1930, published in *Biulleten' oppozitsii*, May 1930, no. 11, p. 25, noted that in response to collectivization (still only partial in Central Asia), "everyone who was linked with the town and had any kind of artisan skills (carpenters, smiths, coopers, saddlemakers, and others) tried to move to the city. . . ."

60. Peter Kruzhin, "False Dawn," in *Soviet Youth: Twelve Komsomol Histories* (Munich: Institut zur Erforschung der UdSSR, series 1, 1959, no. 51), p. 184.

61. Smolensk Archive, WKP 416, 1. 64.

62. Smolensk Archive, WKP 416, 1. 74.

63. *Trud*, 14 July 1933, p. 4.

64. See, for example, the peasant memoirs of dekulakization collected by the Kirovo local historian V. Berdinskii published by A. Dzhapakov in *Trud*, 10 January 1990, and the letters from dekulakized peasants quoted in P. Voshchanov, " 'Kulaki': Sotsial'nyi portret iavleniia," *Komsomol'skaia pravda*, 8 September 1989.

65. Ivan Tvardovskii, "Stranitsy perezhitogo," *Iunost'*, 1988, no. 3, pp. 10–30.

66. Indeed, young people with something that had to be hidden in their family background may have been among the most enthusiastic Stakhanovites and embracers of Soviet values; see, for example, the autobiographical accounts from the 1930s in *Soviet Youth: Twelve Komsomol Histories*.

67. Smolensk Archive, WKP 416, 1. 180.

68. N. Ia. Gushchin, *Sibirskaia derevnia na puti k sotsializmu* (Novosibirsk, 1973), p. 320.

69. Quoted in Gushchin, p. 323.

70. Arutiunian, "Vysvobozhdenie," p. 111.

71. *Molot* (Rostov-on-Don), 23 January 1934, p. 1.

72. Report to first Azovo-Chernomorskaia party conference, *Molot*, 23 January 1934, p. 1. The same happened in the Ukraine, according to Victor Krachenko's eyewitness testimony in *I Chose Freedom* (London, 1949), p. 111.

73. See Nobuo Shimotomai, "A Note on the Kuban Affair (1932–1933)," *Acta Slavica Iaponica* 1, 1983.

74. There were some exceptions to this rule. Peasants (*kolkhozniki* and *edinolichniki*) received passports if they lived within city limits or, in the case of Moscow and

Leningrad, a 100-kilometer zone around the city; and passports were later issued to all inhabitants of frontier zones, including peasants (see resolution of Leningrad oblispolkom, 22 May 1935, "O rezhime v pogranichnykh okrugakh i raionakh Leningradskoi oblasti," *Krest'ianskaia pravda* [Leningrad], 23 May 1935, p. 4).

75. "Ob ustanovlenii edinoi pasportnoi sistemy po Soiuzu SSR i obiazatel'noi propiske pasportov," *Sobranie zakonov i rasporiazhenii*, 1932, no. 84, art. 516; "Polozhenie o pasportakh," *Sobranie zakonov*, 1932, no. 84, art. 517. The first city in which passports were introduced (from mid-January 1933) was Moscow, followed rapidly by Leningrad, Kharkov, Kiev, Minsk, Rostov-on-Don, and Vladivostok. In February, passportization was extended to Magnitogorsk, Kuznetsk, Stalingrad, Baku, and Gorky-Sormovo (SZ 1933, no. 11, articles 60 and 61), and later in the year to Tiflis and Batumi (*Sobranie zakonov*, 1933, no. 46, art. 273).

76. Resolution of Sovnarkom USSR and the Central Committee, "O rasshirenii prava zavodoupravlenii v dele snabzheniia rabochikh i uluchshenii kartochnoi sistemy," *Trud*, 5 December 1932, p. 1.

77. "Ob uvol'nenii za progul bez uvazhitel'nykh prichin," Resolution of TsIK and Sovnarkom SSSR, 15 November 1932. *Sobranie zakonov*, 1932, no. 78, art. 475.

78. "Ob otkhodnichestve," *Pravda*, 20 March 1933, p. 2.

79. *Molodoi kommunist*, 1988, no. 4, p. 85, quoted in Rogalina, p. 163.

80. *Tret'ia sessiia TsIK Soiuza SSR VI sozyva. Stenograficheskii otchet. 23–30 ianvaria 1933 g.* (Moscow, 1933), Bulletin 24, pp. 6–8.

81. *Trud*, 17 November 1932, p. 1.

82. *Pravda*, 28 December 1932, p. 1.

83. A., "Ochistit' goroda ot sotsial'nogo musora," *Trud*, 29 December 1932, p. 2.

84. *Pravda*, 28 December 1932, p. 1, "Dlia chego vvoditsia edenaia pasportnaia sistema." The establishment of a Militia Administration of the OGPU, charged with introducing and implementing the new passport system, was announced in the same issue of *Pravda*. It was headed by G. E. Prokofev.

85. *Trud*, 2 January 1933, p. 2.

86. *New York Times*, 22 January 1933, p. 15.

87. Ibid., 5 February 1933, p. 1.

88. *Sotsialisticheskii vestnik*, 1933, no. 8 (25 May), p. 16.

89. *Sotsialisticheskii vestnik*, 1933, no. 3 (13 February), p. 16. Walter Duranty lifted this report almost word for word and published it (without acknowledgment) in the *New York Times*, 9 April 1933, sec. 4, p. 3.

90. *VII syezd kommunisticheskikh organizatsii Zakavkaz'ia: Stenograficheskii otchet* (Tiflis, 1934), pp. 159–60. For examples from other cities, see *Istoriia industrializatsii Nizhegorodskogo-Gor'kovskogo kraia (1926–1941 gg.)* (Gorky, 1968), p. 276, and *Trud*, 6 January 1933, p. 2.

91. *Trud v SSSR* (1936), p. 7.

92. Vdovin and Drobizhev, p. 109.

93. M. A. Vyltsan, "Trudovye resursy kolkhozov v dovoennye gody (1935–1940 gg.)," *Voprosy istorii*, 1973, no. 2, p. 22.

94. Ibid., p. 24.

95. *Industrializatsiia SSSR 1933–1937 gg. Dokumenty i materialy* (Moscow, 1971), pp. 513–14: 1938 Gosplan memo on kolkhoz labor reserves. Of this group, 2.3 million were village residents who held kolkhoz membership but were basically employed in neighboring enterprises, according to investigations conducted in the first half of 1938.

96. For confirmation by the Supreme Court of the RSFSR of the criminal liability of enterprise officials hiring peasant workers without passports, see *Sovetskaia iustitsiia*, 1934, no. 17, p. 22. For one of many reports of violation, see ibid., 1934, no. 18, p. 23.

97. Historians should treat statistics on "organized labor recruitment" in the Stalin period with the greatest caution. These figures rarely refer strictly to orga-

nized recruitment, i.e., recruitment via contracts between industrial enterprises and kolkhozy, because no bureaucratic entity at central or local level was charged with keeping such statistics. When industrial enterprises were asked to supply "organized recruitment" totals, they might include all peasants hired in groups, all kolkhozniki hired (by formal contracts, in groups without formal contracts, individually on contracts, or individually at the factory gate), all peasants hired, etc.

98. For a range of examples, see *Industrializatsiia SSSR*, pp. 282–83, 288–89, 445–46, and 489–90. The plants often justified their failure to recruit via orgnabor with reference to shortage of accommodation. Enterprises that took orgnabor recruits were required to supply them with housing by the terms of the contracts signed with the kolkhozy.

III

SOCIAL MOBILITY
IN THE COUNTRYSIDE

Stephan Merl

Soviet industrialization in the 1930s involved a high degree of social mobility in the countryside. According to one source, approximately 18.5 million people, predominantly able-bodied young men, migrated to towns and cities to take up work outside the agricultural sector.[1] Millions more in the countryside left field work for jobs in administration or the service sector. Underlying these processes were rampant fears of arrest, deportation, starvation, and disease. The countryside in the 1930s witnessed a continual fight for survival.

Many peasants sought to avoid these traumas in various ways. Taking a very broad definition of social mobility, one might consider the ability to secure a job outside the manual agricultural labor pool as a form of "advancement." Joining the party and taking an administrative job in the collective farm network was one obvious form of such advancement. So was becoming a mechanic or even a Stakhanovite, which sometimes brought the opportunity to leave the state and collective farms under favorable circumstances. This essay, based on studies of the Soviet kolkhoz system, begins by looking briefly at living and working conditions in the countryside, then explores the various forms of ability and opportunity for advancement which constituted, in part, a rural analogue to the industrialization process proper.[2] It should be emphasized, however, that the sources for these interesting topics are limited; in keeping with the goal of the seminar, much of what follows should be considered as suggestive rather than conclusive.[3]

Collectivization involved not only the expulsion from the countryside of millions of relatively well off peasants (kulaks) and the expropriation of their possessions but also a precipitous decline in income for the overwhelming majority of those who stayed on the land. The decline in income was due in part to the loss of sources for income from nonagricultural work, important to the peasants before World War I and during the 1920s. It occurred as well, of course, because of the increasing inability of the peasants to dispose of agricultural production. Before collectivization, peasant money income, especially in the non–Black Earth zone, was largely based on nonfarm activities. As table 3.1 indicates, only some 28 percent of the money income for households in the non–Black Earth zone came from the selling of agricultural products in 1927. In the Ukraine, by contrast, the figure was 49 percent. In the 1930s additional money income was available to kolkhozniki only from off-farm seasonal work. Income from handicraft (kustar) production, which was widely destroyed during collectivization, shrank dramatically; so did income from such sources as providing carts and wagons to transport agricultural production, which had previously been available to those who owned a horse. Only from 1933 onward, when fixed compulsory deliveries were introduced and private plot production encouraged, did the kolkhozniki have the ability once again to dispose of at least a share of their own production.

All of this helped consolidate three broad types of workers in the countryside in the 1930s. At the bottom of the social ladder were the *collective farm workers* (kolkhozniki) themselves, who had no regular income at all (an exception was the collective farms producing cotton after 1935). At the end of 1932 kolkhozniki even lost the right to leave the collective farms without the permission of local authorities. The distribution of produce within the collective farm, which was based on the number of labor units earned, differed greatly between collective farms even within a single district. About 10 percent of all kolkhozes did quite well in comparison with others and generally distributed sufficient food and fodder for the personal needs of their members. Others distributed completely inadequate amounts, even of grain and potatoes. This situation did not significantly change through the 1930s, with the exception of 1937, when a bumper harvest allowed the majority of collective farms to distribute sufficient food and fodder.

The differences in the social well-being of kolkhozniki within the same district were obviously much stronger in the 1930s than between peasant farms in the 1920s, and we can only speculate as to why this may have been so. Collective farms sometimes set different values to the labor unit, the basic claim to income. As a consequence, even a collective farm chairman in a poor kolkhoz might be worse off than a rank-and-file seasonal worker in a neighboring one.[4] In addition, most kolkhozniki profited by thefts of collective farm property, although it is difficult to factor the share of theft into estimates of total income. A further source of differentiation came from the production of private plots, which were necessary for survival and often the only source of any money income. From 1933 onward, production from private plots may have contributed about 50 percent to the total income in money and kind of the average kolkhoz household. The actual total income of a household did not therefore correspond strictly to its share of the number of labor units, leading to a further degree of social

Table 3.1. Money Income of Rural Households in Russia and the Ukraine, 1927

Sown Holdings (in Hectares)	Households (%)	Persons per Household	Money Income (%) from					
			Agricultural Products	Hunting, Fishing, Beekeeping	Nonagricultural Products	Off-Farm Activities*	Borrowing	Other
Grain-deficit zone (i.e., non–Black Earth zone) of the RSFSR								
0– 2.28	50.0	4.15	21.5	2.9	4.2	57.3	6.1	8.0
2.29– 4.47	35.0	5.69	32.2	3.1	3.6	46.1	6.5	8.5
4.48– 8.84	13.8	7.20	40.0	1.9	5.1	38.6	6.4	8.0
8.85–17.58	1.2	9.54	50.6	1.1	3.7	27.8	7.4	9.4
Total/average	100.0	5.23	28.2	2.8	4.2	50.4	6.4	8.0
Ukraine†								
0– 2.28	27.8	3.67	30.4	1.6	1.6	47.8	8.4	10.2
2.29– 4.47	37.1	4.69	46.6	1.2	1.3	32.0	9.2	9.7
4.48– 8.84	25.4	5.70	58.9	1.0	1.5	21.6	8.1	8.9
8.85–17.58	8.3	8.82	67.1	0.5	1.2	14.1	8.1	9.0
Above 17.58	1.4	7.89	72.8	0.3	1.1	11.1	7.1	7.6
Total/average	100.0	4.87	49.1	1.1	1.8	30.2	8.4	9.4

Source: *Denezhnyi oborot v krest'ianskikh khoziaistvakh za 1927 god po mesiatsam* (Moscow, 1929), pp. 44–45, 50, 57.
*Among others, handicraft, trade, hired work in industry or agriculture.
†Representative region for the black-earth zone.

differentiation. How great these differences were is an important task for further research.

A second broad category consisted of *private farmers* who had somehow avoided collectivization. These people were more exposed to the terror of tax and grain procurement campaigns than rank-and-file kolkhozniki, and many lost their property (and their lives), especially in the early 1930s. Nonetheless, some private farmers remained in the countryside and were generally better off than those on collective farms. The most important difference between private farmers and kolkhozniki was the ability of the former to own a work animal and to better dispose of their own agricultural production. In talking about private farmers in the second half of the decade one has to distinguish between invalids and the elderly, who were more or less exempt from further state terror and repression and worked only on their private plots, and private farmers in the Western sense of the word, who were fully engaged in agriculture. This latter group was to be found almost entirely among minority nationalities in the various national republics. There was also, however, a third group—"private entrepreneurs"—who were no longer engaged in agricultural production per se but who worked as hired laborers with their own draft animals and were paid by the collective farms or state and cooperative enterprises for their services. There is some evidence that after the bumper harvest of 1937, some kolkhozniki attempted to buy a horse, quit the collective farm, and join this "private entrepreneurial" group. In total there were about 200,000 rural households of this kind in 1937.

The third broad social category in the countryside consisted of *workers and employees paid by the state,* the only group whose members earned a regular monthly wage. From 1933 onward, these people generally possessed small private plots and produced their own vegetables and other nongrain agricultural products needed for personal consumption. Until 1939, they were also exempted from compulsory deliveries of animal products and potatoes to the state as well as from agricultural taxes.

The number of state workers and employees in the countryside grew steadily during the 1930s, despite the state's effort to keep the number of its employees small, preferring to employ kolkhozniki or private farmers as seasonal employees or day laborers. The majority of workers of the Machine-Tractor Stations (MTS), for example, especially the tractor drivers, were not permanent employees of the state until 1953. In fact, in practical terms, permanent jobs in the countryside were available only to members of collective farm administrations and to the providers of other essential services. Work for the remainder in the countryside in general was highly seasonal, lasting only about 100 working days a year. Only about 1.5 to 1.8 million kolkhozniki (or 5 percent of the collective farm work force) held permanent jobs relating to animal husbandry, and most nonagricultural work—for example, woodcutting or work in construction—was seasonal as well. This had important implications for social mobility and advancement.

One way open to peasants and others in the countryside to "advance" themselves during the industrialization and collectivization drives was by joining the Communist Party. Under the New Economic Policy (NEP), party membership was more or less available to peasants only during the brief period when the leadership turned "its face to the countryside." By 1926 membership was again more difficult. Many in the countryside quit the party or were forced out; on the eve of collectivization and industrialization, membership in rural party organizations was primarily limited to "agricultural workers," a vague category.[5]

Collectivization posed serious administrative problems for the party. As many as several hundred thousand new positions had to be filled while the total number of party members who were classified as peasants was below 200,000. In 1930, consequently, a radical change in admissions policy took place, and by 1933, more than 700,000 peasants had joined the party. The evidence suggests that they were mostly kolkhozniki, since an additional 100,000 classified as "agricultural workers" were also admitted.[6] These figures are summarized in table 3.2.

There is no reliable information on the social status of these new Communists, but it is quite likely that the majority came from poor farms. There is also no information on their motives for joining. Later evidence suggests that political convictions or even a rudimentary knowledge of the political aims of the party itself played only a minor role.[7] We can therefore surmise that many if not most were motivated by the desire for personal advancement, to be better off than the rest of their fellow kolkhozniki. Surveys on peasant communist attitudes in 1927–28 also suggest that many

Table 3.2. Peasant Communists in Soviet Communist Party (VKP), 1929–36

Year	Farmers or Kolkhozniki Admitted as Candidates or Full Members	Increase/ Decrease Members Classified as Peasants at Time of Admission	Expulsions or Resignations*	Advancements to Status of Workers, Employees, or Students*
1929	44,440	+ 6,507	37,933	5,287
1930	171,484	+ 149,365	22,119	3,365
1931	306,393	+ 293,359	13,034	94,611
1932	226,162	+ 155,718	70,444	97,490
1933–36	—	− 466,584	466,584	—

Source: Calculated by author from data in I. N. Iudin, *Sotsial'naia baza rosta KPSS* (Moscow, 1973), pp. 162–64.
*Figures are minimums and include those admitted as "agricultural laborers" and registered as workers at time of admission, who later became kolkhozniki and had their social designation changed. The total number of these cases is approximately 10,000.

Table 3.3. Soviet Communists Registered as Peasants at Time of Admission to Party Who Became Industrial
Workers, Employees, or Students,
1925–37

Year	Number
1925	117,152
1926	112,150
1927	140,147
1928	122,022
1929	114,688
1930	119,975
1931	122,653
1932	217,264
1933	314,754
1937	254,000

Source: Calculated from data in I. N.
Iudin, *Sotsial'naia baza rosta KPSS* (Moscow,
1973), pp. 164f.; *Istoriia kommunisticheskoi
partii sovetskogo soiuza v shesti tomakh*, vol. 4,
pt. 2 (Moscow, 1971), p. 507.
Data are for January 1 of each year; all
figures are minimums.

may have joined the party in order to escape from the countryside
altogether.[8]

Very few of those admitted to the party after the beginning of collectivization, however, had the necessary training or ability to fill leading
positions. Many even lacked an elementary education and were likely
granted admission by local organizations to provide some social "ballast."
At least 200,000 of these new members also seem to have succeeded in
getting positions outside the collective farms themselves, and most probably left the countryside to become industrial workers or students in various institutes and schools (see table 3.3). Among these, at least 30,000
became chairmen or chairwomen of village soviets, many of whom, much
more so than those who left the countryside, would soon fall victim to the
purges.

The majority of the peasants who were admitted to the party in 1930–32,
however, remained in rural areas and worked in lowly kolkhoznik positions. At the time the campaign to send peasant Communists back to
production work began in early 1933, only about a third of the 600,000
party members who were registered kolkhozniki actually filled such leading positions in the collective farm management as chair, brigadier, department head, or accountant. Most held minor administrative posts and
earned their living with little actual work. It was routine for rank-and-file

kolkhozniki to be given some administrative position in the collective farm at the time they were admitted to the party.[9]

In late 1932 the first wave of purges struck rural party members, beginning in the southern grain districts affected by Stalin's famine. By mid-1933 the purge had spread to village party organizations everywhere. As table 3.2 indicates, at least 80 percent of all peasant Communists admitted to the party between 1930 and 1932 who were still living in the countryside in early 1933 were expelled or otherwise forced out.[10]

Among the reasons most frequently given for the expulsion of a rural party member were passivity, "alien class element," "ballast," the lack of morality, and political illiteracy. It is doubtlessly the case that those expelled were primarily in leading positions and included large numbers of men and women in charge of collective farms or village soviets. Many of these people, however, appealed their expulsions and were reinstated.[11] There is also evidence that others were subsequently reinstated in the same position by the district committees even if they did not rejoin the party.

Given the purges, it is hard to assess the effect of membership in the party on a peasant's career. Many clearly "advanced," but few seem to have escaped some form of subsequent degradation, either to the position again of rank-and-file kolkhoznik or to minor posts in collective farm administration and services. Many peasant Communists arrested and sent to prison during the 1932–33 terror were also granted a pardon in 1935.[12] They also seemed to escape in the main the ravages of the Ezhovshchina in 1936–37, perhaps simply because they held such insignificant positions.

By 1937 hardly any rank-and-file kolkhoznik was a member of the party. Of the approximately 180,000 rural Communists who were nonetheless registered as kolkhozniki, about one-third chaired the collective farms while others worked as tractor drivers, brigade commanders, and the like (see table 3.4).

After 1936 very few collective farmers were admitted to the party.[13] In the latter part of the decade, in contrast to 1930–32, those recruited were now primarily agriculture specialists or rural teachers. Thus party membership after 1936 was a reward for success rather than the entry to a new career, although it undoubtedly facilitated further advancement.[14]

Ostensibly intended to increase the efficiency of agricultural production, collectivization actually aggravated the problem of underemployment in the countryside. The destruction of livestock and the smothering of handicrafts resulted in the loss not simply of peasant income but also in thousands of jobs as well. The only new positions created by collectivization were in service and administration, and often the only purpose in creating many of these positions was to provide people with a means of surviving, since the jobs themselves were actually not needed. Actual field work in the collective farms, which largely remained seasonal, became the underprivileged domain of women, children, and youth.

Table 3.4. Jobs of Peasant Members and Candidates of Soviet Communist Party and Communist Youth League, End of 1937

Job	Communist Party		Communist Youth League	
	Number	Percent	Number	Percent
Chair or vice-chair of kolkhoz	48,785	60.4	18,480	16.5
Brigade leader, head of animal farm	17,483	21.6	32,965	29.5
Head of revision committee	6,043	7.5	12,783	11.4
Agricultural specialist*	1,618	2.0	7,240	6.5
Bookkeeper, accountant	3,477	4.3	35,271	31.6
Milkmaid	3,383	4.2	5,074	4.5
Total	80,789	100	111,813	100

Source: *Kolkhozy vo vtoroi Stalinskoi piatiletke: Statisticheskii sbornik* (Moscow-Leningrad, 1939), pp. 60–80.
*Animal technician, agronomist, agricultural technician, veterinary assistant.

Most new collective farm posts were created between 1930 and 1933. By the mid-1930s there were about two million "leading" posts in collective farm administration (chair, brigadier, accountant, agronomist, animal specialist). An additional ten million able-bodied kolkhozniki held minor jobs in administration and service: storekeepers, guards, members of fire brigades, nurses, cleaners, postal and communications workers, office personnel, etc. We can thus estimate that approximately 30 percent of all able-bodied collective farm workers (predominantly men) did not take part in agricultural production. Specific figures for one region are given in table 3.5.

One of the most attractive forms of advancement in the countryside during industrialization and collectivization was to become chair of a collective farm. When collectivization began in late 1929, party leaders apparently thought only industrial workers could be appointed to this post. As Lynne Viola has shown, this led to the dispatch of the "25,000ers" to the countryside, a figure which corresponded to the total number of planned large-scale collective farms.[15]

Most of the 240,000 collective farms in the 1930s were, however, relatively small-scale enterprises, averaging only about eighty households. It was therefore impossible even to attempt to staff them with skilled industrial workers, and most kolkhoz administrators had to be recruited from the peasants themselves. Even among the 25,000ers only about 7,000 actually worked as kolkhoz chairs, predominantly in the Volga, North Caucasus,

Table 3.5. Jobs of Able-Bodied Collective Farm Workers in Novosibirsk Oblast, Early 1939

Job	Number	Percent
Management		
Kolkhoz chair or vice-chair, accountant, etc.	25,100	3.9
Brigade leader, head of animal farm	20,000	3.1
Agricultural specialist	1,300	0.2
Nonagricultural specialist (culture, education and health)	2,500	0.4
Total	48,900	7.6
Outside agricultural production		
Blacksmith, mechanic, locksmith	8,900	1.4
Driver	1,100	0.2
Woodcutter	5,800	0.9
Carpenter, joiner	13,700	2.2
Carter	22,600	3.5
Other service	85,600	13.5
Total	137,700	21.7
In agricultural production		
Animal production (milkmaid, tending cattle or horses, herds)	94,900	14.9
Machinist	6,200	1.0
Horticulture, etc.	21,600	3.4
Manual field worker	326,000	51.4
Total	449,100*	70.7
Grand Total	635,700	100.0

Source: Gushchin et al., *Krest'ianstvo zapadnoi Sibiri v dovoennye gody (1935–1941)* (Novosibirsk, 1975), p. 84.
All figures exclude kolkhozniki absent for seasonal work, study, or service in the army.
*Figure should be 448,700; mistake in source.

and the Ukraine, where they constituted 10 to 20 percent of these positions.[16] The heads of other collective farms were recruited from "politically active" peasants. By 1933 every third collective farm chair was a party member and two-thirds were formerly poor peasants, at least by official designation, a group which was strongly overrepresented among collective farm heads.[17]

It is likely that most of these people held positions in collective farms away from their home districts, although no information is available on the number of collective farm chairs who may have been recruited from the local peasantry for the smaller collective farms. In practice, the regional party committee selected candidates to head the kolkhozy, although by statute the general collective farm assembly was entitled to elect its chair.

Kolkhozy quickly learned, however, how to get rid of someone they didn't want. Consequently, people beginning work as collective farm chairs had little chance to remain in office for more than a few months. Throughout the 1930s approximately half of all collective farm heads were removed from office every year, and most seem to have been discharged after only a few months.[18] Even in the second half of the 1930s only about 35 percent of all collective farms were headed by people who had served in that position two years or longer (see table 3.6). Many of these persons were, of course, scapegoats during the various rural purges who were held responsible for the poor state of the collective farms as a whole.

These official statistics are, however, misleading. Data cover only length of service on a given kolkhoz without giving information about how long a person may have worked elsewhere in the same position. A removal may also have represented a promotion. According to regional data, approximately 5 percent of all collective farm chairs "advanced" each year to either another collective farm or a comparable position outside the kolkhoz—in effect, a promotion. Only between 10 and 15 percent of all collective farm chairs appear to have been discharged for complete incompetence, and most were in their first job as chair. Many, especially women, also seem to have left on their own accord to return to positions of lesser responsibility. Still, the majority of collective farm chairs (about a third of all chairs each year) were removed because of "mistakes." In all likelihood most of these people remained in the confidence of district officials and even if put to trial were usually given light sentences and renominated soon to the same position. Thus the yearly renewal of kolkhoz chairs was probably below 15 percent.[19]

New recruits to the position of collective farm chair came primarily from brigade leaders. These people undoubtedly had some practical knowledge in commanding other people. In contrast, few graduates of agricultural institutes seem to have become collective farm chair.[20] One reason might have been that better qualified people preferred to work elsewhere, although a number of such graduates were found in collective farm positions at levels below that of chairs (accountant, agricultural specialist). The most likely explanation is that better education was no qualification for the job of a collective farm chair in the eyes of the district party secretaries. Throughout the 1930s, of course, collective farms faced impossible and contradictory demands, especially after procurement prices ceased to be sufficient to meet the costs of production.

It is hardly surprising, therefore, to find evidence that "successful" collective farm chairs owed their success primarily to their good relations with local party and soviet organizations, primarily those on a district level. Just as in industry, all leading administrators in a given district had common interests. Above all was the need to appear to fulfill state procurement demands while in fact hiding as much as possible from delivery requirements in order to meet the collective farm's own needs. As elsewhere in the

Table 3.6. Collective Farm Officials in USSR by Length of Service, 1936 and 1938

Job		Service in Years*				Percentage of		
		Less than 1	1–2	2–5	More than 5	Communists	Komsomol	Women
Kolkhoz chair or vice-chair	1936	37.4	27.5	29.7	5.4	33.2†	3.8	2.7
Kolkhoz chair	1938	46.0	19.6	25.2	9.2	17.5	5.5	2.6
Kolkhoz vice-chair	1938					5.0	5.0	3.7
Head of revision committee	1936	32.1	31.6	32.5	3.8	8.3†	5.9	1.8
	1938	47.1	24.6	22.3	6.0	2.6	5.5	3.0
Head of animal farm	1936	38.6	26.3	30.7	4.4	9.2†	5.4	16.1
	1938	43.6	23.8	24.6	8.0	3.6	4.5	18.3
Field brigade leader	1936	28.4	27.2	39.5	4.9	6.8†	4.5	2.7
	1938	40.1	23.8	27.6	8.5	1.8	4.2	4.2
Bookkeeper, accountant	1936	29.3	21.0	39.6	10.1	3.1†	12.6	4.5
	1938	34.9	22.2	30.0	12.9	1.4	14.2	6.2
Team leader	1936	29.7	41.9	26.2	2.2	1.0	4.5	66.8
Tender of horses	1936	34.9	24.0	36.5	4.6	0.9†	1.9	3.2
Milkmaid	1938	38.4	25.5	27.0	9.1	0.8	1.2	100
Veterinary assistant	1938	34.0	28.5	28.7	8.8	1.8	8.6	2.5

Source: 1936: *Trud v SSSR* (Moscow, 1936), p. 326; 1938: *Kolkhozy vo vtoroi piatiletke*, pp. 60–80.
*1936 = 7,030 kolkhozes (3 percent of total); 1938 = 237,568 kolkhozes (98 percent of total).
†Including sympathizers (minor status of candidates, not registered in party).

Soviet economy in this period, a collective farm chair needed experience above all in betraying the state.

Field brigade positions were also a means of advancement in the country-side, as were heads of dairy and livestock farms. People at this level were more often recruited from the ranks of "middle peasants" than were the collective farm chairs. Evidence suggests that the number of middle peasants among field brigade leaders roughly corresponded to the share of middle peasants among all collective farmers in the 1920s.[21]

Data on the gender and age of collective farm management people (table 3.6) suggests that access to these posts was limited. Nearly all management positions were held by men over twenty-five years of age. Few women or younger people were employed, despite several campaigns to promote women in kolkhoz ranks during the 1930s. "Leading positions" for women thus meant children's work or work as deputies of some sort.[22] Only in some areas near the industrial centers in the non–Black Earth zone and in Siberia was the share of women collective farm chairs and brigade commanders above 5 percent, probably because most men had left the collective farms for better positions elsewhere.

Still, collective farm administrative posts were privileged in comparison with seasonal work in the fields since they secured a permanent occupation and were comparatively easy to perform. In addition, collective farm administrators generally earned significantly more labor units than production workers. Even if the number of labor units per working day was small, as in the case of a scrubwoman or a nurse, the fact that the position was a permanent one secured for its holder at least the same amount of labor units as did work in agricultural production (see table 3.7).

On occasion, party leaders attempted to struggle against the proliferation of collective farm positions. The first campaign against unnecessary posts began in 1933 but was largely unsuccessful, partly because the state simultaneously expanded the number of positions for rural militia and guards to protect the collective farm harvests from theft. A second campaign, which did not occur until 1940, was carried through with more vigor.[23]

The mechanization of agriculture in the 1930s also presented opportunities for "advancement," but working conditions in this area, especially at the beginning and at the end of the 1930s, were so miserable that only a few of the trained mechanics or machine operators stayed at their jobs for long periods of time.

Instability in this area of the rural work force began with the nationalization of tractors and their withdrawal from the collective farms in 1929–30. Although they had lost control over their machinery, tractor drivers remained kolkhozniki. They worked in the MTS during seasonal fieldwork (about 100 days a year, on average) and were idle during the winter. Their pay came from the kolkhoz, not the MTS. They were also excluded from state insurance (a big problem in cases of accidental injury or death).

Table 3.7. Kolkhoz Jobs in USSR by Working Days and Labor Units, 1939

		Average per Capita		
Job	Total (Incomplete)	Working Days	Labor Units	Labor Units per Working Day
Agricultural specialist (*polevod*)	3	363	453	1.25
Cultural worker	5	358	511	1.43
Horse tender (*koniukh*)	49	353	459	1.30
Veterinary	14	351	515	1.47
Economist	54	349	514	1.47
Bookkeeper	38	345	625	1.81
Mail deliverer	102	343	289	0.84
Cleaner	83	341	245	0.72
Storekeeper	143	338	419	1.24
Veterinary assistant	56	337	441	1.31
Accountant (animal farm)	28	335	402	1.20
Head of blacksmith shop	36	334	541	1.62
Secretary	24	334	442	1.32
Assistant accountant	115	326	432	1.33
Registrar	66	322	393	1.22
Field brigade leader	279	320	479	1.50
Cashier	64	317	270	0.85
Barber	2	313	446	1.42
Guard (office)	151	312	265	0.85
Blacksmith	234	305	484	1.59
Firefighter	154	293	298	1.02
Agronomist	12	288	460	1.60
Assistant chemist (plant protection)	6	227	217	0.96
Head of kindergarten	100	221	235	1.06
Worker with draft animals in fields	1,488	216	291*	1.35
Team leader in fields	508	198	236	1.19
Manual worker in fields	5,723	143	169	1.18
Total	9,537			

Source: *Sotsialisticheskoe sel'skoe khoziaistvo*, 1941, no. 2, p. 33.
Figures include 132 kolkhozes in 26 oblasti.
*Misprint in source (201) corrected.

In retaining the legal status of kolkhozniki but in fact being seasonal state employees by profession, the biggest problem for tractor drivers throughout the period of industrialization and collectivization was to get paid for the actual work they did. Tractor drivers had to fight with both the collective farms and MTS to be compensated for the labor units that remained the measurement of earnings. Often the collective farms had neither money nor grain to pay their drivers after distributions to their other members, and no collective farm was willing to pay for work done by the tractor drivers on the fields of other farms. Many drivers were thus paid sporadically over the winter and some not at all. In 1931 the drivers' lot worsened when mechanical breakdowns were deemed "kulak" behavior and could land a driver in jail. This happened quite often, in fact, since drivers and other MTS mechanics were quite ill-trained.[24]

Until 1932, therefore, the average tractor driver was probably even worse off than the average field worker on the collective farms. Evidence suggests that as many as 50 percent of newly trained drivers quit their jobs during their first season of work; others dropped out of the training courses. The situation seems to have improved somewhat after a 1933 decree setting a minimum value for the labor unit used to calculate tractor drivers' earnings (2.5 rubles and 3 kg of grain). This was significantly above the average value of labor units earned by kolkhozniki.[25] Still, tractor drivers continued to have difficulty receiving their pay. In the winter of 1933–34 the party consequently instituted a special campaign to secure payment for the 1933 working season.[26] Yet the drivers were still only paid for actual work done in the fields; the burden for time lost due to work interruptions of any sort, even if due to the lack of fuel or replacement parts, continued to fall on their shoulders.[27] Improvements in income significantly reduced the turnover rate from approximately 45 percent in 1933 to about 25 percent in 1934.[28] Between 1934 and 1936 the turnover rate of combine drivers was still around 40 percent and fell only to the 20 percent level in 1937. Since it took two years to fully train a combine driver and was thus quite expensive for the state, the government decided in 1935 to absorb combine drivers onto the state payroll as a means of controlling turnover rates.[29]

Yet becoming a tractor driver was still an attractive job, especially for kolkhoz youth. A 1936 survey showed that 56 percent of all drivers were under twenty-five years old. Thirteen percent were Komsomol members, while fewer than 1 percent were members of the party. The share of women among the drivers was quite small and did not exceed 4 percent. Here too, however, 80 percent of the women were under twenty-five years old; 21 percent were Komsomol members. Of the 7,311 combine drivers included in the 1936 survey, 48 percent were younger than twenty-five and 6 percent were women.[30] Turnover among women tractor drivers was extremely high. Hard working conditions and the difficulties of staying overnight in the fields with male drivers apparently took their toll. New attempts by the party to recruit more women as tractor drivers failed. Only in the non–Black Earth zone and in Siberia, with its serious shortage of male collective farm workers (as a consequence of migration), did women briefly constitute more than 10 percent of the driver work force in the second half of the 1930s.[31]

At the end of 1937 only 10 percent of the tractor drivers trained before 1932 were still at work. Of the half-million drivers trained in 1933 and 1934, 27 percent were still working; of the 650,000 drivers trained in 1935 and 1936, 47 percent were still at work. Turnover remained greatest during the first season of work. Thus only 60 percent of the drivers trained in early 1937 were still on the job at the end of the year.[32]

Recruitment of tractor and especially combine drivers became a problem after 1937. In some districts machinery stood idle as a consequence.[33] One reason why the post remained unattractive for many apparently had to do with the decline in delivery of new tractors after 1936, the poor quality of repair work, and the consequent high rate of breakdowns (due in part to the fact that Soviet tractors were used approximately ten times more hours annually than tractors in the West). Further problems arose from continued fuel shortages, and often it took days and even weeks to get replacement parts or fuel to the fields. As in the earlier years of collectivization, drivers did not earn labor units during this downtime. After 1937, while the total number of drivers remained relatively constant (at around 800,000), turnover remained high. The yearly average for the period between 1936 and 1940 was approximately 250,000.[34] This undoubtedly led to inclusion of tractor drivers in the new harsh rules of labor discipline for state workers in 1940, making it a crime to quit one's job without authorization.[35] In 1938 and 1939 approximately 20 percent of the tractor driver work force and half of the combine drivers apparently quit their jobs in this way.[36]

Many of these people, especially the women, returned to less difficult collective farm jobs where their real incomes were more predictable. Others migrated to towns and sometimes simply left their tractors sitting in the fields. Most drivers, however, apparently had authorization to leave their jobs. About 20 percent a year were recruited into the army. Others advanced into higher-paying positions. Nearly all combine drivers were recruited from the traktoristy; others became tractor brigade leaders or MTS mechanics, remaining on the state payroll. Thus up to one-third of all those leaving their jobs as tractor drivers in the second half of the 1930s stayed in the same professional area.

Incentives and advancement among collective farm workers were also stimulated by the introduction in 1930 of shock work, which served the purpose as well of strengthening labor discipline. By the spring of 1931 at least one million collective farmers were registered as "shock workers." As many as a quarter million were rewarded with premiums.[37] National congresses of collective farm shock workers in 1933 and especially 1935 gave the movement a boost. As in other such gatherings, rank-and-file collective farm women went to Moscow to shake hands with Stalin and discuss "state affairs." In 1935 the gathering was organized to discuss the new draft collective farm statute. According to at least one report, this involvement made a great impression on rank-and-file rural workers.[38]

The year 1935 also saw the introduction of the Stakhanovite movement in the countryside and the decoration of Maria Demchenko as the first Stakhanovite hero of agriculture.[39] Unlike shock work, however, Stakhanovism led to serious trouble in the collective farms. As elsewhere, the intention was to increase labor productivity by substituting higher working norms, which threatened the already miserable income of collective farm workers. Kolkhozniki were soon attacking the Stakhanovites with abandon, beating them up, destroying their animals, even killing them.[40] For obvious reasons, collective farm management and even village authorities were often also not eager to see labor norms increased and colluded in these assaults. If we recall that field work in the collective farms was done primarily by women, it is understandable why the vast majority of rural Stakhanovites were female. In general, male Stakhanovites were chosen from tractor or combine drivers. As elsewhere, most were young.[41]

Despite the risks, a career as a shock worker or Stakhanovite remained attractive for many younger people, especially women. It was a means for some to break away from the patriarchal hierarchy of village society and to win acknowledgment from party and state officials. Often, apparently, close relationships developed between female Stakhanovites and their party patrons.[42] This may well have been the source of much arbitrariness and cheating concerning official production records, which were sometimes reached in miraculous fashion with only one cow or a small area of land.

The first all-Union Exhibition of Agriculture, which opened in Moscow in 1939, gives us some idea about the number of successful Stakhanovites at the end of the decade. Some 168,000 of the best rural workers and managers were nominated to take part, fewer than 0.5 percent of all able-bodied kolkhozniki; 21,000 of them received gold or silver medals and money premiums (of between 500 and 3,000 rubles). In 1940 the number of participants increased to 270,000. Thus about 3 percent of all able-bodied kolkhozniki were probably active Stakhanovites.[43]

Obviously, becoming a Stakhanovite at least offered the possibility of a higher standard of living than that of other collective farm workers, yet most probably received relatively minor awards: clothes, a watch, a radio, a bicycle. Since the value of a labor unit was so small on the average collective farm, even a large number of units did not allow one to advance significantly. Refugees from the countryside interviewed in the Harvard Refugee Project almost sound as if they pity "their" Stakhanovites:

In each kolkhoz you will find about five or six of them. A Stakhanovite is a person who works day and night with his whole soul. If you give him one norm, he'll fulfill two, if two then two and a half. He gets prizes. Oh, the prizes are often little swine who are too weak to live. Let's say a mother sow died, so they give the litter to the Stakhanovites. They call a big meeting, and then in the papers they write he received a sow or a swine. They don't write that he put him in his glove to take him home, and that three days later he died on him under the stove. Well, that's the sort of Stakhanovites that we have. . . .

How do people look on the Stakhanovites? Well, like on fools. . . . They don't like them, because they are then held up as examples and they say, why don't you work as hard as these do. Because of them you have to work harder even though you don't have the same strength.[44]

In all we had about twenty Stakhanovites on the collective farm. Usually there were one or two in a brigade, although in some brigades there were none. Later we had about forty Stakhanovites. They would get a trip to Moscow. They were downtrodden people. They were dark and blank. They believed that they would be taken care of by the Regime. However, in fact if a Stakhanovite did not do well because he lost his health or because he had some family difficulty he was out. He would be fined and sometimes even arrested.[45]

There is thus little evidence that becoming a Stakhanovite was the starting point of a career, although a few Stakhanovites obviously became national heroes. The majority stayed on the collective farms and remained seasonal production workers. The difficulty of the work itself also made it impossible to remain a Stakhanovite for very long.

Finally, a few observations about seasonal work outside the collective farms and urban rural migration. At the height of the industrialization drive in the mid-1930s, about 10 percent of all able-bodied kolkhozniki, predominantly men, worked permanently or seasonally outside the collective farms.[46] Interestingly, there is some evidence that village soviets and even the kolkhoz leadership tried to sabotage the recruitment of seasonal workers, fearing they would lack the numbers needed for the next season's production.[47] Kolkhozniki who took up seasonal work outside their farms were sometimes regarded as "deserters" and their families threatened with expulsion from the collective. On the other hand, seasonal collective farm workers aggressively recruited for essentially forced labor in activities such as cutting wood often refused to go.[48]

To combat this resistance, the state introduced incentives. Those willing to do seasonal work in the mining or peat industry were exempted from agricultural taxes and allowed to receive grain or fodder from the collective farms at low state procurement prices, even if they had left the farms without authorization. Collective farm chairmen who opposed these rewards were themselves threatened with arrest.[49]

Toward the end of the 1930s industrial recruiters were often seen as competitors in the countryside, both with the collective farms and among themselves. Some kolkhozniki signed on with several industrial enterprises at once, cashing the premiums they were given for enrolling but never leaving the collective farm. In 1938 and 1939, several decrees were issued to fight against these abuses, but plans for labor recruitment from the countryside for nonagricultural work (about 3.3 to 3.8 million workers were sought between 1937 and 1939) were seriously underfulfilled (see table 3.8). A special problem of recruitment had to do with skill. Kolkhozniki could often be used only for simple unskilled work. Although about 8.3 million workers from the collective farms finished courses certifying to a "minimum technical competence," this had little effect on permanent out-migration from the countryside, since many proved incompetent and returned to their villages.[50] Nevertheless, despite these problems and the unattractiveness of seasonal work in construction, woodcutting, mining, and other difficult jobs, seasonal work could still be a step to permanent employment in industry, especially for younger people. Adults in the 1930s, largely unskilled and often with strong ties to their families, seem to have worked in the main only one or two seasons away from their villages. Much more attractive for them were posts in village services or even such jobs as food preparers, as in a bakery.[51] Better jobs in the countryside apparently went more often to those who were not already collective farmers, including private farmers. In the first half of the 1930s the state even provided incentives for this category. If the head of a private household took up permanent work in a state farm, for example, the entire family was exempted from agricultural taxes. Probably about one million people in total took up permanent work in the state farms in this way between 1930 and 1935. An additional 1.5 million from both individual and collective farms were hired annually as seasonal state farm workers or day laborers.[52]

Hardly any information is available about the 1 or 2 percent of collective farm households that were annually expelled. About half of them may have been expelled after the principal household worker took up unauthorized work outside the collective. In all likelihood, however, most probably became members of another collective farm or migrated to urban areas.

Overwhelmingly, of course, collectivization created only downward social mobility for the peasants, marked by the loss of nonagricultural income and the ability to dispose of agricultural produce. The general framework was set above all by low state procurement prices in the system of compulsory deliveries. These repressive determinants of rural life during industrialization (and afterward) meant that for the overwhelming majority there was absolutely no possibility of real social advancement for those working in agricultural production. Even Stakhanovites did not constitute

Table 3.8. Seasonal Work in USSR by Peasants outside Agriculture, with Increases in State Workers and Employees, 1925–40

Year	Peasants Working Seasonally outside Agriculture*	New Workers and Employees in National Economy[†]	Migration Surplus of Towns
1925	2,867,000		
1926	3,285,000	1,700,000–1,800,000	
1927	3,145,000	1,100,000–1,200,000	
1928	3,963,000	1,100,000–1,200,000	1,062,000
1929	4,343,000	1,500,000–1,600,000	1,392,000
1930		3,500,000–3,600,000	2,633,000
1931	5,454,000	5,400,000–5,600,000	4,100,000
1932	3,642,000	4,800,000–5,000,000	2,719,000
1933	1,887,000	100,000–300,000	772,000
1934	3,247,000	2,200,000–2,500,000	2,452,000
1935	3,124,000	2,100,000–2,300,000	(2,556,000)
1936	3,104,000	2,300,000–2,600,000	
1937	1,570,000	2,500,000–2,800,000	
1938	2,011,000		
1939	2,315,000		
1940	2,327,000		

Sources: A. I. Vdovin u. V. Z. Drobizhev, *Rost rabochego klassa SSSR 1917–1940 gg.* (Moscow, 1976), pp. 109–20; *Trud v SSSR.* (Moscow, 1936), p. 7; V. P. Danilov, "Krest'ianskii otkhod na promysly v 1920-kh godakh," *Istoricheskie zapiski* 96, 1974, pp. 55–122.
*Includes *orgnabor* (contract between kolkhoz and industrial plant); 1925–29 = economic years 1924/25–1928/29; 1925–29 = seasonal work; 1932–33 = unauthorized seasonal work and orgnabor; 1933–40 = orgnabor only.
[†]Increase counted with regard to retirement.

much of an exception. Collectivization turned agricultural production into the province of the underprivileged (women, children, and youth), but even the widespread passing of males into jobs in collective farm administration should not be interpreted as real advancement, especially in comparison to the 1920s. At best, such improvements in social position only allowed one to maintain the living standard of a poor peasant under NEP.

Only those few jobs in collective farm administration that involved responsibility over others could be thought of as an area of genuine social mobility. Here, however, advancement and repression were strongly connected. Often such mobility led to a quick and disastrous conclusion.

Advancement to kolkhoz managerial positions was also largely limited to adult males. Unlike education in urban areas, education in the countryside did not in general open new career paths. The only exceptions were jobs as accountants, agricultural specialists, and rural teachers. As a consequence, "advancement" took other forms. A job was soon attractive not in terms of the number of labor units it provided but in terms of how hard one had to work for them. Thus the most appealing forms of advancement in the collective farm involved moving to positions which liberated a person from working in the fields.

The problem of finding adequate work for young people in the collective farms thus remained a serious one in the 1930s. The least attractive jobs in field production were the ones most readily available. For young people to advance socially in any significant way therefore meant leaving the countryside entirely. Here the opportunities for young men were significantly greater than for women. In all likelihood, training as a tractor or combine driver offered the best chance for a career outside agriculture. The military was another avenue of escape open almost entirely to men. Most young rural male migrants, however, probably succeeded in escaping the kolkhoz by first taking up seasonal work and making contacts that could subsequently secure a permanent position. By the mid-1930s, therefore, the image of the countryside as an unlimited source for Russia's growing industrial work force is undoubtedly overdrawn. At the very least, it appears that the more attractive jobs in industry were filled by those from the urban areas themselves. Rural migrants, in the main, took unpopular and low-paying jobs such as those in the mines and forests, often with high numbers of injuries and in working conditions similar to those of forced labor.

NOTES

1. *Bol'shaia sovetskaia entsiklopediia*, 3d ed., vol. 24, bk. 2 (Moscow, 1977), p. 16.

2. S. Merl, *Sozialer Aufstieg im sowjetischen Kolchossystem der 30er Jahre? Über das Schicksal der bäuerlichen Parteimitglieder, Dorfsowjetvorsitzenden, Posteninhaber in Kolchosen, Mechanisatoren und Stachanowleute* (Berlin: Duncher & Homblot, 1990); same author, *Bauern unter Stalin: Die Formierung des sowjetischen Kolchossystems, 1930–1941* (Berlin: Duncker & Humblot, 1990).

3. There is hardly any direct information on social mobility in the countryside as far as individual careers are concerned. The known biographies of several hundred Stakhanovites are so stereotyped, especially in terms of social origins, that they are of little value. Legal records and files on the expulsion of party members

provide a glimpse of a very small number of careers, but they do not allow for generalization. Most of what follows is therefore based on indirect information: changes in the number and types of positions; accessibility by sex, age, and education; the turnover rate. For specific references, see S. Merl, *Sozialer Aufstieg.*

4. This becomes particularly evident from the 1940 law on the payment of the kolkhoz chairmen. For the same job a kolkhoz chairman earned between 25 and 400 rubles monthly, depending on the money income of the kolkhoz (*Sobranie zakonov SSSR*, 1940, no. 11, art. 271).

5. See the discussion in S. Merl, *Der Agrarmarkt und die Neue Ökonomische Politik: Die Anfänge staatlicher Lenkung der Landwirtschaft in der Sowjetunion 1925–1928* (München, Wien: R. Oldenbourg Verlag, 1981), pp. 40–49; same author, *Die Anfänge der Kollektivierung in der Sowjetunion: Der Übergang zur staatlichen Reglementierung der Produktions- und Marktbeziehungen im Dorf (1928–1930)* (Wiesbaden: Otto Harrassowitz Verlag, 1985), pp. 98–104.

6. See table 2, *Partiinoe stroitel'stvo*, 1932, nos. 7–8, p. 54.

7. See, for example, *Partiinoe stroitel'stvo*, 1932, nos. 7–8, pp. 53f., no. 21, pp. 46–48.

8. *Derevenskii kommunist*, 1928, no. 8, p. 21; *Izvestiia TsK*, 1928, no. 29, p. 13; Merl, *Anfänge*, pp. 101f.

9. *Partiinoe stroitel'stvo*, 1932, no. 10, pp. 37f.; nos. 19–20, pp. 61–63; *Sputnik kommunista v derevne*, 1932, no. 2, pp. 37–41.

10. The exact number of peasant Communists expelled is not known, however. Between 1930 and 1932 about 100,000 peasant Communists seem to have left the party. Data on the effect of the purge on rural party organizations are available only for 1932–33. While figures for the party as a whole show that about 17 percent of all party members and candidates were expelled in 1933, rural party organizations lost 30 to 45 percent of their members. See *Partiinoe stroitel'stvo*, 1933, nos. 1–2, pp. 27–33; nos. 7–8, pp. 42–44; no. 17, pp. 8–12; *Bolshevik*, 1934, no. 15, pp. 9–23; no. 21, pp. 34–47.

11. S. G. Wheatcroft, "Towards a Thorough Analysis of Soviet Forced Labour Statistics," *Soviet Studies*, 1983, p. 227.

12. *Sobranie zakonov*, 1935, no. 44, art. 365.

13. M. A. Vyltsan, *Sovetskaia derevnia nakanune Velikoi Otechestvennoi voiny (1938–1941 gg.)* (Moscow, 1970), p. 188.

14. T. H. Rigby, *Communist Party Membership in the U.S.S.R., 1917–1967* (Princeton, N.J.: Princeton University Press, 1968), pp. 214–29.

15. Lynne Viola, *The Best Sons of the Fatherland: Workers in the Vanguard of Soviet Collectivization* (Oxford: Oxford University Press, 1987); Merl, *Anfänge*, pp. 331–400.

16. Calculated by the author from data in *Kolkhozy vesnoi 1931 g. Statisticheskaia razrabotka otchetov kolkhozov ob itogakh vesennogo seva 1931 g.* (Moscow, 1931).

17. *Problemy ekonomiki*, 1937, no. 1, pp. 182f.; *Sputnik kommunista v derevne*, 1933, no. 2, pp. 41f.

18. *Sputnik kommunista v derevne*, 1936, no. 17, pp. 15f.; Iu. V. Arutiunian, *Sovetskoe krest'ianstvo v gody velikoi otechestvennoi voiny* (Moscow, 1963), p. 396.

19. See, for example, *Sovetskaia iustitsiia*, 1936, no. 11, p. 5.

20. See *Istoriia sovetskogo krest'ianstva 3: Krest'ianstvo nakanune i v gody velikoi otechestvennoi voiny 1938–1945* (Moscow, 1987), p. 105.

21. Smolensk Archive, WKP 313, p. 88; *Problemy ekonomiki*, 1937, no. 1, pp. 182f.

22. *Na agrarnom fronte*, 1935, nos. 2–3, p. 127.

23. *Pravda*, September 12, 1940; *Pravda*, April 7, 1941.

24. *Sobranie zakonov*, 1931, no. 9, art. 104.

25. *Sobranie zakonov*, 1933, no. 60, art. 361.

26. *Sobranie zakonov*, 1933, no. 66, art. 399.

27. *Sobranie zakonov*, 1933, no. 60, art. 361.

28. Iu. V. Arutiunian, *Mekhanizatory sel'skogo khoziaistva SSSR v 1929–1957 gg.*
Formirovanie kadrov massovykh kvalifikatsii (Moscow, 1960), pp. 29, 38, 46.

29. *Sobranie zakonov*, 1935, no. 21, art. 164.

30. *Trud v SSSR. Ezhegodnik* (Moscow, 1936), pp. 325–27.

31. *MTS vo vtoroi piatiletke* (Moscow-Leningrad, 1939), pp. 95f.

32. Calculated from data in ibid., p. 95.

33. *Sotsialisticheskoe zemledelie*, June 17, 1939; March 20, 1940.

34. Arutiunian, *Mekhanizatory*, pp. 29, 38, 46; Arutiunian, *Krest'ianstvo*, p. 109.

35. *Izvestiia*, July 17, 1940.

36. *Sotsialisticheskoe sel'skoe khoziaistvo*, 1941, no. 1, p. 27.

37. Calculated from data in *Kolkhozy vesnoi 1931 g.*, pp. 113–15.

38. See P. Angelina, *Meine Antwort auf einen amerikanischen Fragebogen* (Moscow,
1949), pp. 39–41.

39. Harvard Refugee Project, interview B 67.

40. See, e.g., Smolensk Archive, WKP 202, p. 195.

41. *Sotsial'nyi oblik kolkhoznoi molodezhi. Po materialam sotsiologicheskikh obsledovanii
1938 i 1969 gg.* (Moscow, 1976), pp. 20–25, 176–79.

42. See, for example, Smolensk Archive, WKP 197, pp. 133f.

43. *Sobranie zakonov*, 1939, no. 13, arts. 86 and 87; N. V. Tsitsin, *Vsesoiuznaia
sel'skokhoziaistvennaia vystavka 1940 goda* (Moscow, 1940), p. 10.

44. Harvard Refugee Project, interview A 275.

45. Harvard Refugee Project, interview A 407.

46. *Bolshevik*, 1935, no. 10, pp. 53f.

47. See *Voprosy truda*, 1933, no. 6, pp. 21–25; Smolensk Archive, WKP 201, pp.
204–7.

48. Smolensk Archive, WKP 98.

49. *Pravda*, February 14, 1938.

50. Bolshevik, 1941, nos. 7–8, p. 39.

51. Harvard Refugee Project, interview B 124.

52. Calculated from data in *Sotsialisticheskoe stroitel'stvo*, 1936, p. 553.

IV

PEOPLING MAGNITOSTROI
THE POLITICS OF DEMOGRAPHY

Stephen Kotkin

> What is Magnitostroi? It is a grandiose factory for remaking people. Yesterday's peasant . . . becomes a genuine proletarian . . . fighting for the quickest possible completion of the laying of socialism's foundation. You are an unfortunate person, my dear reader, if you have not been to Magnitostroi. I feel sorry for you.
>
> A visiting Moscow correspondent[1]

In March 1929 the first party of settlers arrived on horseback at Magnitostroi to prepare the snow-covered site for the coming construction season. Their immediate task was to build some barracks and a small bakery, organize a workers' cooperative, and recruit more people.[2] By the middle of the summer the railroad link was completed and the first train arrived at the site decorated with banners: "The steel horse breathes life into the Magnitogorsk Giant. Long live the Bolshevik Party!" Many of the several thousand people present had never before seen a train, but the train had perhaps never before seen such a wild and isolated place.

While the site had obvious advantages in terms of operating a steel plant, the hinterland surrounding Magnitostroi lacked any of the elements necessary to sustain a large construction. There were almost no trees, and neither coal nor any other source of energy. There were few established agricultural centers; indeed, there was virtually no good pasture land. The severe continental climate with long and bitterly cold winters exacerbated by brisk winds from the Arctic and unbearably hot and dry summers rendered the steppe even more inhospitable. What was worse, there were no nearby population clusters from which the construction site could draw its inhabitants.[3] The nearest urban center, Cheliabinsk, was several hundred kilometers away, and primitive rail connections made it seem much farther.[4]

Without sustenance from its own hinterland and far from a larger urban center that might have served as a logistical support base, Magnitostroi was utterly dependent on long-distance rail. Everything had to be brought in: supplies, machines, and especially people. Perhaps as few as twenty-five people were in the original party that arrived in March 1929. But by the fall of 1932 *Pravda* announced that the population on the site had reached 250,000.[5] From twenty-five people to a quarter million in three and a half years—who were they, where did they all come from, how did they get there, and what became of them?

In answering these questions, it must be kept in mind that Magnitostroi was more than a construction site for a colossal and technologically advanced steel plant; it was also a political device. At Magnitostroi, the busy pamphleteers tirelessly pointed out, "it is not only the mountain and the steppe that are being rebuilt. Man himself is being rebuilt."[6] Accordingly, an analysis of the peopling of Magnitostroi must treat both the importation of a large population to a previously almost-uninhabited location and the ultimately even more challenging task of transforming each incoming individual into a specific kind of urbanite.

In their attempts not merely to populate Magnitostroi but to populate it with people who lived and thought in new ways, the authorities were confronted with subtle and not-so-subtle forms of resistance and with unforeseen contingencies that necessitated reformulations in their strategies. As the new population programs unfolded, the leadership's resolve showed itself to be greater than its abilities to control the course of events it had set in motion. The methods to which the Bolsheviks resorted for realizing their ambitious transformational goals remained predictable even as the results of their policies continued to surprise.

Squeezing the Village into the City

There were several ways to reach Magnitostroi, but first of all, in keeping with Bolshevik practice, people were "mobilized," that is, ordered to the site by party, government, or trade union organizations. The office of Magnitostroi itself, housed in the cozy quarters of the grandest building in Sverdlovsk, was suddenly mobilized in mid-1930 and sent to the site.[7] According to one contemporary, "many specialists did not feel like moving from the oblast center city, where there were theaters, cinemas, and other cultural activities, to the bare, wild steppe."[8] Another member from the original group recalled that "many greeted the [relocation] notice as a personal tragedy. It was very difficult, even pitiful, to forsake the comfort of one's own apartment in the busy and well-known city. And for what? To settle God knows where, in the middle of some deserted mountain of the steppe."[9]

Vesenkha sent many "specialists" to Magnitostroi on temporary assignment *(komandirovka)*. Although these consultants were housed in the comparatively comfortable quarters of Magnitogorsk's Central Hotel, they did not relish the duty. "In the hotel," recalled one contemporary, "the majority of residents were employees from the administration who would gather at night to discuss whose assignment ended when." A favorite trick of these people was to put in for a short "vacation" and not return.[10]

Graduates of higher education institutions were looked upon as prime material for mobilizations. Vesenkha sometimes dispatched entire classes (up to 200 people or more) of a technical or trade school immediately upon graduation.[11] In a similar vein, some of those sent to Magnitostroi had just been "graduated" from the Red Army. When construction resumed on the rail link in spring 1929, an entire army regiment was sent, and in 1930, almost a thousand demobilized soldiers were sent to Magnitostroi.[12] Magnitostroi sent representatives as far as the Belorussian military district to gather in demobilized soldiers before they could disperse.[13]

In the directives for mobilization, the authorities paid particular attention to party members and skilled workers. In May 1930, for example, the Central Committee ordered "Communists" and "skilled" workers to be sent to Magnitostroi from Dneprostroi, Turksib, and other construction sites.[14] Such mobilizations were frequent and numerous, and usually effected with great commotion and fanfare. One party official sent to the site in 1931 as part of a special mobilization of twenty "leading" party activists recalled how a deputy in the Central Committee Organization Department broke the news about their mobilization:

> "Comrades, you're going to Magnitka. And do you know what Magnitka is?"
> "No, we haven't a clue."
> "Unfortunately, neither do we, but you're going to Magnitka all the same."[15]

The party's whim—more precisely, the whim of functionaries within the layers of the *apparat*—was a force which could strike at any moment.

All local party officials were of course assigned to their posts, but given the demand everywhere for party workers, such political mobilizations never involved large numbers. Moreover, not all of those lower-level party members and their counterparts in the larger ranks of the Komsomol who were sent actually made it to the site. Despite the fact, for example, that the Moscow Komsomol continually mobilized hundreds of Komsomolites for Magnitostroi in 1930, all told only twenty or so individuals arrived on the site, including five girls not allowed by law to work eight hours; some of the others in the group of twenty were called up for military service immediately after arrival. The Urals oblast Komsomol sent more than 100 Komsomol activists, but only fifteen made it to the site.[16] Despite the mixed and often meager results, however, mobilizations of political workers continued (a bit later, a handful of party members who had belonged to the various "oppositions" were exiled to Magnitostroi).[17]

Mobilizations were often connected with the transfer of an important official, who would bring along associates. For example, when Iakov Gugel from the Mariupol factory was named the new head of Magnitostroi in January 1931, he arrived on the site and, wrote one eyewitness, "behind him stretched a string of hundreds of people."[18] But the people Gugel attempted to bring with him to Magnitostroi had a hard time leaving Mariupol. "For a long time they didn't want to let us go," recalled Reizer, who became the head of open-hearth construction under Gugel. "Then came an order directly from Ordzhonkidze," which was heeded.[19] In other cases, however, even phone calls from the offices of the People's Commissariat of Heavy Industry could not "liberate" mobilized workers and specialists from their factories.[20]

Most people, though not pleased with being sent to Magnitostroi, expected upon arrival at least to see large blast furnaces, steel mills, and a shiny socialist city. Instead, what greeted them were the empty expanses of the steppe and the primitive conditions of their new life, transforming their trepidation at having been mobilized into outright panic.[21] In 1932, for example, one Tomilov was sent to Magnitostroi with a group of workers from Mariupol. With him came his wife, who, upon seeing the place, screamed: "Where have we come, like exiles!"[22] In fact, a few of those mobilized were "prisoner specialists," older engineers victimized in the 1930 Industrial Party Trial and sentenced to exile[23] (although Tomilov's wife probably had in mind the "political" exiles of the tsarist days).[24] Be that as it may, it was certainly one of the many paradoxes of the times that Magnitogorsk, the most potent symbol of the heroic building of socialism, could also be a place for exile.

Another vital but small contingent of people brought to the site by Soviet authorities were the foreigners, of which there were essentially three groups. One consisted of political refugees from Europe who had fled east in quest of freedom and who, upon crossing the Soviet border, had promptly been arrested. During 1932 and 1933, some of these border crossers were shipped to Magnitogorsk and placed under GPU surveillance. During the latter part of the 1930s virtually all of these people were deported farther east.[25]

A second group of foreigners consisted of hired technical personnel. Most of the highly qualified specialists went to Magnitogorsk on individual contracts with Amtorg or were sent by the Western firms that had contracted to design, equip, and supervise the construction. By late 1930 there were eighty-six American engineers representing various European and American firms.[26] Beginning already in 1931 and continuing for the next two years, however, some foreign specialists were recalled by their companies when disagreements arose between the companies and Soviet authorities, and by 1933 the number of "valiuta," or foreign-currency Americans, had shrunk to seven.[27]

The third group of foreigners consisted of those who had come to the

USSR on tourist visas but were looking for work. Upon arrival they usually went to the offices of some construction trust or industrial enterprise, where they were gladly enlisted and sent to sites such as Magnitogorsk. In the mid-1930s there were some 200 skilled German workers working for rubles in Magnitogorsk (among them the future East German party chief, Erich Honecker), a good number of them members of communist or socialist parties who had their own understanding of socialism.[28] Similarly, as of 1933 there were around seventy American workers, including thirty who were members of the Soviet Communist Party (one of whom was John Scott). Many of the American workers were returning emigrants.[29]

Altogether, despite discrepancies in the sources, it seems that the number of foreign specialists and workers in Magnitogorsk, excluding refugees, probably did not exceed 1,000, with fewer than that at any one time.[30] In this way, the number of foreign workers and specialists at Magnitostroi probably matched that of the Soviet specialists and officials who were mobilized—a very small number of the total that came to the site.

Still, mobilizations never ceased. Both the Central Committee and the People's Commissariat of Heavy Industry considered commanding people to go wherever these authorities felt they were needed an indispensable method of administration. The Bolshevik leadership would have decreed the whole country mobilized if it had thought it could succeed. In a way, it did just that, as mobilizations by command gave way to mobilizations by exhortation, or "recruitment."

Recruitment *(orgnabor)* was the sole way that ordinary Soviet citizens— those who were neither foreigners, demobilized Red Army soldiers, party officials, nor specialists—were supposed to reach the construction site. Accordingly, industrial trusts and construction sites were empowered to negotiate with collective farms, offering raw materials and machines in exchange for labor power. The authorities also called for greater efforts to recruit members of workers' and white-collar employees' families, members of artisanal cooperatives, laborers, and noncollectivized "poor" peasants. At the same time, the People's Commissariat of Labor had local labor bureaus in each oblast and, according to a Soviet scholar, in the second half of 1931 the People's Commissariat of Labor for the RSFSR recruited 12,655 workers from the Central Black Earth Region, including 7,205 for Magnitostroi. The next year 22,520 people were recruited from the same region, 2,250 of whom were for Magnitostroi.[31]

Despite these impressive numbers, however, I. A. Kraval of the People's Commissariat of Labor reported on 25 January 1931 that his commissariat was not up to the task of supplying Magnitostroi and other large projects even farther east with the mandated quantities of labor power. In response, on 27 March 1931 an important meeting was called with representatives of the All-Union Council of Trade Unions (VTsSPS), Gosplan, the Labor Commissariat, and Vesenkha, and various measures were suggested for redoubling recruiting efforts. Vesenkha, for example, was finally allowed to recruit labor power for its industrial and construction centers on its own (a serious encroachment on the Labor Commissariat's turf). But the real consequences of these reports and meetings would become apparent only later that spring.[32]

Like all large construction concerns, Magnitostroi had its own recruitment apparatus that sent representatives into officially designated areas of the country.[33] *Verbovshchiki,* or recruiters, went to villages and told of the wonders of the world-historical giant being built at the foot of the iron-ore deposits, offering free rail transportation to the site and the promise of work clothes and a bread card upon arrival. After July 1930 they could also offer an extra month's pay to those who put in five months on the site, and they often gave recruits "advances" to see them to the site.

Such recruitment efforts were supported by a national press campaign. Every major newspaper carried exhortations to work on the new construction sites, Magnitostroi especially: "Tebia zovet Magnitostroi! (Magnitostroi is calling you!)" Documentary films and newsreel footage about the great construction were shown in factories and movie houses.[34] Sometimes worker-correspondents would visit factories and construction sites to stump for recruits, handing out train tickets right there. "Evenings," or night-time discussions, on Magnitostroi were conducted in factories and other institutions.[35] One former Red Army soldier and tractor driver, F. Kadochnikov, recalled how such recruitment pitches were made:

> I first heard about Magnitka in my political training classes at the Frunze Artillery School, in Odessa. The commissar explained that, near the Ural river, they were going to build a gigantic metallurgical factory and a large modern city. He asked: "Who wants to go to this shock construction site?" More than ten hands shot up—all were from the Urals.[36]

Some potential recruits were more cautious, sending "scouts" to the site to investigate the promises of adventure and good pay and report back to the collective on what the actual conditions were.[37]

Other construction sites proved an especially good source for recruitment, particularly when various short-term goals were nearing completion. Viktor Kalmykov, who was featured in a special photographic essay on the newcomers, was one of hundreds who went to Magnitostroi after preliminary foundation work had been finished at the Stalingrad tractor site in 1930.[38] In the enthusiasm of the moment, entire work gangs would sometimes declare their desire to participate in the building of socialism at Magnetic Mountain. Such was the case with Khabibullin Galiullin, a Tatar, who was recruited along with some fifty compatriots from a construction site in Moscow.[39] In such cases the line between recruitment and mobilization became blurred.

The press campaign and other recruitment efforts were supplemented by letter writing to friends and relatives back home, some officially sponsored but much of it spontaneous, by those already living at the site.[40] "At that time there was so much in the papers about the building of the new cities, and about industrialization, and we young people were all enthusiastic about the new cities," explained Masha Scott. "My sister had already gone to Magnitogorsk and she wrote me how interesting it was, how nice, how it was something new." A student in Moscow at the time, Scott boarded a train and upon arrival took up residence with her sister and brother-in-law.[41]

But recruitment in all its forms met many obstacles. Industrial enterprises, compelled to enter into agreements to provide workers for Magnitostroi, sent far fewer people than had been agreed upon, if they sent anyone at all.[42] Magnitostroi signed agreements with dozens of factories to send skilled workers, but these workers were needed where they were. As for the supposed reserves of the collective farms, they supplied no more than 11 percent of all those who came to the site in 1932 and only 6 percent in 1933.[43] Collective farm chairmen reportedly concealed recruitment announcements from members and lied to them about the requests being made to collective farms for supplying construction workers.[44] Moreover, the traveling recruiters were apparently not very capable or trustworthy. In the second half of 1930, for example, of the sixty-five recruiters sent out by Magnitostroi, thirty-six returned without having recruited a single person, in the process spending 200 to 2,000 rubles each.[45] And even those few people actually recruited did not always make it all the way to the site. The recruiters "were clever; they promised the moon and brought with them brochures," recalled one recruit, "but many recruits disappeared before reaching Magnitostroi, some even drinking their advances, while many left just after arrival."[46]

Locally known recruiters were often the most successful,[47] but they too faced many obstacles, as the following story about the efforts of a Novostal' agent illustrates. "A recruiting agent for Kuznetskstroi came to our village," an eyewitness recalled. "Two thousand people showed up at a meeting. He spoke about the details of the contract and tried to paint a rosy picture. But we were experienced workers, and so we didn't believe him. He flopped and was powerless to recruit even a fraction of our village." But this was not the end of the story. The narrator of this vignette had himself gotten a telegram from an old acquaintance who now worked for Magnitostroi and who had asked him to go to the site, which he did. And after reaching the site, he was sent back to his village to recruit, at which time he discovered the presence of the Novostal' agent. "Since I was well known and trusted," the local explained, "already on the second day my neighbors began knocking at my door." But anyone wanting to sign up with him had somehow to bypass the spurned Novostal' agent, who refused to leave the village. A list of around 200 names was compiled and sent to Novostal' headquarters, and a new agent came with 15,000 rubles advance money to pick up the workers for Magnitostroi. Yet even this was still not the end of the story, for most of those on the list belonged to the local trade union, which naturally refused to let its workers go. This meant that they would be without valid travel documents and thus would have difficulty using the advance to buy the train tickets. Recruitment was a tricky business.[48]

In fact, the overwhelming majority of people went to Magnitostroi not through recruitment but haphazardly, by what was called *samotek*. Official statistics, heavily biased to demonstrate the success of recruitment, nevertheless could not conceal its failure. In 1931, 48 percent of all workers who came to the site were supposedly recruited; in 1932, 29 percent, and in 1933, 24 percent. These already meager numbers should be reduced still further because not everyone "recruited" made it to the site, while even those who made it often did not stay. Even top officials recognized that the policy of organized recruitment never amounted to much more than whistling in the dark. To central authorities doggedly determined to supervise unobstructed the country's labor supply but unable to carry out their desire in practice, a change in strategy was called for. As it happened, a solution of sorts presented itself in the form of new policies toward the village that accompanied the industrialization drive.

After a series of increasingly burdensome taxes and other means of harassment, on 30 January 1930 the Central Committee adopted a resolution formally calling for the "liquidation of the kulaks as a class."[49] "Dekulakization" had already been taking place in some areas, but now it became an officially declared policy, and persons accused of being "kulaks" or "kulak henchmen" had their property confiscated and were forbidden "to join" the collective farms. Many were shot; the rest were sent to camps or "sentenced" to exile with forced labor and deported to the North, Siberia, the Urals, Kazakhstan, or remote areas of their own regions.[50] A second and far larger wave of "kulak" deportations occurred following a formal decision by the leadership in February 1931[51]—that is, right in the midst of the nervous top-level discussions on labor shortages at all the major construction sites of the Five-Year Plan, including Magnitostroi. In short, the aforementioned 27 March 1931 panicked meeting on the shortfall in the labor supply for Magnitostroi and other large construction sites found its resolution in deportation.

Tightly packed boxcars carrying dekulakized peasants began to arrive at Magnitostroi in May 1931 and continued to do so throughout 1931 and 1932.[52] (In the month of June 1931 alone the population at Magnitostroi jumped some 50,000.[53]) One Soviet eyewitness to their arrival recalled when

> they began to drive the special resettlers to Magnitogorsk. An extraordinary plenipotentiary arrived. They called for me. A car came at 1 A.M., and I rode to them. Comrade Iakov Semenovich Gugel, the chief of the construction, was there. The plenipotentiary turned to me and asked my name. Then he asked: "Do you *(ty)* know who you're speaking with?" I said, "I don't know you *(vy)*." He answered: "Here's how you can help me. In three days there will be no fewer than 25,000 people. You served in the army? We need

barracks built by that time." . . . They herded in not 25,000, but 40,000. It was raining, children were crying, as you walked by, you didn't want to look.[54]

Of course, the barracks were not built in three days or even three months. Instead, the peasant exiles, who numbered upwards of 40,000 men, women, and children, lived in tents.[55] If the scientific authority of class analysis and the pliability of class categories—when combined with the Bolshevik leadership's eagerness to resort to state-organized violence—helped to make possible the deportations, so the deportations facilitated the authorities' ambitious plans for the new construction sites.

Deportations from villages coincided with a thirst for labor in cities and at construction sites that existing urban populations could not come near to satisfying. During the First Five-Year Plan, urban unemployment in the Soviet Union was proclaimed "liquidated." Yet while the construction sites helped to eliminate registered unemployment, the unemployed could not have provided the number of people needed for the construction projects: those officially counted as unemployed disappeared like a pitcher of water poured into the sea.[56] In fact, it was not the unemployed from the cities who were peopling the new construction sites but peasants from the villages. And peasants were being driven from the villages, sometimes at gunpoint, sometimes out of hunger and desperation, and in many cases out of genuine enthusiasm to see the cities.

Significant movement from countryside to city had been occurring ever since the emancipation of peasants in 1861. Within the Urals, *otkhodniki*, or peasant seasonal workers, traditionally left the villages for temporary work in timber, mining, or construction. This movement, which had essentially ceased during the Civil War but was renewed during the NEP, increased considerably during the First Five-Year Plan, when the number of otkhodniki to the Urals region was estimated to be 148,000 on 1 January 1931, 205,000 on 1 June 1931, 301,000 on 1 August 1931, and 424,800 on 1 January 1932.[57] These numbers are large. Indeed, N. Efremov, the Soviet historian who provided them, claims that the 1932 total for otkhodniki represents more than 25 percent of all people of working age living in the Urals at the time.

That Magnitostroi, a place to which obviously no otkhodnik had ever traveled before (because it did not exist), was now receiving an influx of something resembling otkhodniki in tremendous numbers shows that with collectivization otkhod was undergoing transformation. This is not the place to examine the complicated otkhod issue in depth.[58] While statistics on otkhod per se are inconclusive, reflecting the confusion which prevailed at the time and continues to baffle scholars to this day, there can be no doubt that the number of those traveling from villages to cities and construction sites was increasing dramatically.[59]

For the Bolshevik leadership, however, the point was not to increase otkhod but to render it unnecessary by the permanent transfer of peasants to the cities. Accordingly, one of the main tasks at the new construction sites was to transform the construction industry into a year-round activity, eliminating its seasonal character, which was determined by weather and the rhythms of agriculture. This effort was particularly evident at Magnitostroi, where, among other things, winter concrete work was done outdoors in bitterly cold weather. There was even a special decree *(prikaz)* on work in cold weather: below −20°C, frequent breaks and more frequent shift changes were called for, while no work was supposed to be done when the temperature reached −41°C.[60] These guidelines, even if not always followed, indicate that construction work was indeed being conducted in winter and that the seasonal character of construction, one of the basic structures of the otkhod system, had at least been partially undermined. Indeed, Efremov claims that of the 424,000 otkhodniki tabulated by January 1932, over 250,000 stayed on in the cities permanently,[61] meaning that despite his use of the contemporary designation attached to these people, technically they were no longer otkhodniki.

Whether as temporary, seasonal workers or as one-way out-migrants, therefore, it was those lumped into the category of otkhodniki who were helping to people the new construction sites most extensively. During the First Five-Year Plan the urban population of the Urals climbed 1,172,900, from 1,635,000 (1928–29) to 2,807,000 (1932). During the same period, the village population declined over 600,000.[62] Clearly, the countryside was populating the cities of the Urals, but which countryside?

According to one Soviet scholar, 70 percent of the new urban population in the Urals came from within the region.[63] That may have been so for the region as a whole, but the one year for which detailed data were available to me on the region of origin for the population coming into Magnitostroi, 1931, shows a different picture (see table 4.1).[64] As is evident from the table, the largest single category consisted of people whose region of origin was unspecified. No doubt many of these people came from within the Urals region, but it is impossible to conclude that the majority, let alone 70 percent, of all in-migrants did. Indeed, in 1931 at least 55,000 out of the 116,000 did not come from the Urals.[65]

Consider again the dekulakized. One Soviet source asserts that between 1930 and 1932, 15,200 "kulak" families in the Urals were deported (how many more escaped deportation but had to flee?), although it gives no indication of their destination.[66] Some certainly were sent to Magnitostroi. But according to John Scott, the majority of dekulakized at Magnitostroi came from Kazan and its surrounding districts, and according to a Soviet source they came from Kazan and the Ukraine.[67] It seems clear from the example of Magnitostroi that, both through deportations and the transformation of otkhod, the Urals region was experiencing an influx of population from outside, particularly from the territories to its immediate west.

Table 4.1. Origin of Incoming Population, Magnitostroi, 1931

Region of Origin	Method of Origin			
	Plan	Recruited	Samotek	Total
Urals	12,930	13,022	5,156	18,179
Tatar ASSR	10,795	9,091	1,649	10,668
Bashkir ASSR	?	3,646	1,306	4,952
Middle Volga Krai	12,030	5,451	2,142	7,592
Nizhnyi Novgorod Krai	7,470	2,989	514	3,502
Western Oblast	16,000	7,273	582	7,856
Ivanov Oblast	7,680	3,746	186	3,932
Kazakhstan, Krighizia, Central Asia, Central Black Earth	?	10,905	6,650	17,555
Unspecified	—	—	42,471	42,471
Totals	?	56,052	60,655	116,709

That Magnitostroi was primarily peopled from villages outside the Urals, through deportation and the transformation of otkhod, can be highlighted by a brief examination of the national composition of the site's population.[68] Although few data on nationalities were available, some percentages, apparently based on official statistics, did appear in a 1931 pamphlet (it is unclear if the figures are for the beginning or the middle of the year).[69] Russians are given at 83.7 percent, Ukrainians 6.8 percent (around 8,000 people), White Russians 1.57 percent, Tatars 2.7 percent (around 3,000), Bashkirs 1.37 percent, with no other groups above 1 percent. Kazakhs are not listed, but the local newspaper revealed that some 4,000 Kazakhs "came" to the site at some time.[70] It seems, then, that there were at least 1,000 or so Bashkir, 3,000 Tatar, 4,000 Kazakh, and 8,000 Ukrainians, or a total of some 16,000 non-Russians, at Magnitostroi in 1931.[71]

Despite the population's overwhelmingly Russian character, these scattered figures indicating the presence of a sizable number of non-Russians at Magnitostroi are suggestive, for although bordered to the west by Bashkiria and Tataria and to the south by Kazakhstan, the Urals had had a population according to the 1926 census that was 91.21 percent Russian. In the words of one geographer (writing just prior to the founding of Magnitostroi), the Urals region was "a Russian island surrounded by a sea of nationalities."[72] In other words, by 1931 there were significantly higher proportions of non-Russians at Magnitostroi than had been the case previously for the Urals.

The Ukrainians are a good example. Notwithstanding the fact that Ukrainian peasants had been migrating eastward in large numbers since the end of the nineteenth century, it seems that few settled in the Urals.[73] In fact, in 1926 Ukrainians comprised less than 1 percent of the population in the Urals, a figure so small that allowances for the notorious un- derreporting of Ukrainian nationals outside the Ukraine could not alter it significantly. In contrast, Ukrainians at Magnitstroi in 1931 comprised almost 7 percent of the total population. Many perhaps had been deported to Magnitostroi, while of those who came "freely" very few would have been otkhodniki in the original sense of the term, given the distance involved.

In sum, the (at least) 16,000 Bashkirs, Tatars, Kazakhs, and Ukrainians present at Magnitostroi in 1931 could hardly have been indigenous to the Urals. They came from elsewhere, as seems true of half, at the very least, of Magnitostroi's aggregate population. The village outside the Urals was "peopling" Magnitostroi. With mobilizations producing no more than a drop in the ocean and recruitment a disappointing failure, the Bolshevik leadership, having created chaos in the countryside with the radical policies of collectivization and dekulakization, was in effect "squeezing" people out of the village—Russians, Ukrainians, Tatars, Kazakhs—and trying to direct them to distant destinations, such as Magnitostroi.

The Struggle for Cadres

> The conductor announced that we had arrived in Magnitogorsk. From the train a motley crowd quickly poured out. The clothes of the newly arrived were primarily home-spun. Only a few wore jackboots or shoes. The rest wore bast sandals. Waiting until the flow of new construction workers dis- persed, I started along. Along the way horses were carrying bricks, cement, and logs. From the left could be heard incessant hammering, resembling machine-gun fire. I caught up to the horse laden with cement. Behind the horse was walking a tall, lean, unshaven *muzhik*. I asked him, what was that hammering? The *muzhik* answered severely: "You mean you don't know! They are building a blast furnace [*domna*]. It will be bigger than all the others on the earth!" What a blast furnace was, I didn't know, and I didn't ask.[74]

Who were the people congregated at Magnitostroi? How could they be categorized? What could be expected of them?

A countrywide sampling of members of the Metal Workers Union in 1932–33 indicated that 57.2 percent of all such workers at Magnitostroi were "peasants."[75] (And how many of those listed as "workers" had been peasants until rather recently?) Another Soviet source expressed concern that as many as two-thirds of all those on the construction site had no previous industrial experience, and very few had any "skills" beyond wield- ing an axe.[76] Also, in 1931, when the criteria for literacy were not very stringent, as much as 30 percent of the Magnitogorsk work force was pronounced illiterate or semi-literate.[77] Finally, the population at Magnitostroi was generally young—as of 1 January 1933, almost half the workers were under twenty-four years of age[78]—and primarily male.[79] Here, then, was the bulk of the new people who would build socialism and populate the new city, as they appeared to the agents charged with characterizing them: former villagers, young, male, unskilled, and either illiterate or semi-literate.

Such a profile of the country's new work force—which applied, although to a lesser degree, to other cities and factories throughout the Soviet Union[80]—caused the Bolshevik leadership considerable alarm: a pro-letarian revolution, it was felt, needed a "real" proletariat, not a peasant work force. In the leadership's thinking, "consciousness" was strongly dependent on social background. The much-feared "peasantization" of the urban work force and city population induced the leadership to commis-sion numerous studies and censuses of the politically vital proletariat and to issue various decrees and instructions, all of which made clear that the authorities were inclined to take special measures to address what they perceived to be a critical problem. That problem was defined in a specific way, the analysis of which requires step-by-step treatment.[81]

In its simplest form, the point was as follows: when completed, the Magnitogorsk Works was going to need a large number of workers—19,500 workers, according to a 1931 Vesenkha calculation (up from the original projection of 14,610). Of that work force, 7,000 were to be sup-plied by other factories, 2,000 would come from active recruitment by the factory, another 2,000 from the factory's training programs, and the rest, 8,000, simply from among the workers of the construction site itself.[82] In other words, even with the overly optimistic assessment of how much of the operating personnel would come from other factories, the majority (8,000 plus 2,000) were to come from the population already at the site. Yet how were they going to make skilled workers and urbanites out of the people on hand? Machines and equipment could be imported, but operating per-sonnel could not. As one Soviet historian wrote, "the most important problem in the construction of the factory was supplying it with cadres."[83]

Indeed, for the authorities, creating a skilled work force at Magnitostroi was understood as a "struggle for cadres," cadres in the sense of qualified technicians. To begin with, the authorities reasoned that they needed some sort of mass training program for the peasants that lacked industrial skills. To this end, they sent potential workers by the thousands to Verkhne-Uralsk, fifty kilometers north of the site, where they were enrolled in "courses" that were based on the pedagogical methods of the Central Institute of Labor.[84] In a few weeks, these youngsters would learn, for example, how to lay bricks. But when they returned to the site, there were no bricks to be found, a situation that led to the questioning by local authorities of sending inexperienced workers to training schools. Not sur-prisingly, such mass training schools away from the site were soon aban-doned and replaced by on-the-job-training supplemented by all sorts of makeshift courses, circles, technical hours, night schools, and brigade schools.[85] To a great extent, the subject matter of the training did not matter, for training experts discovered that "experience shows irrefutably that workers who were in training courses, no matter how brief, mastered the production process faster than those who were not, commanded complicated machines better, and showed higher productivity with less idle time."[86] It was the inculcation of new attitudes, habits, and rhythms of work that were the key, and these could be (indeed, had to be) acquired in the "heat of construction."

Building factory shops and creating factory operating personnel went hand in hand, and in the words of the popular contemporary expression, people "grew like mushrooms" on the site.[87] As a leading historian of Magnitogorsk has written, "thousands of workers of the Magnitogorsk complex in a very short time traversed the path of unskilled laborer, *zemlekop*, master, brigadier, foreman, and so on."[88] It should be added that the on-the-job, as-you-go, trial-by-fire training applied to so-called engineers as well as laborers. In 1931 less than two-thirds of the "engineers" on the site had higher or middle-level educations, and certainly only a handful had real engineering experience.[89] As late as 1935, when there were 1,465 "specialists" at Magnitostroi, 70 percent had no technical training and were qualified as specialists solely "from experience."[90]

But acquiring technical skills formed just one element of the larger goal. "The struggle for cadres in Magnitostroi," a Soviet scholar has written, "was a struggle for the rearing of workers coming from the village in the spirit of socialist relations to labor."[91] In other words, the Magnitogorsk factory was not only to supply the country with metal; it would also supply it with a proletariat, and the creation of a proletariat was not simply a question of producing skilled workers, but skilled workers who were "socialist." The struggle for creating skilled workers was equally a struggle for instilling political allegiance, which in turn was part of the establishment at Magnetic Mountain of "Soviet power." At Magnitostroi Soviet power did not arise automatically from a decree; nor was it based solely on the party and the police. Soviet power existed through the people's belief and participation in it.

Pamphleteers, whose ranks served as a graphic manifestation of the existence of a battle for the allegiance of the people, were finely attuned to what was at stake in such a battle, as the following conversation, which reportedly took place on the site in the first years, shows:

> "Did you catch that, old woman? A Giant is being built. There's going to be a factory here. It will make iron."
> "Why are you bothering me? You're accursed. They're not going to build anything here. The Bolsheviks are only fantasizing. Agitating the people."

The old woman, who lost two sons in the Civil War and had another leave her, roared that the Bolsheviks "sit on our necks! They suck our blood!"[92]

And it was not just old women who spoke thus (although we cannot expect the pamphleteers to give us examples) or whose attitudes and allegiances constituted an arena of contestation. Let us, for example, examine the issue of the associations and groupings of the workers who arrived on the site.

Many of the peasants came to the site in traditional groups of migrant villagers known as artels whose leaders were generally older peasants, men who commanded absolute loyalty from the other members and brooked no incursions into their authority. One enthusiastic party member explained what he thought was at stake here:

> An artel was completely composed of fellow villagers, and people came to the site as artels. In general, we did not have the right to interfere in their affairs. They divided the wages among themselves. Every artel had its own tradition [for dividing wages]. In the artels they had their own "masters of the first hand," "masters of the second hand." To the master of the first hand, they gave more money, to those of the second a little less, and so on. It did not depend on how a person worked, but only on his position. These traditions were strongly maintained. . . . We had to smash [*razbit'*] the artels.[93]

That artels might somehow coexist with Soviet, that is, Bolshevik, power seems not to have been considered.

Instinctively suspicious of even a hint of an alternative center of authority, the Bolshevik leadership at Magnitogorsk, following national directives, adopted several strategies for curbing the power of the local artels. First, they introduced piece rates, trying to tie wages to individual job performance. This policy was of course resisted by the artels, and by itself would have had no effect.[94] But in addition, the authorities sought volunteers among the artel members to form "brigades," in the hope that the brigades, led by "new men," would drown out the artels. This approach seems to have had some effect. True, "there were cases in which old artel leaders somehow became brigade leaders," recalled one participant, "but in the majority of cases brigadiers were 'new' people."[95]

Despite certain surface resemblances between the artel and brigade forms of organization, and despite the periodic continuities in leadership, there could be no doubt that with this tactic the local Bolshevik leadership began to make inroads into the power of the artel leaders.[96] But breaking the authority of the artel leaders was just the beginning. In forming brigades, the local authorities tried not only to undermine the old allegiances but, more importantly, to create new ones. In this critical task they were aided by the trade union organization and especially the Komsomol, which, along with the brigade, served as a Bolshevik wedge between the powerful artel leaders and the artel members.

It was at Magnitostroi and other large construction sites that, beginning in 1930, the Komsomol became a mass organization.[97] Entrance into the Komsomol occurred in waves. Membership in Magnitogorsk rose from just over 3,000 as of 1 January 1931 to 14,241 by 1 January 1932. Virtually all the new members had joined during 1931.[98] In 1930 Magnitogorsk was declared the first-ever all-union Komsomol construction site,[99] and a traveling brigade from the newspaper *Komsomol'skaia pravda* set up an office there in a railroad car and in September 1930 began issuing *Komsomol'skaia pravda na Magnitostroe.* By October the paper became *Magnitogorskii komsomolets,* purportedly the first city Komsomol newspaper in the USSR.[100]

As the Bolshevik authorities at Magnitgorsk discovered, the Komsomol could be used for everything from night watches protecting the site to making the rounds in the barracks to fight carousing. Komsomolites were particularly active in the campaigns for the liquidation of illiteracy (and not just their own), and they also played a key role in construction work: blast furnace no. 2 was christened "Komsomolka," as virtually everyone working on it joined the Komsomol. "The Magnitogorsk Komsomol," wrote one of the first directors of the site, Iakov Gugel, "was the most reliable and powerful organizing force of the construction."[101]

The effectiveness of the new organizational strategy centered on the Komsomol and the brigade was developed through the devices known as socialist competition and shock work. It is not possible here to examine socialist competition and shock work in detail. For the moment, it will suffice to illustrate how these instruments were used in the programs for "peopling" Magnitostroi through a vivid example. Soviet sources celebrate the construction in 1930 of a dam on the Ural River to supply the steel factory with water as the first great event in the history of Magnitogorsk. Such a construction would seem a simple and straightforward matter, yet it turned out to be anything but that.[102]

Excavation work for the dam began on 26 July 1930. At first, the work went poorly. There was virtually no mechanization, not enough laborers to make up the difference, and in any case no one seemed to know what to do.[103] In August representatives of the Central Control Commission— Workers' and Peasants Inspectorate (TsKK-RKI) visited the site of the future dam and sounded the alarm: "The dam is in danger!" A new local party organization was formed that, on 21 August, issued a special decree on the dam. Speeches were made, mobilizations were ordered, brigades were organized, shock work began: "Everyone to the dam! Everything for the dam."[104]

In extremely cold temperatures, work went on around the clock (one brigade reportedly remained at its "post" heroically for thirty-six straight hours). Meals were skipped, and workers were often called back to the job for emergencies immediately upon returning home after long shifts.[105] There were not enough heaters to keep the cement from freezing, and sometimes, when the electricity went down, cement was mixed by hand.[106] "The chronicle of these days," wrote a journalist, "is a long list of cubic meters, of cement mixes, of Komsomol mobilizations, of emergency duty, and of storming nights."[107]

In a time-honored tradition, the authorities attempted to compensate for the low skill level among the builders with the greater motivation derived from a sense of higher purpose. Not everyone shared the same level of commitment, however, judging by the posters that were put up: "Entrance for all absentees and shirkers is blocked!"[108] A "black" bulletin board carried the names of everyone who did not show up or "deserted" his or her post and thus "betrayed" the construction, and a "penalty" brigade was formed to combat absenteeism by seeking out the deserters and slackers to embarrass and shame them back to the job.[109]

On 3 September 1930 someone came up with the idea, inspired by the experience of the famed Dneprostroi hydroelectric dam, of having a "socialist competition" between the left and right banks of the river: first side to reach the middle wins.[110] The American consultants in charge of overseeing the dam construction protested vehemently (to no avail) that there would be serious consequences if the two sides did not meet properly. To the Americans, the socialist competition was a technically unsound gimmick.[111] Others protested the socialist competitions for different reasons, as one Soviet partisan recalled:

> We spoke about socialist competition with the leader of an artel—a strong, tough old guy in a red calico peasant shirt, girded with a patterned sash. He listened to us with a reserved expression on his face. It seemed that he understood everything, and was agreed. . . . And then the old carpenter exclaimed: "It's not your business to teach me how to work faster. With my axe I've brought forth dozens of churches and no one hurried me, nor told me that I worked slowly."[112]

And not just old "peasants" but new men in the "brigades" resisted the socialist competitions as well.[113] One journalist revealed that some of the peasants had their own competition: who could eat the most bread.[114] Expressing some public resistance to the terms of work seems still to have been possible, but not long after it was begun the dam had become, just as the construction as a whole would, a highly charged field of political reckoning.

As further evidence of the political significance engulfing the construction of the dam, the local leadership decided, against all technical considerations, that it should be finished in time for the 7 November holiday. But even this was not enough, for to this propitious date "counterplans" demonstrating greater ambition (and thus allegiance) were proposed: 1 November, then 15 October. In fact the dam, which was named in honor of the ninth Komsomol Congress, was reportedly finished in early October—a "record" of just seventy-four days (as opposed to the 120 supposedly proposed by the Americans). The right bank won (by varying degrees, according to different accounts). Banners were hung, speeches were given, "heroes" were decorated, and busts of Lenin and Stalin were made from the cement. The atmosphere was described as "saturated" with labor enthusiasm[115] (although at first, as one Soviet journalist tells it, the workers had not even been able to pronounce the word *enthusiast*[116]). Aleksandr Voroshilov (no relation to the marshal) composed a poem, "Pervaia Pobeda" (The First Victory), which is how the story of the dam is known in Magnitogorsk to this day.

Did it matter that it was soon discovered that the dam was not deep enough and the water froze, so that the local authorities had to beg Moscow to send dredging explosives?[117] Or that the water shortage became so acute that the same authorities begged Moscow for a water specialist to be sent immediately and began to build makeshift pipelines to distant streams? That this chronic water shortage persisted for years?[118] And what of the fact that the capacity of the factory in the meantime had been raised considerably, so that the dam was utterly inadequate even as it was finished, and that a whole new dam, over five times larger, had to be begun almost immediately; that when the second dam was completed (planned for 1932, it was not finished until 1938), the original dam was submerged? This all meant nothing.

What mattered instead was the fact that the dam had been built—not only built but built ahead of schedule—and in the process hundreds of youths had come of age as loyal partisans of the cause. As the dam was being built, the number of shock workers skyrocketed during the building of the dam from 1,635 to over 6,000 in one month.[119] And their "enthusiasm" soared.[120] "As at a military front, where the will to victory decides the success of battle," wrote Iakov Gugel, "so on the construction front of Magnitka, enthusiasm and labor upsurge became deciding forces."[121] This was not a dam but a gigantic crusade in which the lowest individual could become a great hero by straining to pour an extra load of cement. In a way, experiences on the construction site, such as building the dam, cemented Soviet power as much as the production of the steel plant itself would. "The Magnitogorsk dam," wrote one pamphleteer, "was a school at which people began to respect Bolshevik miracles."[122] With the storming and the socialist competition on the dam project, Soviet historians subsequently wrote, "the authority of the party soared."[123]

Surrounded by empty steppe as far as the eye could see, hounded by freezing cold and blizzards, with little food or warm clothes, living in a crowded barrack and working sixteen-hour shifts moving earth in horse-drawn carts or pouring concrete in the dead of night—Magnitostroi workers soon divided into those who believed in the dream, in the great future, and those who did not. And allegiance was what Magnitostroi was, in a way, all about.

A group of young enthusiasts, working double shifts, whole days without rest and with little food, met to discuss the work on blast furnace no. 2, "their" furnace, the Komsomolka. One of them opened the meeting by asking, "Does anybody have any suggestions?" Someone else was quoted as saying, "What kind of suggestions could there be—everybody straight to the site for a subbotnik." And if we are to believe the credible account from which this conversation is taken, the youths "worked until dawn."[124] Such pathos was genuine, and it was widespread. "Everyone, even the laborers, felt that Magnitogorsk was making history, and that he, personally, had a considerable part in it," wrote John Scott, himself deeply affected by the enthusiasm of the crusade. "This feeling was shared to some extent even by the exiled kulaks."[125]

But perhaps not everyone was as enamored of the great construction as Scott. And what about those who refused to be caught up in the excitement, who refused to perform all the outrageous requests that were made of them, who voiced an alternative view, even if on a seemingly trivial matter? They were branded "class enemies," regardless, of course, to which class they belonged (either by birth or occupation). Here, for example, are the words attributed to Komissarov, a Donbass miner who had come to Magnitostroi: "Why are we working here? There is no bread, they pay us no money, there are no apartments, the chow is lousy, they don't give us any work clothes. Is this living?"[126] From these undeniably true observations it was concluded that Komissarov, thirty years a miner, was a "class enemy." In the logic of the struggle, anyone who asked for more rations, for better work, for more pay, for anything at all, "threatened" to undermine the whole enterprise, to bring the entire revolution to a halt. Such people were dubbed "kulaks" or "kulak henchmen," people with a "doubtful past," and were subjected to humiliations, to comrade courts, to expulsion from the site, and to arrest.[127]

From the very beginning in Magnitogorsk, before the cement foundations were even poured, class enemies, right opportunists, and counterrevolutionaries were being "unmasked."[128] And every such "discovery" brought new exhortations to struggle harder and achieve more.[129] The so-called struggle for cadres at Magnitostroi, where even "neutrality" could seem as suspicious as opposition, was an intricate political encounter. What the Red Army had been for the regime in the 1920s, the new construction sites became in the 1930s: its device for transforming and assimilating the peasantry into the collective crusade, "the revolution," the building of socialism, the Five-Year Plan—in short, the new civilization.

The Art of Managing an Artful Resource

By the end of the First Five-Year Plan, according to one source, there were 305,000 people on construction sites in the Urals, compared with 42,000 at the beginning.[130] More than half of these would have been at Magnitostroi. It was the biggest construction site in the Union. By the end of 1931, when the population of Magnitostroi was closing in on 200,000, the population of Karaganda was 96,000.[131] At Novokuznetsk in 1931 there were said to be exactly 45,903 people, with another 5,862 across the

Table 4.2. Labor on Hand by Month, Magnitostroi, 1931

Month	On Hand First of Month	Came	Left
January	18,865	3,597	3,853
February	18,609	4,398	3,402
March	19,605	8,570	5,934
April	22,241	9.391	7,166
May	24,446	17,640	9,826
June	32,280	17,292	10,825
July	38,747	10,983	12,694
August	37,006	8,693	11,447
September	34,252	10,381	9,421
October	35,162	8,003	10,072
November	33,093	10,350	10,797
December	32,666	7,440	7,835

river and six miles away in old Kuznetsk.[132] Magnitostroi dwarfed the largest of the other "shock" *(udarnyi)* construction sites.

But Magnitostroi, the biggest shock construction site in a country that worshipped bigness, did not have enough "labor power," even of the "unskilled" variety. In 1931, when the construction plan called for 47,105 semi-skilled workers, the monthly average, no higher than 33,000, left the site some 14,000, or 30 percent, short. Table 4.2 gives a detailed breakdown for labor on hand by month in 1931.[133] The planned targets of labor power were not met even during the peak months. For Soviet officials, for whom population was a resource to be managed no less than it was for officials of other European states, the chief cause of the labor shortfall in Magnitogorsk was not insufficient arrivals but excessive departures—a problem that attracted considerable attention.

What the authorities called labor fluidity *(tekuchest',* literally "leakage") existed in the Urals before the establishment of Magnitostroi.[134] Indeed, the authorities probably hoped that Magnitostroi would become a magnet that could draw in and retain the large roaming population. And crammed trains did come to Magnitostroi regularly, even if there was as yet no train station there, as expressed in this ditty from the barracks:

> Ekh mne Milka napisala—
> Vstrechai, milii, u vokzala.
> Telegrammu Milke dal:
> Privozi s soboi vokzal.

> My arriving Mila wrote to me—
> Let's meet, honey, at the station.
> I sent Mila a telegram:
> Bring the station with you.[135]

No matter: an incoming train approaching the site would simply come to a halt where a sign—"Magnitogorskaia"—had been placed on an uncoupled boxcar that sat on a siding, and unload its human cargo, or labor power, anyway. "Thousands would get off," one pamphleteer wrote. "[They] were carrying homemade knapsacks. They would ask: are there felt boots, work pants? Is there butter, how is it with eggs, can one find milk? Are people joining trade unions?"[136] Arrivals were greeted, asked a series of questions about their point of origin, social status, skill levels, etc., and signed up for work on the spot. The construction sites themselves had become "recruiters."

If people were streaming into Magnitostroi, they were also streaming out. Vissarion "Beso" Lominadze, for a while city party secretary in Magnitogorsk, presented figures for the number of those workers who had come and gone from Magnitostroi (see table 4.3).[137] Since the average number of workers on the site was around 30,000, by early 1934 almost ten times as many workers had passed through the site than were at hand. Indeed, who had not been to Magnitostroi!

> You tell someone you're going to Magnitostroi, and everywhere you hear: "Magnitka, I'm going there," or "I just came from there." Somebody says he has a brother there, somebody else is waiting for a letter from his son. You get the impression that the whole country either was there already or is going there.[138]

Many people in fact came and left several times in the course of a single year.[139]

People were coming and going by the tens of thousands, and in between, they were not staying very long. Of the 116,703 who left during 1931, 30,756 registered their exit, and of those who complied with the mandatory exit registration, fully 27,649 people (90 percent) had been at the site less than six months; 16,031 (over 50 percent) had been there less than three.[140] According to another official source, in 1931 the average length of stay for a worker was 82 calendar days.[141] And it was not only the workers who were leaving. In 1931 almost 3,000 white-collar employees

Table 4.3. Workers Arriving and Departing Magnitostroi, 1930–33

Year	Came	Left
1930	67,000	45,000
1931	111,000	97,000
1932	62,000	70,000
1933	53,000	53,000
Total	293,000	265,000

(*sluzhashchie*—there were around 6,000 on hand in March 1931) left the site. The average length of stay for employees was 186 days; for engineering and technical personnel, 221 days.[142] Only the handful of top-level administrative personnel, the one thousand or so highly skilled workers, and the 40,000 dekulakized exiles behind barbed wire were not fleeing the famed construction site.

Many people left legally and without reproach. A few hundred, for example were called up for service in the Red Army.[143] More important, many departed after having completed the terms of their work contracts. Out of desperation to entice workers to the site, six-month and even three-month contracts were offered to workers, who were then free to leave, as some apparently did.[144] Of the 30,756 who registered their departure in 1931, 6,130 (20 percent) did so after having completed the terms of their contracts.[145] Many young construction workers considered production as a supplementary income to their basic earnings in agriculture.[146] Some were probably returning to the villages to take part in the land redistribution and to look into reports of hard times or trouble. In short, given the high demand for labor and the woeful inadequacy of the recruitment apparatus, Magnitostroi had no choice but to accept all comers, however long or short a time they agreed to stay, and many agreed to stay only briefly.

Others, however, were leaving out of dissatisfaction, for even by the standards of the day, living conditions on the site were harsh. Most workers for the most part lived in filthy, overcrowded barracks. There was a severe shortage of warm work clothes, little to do besides work, and the food and service in the public dining halls was generally despised. Moreover, by the fall of 1931 (well before the onset of the famine), food shortages began, and getting even bread became a problem.[147] True, some people stayed despite the wretched living conditions. D. D. Lushenko, sent from Moscow in 1931, recalled a few years later that

> there were forty of us sent. All the others have gone back. Back then it's true, living conditions were not so hot. My group tried to get me to leave Magnitka and go back, but I said that there's no defender of Soviet power who is afraid to endure all difficulties. I am going to stay the length of my mobilization period, and then I'll return. I worked my year, and I then stayed on to work. And look, I'm working in Magnitogorsk three years.[148]

But many more fled. Even the vaunted Komsomolites were bolting.[149] If as of 1 January 1933 there were 11,000 Komsomolites, one year later there were only 5,400. Some 800 had been kicked out, another 1,000 were known to have quit and were taken off the rolls, and the rest just evaporated.[150] Some of those "voting with their feet," as if in confirmation of Lenin's apt phrase, literally left on foot, just setting out for the Ural mountains in the distance.[151]

Magnitostroi became a revolving door, a literal "labor exchange" in the form of a railroad junction.[152] The train, that ally of the Bolshevik leadership and its bureaucrats and planners, was being used against them: construction workers were using the trains to tour the country. As one Soviet historian has written,

> Such workers knew everything: what kind of lunch they served at Stalingrad, what kind of industrial goods they had at the distribution points of Dneprostroi, what kind of wages were paid at Magnitka. In one season they succeeded in visiting all the huge construction sites of the Union—having seen that everywhere there were recruiters who paid for trains without asking you for birthplace or social origin, but only that you take up work.[153]

In 1931 alone, the bacchanalian fluidity cost Magnitostroi seven million rubles in transportation costs and another two million in lost work clothes.[154]

At least initially, the creation of new construction sites such as Magnitostroi had not resulted in the establishment of stationary working populations, but instead further fueled the fluidity. The Bolshevik leadership concluded not that people were taking advantage of the confused situation and traveling perhaps in part out of a sense of genuine adventure but that the harsh living conditions were understandably driving workers from the new construction sites. This state of affairs was called a "disease" of the construction sites and a "blight" on the Five-Year Plan. And how deeply it seemed to be embedded: in a speech delivered before a select audience in Magnitogorsk in 1933, for example, Sergo Ordzhonikidze went so far as to decry the "suitcase mood" *(chemodannye nostroeniia)* among even the comparatively privileged leading personnel. If in Magnitogorsk the stalwart leaders "felt as if on a temporary business trip" *(komandirovka)*,[155] how were the humbler to feel? But little would change, central authorities reasoned, until concrete steps were taken to improve living conditions—and to do something else as well.

In fact, the authorities at Magnitostroi tried to combat the dread fluidity in several ways. They declared mandatory registration for anyone leaving the site and deployed workers' watchgroups *(zaslony)* to enforce the decree. But given the conditions at the site, such a policy was unenforceable. Beyond restrictions, however, there were various incentives for those who agreed to stay, such as advances for workers to bring their families to Magnitogorsk or preferential supply allotments for those who had stayed at the site for a certain period: a little extra bread, maybe some more sugar—at least that what was stamped on the paper, though the supply depot often found it impossible to comply.[156] A popular approach was to give the workers plots of land on which they could grow potatoes and other vegetables, and according to one party official, this helped somewhat.[157] Above all, there were much-publicized campaigns to get the workers to sign contracts to stay until the end of construction, or at least the end of the Five-Year Plan. But these proved to be no more enforceable than the system of mandatory exit registration. "Thousands signed up," one soviet eyewitness remarked of the solemn pledges, but "then most left anyway."[158]

Ordinary people seemed to be holding all the cards. Here is how one petty official at Magnitostroi characterized his attempts to battle the labor fluidity: "They called me on the phone and told me that the *Dnepropetrovtsky* were leaving. . . . A scandal! I had to go straight to the barrack. What's the matter? They said they had been cheated, they get sent to work where they can fall and kill themselves, and so on. I spoke with them for two hours, and they stayed."[159] Not everyone could be talked out of leaving, and in any case a situation which required them to beg workers to stay was one the authorities would tolerate only so long.

It is against this background that we can begin to understand the reintroduction of the old tsarist internal passport system, announced by Sovnarkom on 28 December 1932. The immediate cause for the "passportization" of the urban population might well have been the fear that famine conditions in the countryside would drive the peasants en masse into the cities in search of food. But there can be no doubt that the Bolshevik leadership was also trying to bring some order to the construction sites. Seen from the vantage point of the peopling of Magnitostroi, passportization appears not as the culmination of a premeditated policy designed to establish total control over the populace but rather as a typically heavy-handed Bolshevik improvisation to combat a problem their policies had done so much to create. Still, what stands out is the leadership's willingness to employ any means necessary to advance its aims, and to express all such radical measures in the sanctifying language of defending "the revolution."

In Magnitogorsk passportization was announced on 10 February 1933, and individuals were required to present valid documents at their place of work beginning immediately. From 15 February until 25 April, all those in charge of the various construction objectives were to turn in lists of their workers with name, year of birth, place of origin, current residence, and job title. Beginning 1 March, all hiring was to be done strictly upon the presentation of a valid passport. A brigade was sent from Moscow to ensure that the passport campaign was taken seriously by enterprise bosses (normally more preoccupied with industrial tasks) and that no passports "fell into the hands of the class enemy."[160]

True to the political quality that came to envelop every aspect of human activity, the first internal passports were given out with much fanfare at a meeting in the dining hall of the elite rolling mill construction group. There were speeches on the building of socialism, on the building of new cities, and on cleansing Magnitogorsk of "parasitic" elements. "The class enemy is stretching out its hand to snatch a passport!" the newspaper warned. "We must strike that hand!"[161] By April it was reported that the passportization was practically complete, but unfortunately the number of passports issued was not made public.[162] On the other hand, it seems that some 2,000 people had their outstretched hands struck, so to speak, and were banished from the city, while another 18,000 did not even try to stretch out their hands but just fled.[163]

But registering the entire population tested the endurance and skills of the local authorities, who, though not afraid to exercise their wide powers, were numerically overmatched.[164] During the passport campaign, on a normal day at a small neighborhood militia station hundreds of people would come to request immediate signatures or documents, to air complaints, or to comply with demands to provide further information.[165] The staff was too small to handle the volume, slip-ups occurred, and some cases deemed suspicious could not be fully investigated, while others escaped investigation altogether. Some people survived for decades under a false identity with bogus documents. Some even survived entirely without documents, hired by enterprises desperate for labor power.[166]

Not surprisingly, documents were particularly valuable objects, among the first things stolen from an apartment by a thief. Escapees from the corrective labor colony mugged the first people they encountered for their documents.[167] And it seems that those precious items, documents, were being "lost" all the time. If the loss of a particular document was duly reported in the newspaper, the person was entitled to obtain a replacement. During 1936, for example, there were many days when there were lists of twenty or more lost and no longer valid documents. Where did those lost documents go? A market in documents had arisen.

In 1936, during what seems to have been an unannounced campaign to root out bogus documents (for which today's researcher can be grateful), the newspaper reported on what it called the case of the "factory for bogus documents." One Popik decided to change his social position from middle to poor peasant. He made his own official seal to stamp the forged documents. Seeing how easy it was, he evidently decided to make a business of his newly discovered craft. He stole blank trade union booklets and membership cards and was able to write them up as necessary, applying the official seals in his possession. When he was arrested, the authorities found blank forms and seals at his place of residence. For his counterfeiting operation, the extent or duration of which is not recorded, he was given three years' "loss of freedom."[168]

Such activity as practiced by Popik was facilitated by the absence, until 1938, of photographs in passports.[169] People could and sometimes did try to rework some of the details on their passports.[170] But just to be safe, one could take advantage of the underground market in the kinds of documents one needed to obtain a passport, making sure that the passport itself would not need homemade "emendations."[171] Everyone knew that one could buy or obtain important documents, if only from newspaper accounts intended to expose the practice.[172] Some people simply created their own documents.[173] Particularly popular seems to have been the technique of forging letters from officials, detailing invented positions a person supposedly held to obtain work (and thus new, unimpeachable documents).[174]

Those who plied the documents market evinced an awareness of the importance of having not simply valid documents but ones that described activities that were valued. If one of the effects of the passport campaign was to generate a proliferation of illegal activities involving documents, another was to demonstrate—at the margins of legality, in the forged and phony documents—the outlines of the new boundaries of social and political life, the new rules of the game, of who one should or should not claim to be.

Passports were but one element of the new approach to population management, for on 13 October 1932, just prior to the announcement of the passport campaign in Magnitogorsk, there was a city soviet decree, following a directive from central authorities, to establish mandatory registration of local residence (propiska) at the militia stations of all Magnitogorsk citizens over sixteen years of age. The registration was to be enforced by the individual in charge of a given residential building (kommendant, starshii, zavobshchezhitiem). (Foreigners too were required to register.) Furthermore, through the rationing system then in force, supply officials were instructed to give out products only when shown a receipt proving local registration, and all outstanding wages were to be paid only upon registration. Particular attention was to be paid to the fulfillment of military obligations. The documents acceptable for registration included birth or marriage certificates, a note from the place of employment, military service papers, trade union membership card, school or student identification. Those without valid documents could obtain a three-month temporary registration. False documents would be penalized.

The registration system was the necessary complement to passports; within the city, passports meant little without it. In turn the registration system was predicated on "control" over places of residence. But such a watchdog system was partially undermined by both lack of staff and the nature of the housing and urban geography of Magnitogorsk, which was spread out over twenty kilometers.

To a certain extent, the less than strict registration system provided considerable slack in the operation of the city's passport control. And yet the registration system could be quite troublesome for residents.[175] Indeed, despite the give and take, the document shuffle was a tricky and dangerous game. There were periodic "exchanges" of documents, and not just of party cards but also of Komsomol and trade union cards, even driver's licenses.[176] The newspaper reported that in 1936, 9,390 passports were exchanged.[177] And document exchanges could be harrowing, the least little suspicion—not to mention the anonymous affidavits from peers or neighbors—setting off an investigation. Although the militia and other authorities were not very organized or efficient, with all the registrations, re-registrations, questionnaires, document exchanges, and anonymous informing and denunciation, exposure could occur at any time. Many of those arrested for petty criminal activity turned out to have phony passports or none at all.

The continuous registration of the entire population was a major operation requiring considerable effort and resources that often overtaxed the local officials. Indeed, authorities were still battling the hiring of workers without propiski, with only temporary propiski, or with phony documents as late as 1938.[178] But by this time the document battle was heavily weighted in the authorities' favor. Some people continued to live and work under their adopted identities, and the document market never entirely disappeared. But the penalties became greater, the police net wider, as trains in and out of the city began to be patrolled systematically and local cinemas and other public places were subject to spot document inspections.

To be sure, migration in and out of Magnitorgosk continued after the passport system went into effect.[179] But as Raphäel Khitarov, city party secretary, proclaimed on New Year's Day, 1936, "the days when being sent to Magnitogorsk was considered a painful ordeal and when the majority of workers felt like temporary visitors are over. Gone are the days when the construction site resembled a revolving door."[180] By this time, managing the movement of the population had become "regularized," and Magnitogorsk's population movement came to resemble what were deemed "normal" migration patterns for established cities.[181]

The Politics of Demography

Securing a sufficient supply of "labor power" is a critical goal for the management of any industrial undertaking.[182] In the Soviet Union during the 1930s, when the entire country was one large industrial undertaking managed by the state and a "free" labor market on which individuals sold their labor power to the highest bidder was thought to be characteristic of capitalism and thus inimical to socialism, the provision of labor power seemed to fall naturally within the province of central planning. All population movement was thus considered a question of how the Soviet state could best direct the supply of labor to further not simply the speedy development of heavy industry but also the reforging of the population's makeup and potential usefulness. Such state direction of population movement over so large a country proved to be a formidable task indeed, but one that the Bolshevik leadership did not shrink from even after the enormity of this proposition began to hit home.

The "peopling" of Magnitostroi can be read as a case study in the Bolshevik leadership's crude methods of administration and rule and in the resourcefulness of individuals when confronted with difficult choices. Much of the peasantry was confined to the new collective farms. For the rest the authorities took away the village and "offered" the city. For some the offer came in the form of deportation, while others could and often did turn the offer to their own advantage, touring the countryside. When these mobile peasants were joined by those desperately in search of food, the regime took strong measures to deter the whirlwind labor fluidity and tried to fix those peasants-cum-construction workers at the new construction sites permanently with the passport and propiska systems.

But these draconian measures proved easier to declare than to enforce. Neither the size and efficiency of the police nor the level of document technique permitted the full realization of the passport system. And these built-in limitations, in the face of the uncompromising inflexibility of the system's goals and rules, made likely the adoption of tactics for the circumvention of the new restrictions. Several methods for falsifying documents or for getting by without them—even a market in illegal documents—arose. It was a game of unequal risk for the two sides; nevertheless, it was a two-sided game: many people were forced to play the dangerous game, yet the authorities were compelled to expend considerable efforts putting it into play.

At the same time, the goal of populating the construction site at Magnetic Mountain had been reached, albeit at greater cost than had been anticipated. The authorities' unwavering insistence on the right to command individuals' relocation and, above all, their readiness to use force certainly made the daunting task less difficult. But even more to the point, the horrendous situation in the village contributed mightily to the Bolshevik leadership's efforts to create a large permanent population at Magnitostroi. The people streaming into Magnitostroi resembled refugees, and their large numbers and the circumstances that impelled them on their journeys gave the impression that war was raging outside the territory of Magnitostroi, as, in a sense, it was.

Still, from the authorities' point of view, populating Magnitostroi was a remarkable achievement: in the chaos and dislocation of the 1930s— admittedly engendered by their own policies of compulsory collectivization and forced-pace industrialization—the authorities nevertheless managed to bring in and maintain some 200,000 people at an isolated location under harsh and difficult conditions. But the authorities were not concerned solely with populating the site with a certain number of people. Just as important was the process of "training" those people, of teaching them to work and to work in specific ways, of encouraging them to think of themselves in new ways, and of tying them to the larger goals of the construction of a new socialist world.

NOTES

This essay is from Stephen Kotkin, *Magnetic Mountain: Stalinism as a Civilization* (Berkeley: University of California Press, 1993). The author gratefully acknowledges the comments of Reginald Zelnik, Martin Malia, Laura Engelstein, Robert Johnson, and the other participants of the conference.

1. R. Roman, *Krokodil v Magnitostroe* (Moscow, 1931), p. 5.

2. Their travails were reported in *Torgovo-promyshlennaia gazeta*, 28 July 1929. The recollections of the group's leader, Andrei Sulimov, can be found in *Magnitostroi: Informatsionny biulleten'*, June 1931, pp. 55–56. Long celebrated as the person who received the first *putevka* to Magnitostroi, Sulimov was later accused of Trotskyism and arrested.

3. In 1928 the population of the entire *raion* in which Magnetic Mountain was located, part of Troitsk *okrug*, was about 12,900. Tsentralnyi gosudarstvennyi arkhiv oktiabr'skoi revoliutsii [TsGAOR], f. 7952, op. 5, d. 308, l. 83. In the United States, which also experienced a form of internal colonization through industrialization, few large-scale industrial ventures were located in places nearly as remote as Magnitogorsk. Moreover, the United States had the advantage of receiving a continual influx of immigrant labor. See, for example, the experience of the great American steel center, Pittsburgh, as described by Nora Faires, "Immigrants and Industry: Peopling the 'Iron City,'" in Samuel Hays (ed.), *City at the Point: Essays on the Social History of Pittsburgh* (Pittsburgh: Pittsburgh University Press, 1989), pp. 3–31. Faires is concerned with what was called "Americanization," a campaign for acculturation that formed an important micropolitical context in the training of America's immigrant labor force. Americanization was in many ways akin to the process of Sovietization that is analyzed in this essay. It should be kept in mind that some immigrants to the United States could exercise an option that was denied to Soviet citizens: starting their own legal private businesses.

4. "Back then [1930]," wrote one young worker in the mid-1930s, "it seemed to me and others in the train that Cheliabinsk, which we were seeing for the first time, was a large rich village, and not a city." He added that this was not his impression of Sverdlovsk, the "capital" of the Urals, where he had just been. TsGAOR, f. 7952, op. 5, d. 317, l. 28.

5. *Pravda*, 25 October 1932. This seems to have been a slight exaggeration. Throughout the remainder of the 1930s semi-official estimates put the population at between 200,000 and 220,000. *Magnitogorskii rabochii*, 17 August 1934, 9 February 1936, 18 December 1936, 9 January 1937. Between 1929 and 1932 the population grew quickly but unevenly. In September 1929, there were 30,000 people at the site; in December 1929, 60,000, according to estimates given by the city planning commission chairman. *Magnitogorskii rabochii*, 11 July 1938. In October 1930 there were some 72,000. At the time of the first local census, January 1931, the population was given at 70,386. MFGAChO, f. 16, op. 1, d. 5, l. 13. In March 1931, within two years of the arrival of the first party, there were 83,200 people. By May 1931 the population passed 100,000, and another 50,000 were added in the month of June alone. By the end of the summer in 1931 it approached 195,000, *Magnitostroi v tsifrakh* (Magnitogorsk, 1932), p. 327. A different estimate put the population in January 1932 at 175,000. Tsentralnyi gosudarstvennyi arkhiv narodnogo khoziaistva [TsGANKh], f. 4086, op. 2, d. 116, l. 21. The same figure was given in *Magnitogorskii komsomolets*, 10 September 1931. In February 1932, however, the journal *SSSR na stroike*, 1932, no. 1, estimated 165,000. These differences arose because of the high mobility and also inconsistency in the inclusion and exclusion of prisoners in official statistics.

6. V. P. Polonskii, *Magnitostroi* (Moscow, 1931), p. 78. Polonskii, a founder and editor of the journal *Pechat' i revoliutsiia*, died in the Magnitogorsk hospital barracks,

24 February 1932, of typhus, as reported in the local literary journal, *Za magnitostroi literatury*, 1932, no. 1, p. 19.

7. The office was opened in 1925 as the Urals planning bureau, which was changed in 1927 to the Urals branch of Gipromez and again in 1928 to "Magnitostroi." Valentin G. Serzhantov, "KPSS—Vdokhnovitel' i organizator stroitel'stva i osvoeniia magnitogorskogo kombinata im. tov. Stalina—Moshchnoi metallurgicheskoi bazy strany, 1929–1937 gg.," candidate's dissertation, Moscow, 1959, p. 121 (citing Partiinyi arkhiv cheliabinskoi oblasti [PAChO], f. 343, op. 3, d. 4, l. 115). The building, the famous Sverdlovsk Passage, had belonged to a merchant. Pachinskii, *Iunost' Magnitki* (Moscow, 1981), p. 37. The new office at the site was a little log cabin on which was written the grandiose designation: "VSNKh SSSR. Kontora Magnitostroia." Iurii G. Petrov, *Magnitka* (Moscow, 1971), p. 30. About 170 people made the move, according to Leonid G. Ankudinov, a member of the group. *Magnitostroi* (Cheliabinsk, 1979), p. 9.

8. Lev Polonskii, *Magnitka zovet* (Baku, 1972), p. 25. After having permitted Magnitostroi's office to be comfortably lodged far from the site in the "capital" city of the Urals for over two years, the central authorities ordered its immediate relocation, which, for no apparent reason, had to be carried out in the greatest haste. One contemporary recalled: "Step by step the offices of Magnitostroi grew larger and larger until they occupied a huge area of the Sverdlovsk Passage. It was all very cultured. No one felt as if he was at a construction site. It was marvelous. The construction task itself was chic, the largest in the Union. They ordered a sign made from gold letters—Magnitostroi—for the Passage building. Everything was wonderful. Everyone came to work at 9 A.M. with his briefcase and left around 3 P.M. Then came the announcement: 'Everybody's going to the site tomorrow!' Imagine what that meant! Just to pack up the files we needed at least a week. . . . Everyone was in a panic. What is this?" TsGAOR, f. 7952, op. 5, d. 308, l. 78. Another participant provided the answer: "an evacuation." Ibid., d. 342, l. 1. The impatience of the central authorities was made a mockery of, however, when the train ride carrying the offices and personnel from Sverdlovsk to the site—a distance of under 800 kilometers—took six days. Ibid., d. 311, l. 6.

9. Polonskii, *Magnitka zovet,* p. 25. On the day of departure there were many tearful faces at the platform in Sverdlovsk. TsGAOR, f. 7952, op. 5, d. 308, l. 78. The offices of Kuznetskstroi were initially located in Tomsk, a two-day train ride from the construction site. Sergei Frankfurt, *Men and Steel* (Moscow, 1935), p. 26.

10. TsGAOR, f. 7952, op. 5, d. 316, l. 18.

11. TsGAOR, f. 7952, op. 5, d. 315, l.46; and d. 314, l. 16.

12. Serzhantov, "KPSS—Vdokhnovitel'," pp. 101–4. In December 1929 another 270 former Red Army soldiers arrived at Magnitostroi. Valentin Serzhantov, "KPSS—Vdokhnovitel' i organizator sozdaniia magnitogorskogo kombinata—Moshchnoi metallurgicheskoi bazy strany (iz istorii stroitel'stva magnitogorskogo zavoda v 1929–1930 gg.)," *Uchenye zapiski cheliabinskogo pedagogicheskogo instituta* (Cheliabinsk, 1956), tom 1, vyp. 1, p. 168. See also I. V. Antipova and M. I. Shkolnik, "Iz istorii sozdaniia magnitogorskogo metallurgicheskogo kombinata (1929–1931 gg.)," *Istoriia SSSR*, 1958, no. 5, pp. 33 (citing PAChO, f. 344, op. 3, d. 111, l. 425).

13. TsGAOR, f. 7952, op. 5, d. 309, l. 136.

14. Aleksandra V. Seredkina, *Bor'ba magnitogorskoi partiinoi organizatsii za sozdanie giganta chernoi metallurgii—MMKa. V pomoshch' lektoru* (Magnitogorsk, 1958), p. 10 (citing PAChO, f. 349, op. 3, sv. 2, d. 7, l. 1 ob.).

15. TsGAOR, f. 7952, op. 5, d. 309, ll. 6–7.

16. Nikolai Markevich, *Rozhdeniie giganta* (Moscow, 1930), pp. 9–12.

17. Later, as the completion of various factory shops neared, a number of mobilizations of managers and skilled operating personnel from Donbass factories was ordered.

18. TsGAOR, f. 7952, op. 5, d. 342, ll. 12–14. The same scenario was reenacted in 1933 when Avramii Zaveniagin became the new chief of the factory.

19. TsGAOR, f. 7952, op. 5, d. 312, ll. 118–19. Once pried loose, mobilized skilled workers and officials went to Moscow, to the famous offices at Ploshchad Nogina of the People's Commissariat of Heavy Industry (the former Delovoi Dvor), where they made the rounds of officials in charge of the nation's industry: Gurevich, the head of GUMP; Moskvin, the head of personnel at NKTP; Semushkin, Ordzhonikidze's secretary; and finally "Sergo" himself, who delivered legendary five-minute pep talks before sending his "troops" off as if into battle.

20. TsGAOR, f. 7952, op. 5, d. 305, l. 84.

21. The following recollections of one mobilized worker at the offices of the steel trust are indicative: "One saw an interesting picture in the offices of Vostokostal' among the mobilized, mostly old specialists, whose wives sometimes begged tearfully not to be sent to Magnitostroi or Kuznetskstroi, produced hundreds of slips of paper, and claimed objective reasons. Many even got away with it, but the majority with a reluctant heart and tearful farewells . . . went into 'political exile' [*ssylka*], as they said back then." TsGAOR, f. 7952, op. 5, d. 315, l. 40.

22. TsGAOR, f. 7952, op. 5, d. 313, l. 1. Among those mobilized, recalled Magnitogorsk party official Dmitrii Gleizer, "everyone had the same thought: what was the quickest way out of Magnitka at any price." (Ibid., d. 306, l. 13.) But such people were not generally permitted to leave. For example, M. N. Zuev, an open-hearth furnace operator, was sent to Magnitogorsk from Mariupol and, in his own words, "not allowed to leave." (Ibid., d. 300 ll. 61, 70.)

23. Scott estimated twenty-five such prisoner specialists. John Scott, *Behind the Urals: An American Worker in Russia's City of Steel,* enl. ed. prepared by Stephen Kotkin (Bloomington: Indiana University Press, 1989), pp. 286–88.

24. "And truthfully," added Tomilov, "all you saw here were prisoners [*itekovtsy*]."

25. Scott estimated that "there were approximately 2,000 Poles, mostly Jews; 200 Finns, mostly ex-smugglers; 50 Bulgarians; 30 Germans; and a few Rumanians and Turks." *Behind the Urals,* pp. 288–89.

26. U.S. National Archives 861.5017/569. Of the various company contingents, the McKee group, by far the largest, had some thirty engineers at any one time. Engineers of the McKee group were changed frequently, so that as many as eighty may have come and gone. Ibid., 861.5017/452. Another American company, Koppers, had about fifteen or eighteen in its party.

27. *Moscow News,* 26 May 1933. Soviet authorities did attempt to keep some of these specialists by signing them to ruble contracts, and some foreign specialists did in fact stay on under the new terms. Virtually all of the most qualified foreign engineers and technicians, however, were gone by the middle of the 1930s, although short-term visits by foreign consultants continued.

27. One Soviet eyewitness later recalled an incident in the early 1930s: "The party and trade union organizations, together with the economic leadership, called a meeting of foreign workers and specialists at which there were twenty-six Germans. Many foreigners came to the meeting with books of Marx and Lenin and began to cite the texts in order to show the incorrect treatment of the working class by our organizations." What, if anything, resulted was not clarified. TsGAOR, f. 7952, op. 5, d. 306, l. 16.

29. In general, workers tended to stay longer than specialists and engineers. Some workers married Soviet women, adopted Soviet citizenship, and hoped to remain permanently. But by 1938 a foreign worker in Magnitogorsk was an anamoly. During the witch hunts of 1937 and 1938, those who retained their foreign passports were forced from their jobs and had to leave the city, while those who had become Soviet citizens in many cases were arrested and disappeared.

30. One Soviet source put the number as of February 1932 at 310 (131 special-

ists and 179 workers), plus another 180 family members, or a total of about 500, representing seventeen countries. P. G. Matushkin, *Uralo-kuzbass* (Cheliabinsk, 1966), pp. 299–300. A different source indicated that during the years 1929–35, 752 foreign specialists at one time or another lived and worked in Magnitogorsk, of whom approximately two-thirds were highly skilled and more than one-third were Communists or socialists. About half were Germans, the next largest group were Czechs and Slovaks, then came Americans, Italians, and others. A. T. Kolotilin, "Inostrannye trudiashchiesiia na Magnitostroe," *Tvorcheskaia deiatel'nost' rabochego klassa Magnitki*, Magnitogorskii Gorno-Metallurgicheskii Institut, Sbornik no. 49 (Magnitogorsk, 1967), p. 20 (citing MFGAChO f. 99, op. 8, d. 1–777; this wealth of material on the foreign specialists remained "closed" through 1991). A later article, in *Iunost' Magnitki*, p. 76, also gave a figure of 752, citing unspecified Chelianbinsk oblast archives. Yet a third source claimed 992 foreigners in Magnitogorsk by 1932–33, of whom 434 were Communists (174 foreign parties, 260 Soviet). N. P. Sharapov, "Ob uchastii inostrannykh rabochikh i spetsialistov v sotsialisti-cheskom stroitel'stve na Urale (1930–1934)," *Voprosy istorii KPSS*, 1966, no. 3, p. 78. According to data from Soviet archives, as of April 1932 there were over 3,000 foreigners with their families in the Urals. Sharapov, "Ob uchastii," p. 71 (citing Arkhiv Sverdlovskogo Filiala Instituta Marksizma-Leninizma pri Tsk KPSS [PASO?], f. 4, op. 10, d. 1109, l. 79.). By the middle to late 1930s, according to another source, there were perhaps as many as 7,000 foreigners in the Urals (this number must include deported refugees). P. G. Matushkin, *Druzhba, solidarnost'* (Cheliabinsk, 1960), p. 29. The number of foreigners throughout the USSR during this time was large. One Soviet source reported in 1936 that 6,800 foreign specialists were working in heavy industry in 1932. American-Russian Chamber of Commerce, *Handbook of the Soviet Union* (New York, 1930), p. 347. According to a contemporary German periodical, by the summer of 1932 there were some 10,000 foreign *Mitarbeiter*, of whom 7,000 were workers (half of these Germans) and the rest specialists. This seems to be an underestimate. *Osteuropa*, June 1932, pp. 509–21, and July 1932, pp. 591–99. That same source indicates that Amtorg was yet to process the applications of 100,000 Americans seeking work in the USSR. (In the absence of diplomatic relations, it was far more difficult for Americans than for Germans to go to the USSR for work.) In any case, the total number of foreigners working in the USSR during the 1930s certainly exceeded 10,000 and, given the number employed at Magnitogorsk alone, could very well have been many more.

31. V. N. Eliseeva, "Istoriografiia voprosa o soiuze rabochego klassa i krest'ian-stva v khode stroeitel'stva MMK," *Istoriografiia istorii sozdaniia i ravvitiia soiuza rabochego klassa i krest'ianstva na Urale* (Sverdlovsk, 1982), p. 141 (citing Gosudar-stvennyi Arkhiv Voronezhskoi Oblasti, f. 1439, op. 4, d. 267, ll. 55–60; and TsGAOR, f. 5515, op. 17, d. 375, l. 103, and d. 533, ll. 230–31).

32. Zuikov, *Sozdanie tiazheloi promyshlennosti na Urale* (Moscow, 1971), pp. 226ff. (citing TsGANKh, f. 4372, op. 28, d. 243, l. 28.).

33. Magnitostroi could recruit in the Urals, the Ukraine, and selected parts of Ivanovskaia and Moskovskaia oblasts. V. N. Eliseeva, "O sposobakh privlecheniia rabochei sily v promyshlennost' i stroitel'stvo v period sotsialisticheskoi in-dustrializatsii SSSR (1926–1937 gg.)," *Izvestiia Voronezhskogo gosudarstvennogo pedago-gicheskogo instituta* (Voronezh, 1967), tom 63, p. 57.

34. Antipova and Shkol'nik, "Iz istorii," p. 34. I saw some of them in the documentary film archives in Krasnogorsk at the Tsentralnyi gosudarstvennyi arkhiv kinofotodokumentov.

35. V. G. Serzhantov, "KPSS—Vdokhnovitel'," p. 101.

36. *Iunost' Magnitki*, p. 44.

37. TsGAOR, f. 7952, op. 5, d. 303, l. 20. One memoir contains an example of what advice was given to those arriving at the site by people who had already been recruited:

A group of pitiful fellows who were sitting with drooping expressions began to look at us new arrivals.

"Hey, you new guys, you're clean. Where are you from?"

"From Dneprostroi."

"Well, get out of here as quick as you can."

As we shall see, many took the advice. TsGAOR, f. 7952, op. 5, d. 308, l. 55.

38. "Gigant i stroitel'," *SSSR na stroike*, 1932, no. 1. Kalmykov is shown in the proverbial *lapty*, or bast sandals, arriving at the site with all his worldly belongings. His communal barrack is depicted, and a reenactment of his marriage at the ZAGS to a German woman is also shown. In the Komsomol document exchange of 1932, Kalmykov had ceremoniously received the first new card. *Koordinaty podviga*, p. 163. Selected as the Magnitogorsk delegate to a Moscow conference of shock workers, he came back in a fashionable new coat and cap. Petrov, *Magnitka*, p. 83. In 1938 Kalmykov was arrested and shot as a German spy. His wife and children were ostracized and haunted, then arrested and deported.

39. *Slovo o Magnitke*, pp. 48–51.

40. Excerpts from seven letters, apparently written to friends and relatives at the behest of authorities, can be found in Z. Ostrovskii, *Magnitostroi* (Moscow, 1931), pp. 41–45.

41. Quoted in Pearl S. Buck, *Talk about Russia (with Masha Scott)* (New York, 1945), p. 91. Sometimes enthusiasm for city life was mixed with other motivations, such as the desire to avoid famine, that also spurred relocation to Magnitostroi. Often several factors worked together. One man from the Northern Caucasus received several enthusiastic letters from his brother at Magnitostroi. When the latter came home to the Caucasus for a brief visit in 1931, the younger brother decided to go back with him to Magnitogorsk. Later the younger brother himself returned to the Caucasus in 1933 to fetch the rest of his family. "I had heard nothing from my family, and 1933 in the Caucasus was an alarming time," he wrote, explaining why he went home that year. "I worked that summer and sent my mom and sister on to Magnitogorsk, then followed." TsGAOR, f. 7952, op. 5, d. 300, 11. 129–44.

42. In Sverdlovsk, for example, industrial enterprises were supposed to send 1,000 workers to Magnitostroi by June 1930 but sent only 300. Eliseeva, "Bor'ba za kadry," pp. 205–8.

43. *Stroitel'stvo i ekspluatatsiia*, p. 83.

44. Eliseeva, "O sposobakh," pp. 47–49 (citing TsGANKh, f. 7446, op. 8, d. 83, ll. 68–70).

45. Eliseeva, "O sposobakh," pp. 55.

46. TsGAOR, f. 7952, op. 5, d. 300, l. 49.

47. For example, E. A. Goncharov was sent to Magnitostroi in December 1929 along with the whole trade union and party "active" of his technicum. In March 1930 Goncharov was sent back to his native Tambov Guberniia to recruit: "I went to Voronezh, found my former comrades there and got them to sign up. I went to the Labor Distribution Department from which I got unofficial permission to recruit 500 people. . . . I recruited 300 from Kalinka village and 186 from Gudovo:. . . . many of these workers had worked with me earlier, . . . so that my workers came with me out of trust. The village soviet also helped me, as I was recognized as a former worker and a local. . . . Within the course of a month, I brought them to Magnitostroi. Everyone to the last person went the distance—no one bolted along the way." Goncharov earned 1,500 rubles for his efforts, a hefty sum. TsGAOR, f. 7952, op. 5, d. 306.

48. Without documents, they could have been taken for fleeing "kulaks." Indeed, it is possible that this entire story was concocted by the narrator to explain

why 200 men arrived at the site without documents! TsGAOR, f. 7952, op. 5, d. 315, l. 80.

49. N. A. Ivnitskii, *Klassovaia bor'ba i likvidatsiia kulachestva kak klassa 1929–1932* (Moscow, 1972), p. 178.

50. Moshe Lewin, *Russian Peasants and Soviet Power: A Study of Collectivization* (Evanston, Ill., Northwestern University Press, 1968), pp. 482–513.

51. Robert Conquest, *The Harvest of Sorrow* (New York: Oxford University Press, 1986), p. 123.

52. TsGAOR, f. 7952, op. 5, d. 200, l. 98. In contrast, the first peasant exiles began arriving in Kuznetsk in the fall of 1930. According to Frankfurt, they were primarily from within Siberia. Later, in July 1931, "several thousand" peasant exiles arrived in Kuznetsk from the central regions of the USSR. Frankfurt, *Men and Steel*, pp. 139–40.

53. *Magnitostroi v tsifrakh*, p. 321.

54. TsGAOR, f. 7952, op. 5, d. 306, l. 8. The speaker is E. A. Goncharov.

55. Scott estimated that "by the end of 1933 this tent colony was composed of about 35,000 persons. Ten percent or more of this colony died of exposure and malnutrition during the winter [1932–33]. Practically no children under ten lived through the winter of 1932–33. . . . The four or five thousand who died during the winter of 1932–33 were replaced by newcomers who were mostly runaway peasants from other colonies. The total population of the Magnitogorsk colony, about 30,000 or 40,000, thus remained constant." At the time, the total population at the site numbered around 190,000. *Behind the Urals*, pp. 281–84. Other foreigners present in the city when the dekulakized arrived and in some cases holding positions of high responsibility unanimously confirm Scott's estimates of around 40,000 peasant exiles, or about one-fifth of the total population at the site. For example, Raymond F. Stuck, "Russia as I Saw It," p. 65; and Stadelman, in a 30 November 1932 debriefing at the U.S. Embassy (Berlin), 861.5017/569.

56. Unemployment was a volatile domestic political issue in the USSR during the 1920s. According to the leading scholar of the Soviet economy, mass unemployment disappeared completely at the latest by the end of 1931. R. W. Davies, "The Ending of Mass Unemployment in the USSR," in David Lane (ed.), *Labor and Employment in the USSR* (New York: New York University Press, 1986), pp. 19–35; see also L. S. Rogachevskaia, *Likvidatsiia bezrabotitsy v SSSR, 1917–1930 gg.* (Moscow, 1973). Although by the fall of 1929 in the Urals oblast there were only 1,491 registered unemployed and shortly thereafter the category disappeared altogether (registered unemployment ended in the Urals even earlier than in the USSR as a whole), in 1928 there had been only 42,908 registered unemployed. Eliseeva, "O sposobakh," pp. 39–40 (citing GASO, f. 88, op. 2, d. 432, l. 277).

57. N. V. Efremov, "K Voprosu o roli kollektivizatsii v perekhode k orgnaboru rabochei sily dlia promyshlennosti Urala," *Iz istorii zavodov i fabrik Urala. Sbornik statei* (Sverdlovsk, 1963), vyp. 2, pp. 208–9. One must wonder about how such statistics were gathered. One reliable scholar has suggested that attempts to register and direct otkhod, through such places as the *korrespondentskie punkty*, proved futile. Eliseeva, "O sposobakh," pp. 43–4.

58. See A. M. Panfilova, *Formirovanie rabochego klassa SSSR v gody pervoi piatiletki (1928–1932)* (Moscow, 1964), p. 8, n. 6, for a bibliography of contemporary sources.

59. One scholar examined the relevant Soviet sources thoroughly, only to conclude that the data are contradictory and confusing. Nobuaki Shiokawa, "The Collectivization of Agriculture and Otkhodnichestvo in the USSR, 1930," *Tokyo Daigaku: Shakai Kagaku Konkyujo*, Annala 1982–83, pp. 129–58. While some of some on the move were not peasants but traders, shopkeepers, and urban artisans, many of those peasants included in the statistics must have been fleeing collectivization (rather than looking for seasonal work).

60. *Magnitogorskii rabochii,* 30 December 1932.
61. Efremov, "K voprosu" (citing GASO, f. 922, op. 1, d. 150, l. 191).
62. A. I. Paiskova, "Nekotorye dannye po vopsrosu formirovaniia rabochego klassa Urala v gody pervoi piatiletki," *Iz istorii zavodov i fabrik Urala* (Sverdlovsk, 1963), vyp. 2, pp. 228–30 (citing GASO, f. 1812-r, op. 1, d. 19, ll. 115, 101).
63. Efremov, "K voprosu," p. 214.
64. The table is adapted from a table reproduced, without citation, in Serzhantov, "KPSS—Vdokhnovitel'," p. 183. The source may be TsGANKh, f. 4086, op. 2, d. 119, l. 22, where a similar table can be found.
65. Incomplete data for 1933 arrivals, asked their region of origin during the residency registration, or *propiska,* are as follows:

Urals	14,001
Central Black Earth Region	9,369
Mid-Volga Territory	5,911
Kazakhstan	3,293
Bashkiriia	3,101
Ukraine	2,033
Other	3,895
Total	41,603

The same source gives a figure for total arrivals for 1933 as 46,497, meaning that the places of origin of more than 5,000 people are inexplicably missing from the table. Taking the data in the table, only slightly more than one-third of all arrivals would seem to have begun their journey to Magnitogorsk from within the Urals. MFGAChO, f. 16, op. 1, d. 29, l. 40; d. 42, l. 92.
66. *Istoriia Urala* (Perm, 1965), tom II, p. 258. This number seems extremely small. In Kazakhstan, with about half the population (but where the political situation admittedly was different), some 40,000 households were dekulakized, while another 15,000 fled or "self-dekulakized." B. A. Tulepbaev, *Torzhestvo leninskikh idei sotsialisticheskogo preobrazovaniia sel'skogo khoziaistva v Srednei Azii i Kazakhstane* (Moscow, 1971), p. 199.
67. Scott, *Behind the Urals,* p. 281; TsGAOR, f. 7952, op. 5, d. 306, l. 14.
68. Soviet historians ritualistically praise the great number of nationalities present at Magnitostroi, with some sources claiming thirty or even forty (without providing detailed data). For example, Galiguzov and Churillin, *Flagman,* p. 28. Similar vague assertions can be found in contemporary pamphlets and propaganda literature.
69. A. Zverev, *Na stroike giganta* (Sverdlovsk, 1931), p. 78.
70. *Magnitogorskii rabochii,* 2 November 1936. It is highly likely that they were forcibly brought in. In one memoir the Kazakhs are called "special resettlers," as were the dekulakized. TsGAOR, f. 7952, op. 5, d. 304, l. 5. There was also a sizable contingent of Kazakhs at Kuznetsk, an even greater distance from Kazakhstan. Frankfurt, *Men and Steel,* pp. 136–39.
71. Another chance piece of evidence indicates that as of May 1930 there were only 500 *natsmen (natsional'noe menshinstvo)* workers at Magnitostroi, but that by July 1931 there were 11,000 (out of 65,000). TsGAOR, f. 7952, op. 5, d. 384, l. 324; and *Magnitogorskii rabochii,* 10 July 1931. Reflecting the presence of sizable groups of such nationals, the local newspaper for a while was issued in a Bashkir-Tatar (1931–35) and a Kazakh (1934–36) edition. One source indicates that the Tatar-Bashkir edition had a *tirazh* of 3,000 copies (it was apparently also made available outside Magnitogorsk). Eliseeva, "Bor'ba za kadry," pp. 223–24. Reductions over time in the number of a particular nationality within the aggregate *natsmen* cannot be excluded, although the discontinuation of the non-Russian versions of the local

newspaper can be explained by the fact that the Tatar learned Russian while the Kazakh edition was absorbed by a national newspaper.

72. P. N. Stepanov, *Ural'skaia oblast'* (Moscow, 1928), p. 36.

73. Ihor Stebelsky, "Ukrainian Peasant Colonization East of the Urals, 1896–1914," *Soviet Geography: Review and Translation* 25, November 1984, no. 9, pp. 681–94.

74. The recollections of G. M. Glushkov, a Komsolite mobilized to Magnitostroi, quoted in *Iunost' Magnitki*, p. 59.

75. VTsSPS. *Profsoiuznaia perepis' 1932–33 gg.* (Moscow, 1934), pp. 75, 98–99. The percentage of peasants in ferrous metallurgy for the USSR as a whole was given as 43.6.

76. Eliseeva, "Iz istorii proektirovanii," p. 147.

77. *Magnitogorskii rabochii*, 6 March 1932.

78. *Stroitel'stvo i ekspluatatsiia*, p. 82. Impressionistic accounts unanimously agree that youths were everywhere in evidence. "There was not one person in the barrack over 35 years old, and not many over 25," according to John Scott. "Magnitogorsk was built by young people." John Scott, " 'Magnetic City,' Core of Valiant Russia's Industrial Might," *National Geographic* 83, 1943, no. 5, p. 546.

79. According to the January 1931 census, of the 70,386 people found to be at the site, only 27,840, or around 35 percent, were women (this included the population of the city proper and the adjacent villages, where more than 11,000 women were recorded and the ratio of men to women was one to one). MfGAChO, f. 16, op. 1, d. 5, l. 13. A journalist wrote that in April 1931, at a time when there were over 80,000 people on the site, there were only 7,000 women (of whom 3,000 were employed outside the home), but even though journalists usually had access to unpublished data, this seems mistaken. Zverev, *Na stroike giganta*, p. 84. According to official sources, the number of women workers reached 5,000 in December 1931, by which time there were some 40,000 working men. By 1941 women workers totaled 8,311, almost 30 percent of the labor force. As reported in *Tvorcheskaia deiatel'nost' rabochego klassa Magnitki* (Magnitogorsk, 1967), p. 28 (citing MFGAChO, f. 99, op. 10, d. 1119, l. 1); see also *Magnitostroi v tsifrakh*, p. 270. After the 1931 census, the population began to climb precipitously, but the ratio of females to males does not seem to have reached something approaching parity until 1935. Data for 1932, contained in a statistical report sent to the center, show a population at Magnitostroi of 155,000, of whom 71,300, or 46 percent, were women. These figures did not include prisoners, for whom the population was estimated at 200,000. Data for 1935 show a population of 204,234, 101,444 of whom were women. These were called "working" figures and other conflicting figures were given elsewhere in the document, indicating that they were rough estimates. MFGAChO, f. 16, op. 1, d. 34, l. 2; d. 40, l. 53. Another indication of the gender of those on the site in the first years is that in March 1931, out of a total population of 83,200, only 29,611 were dependents. See *Magnitostroi: Informatsionnyi biulleten'*, 1931, no. 2, p. 43. Far from a majority of the men seem to have been married, and of those who were, not all had had their families with them, at least in the early years. It comes as no surprise, therefore, that "there was prostitution. Of course, they hushed it up. We had a few girls in the Stal'most trust. They worked in assembly, they did marking off work. . . . They began to 'date' [*progulivat'*, literally: play hooky from work]. Expensive things started appearing on them—silk stockings, silk dresses." TsGAOR, f. 7952, op. 5, d. 300, l. 44. This is the single mention of prostitution in all the sources encountered by this researcher.

80. On this point, in addition to Panfilova, *Formirovanie*, see the work of Rashin, Goltsman, and many others, summarized and discussed in John Barber, "The Composition of the Soviet Working Class, 1928–1941," CREES Discussion Paper, Birmingham, 1978.

81. The "peasantization" of the work force and its supposed consequences for determining attitudes and shop-floor practices have been principal themes for most subsequent researchers investigating the formation of what is usually referred to as the Soviet working class. These scholars neglect to consider *why* such plentiful sources on "peasantization" exist and how such sources were generated—and what the answers to *these* questions portend for the more sociologically oriented questions replicated from source material.

82. Eliseeva, "Bor'ba za kadry," p. 210.

83. Eliseeva, "Iz istorii proektirovanii," p. 145.

84. Serzhantov, "KPSS-Vdokhnovitel'," p. 108, 200.

85. Serzhantov, "KPSS-Vdokhnovitel'," p. 204.

86. V. Bulgakov, *Za obraztsovoe kul'tobsluzhivanie novostroek* (Moscow, 1932), p. 33.

87. The journalist Semen Nariniani offered an analogy to understand the maturation of workers: "childhood"—earth moving, when they are still people of the land; then "adolescence—cement work, when they are already former people of the land; and finally "youth"—steel assembly, when they have become people of the future. Nariniani, *Doroga v sovershennoletie* [1932?], p. 22.

88. Eliseeva, "Bor'ba za kadry," p. 221.

89. Ibid., p. 226.

90. Serzhantov, "KPSS-Vdokhnovitel'," p. 209 (citing MFGAChO, f. 99, op. 9, d. 18, l. 31). Experience was a good teacher, but as Scott wrote, "obviously many of the [unskilled] laborers had to do the work of skilled workers. The result was that inexperienced riggers fell and untrained brick layers laid walls that did not stand." These were also "new men." *Behind the Urals*, p. 73.

91. Eliseeva, "Bor'ba za kadry," p. 233.

92. E. Korin, *Na novykh putiakh* (Moscow, 1931), p. 14.

93. TsGAOR, f. 7952, op. 5, d. 309, ll. 88–89. See the study by David Hoffmann, "Urbanization and Social Change during Soviet Industrialization: In-Migration to Moscow, 1929–1937," Ph.D. dissertation, Columbia University, 1990. Hoffmann demonstrates that during the First Five-Year Plan artels were widespread and argues further that they persisted for years and continued to influence worker attitudes and organization. While the former point seems indisputable, the latter may be partially true in some sense but fails to assess the political confrontation that the artels' existence brought on.

94. Two years later, in July 1933, one-quarter of all construction workers were still not being paid individually. *Stroitel'stvo i ekspluatatsiia*, p. 83.

95. TsGAOR, f. 7952, op. 5, d. 309, l. 140.

96. By June 1931, what had been the site's 850 artels had "become" 530 brigades. Antipova and Shkolnik, "Iz istorii," p. 37. See also the recollections of former Komsomolite A. Grebenichenko, as cited in A. P. Orlova, "Rol' komsomola v organizatsii i razvitii massogo sorevnovaniia na stroitel'stve magnitogorskogo metal-lurgicheskogo kombinata (1929–1933 gg.)," in *Iz istorii KPSS za pobedu sotsialisticheskoi revoliutsii i postroenie kommunisticheskogo obshchestva* (Moscow, 1971), vyp. 2, pp. 161–62.

97. Membership in the Urals Komsomal increased from 132,000 in 1929 to 248,000 in 1932. *Istoriia Urala* (Perm, 165), p. 278.

98. Orlova, "Rol' komsomola," pp. 159–60 (citing PAChO, f. 525, op. 12, d. 679, l. 167; and f. 1101, op. 1, d. 16, l. 50).

99. V. N. Zuikov, "Komsomol na stroitel'stve i osvoenii magnitogorskogo metal-lurgicheskogo kombinata imeni Stalina (1929–1933 gg.)," candidate's dissertation, Sverdlovsk, 1950.

100. T. N. Reshetko, "*Komsomol'skaia pravda* na Magnitostroe," *Deiatel'nost' KPSS po sozdaniiu material'no-teknicheskoi bazy kommunizma* (Cheliabinsk, 1976), vyp. 10, pp.

131–32. The tradition of the all-union Komsomol construction site carried through to the 1980s with the so-called BAM, or Baikal-Amur railway.

101. Iakov Gugel, "Vospominaniia," p. 326. The heroic role of the Komsomol in "socialist construction" has been mythologized in several films, such as the 1943 "Komsomol'tsy" (TsGAKFD 1-9689). It would seem that the trade unions also experienced rapid growth at Magnitostroi, but, curiously, not a single source gives statistics on membership nor exalts the role played by trade unions.

102. There was an uproar over the design. The original "Soviet" design for an earthen dam, supposedly better able to withstand the low temperatures, was scrapped in favor of the proposal by McKee, which advised building a concrete dam like the ones in Minnesota (a cold-weather region). The fight between the American and "Soviet" designs, which took the form of a debate over the technical merits of each plan, became a matter of pride, as Soviet "specialists" resented having to accede to the greater expertise and experience of the American specialists. It took numerous telegrams and ultimatums from Moscow to get the authorities at Magnitostroi to follow the American design. Ironically, the so-called Soviet design, for which the local authorities lobbied, was the work of one Vaida, who, as it turned out, was not a Soviet but a Hungarian enthusiast, brought to Magnitostroi from Dneprostroi. Vaida was later arrested and sent to the great Gulag dam project Belomostroi, where he finally got the chance to supervise construction of an earthen dam. TsGAOR, f. 7952, op. 5, d. 336, ll. 40–2, 60; d. 402, l. 10.

103. V. K. Korolkov, "Bor'ba KPSS za sozdanie Magnitogorskogo metallurgicheskogo kombinata, 1929–1931," candidate's dissertation, Leningrad, 1955, p. 129 (citing PAChO, f. 349, op. 3, sv. 2, d. 6, l. 170).

104. Nariniani, Na stroike mirovogo giganta, pp. 21–24; Galiguzov and Churillin, Flagman, pp. 34–35.

105. Korin, Na novykh, pp. 54–55.

106. A. Baranov, Magnitogorskaia plotina (Sverdlovsk-Moscow, 1931), pp. 11–36.

107. Nariniani, Na stroike, p. 22.

108. Korin, Na novykh, p. 51.

109. Baranov, Magnitogorskaia plotina, p. 22.

110. Korolkov, "Bor'ba KPSS za sozdanie," p. 131.

111. "The Americans were not inflamed by the enthusiasm," recalled one Soviet worker. "People checked their watches by their arrival to and departure from work." Whether accurate or not, this vignette certainly captures the main point: the construction had been made a political test of allegiance, and there was no avoiding the political implications of one's actions. TsGAOR, f. 7952, op. 5, d. 366, ll. 20–21.

112. The recollections of A. Grebenishchenko, as quoted in Orlova, "Rol' komsomola," p. 161, from Magnitogorskii rabochii, 27 April 1966.

113. Baranov, Magnitogorskaia plotina, pp. 31–32.

114. Bulgakov, Za obraztsovoe, p. 17.

115. Gugel, "Vospominaniia," p. 322.

116. Korin, Na novykh, p. 52.

117. TsGANKh, f. 4086, op. 2, d. 42, l. 5.

118. TsGAOR, f. 7952, op. 5, d. 412, ll. 6ff.

119. The number of shock workers was: February 1930, 1,090; September 1930, 1,635; October 1930, 6,064; January 1931, 10,000; January 1932, 18,927. The total number of workers in January 1931 was 18,865; in January 1932, 32,666. Orlova, "Rol' komsomola," pp. 164–65 (citing PAChO, f. 1101, op. 1, d. 17, l. 38); Stroitel'stvo i ekspluatatsiia, p. 82.

120. Here are the purported words of a young shock worker, Viktor Kalmykov: "Inside something burns, something you can't express in words. For example, our right bank is engaged in competition with the left. I always go on over there to have a look, how're things with them. I look over at the shore and I see Levitskii. . . . That

little Levitskii is bypassing us again. So what. Me and the boys just go at it that much harder." As quoted in Korin, *Na novykh*, pp. 55–56.

121. Gugel, "Vospominaniia," p. 32.

122. Nariniani, *Doroga*.

123. Antipova and Shkolnik, "Iz istorii," p. 37.

124. Petrov, *Magnitka*, pp. 63–64.

125. Scott, " 'Magnetic City,' " p. 544.

126. Korin, *Na novykh*, p. 61.

127. Nariniani, *Na stroike*, pp. 57–58.

128. Zverev, *Na stroike giganta*, p. 67; Antipova and Shkolnik, "Iz istorii," pp. 49–50.

129. For example: "Official notice of a young brigade of assembly workers. Having heard the report and the uncovering of a counterrevolutionary group at Magnitostroi, which was trying to foil our construction, in answer we ask to be received into the ranks of the Komsomol, in order, under the leadership of the party, to fight for socialism." Zuikov, "Komsomol," p. 197 (citing Arkhiv Magnitogorskogo GK VLKSM, d. 50, l. 13).

130. *Ural'skii rabochii*, 12 February 1933.

131. A. F. Khavin, *Karaganda—Tret'ia ugol'naia baza SSSR* (Moscow, 1951), pp. 81–82. At the beginning of 1931, the population at Karaganda had been around 5,000.

132. *Kuzbass: Rezul'taty perepisi gorodskogo naseleniia 1931 g.* (Novosibirsk, 1931), p. viii.

133. *Magnitostroi v tsifrakh*, pp. 236–37, 242.

134. In 1928–29, according to the then Urals oblast party secretary Shvernik, 300,000 people came to industrial enterprises in the Urals and another 260,000 left. As cited in V. V. Feldman, "O nekotorykh voprosakh formirovaniia sotsialisticheskogo rabochego klassa Urala," *Iz istorii rabochego klassa Urala. Sbornik statei* (Perm, 1961), pp. 306–19 (citing TsGAOR, f. 5451, op. 14, d. 15, l. 8).

135. Reprinted in Polonskii, *Magnitka zovet*, p. 23.

136. As an enticement, he claimed that "they give out bread and makhorka, some herring." Z. Chagan, *U podnozh'ia Magnitnoi gory* (Moscow, 1930), p. 7.

137. It is possible that the figure of 67,000 for 1930 is a typographical error and should have read 57,000. *Magnitogorskii rabochii*, 15 and 20 January 1934. It is important to emphasize that these figures are for Magnitostroi, and not for the parallel organization, Koksostroi. Since Koksostroi had approximately 4,000 workers, at a rate of ten times the total, we could increase the numbers of those who came another 35 to 40,000. The mine also had a separate administration, and so its workers, a thousand or so, were not included. Nor are so-called cadre workers included, i.e., those workers who were relatively skilled and had been sent on order by other factories. Alternative figures are given in *Magnitostroi v tsifrakh*, pp. 242–43, and *Stroitel'stvo i ekspluatatsiia*, p. 83. Yet another set of figures from oblast archives (GAChO, f. 1373, op. 1, d. 69, l. 7) are given in Eliseeva, "Iz istorii proeketirovanii," p. 147. Despite the differences in these figures, the order of magnitude remains constant throughout.

138. TsGAOR, f. 7952, op. 5, d. 342, l. 10.

139. TsGAOR, f. 7952, op. 5, d. 300, l. 50; and d. 311, l. 36.

140. *Magnitostroi v tsifrakh*, pp. 250–51. Slightly different figures are given in TsGANKh, f. 4086, op. 2, d. 119, ll. 25–26: total registered exit, 30,755; less than six months on site, 27,914. The differences are minuscule.

141. TsGANKh, f. 4086, op. 2, d. 119, ll. 21–22.

142. TsGANKh, f. 4086, op. 2, d. 119, ll. 25, 26. For the total white-collar employees: *Informatsionnyi biulleten'*, 1931, no. 2, p. 43.

143. *Magnitostroi v tsifrakh*, pp. 250–51.

144. *Magnitostroi,* 1931, nos. 9–12.

145. *Magnitostroi v tsifrakh,* pp. 250–51.

146. Eliseeva, "O sposobakh," p. 70.

147. TsGAOR, f. 7952, op. 5, d. 309, l. 38; and d. 300, l. 44. A third memoir says that "interruptions in supply began in the fall of 1932." Ibid., d. 312, ll. 296–97.

148. TsGAOR, f. 7952, op. 5, d. 301, l. 69.

149. *Magnitogorskii komsomolets,* 10 January 1932.

150. *Magnitogorskii rabochii,* 20 January 1934.

151. TsGAOR, f. 7952, op. 5, d. 309, l. 39.

152. Railroad stations that had been converted into labor exchanges could also become, during the famine, showcases of human misery. But the famine could not be mentioned. V. Budrov, "U vorot Donbassa," *Za industrializatsiiu,* 2 February 1933.

153. Eliseeva, "O sposobakh," p. 58 (citing TsGAOR, f. 7952, op. 5, d. 72, ll. 36, 29).

154. Serzhantov, "KPSS-Vdokhnovitel'," p. 184.

155. TsGAOR, f. 7952, op. 5, d. 361, l. 28.

156. TsGAOR, f. 7952, op. 5, d. 304, l. 11.

157. TsGAOR, f. 7952, op. 5, d. 309, l. 45. Workers were also given money to purchase cows, which around this time cost just under 2,000 rubles. Ibid., d. 315, l. 64.

158. Korolkov, "Bor'ba KPSS za sozdanie," pp. 139–40.

159. TsGAOR, f. 7952, op. 5, d. 307, l. 145.

160. *Magnitogorskii rabochii,* 12 and 15 February 1933.

161. *Magnitogorskii rabochii,* 17 February 1933.

162. According to one newspaper report, in 1934, 35,262 three-year passports were issued, while the following year 34,678 five-year passports, along with 14,320 three-year ones, were issued. But there is no indication of what percentage of the total number these figures represented. *Magnitogorskii rabochii,* 21 October 1936.

163. Orlova, "Rol' komsomola," pp. 153–72 (citing PAChO, f. 234, op. 1, d. 243, l. 208). In a speech a few months later, Beso Lominadze asserted that 52,000 people without the right to a passport were deported *(vyslany)* from Magnitogorsk during the passport campaign. *Magnitogorskii rabochii,* 15 January 1934. This figure was repeated (without reference) in an unpublished manuscript by V. Shklovskii, "Poezdka v Magnitogorsk." It is clearly an exaggeration. TsGAOR, f. 7952, op. 5, d. 380, l. 4.

164. As of 1 March 1933, Narpit, the city food trust, had 4,360 employees, 3,812 of whom presented themselves for a passport (meaning that 548 people, around 12.5 percent, simply fled). Passports for three years were issued to 657 people; for one year, to 1,495; and for three months, to 1,566. Another 90 or so were denied passports, of whom 20 had their files turned over to the courts for further investigation. It should be emphasized that more than one-third of Narpit's employees would have to be reexamined after only three months, and more than two-thirds after one year or less. Narpit was notorious as a supposed refuge for unsavory elements, but even if in other organizations more passports of greater duration were issued, the bulk of the city's population would still have to be reissued passports within only three years. And complaints or denunciations during that interval that needed to be checked out could pile up. TsGAOR, f. 7952, op. 5, d. 294, ll. 39–42.

165. *Magnitogorskii rabochii,* 11 April 1936.

166. TsGAOR, f. 7952, op. 5, d. 366, l. 15.

167. *Magnitogorskii rabochii,* 9 August 1936.

168. *Magnitogorskii rabochii,* 6 March 1936.

169. *Magnitogorskii rabochii,* 27 January 1938. And this process did not happen

immediately, judging by the complaints made by officials that managers inside the shops, where the photographing was to take place, were not paying sufficient attention to it. MFGAChO, f. 10, op. 10, d. 1096, l. 259.

170. *Magnitogorskii rabochii,* 9 May 1936.

171. One case was reported in the local newspaper of a person who for twenty-five rubles bought documents with a new family name to be used in obtaining a passport. *Magnitogorskii rabochii,* 6 April 1936.

172. For example, one pickpocket, when apprehended, turned out to have four different passports, which he probably would have sold for the right price. *Magnitogorskii rabochii,* 16 May 1936.

173. Ivan Kozints, for example, wrote himself out a diploma from the Kharkov Technical Institute and passed himself off as an engineer (which in those days [1931] was not overly difficult). He worked in that capacity at various factories, ending up as an engineer in the Mining Administration at Magnitogorsk, until he was "unmasked." Significantly, he also claimed to have served in the Red Army. *Magnitogorskii rabochii,* 20 March 1931.

174. *Magnitogorskii rabochii,* 16 March 1936.

175. For example, one woman who had allegedly stolen the daily receipts from a dining hall and fled Magnitogorsk turned up in the city again and was nailed by the militia during the mandatory *propiska. Magnitogorskii rabochii,* 20 November 1936.

176. *Magnitogorskii rabochii,* 26 January 1936.

177. *Magnitogorskii rabochii,* 21 October 1936. The announcement neglected to mention the reason, but it is likely the passports were being exchanged in part to eradicate bogus ones.

178. *Magnitogorskii rabochii,* 16 February 1938.

179. In 1933, as the passport system was being introduced, 32,852 people came to Magnitogorsk and another 21,421 left. During 1934, the first full year of operation of the passport system, 53,369 people arrived in Magnitogorsk and 33,333 left—a net gain of almost 20,000 people. MFGAChO, f. 16, op. 1, d. 42, l. 92. In 1935, 29,900 arrived and 21,020 left; in 1937, 24,501 and 25,564. In the first six months of 1938 (no yearly data were available), there were 7,663 registered arrivals and 10,783 departures, and in 1939, the figures were 20,248 and 19,673, respectively. Ibid., d. 72, l. 21, 45; d. 73, l. 21,; d. 102, ll. 2–53. According to a different archival source (TsGANKh, f. 4086, op. 2, d. 933, l. 22), however, in 1934, 33,329 people came and 25,008 left. So large a discrepancy in the measurement of population movement may reflect a bureaucratic error in reporting. The main point is that movement persisted after passportization; whatever the precise figures, the number of people entering or leaving the city was in the tens of thousands. Still, caution seems advised by the discrepancy in the numbers reported by officials as well as by indications that the registration system (particularly in the case of departures) may not have been perfect. Magnitogorsk statisticians conducted a survey of two buildings to ascertain the accuracy of the migration data. In one building with 219 registered residents (in 32 apartments), only 166 people were discovered to be residing there. Sixty-seven people had left the city without registering their departure and another 14 people were living in the unit without having registered (presumably recently born children). In the other building surveyed, of the 217 registered residents, all but one was actually in residence, and no one was living there without registration. Unfortunately, the report of the survey made no indication of the representativeness of the buildings and hence the significance of the findings. Ibid., d. 72, l. 31.

180. *Magnitogorskii rabochii,* 1 January 1936. Whereas during the first nine months of 1936 "several thousand" workers (not tens of thousands) left the construction trust, in the last four months of 1937, only around 1,500 construction workers were lost. Ibid., 18 December 1936 and 25 January 1938. There seems to

have been a constant shortage of construction workers, a problem made more acute toward the end of the decade when large-scale construction was renewed. In early 1940 it was reported that 1,000 Belorussian families had been imported to Magnitogorsk, with another 1,000 to come later. Ibid., 1 and 5 January 1940.

181. This is reflected in the language used by management officials, for example MFGAChO, f. 16, op. 1, d. 42, l. 62. Compare the data published for Khar'kov, whose population between the censuses of 1926 and 1939 doubled (as did that of Moscow and Leningrad) in M. V. Kurman and I. V. Lebedinskii, *Naselenie bol'shogo sotsialisticheskogo goroda* (Moscow, 1968), pp. 27, 64.

182. Compare the process for the industrial town of Bochum, as described by David Crew, *Town in the Ruhr* (New York: Columbia University Press, 1979). In the course of demonstrating how infrequently German workers secured stable employment with family-sustaining incomes, Crew furnishes ample evidence of employers strategizing about how best to exercise social control of the labor force.

V

THE MANAGEMENT OF SOVIET INDUSTRY, 1928–41

R. W. Davies

Since the end of 1986 a number of remarkable publications have appeared in the Soviet press concerned with the management of the economy in general and of industry in particular in the Stalin years. The Soviet literature presents the Stalinist industrial system as an "administrative-command system" controlled primarily by directives for which Stalin was personally responsible. The present essay argues that three major modifications need to be made to this simple model. First, as the essay in this volume by Lewis Siegelbaum and Ronald Suny suggests, the research of Granick, Berliner, and other Western scholars has shown that managers and even engineers were not simply passive recipients of orders; their behavior substantially modified the way in which the system operated. Second, although, particularly in the post-1937 years, Stalin's personal instructions were the ultimate authority, even after 1937 industrial managers sought to influence the policies of Stalin and the center, and the orders they received. Sometimes they succeeded in modifying them substantially. Third, I think it is the case, as I shall briefly try to illustrate at the end of this essay, that "market" or "quasi-market" features of the economic system existed in this period that are not incorporated in the Soviet version of the administrative-command model, notably the peasant free market and the quasi-market for labor.

Recent Soviet Views of the Stalinist Industrial System

Among the documents concerned with the management of the Soviet economy in the Stalin years that have been published since 1986 are three impressive novels. The fictionalized biography of Tevosian (as "Onisimov") by Aleksandr Bek, a well-known industrial journalist, had already been published in the West.[1] Anatolii Rybakov's *Children of the Arbat* features a leading character largely based on Tevosian's even more famous contemporary Zaveniagin (as "Riazanov"). It also includes "Budiagin," a composite figure based on Ordzhonikidze's close associates.[2] Sergei Antonov's account of the construction of the Moscow Metro features Kaganovich in the wings as the responsible Politburo member.[3] New firsthand accounts of economic management in the Stalin period have also appeared, including a metallurgist's comments on Bek's novel[4] and a revised and much franker version of an account of top-level decisions about armaments published by S. L. Vannikov in 1968–69. Vannikov was people's commissar for armaments between January 11, 1939, and June 9, 1941, and people's commissar for ammunition from February 16, 1942, to 1946.[5]

Such sources have to be handled with great caution. In their imaginative reconstruction all novelists go beyond the strict historical evidence; but Rybakov's novel in particular is much less careful than the author believes.[6] The reminiscences by Stalinist economic managers suffer not merely from the usual defects of all reminiscences, particularly those prepared long after the event, but were also censored and manipulated in accordance with the political conditions at the time of publication, as the two versions of Vannikov's memoirs eloquently testify.[7] But these are indispensable sources for understanding economic management under Stalin, and I believe they can be used if due care is taken.

The novels have already had a huge readership in the USSR and have been the subjects of much public discussion. Perhaps the most interesting and influential comments are those on Bek's novel and his portrait of Tevosian by the well-known economic reformer subsequently appointed mayor of Moscow, Gavril Popov.[8]

Tevosian was fanatically devoted to his work, incorruptible, modest in his personal needs, but above all obedient to the will of Stalin. His energy saved the steel industry, of which he was people's commissar from May 17, 1940, from the near-stagnation which followed the purges of 1937–38. But his obedience led him to waste enormous sums on a useless invention which had Stalin's support, while his reliance on the conservative specialists in his department led him to ban experiments on a valuable technical innovation proposed by a factory director.

Popov's review uses Bek's portrait of Tevosian to analyze the Soviet economic system. The subtitles of Popov's essay indicate the thrust of his argument: (1) the Administrative System; (2) Administrative Style; (3) the Administrator; (4) Breakdowns in Administration; (5) Breakdown in Scientific-Technical Progress; (6) the Crisis of the Administrative System. According to Popov, the novel exemplifies the Administrative System of the Stalinist economy:

> The basis of the system is the centralization of decisions and punctual, undeviating, over-riding fulfillment of directives from Above and particularly from Stalin—the Boss. Not pitying himself, intensifying above all his own

personal work, Onisimov [Tevosian] "holds the ministerial *apparat* in a state of tension". . . .

This is a system of specific and detailed management *in natura*. It is a system of continuous operational management of the course of production from the center. This is the Administrative System.

Two further important points stressed by Popov, referring primarily to the postwar period, help to place the system of the 1930s in its historical context. First, Tevosian's own quality as an economic manager deteriorated, as he steadily became unaccustomed to independent thinking. But at least such administrators as Tevosian and his boss Ordzhonikidze came to the Administrative System with a life experience from outside it, in the revolutionary underground and Civil War. With their successors, lack of independence was built into their managerial behavior from the beginning of their careers. The system contained within itself its own degeneration.

Second, Popov argues that the Administrative System is not coterminous with the Stalin dictatorship. Tevosian, believing that independent thought was permissible after Stalin's death, criticized in 1957 Khrushchev's scheme to replace the industrial ministries by regional economic councils. He was promptly dismissed and posted abroad. In his final section, "What was Onisimov's Mistake?" Popov uses this incident to illustrate his view that the Administrative System has continued till the present day: terror and fear have gone, but the System in principle remains. This is a distinction similar to T. H. Rigby's between the "mono-organizational society combined with personal dictatorship" of the Stalin period and the "mono-organizational society without personal dictatorship" which followed the death of Stalin.[9]

Popov's careful reflections and similar published and unpublished analyses of the Soviet past by those who shared his approach must have been a major influence on Gorbachev's report of November 2, 1987, on the occasion of the seventieth anniversary of the October Revolution.[10] Like some other major Soviet official reports, the historical sections of Gorbachev's report give the impression of having been written by several rival hands. The most impressive passages discuss what Gorbachev calls "the administrative-command system of party-state management of the country," an almost explicit reference to Popov's Administrative System. Unlike Khrushchev, who presented the "cult of personality" as a more or less accidental distortion of the normal socialist system, Gorbachev presents the administrative-command system as providing the prerequisites for the emergence of the Stalinist repressions. In several passages of the report Gorbachev expressed his strong support for both industrialization and, on the whole, the collectivization of agriculture. But he added the important qualification that their emergence had been associated with the emergence of the administrative-command system and with the accompanying growth of bureaucratism. In this context he gave a very cautious appraisal of the economic results of the system:

The corresponding structure of administration and methods of planning began to be established. In industry, at the size it was then, when all the basic objects of the industrial building were literally visible, such methods and such a system of administration in general gave their results. But such a strict system of centralization and commands was impermissible in solving the problems of the transformation of the countryside.[11]

Moreover, the system had even more serious consequences in social and political life. According to Gorbachev:

the administrative-command system . . . affected the whole political and social life of the country. Firmly established in the economy, it also spread to the superstructure, limiting the development of the democratic potential of socialism, and restraining the progress of socialist democracy.[12]

The picture painted here is of a system of economic management primarily based on the issue of commands from above, or even from a single individual. Such an impression is not all that different from that conveyed by Western scholars in the heyday of totalitarian theory, as discussed by Lewis Siegelbaum and Ronald Suny. However, it would be misleading to suggest that late Soviet thinking about Stalinist industrialization merely recapitulates earlier Western views.

Several recent publications, for example, have sought to provide evidence that Stalin's personal rule did not go unchallenged. Thus in a 1988 article on Khrushchev, Fyodor Burlatsky wrote:

He was a representative (*vyrazitel'*) of the trend in the party which was represented in other circumstances and probably in other ways by politicians who were different from each other in many ways such as Dzerzhinsky, Bukharin, Rykov, Rudzutak and Kirov. They were supporters of the development of NEP and democratization, and opponents of coercive measures in industry or in agriculture, and still more in culture. In spite of the cruel Stalinist repressions, this trend never died.[13]

This is tantalizingly unspecific. In another 1988 article, Mikoyan's son, citing the old Bolshevik A. V. Snegov, reported that at a "Central Committee" (i.e., Politburo or Orgburo) session sometime in 1931, chaired by Kaganovich, several of those present, including Kartvelishvili, first secretary of the Trans-Caucasus regional party committee, strenuously objected to Stalin's proposal that Beria be appointed second secretary of the Transcaucasian committee, and the proposal found no support (Ordzhonikidze was said by Mikoyan to have deliberately absented himself from the meeting). Mikoyan's son comments: "It is interesting (*liubopytno*) that at that time, apparently, disagreement could still take place. So far opponents able to express and defend other points of view had not been removed."[14]

Finally, an article on the postwar Leningrad affair suggests that A. A. Kuznetsov, one of its victims, deliberately underemphasized the name of

Stalin and stressed the name of Kirov in his speeches, following the tradition which developed in Leningrad under siege; he also used his position as the Central Committee secretary responsible for cadres to attempt to find out the truth about Kirov's assassination. The author comments that such people as Kuznetsov were innocent before the party and the people but asks whether they were innocent "before the criminals, adventurists and careerists who were creating an arbitrary system": "Perhaps there were those who did not believe in the cult? Who did not reconcile themselves with it? And who in the end resisted it? I dare to believe and assert: Aleksei Aleksandrovich Kuznetsov *was not an innocent sacrifice.*"[15]

The evidence provided in this instance is circumstantial and rather vague. In general many Soviet writers nowadays are likely to seek out every scrap of evidence about resistance to the repression and most unlikely to present scrupulously evidence showing that Stalin had a sensible policy about anything.

Industrial Policy and Soviet Management

The question thus arises: how far and in what ways were the industrial policies of Stalin and the Politburo influenced by party and industrial officials and managers at various levels? I consider two subperiods: 1929–33, when the system was in the process of formation under the impact of an unprecedented emphasis on investment in the capital goods industries, and 1938–41, following the Great Purges, the years of intensive rearmament before the German invasion of June 22, 1941.

1929–33

The policies of forced industrialization and the collectivization of agriculture with which Stalin is personally identified emerged triumphant in these years. But there is strong evidence that the Politburo did not obediently or automatically endorse Stalin's policies in 1929–30. Jonathan Haslam's work on Soviet foreign policy in the 1930s reveals a Stalin who in the early 1930s often left the conduct of foreign affairs to Litvinov.[16] In my own work on the early 1930s, it has become increasingly clear that members of the Politburo continued to argue with "Koba," particularly, but not entirely, on issues where they had a special competence. In economic affairs, there is strong evidence that opposition developed within the Politburo to the course of collectivization sanctioned by Stalin; at one meeting nearly all members may have opposed him.[17] In 1931–32 the protracted dispute about the planned rates of industrial growth undoubtedly involved acrimonious discussions behind the scenes at the top level in the party, though the position of Stalin in this dispute is by no means unambiguous. In 1932–33 the growing famine and the economic crisis led to a profound crisis of confidence within the party.

A more detailed examination of industrial plans in 1929–33 will help to establish how decisions were taken and to assess the influence of the leading industrial administrators and the technical and economic specialists on the outcome. This exercise will also reveal the considerable difficulties involved in handling the inadequate sources at present available.

The course of events may be briefly summarized. The "optimum" variant of the First Five-Year Plan, adopted in the spring of 1929, was already extremely optimistic and had been strongly resisted by many technical specialists and economists in Gosplan and Vesenkha. Between the spring of 1929 and the summer of 1930 every component of the plan was increased, largely as a result of pressure from Rabkrin (at this time headed by Ordzhonikidze). Thus the pig-iron plan for 1932–33, some seven or eight million tons on the proposal of the Vesenkha specialists, rose to ten million tons in the Five-Year Plan of spring 1929 and was increased to seventeen million tons by the sixteenth party congress in June-July 1930. The 1931 annual plan, the most ambitious in Soviet history, assumed that the revised plans would be achieved in full. The 1932 plan was less extravagant but still extremely overambitious. In the midst of economic crisis and growing famine, the annual 1933 plan and the broad goals for the 1933–37 Five-Year Plan announced at the January 1933 Central Committee plenum marked the return to realistic planning.

There is ample evidence that many factory managers and industrial specialists and administrators resisted the unrealistic plans. This is not quite the whole story. Some specialists supported the upward revision of the plans. Technologists on the staff of Vesenkha advocated reforms, such as the continuous working week *(nepreryvka)*, which were damaging to industrial plants in the long run but in 1929–31 enabled production to be pushed up.[18] And Rabkrin had its own specialists, including foreign specialists such as the notorious Dr. Karner, director of a small German iron and steel works. He backed proposals for extremely high efficiency coefficients in the southern iron and steel trust Iugostal, which were an essential element in the exaggerated Five-Year Plan for the industry.[19] But Karner was an exception: nearly all foreign specialists who recorded their views opposed, perhaps a little too firmly, the notion that American or German levels of utilization could be achieved under Soviet conditions.[20]

Throughout the winter of 1929–30 complaints appeared in the press about the hostility of managers and specialists to increases in the plans or to the existing level of the plans. In December 1929 Kuibyshev condemned those who criticized the high targets.[21] In March 1930 S. Kosior noted that "in many factories and mines the management and technical personnel formed the firm opinion that the programs are exaggerated and cannot be fulfilled."[22] In May *Izvestiia* claimed or admitted that "some leaders of industrial enterprises, a certain part of the engineering-technical personnel, and even in some places the voluntary organizations of the workers, consider that the high rates of development of the economy, and particularly of industry, are a temporary transitory phenomenon."[23] At the sixteenth party congress in June–July, Mezhlauk claimed that both the seventeen-million-ton plan for pig iron and the Ural-Kuznetsk project had been adopted by the party "against the soviet apparatus, which hestitated, doubted and did not know what to do."[24] In his autobiography Bardin, chief engineer of the Kuznetsk part of the project, admitted that he had resisted the proposed increase in capacity of the plant at the end of 1929.[25]

It should be remembered that these objections were being voiced at a time when many specialists had been arrested for wrecking activities; the accusation of advocating low production targets was often prominent. Open opposition to the plans required considerable courage. Syrtsov, in his famous critical speech of August 30, 1930, remarked that factory directors believed that the plans were unrealistic but lacked the civil courage to oppose them.[26] Even so, during the autumn the Soviet press published numerous reports that factory directors and industrial officials were resisting the "counterplans" that were a fashionable method of increasing factory and branch plans at that time. The industrial newspaper wrote of the counterplan that "as a rule it is not greeted with joy by economic officials, and it is sometimes even held off at bayonet point."[27] It was in August that Kuibyshev, then still chairman of Vesenkha, is reported to have come to the conclusion that capital investment in 1931 would be too low to enable the seventeen-million-ton pig-iron plan to be achieved in the economic year 1932–33.[28] It seems safe to assume that he came to this conclusion after receiving advice from Vesenkha officials.

The 1931 plan, with its proposed increase of industrial production by as much as 45 percent in a single year, aroused fresh resistance. According to an émigré source, the chief assistant to the nonferrous-metals combine objected to the plan to produce 150,000 tons of copper and was dismissed.[29] A leading Vesenkha official reported that some senior managers and mine managers in the coal industry displayed "lack of faith in the rates of growth approved by the party."[30]

During the first few months of 1931, almost every industry fell badly behind the plan. In June a report from the medium engineering combine to the Vesenkha presidium noted "a certain perplexity of leading personnel at a number of factories"; "in many instances energy was directed to a considerable extent to proving that the targets could not be fulfilled."[31] After the results for the first six months became known, the financial journal *Finansovye Problemy* noted that "individual voices have been heard both in the Soviet administration and inside our party to the effect that the failures in the first half of 1931 will make it necessary to pose the question of reexamining the annual plan."[32] In circumstances when open opposition to official policies was increasingly impossible, a headline in the industrial newspaper drew attention to the disquiet behind the scenes: "Do Not Whisper that the Plan Is Unrealistic!"[33]

Similar reports continued to appear intermittently in the course of 1932.

Among the most striking was a thinly veiled criticism of the iron and steel plans published in the industrial newspaper by a senior metallurgist.[34] He pointed out that the 1932 plan proposed to install as many as twenty-four new blast furnaces but that only nine had been installed in the first eight months of the year. To achieve the plan, equipment to a value of 750 million rubles would be required, but only 150 million rubles was available. "In the capital investment plan for 1933 there is a very great deal to be said for the need *to place the main emphasis on completing projects carried over into 1933; preparation for new construction should begin only after the actual completion and start-up of projects already being built.*"[35]

While all these complaints were being voiced, the Politburo gradually and painfully adjusted the plans downward toward reality. The decisive change came at the beginning of 1933 and was encapsulated in Stalin's sensational announcement of the shape of future plans at the Central Committee plenum of January 1933:

> Even if we wanted to, we could not carry out . . . a policy of accelerating rates of growth to the maximum during the Second Five-Year Plan, especially in the first two or three years. . . .
>
>   During the First Five-Year Plan the annual increment to industrial production was on average 22 percent. I think that for the Second Five-Year Plan it is appropriate to take an average annual increment to industrial production of 13–14 percent as a minimum.[36]

For Stalin, the 1931 plan, with its 45 percent growth rate, had already become a forgotten episode in the history of planning.

How far was the shift to more realistic planning at the beginning of 1933 a response to the open and muted pressure during the previous three years from the industrial specialists and administrators? Perhaps such pressure was hardly necessary. In the years 1931 and 1932 industry continuously failed to achieve its plans. Pig-iron production was 4.9 million tons in 1931 and 6.2 million in 1932, and most of the new blast furnaces were far from complete. It must have been increasingly obvious to the most enthusiastic Bolshevik that it was impossible to produce ten million tons in 1932–33, let alone seventeen million tons. But the change in the approach of the party leadership to planning was more fundamental than a mere recognition of failure. Stalin's speech heralded a more or less permanent shift to much more realistic planning.

Soviet publications by participants in these events provide tentative evidence about the influence of technical specialists and administrators on this change of approach.

According to these accounts, the realism of the annual and five-year plans for the iron and steel industry, which were at the heart of all Soviet planning, began to preoccupy members of the Politburo in the course of 1931. Sometime during the summer Ordzhonikidze, who as chairman of Rabkrin had led the campaign for the seventeen-million-ton plan, suggested to the metallurgical engineer A. S. Tochinskii, with whom he had been acquainted since 1918, that "perhaps the plan is not realistic." After some hesitation Tochinskii replied that there was "Manilovshchina" in the plans received by factories because they were not based on specific conditions (Manilov is a dreamy, complacent character in Gogol's *Dead Souls*). He strongly criticized Rabkrin and Dr. Karner: Karner had "pedantically estimated" how much each furnace would yield on the basis that all necessary resources were available. "A psychological situation is created; you won't reach the plan, and so you don't care whether you get 80 percent or 60 percent." Tochinskii also told Ordzhonikidze that many new leaders of industry "led with their vocal cords" but were afraid to reveal the real position. He then produced a notebook containing estimates of the possible production of each work in the southern iron and steel industry and bluntly told Ordzhonikidze that a realistic plan for 1931 would be a mere five million tons of pig iron, less than in the previous year. His figures proved to be approximately correct. Ordzhonikidze was evidently impressed by Tochinskii's evidence. A few months later, on November 9, 1931, he summoned him to a session of the Central Committee commission on metallurgy, which was discussing the 1932 plan; the session was attended by two other Politburo members, Voroshilov and Rudzutak.[37]

In the summer of 1931 preparations for the Second Five-Year Plan (1933–37) were also under way. On August 11 Kuibyshev, who became chairman of Gosplan after Ordzhonikidze took over Vesenkha in November 1930, presented reports about the iron and steel industry to the Central Committee (i.e., the Politburo) and Sovnarkom. In these reports he proposed a reduction in the pig-iron target for 1937 from sixty to forty-five million tons. In the same month a metallurgical conference which met under the auspices of the Politburo and Sovnarkom concluded that this reduced figure was still too high. It therefore resolved to reexamine the plan "taking into account the exchange of opinions" at the conference, on the basis of a 1937 target for pig-iron production of only twenty-five–thirty million tons. The conference also prudently decided to seek the opinions of Stalin and Molotov, who were not present. When it reassembled, it was informed of Stalin's counterproposal, that a "precise figure" of twenty-five million tons should be approved for 1937, and duly accepted it.[38]

Both the 1932 annual plan for iron and steel and the revised target for 1937 were still a long way from realism. The Soviet source I have cited gives the impression that under Tochinskii's influence the 1932 plan for ferrous metals was realistic. But the pig-iron target adopted by the Politburo on November 10, 1931, was nine million tons, and a counterplan of ten million tons later acquired more or less official status.[39] In the event, only 6.2 million tons was produced in 1932. Stalin's "precise figure" of twenty-five million tons for pig iron production in 1937 also proved to be too high. In the course of 1932 and 1933, it was eventually reduced first to eighteen million tons and then, in accordance with a dramatic proposal by

Ordzhonikidze at the seventeenth party congress, to only sixteen million tons.[40] Realism was at last almost achieved: production in 1937 amounted to 14.5 million tons (though the plans for some other major industries were still too optimistic).

An even more interesting event occurred on the occasion of the January 1933 Central Committee plenum: a consultation about planning between Stalin and Zaveniagin. According to a *Pravda* journalist, Zaveniagin told him:

> Just before the plenum Sergo [Ordzhonikidze] and I were with comrade Stalin. He asked what I thought was the main thing in industry. I answered: "assimilation" [*osvoenie*]. He tried to push me in different directions, asked me about the importance of supply, transport, and personnel, and like a *vas'ka-vstanka* [rocking doll] I kept coming back to my point of view, and insisted: "assimilation."[41]

No doubt Zaveniagin was not the only person consulted by Stalin, and this was in any case not as entirely new an idea for Stalin as Zaveniagin implied. In January 1932 the seventeenth party conference asserted that "mastering technology" *(ovladenie tekhnikoi)* was an urgent necessity; this notion of "mastering" was close to the notion of "assimilation."[42] In the summer of 1932, in a letter to heavy industry, Stalin wrote that "we have a passion for construction, and that's excellent, but we lack the passion for mastering [*ovladenie*] production."[43] Nevertheless, there was an important change of emphasis at this time. At the January 1933 plenum, Stalin emphasized assimilation much more strongly, treating what had previously been a subtheme of party policy as the main key to successful development. Stalin closely linked assimilation with his call for a switch to a slower pace of industrialization. During the Second Five-Year Plan, with its slower rate of growth, he insisted, the passion for construction must be complemented by concentrating on "enthusiasm and passion for *assimilation* of new factories and new technology, a serious improvement of labor productivity, a serious reduction in costs."[44] A few days later, on January 12, Iaroslavsky told the *Pravda* editorial team that this was "a real change of direction in the policy of industrialization."[45]

If this account is reliable, it provides a remarkable example of the way in which both Ordzhonikidze and Zaveniagin, a Soviet-trained, rapidly promoted engineer, themselves modified their revolutionary enthusiasm by acquiring some of the professional realism of the older specialists, then played an important part in winning Stalin over to this approach.[46] But it seems to me that the available evidence does not enable us to interpret these events as a straightforward battle between Ordzhonikidze, backed by the "technostructure," and Stalin and Molotov on behalf of the "political structure." Ordzhonikidze seems to have taken a long while to conclude that the Rabkrin plans could not be achieved. We have seen that at the end of 1931 he supported an exaggerated iron and steel plan for 1932. His cry from the heart at the October 1932 Central Committee plenum seems genuine: construction of the iron and steel industry "is a huge task, we torment ourselves, we bang our heads against it, and we learn. . . . We thought we could construct Magnitka in two or three years. It didn't come off, we strained every nerve, but it didn't come off."[47]

On the other hand, Stalin, who had vigorously defended the higher targets in February 1931, on the available evidence appears (no doubt wrongly) to have accepted moderate plans ever since August 1931. The growth rates for 1933–37 which he advocated at the January 1933 plenum were *lower* than those eventually accepted at the seventeenth party congress a year later.[48] Obviously much remains mysterious about the relationship between industry and the Politburo in those years; what is clear is that there was a dialogue, not a simple *diktat*.

1938–41

The extensive arrests and executions from 1936 onward of industrial officials and managers at all levels from the head of Gosplan to factory foremen resulted in the rapid promotion of Soviet-trained specialists. Men such as Zaveniagin, Tevosian, Vannikov, Shakhurin, Iakovlev and Emelianov were promoted to very senior positions. This resulted in a considerable enhancement of Stalin's power. How did it affect the process of decision making and policy making in industry? The reminiscences and biographies of some of the leading actors provide useful material.

The evidence from both admirers and critics of Stalin confirms both his willfulness and his uncontrollability. His colleagues and his advisers bent to his will. Vannikov describes how Zhdanov, in a discussion about the 107-mm gun, "unfortunately took Stalin's comments to indicate approval of G. I. Kulik's project, and this influenced his future attitude to this question."[49] On another issue "I was angered to hear military engineers express views contrary to their experience and knowledge, solely because Stalin had expressed liking for [them] the previous day."[50] For his own part Vannikov frankly admits: "The then leaders of the People's Commissariat for Armaments, including myself, while having a correct attitude, did not, however, display enough firmness and principle, and carried out orders which we considered harmful for the state. And we were influenced not only by a sense of discipline, but also by the desire to avoid repressions."[51]

This environment of fear and suspicion corrupted major and minor decisions about the defense industry. Leading designers were arrested and perished; senior industrial officials and factory management were persecuted by the NKVD for failures which were not their fault.[52] In the last couple of years before the war, Stalin pressed ahead with unwise plans for "a fleet for seven seas and oceans" and gave orders that new armaments factories were to be constructed in the Ukraine, where they would be invulnerable only on the unrealistic assumption that an aggressor would not succeed in penetrating Soviet borders.

But debate at the top had not ceased. According to Vannikov, the draconian legislation enforcing tighter labor discipline in June 1940, which might be thought of as a typical Stalin measure, was approved reluctantly by Stalin after frequent requests from the commissariats.[53] Stalin often acted as arbiter between the commissariats and (where his pet prejudices were not involved) struggled desperately to hear the rival points of view. At the Defense Committee the Commissariat for Foreign Trade nearly persuaded Stalin to stop importing an expensive machine tool with the argument that it would cost a boatload of wheat.[54]

Behind the clashes at the top, within the commissariats the people's commissars in their turn were subjected to pressure and persuasion from more junior industrial officials. Vannikov describes how his deputies insisted that he should phone Voznesenskii to try to reverse the decision of a commission headed by Molotov. The commission had decided to switch the rifle factories to the production of self-loading rifles in 1941 and to cease producing ordinary rifles altogether. Voznesenskii crudely told Vannikov to stop his "sabotage and red tape." Vannikov's deputies then insisted that he should appeal to Stalin. After four hours Stalin phoned back with the news that the Politburo agreed. Vannikov comments that without the pressure on him from his deputies the Soviet Union would have been left without a single operating rifle factory in the worst period of the war.[55]

In the command economy technical innovations have to be endorsed from above. Soviet publications report many cases of "false innovators" who succeeded in imposing their ideas on a Stalin and a Politburo desperately anxious to achieve technical primacy in their military race with Nazi Germany.

In one case, wretched Kulik, then head of the Chief Artillery Administration, on the basis of a misreading of the technical level of German tanks, persuaded Stalin to cease production of 45- and 76-mm guns, shifting all production to the 107-mm gun; the decision was reversed, after much waste, a month after the German invasion.[56] (Will someone write a learned essay rehabilitating Kulik one day, a companion to that long-awaited volume on "Zinoviev as hero and theorist?"[57]) Another case occurred in the summer of 1940, when Iakovlev was deputy commissar for aviation responsible for research and development. A designer complained to the Politburo that Iakovlev had blocked his design for a new aircraft because he was afraid of competition. A full meeting of the Politburo allocated resources to the complainant; his aircraft crashed on its first flight.[58] In a third case, an engineer persuaded the head of the relevant department of the Red Army to support his new type of tank armor-plating. He presented a good case in nontechnical terms to a commission chaired by Molotov at which Stalin was present, describing his metal as "armor which defends in being destroyed." Stalin commented "There you are, dialectics in action!" and gave the project his support. The skeptical Emelianov, then in charge of research in the Armor-Plating Administration of the People's Commissariat for the Defense Industry, acquired a sample of the metal and submitted it to an official test without the military realizing that the new metal was involved. The metal was completely destroyed, and the project was dropped. Emelianov claims that, in order to protect the military from Stalin's wrath, he joined with them in persuading Stalin to concentrate on armor which would resist shells as well as bullets.[59]

This last example of a poor innovation being brought to a halt without Stalin being fully aware of what was going on illustrates how a technologist was able to sidetrack one of Stalin's decisions. On another occasion a good innovation was pushed through by stealth. An enlightened military representative endorsed a scheme to cast tank turrets experimentally in whole units rather than forging and welding them. The prototypes were produced at a shipyard with the approval of Emelianov, who was then head of the metal administration of the People's Commissariat for Shipbuilding. When this type of turret was compared with the existing forged and welded turrets at the Committee of Defense, Voroshilov was astonished to find that they had undertaken this work on their own initiative. The experiment was endorsed by the committee. At the subsequent meeting of the Politburo its advocates answered Stalin's questions incompetently, and it looked as if the new type of turret would be blocked. But Savelev, who then worked in the Politburo Secretariat, helped Emelianov to get the project approved by advising him that he should draft a resolution which gave permission for cast turrets to be produced *as well as* welded; this was endorsed by Stalin.[60]

It is not always clear, of course, whether an innovation is "poor" or "good." Marshal Voronov argues that the story of the 107-mm gun was rather more complicated than Vannikov suggested.[61] Kudriavtsev, who was engaged in work on a "poor" technology for smelting iron that was reluctantly supported by Tevosian on Stalin's orders, points out that this mistake did not seem so bad when considered in a comparative context. Soviet experiments with this innovation were brought to an end by the decision of a government commission in 1954, the year after Stalin's death. But work on the same technology continued unsuccessfully in the United States until 1964.[62]

Plenty of unambiguously "good" innovations were taken up by the administrative system between 1929 and 1945; only this can explain the high quality of Soviet tanks and aircraft at the height of the Second World War. Some Soviet participants present their story as if these successes were invariably achieved in opposition to Stalin. But Iakovlev's Stalin on the whole encourages successful innovation; on one occasion, for example, blocked by bureaucracy, Iakovlev successfully appealed to Stalin to allow him to design a lightweight jet engine.[63] Others present Stalin as their principal supporter, notably the famous artillery designer V. G. Grabin, who describes how he received support from Stalin against Tukhachevskii when the latter was overenamored with a universal gun which he wrongly believed was becoming standard in the United States.[64]

This was a brutal and devious world. The people's commissar for armaments was arrested early in June 1941; after the German invasion, still in prison, he was ordered by Stalin to prepare an assessment of the armaments situation in the light of wartime developments of which he knew nothing.[65] Iakovlev describes in some detail the atmosphere of fear and provocation which surrounded him for several years before Stalin's death.[66] The leading armaments designer, Shpitalnyi, is said to have accused industrialists of sabotage when production went wrong because of defects in the designs; he also destroyed the designs of rivals who had been arrested.[67] From such accounts we get the impression that the repressive machine used so ruthlessly by Stalin during the Ezhovshchina had acquired a life of its own, weaving tales of plots and intrigues in which both Stalin and his policemen were unable to distinguish fact from fantasy.

Nevertheless, the political leaders and the technologists continued to work together in amity, rivalry, and hatred. Designers, engineers, and technicians appeared before Stalin or before commissions headed by Molotov, Voroshilov, Zhdanov, or Voznesenskii. Technological and production decisions were thrashed out, sometimes after stormy debate. The senior managers of industry were subordinates in the achievements and failures of the Administrative System, but they were influential subordinates.

The Administrative System and the Market

A further important set of issues has so far not been dealt with directly in this paper. In 1930 the future socialist system was expected to operate entirely through direct planning. The market, trade, and money were to be abolished. Labor as well as products would be directly allocated by central and local authorities. Rationing would probably be permanently retained. In the early 1930s this model underwent considerable modifications. By 1933 the personal plot of the collective farm household and the kolkhoz market at free prices were legalized features of the system. In socialized trade by 1935, the rationing of food and consumer goods had been replaced by limited consumer choice at fixed prices. In industry itself, labor was on the whole not allocated (except in the growing forced-labor sector). Workers were free to change their jobs and were paid money wages differentiated by skill, by work done, and to a certain extent by scarcity. There was a quasi-market for labor. Costs plans, and *khozraschet* generally, were an increasingly important aspect of the plans of every industry and factory. In all these respects the actual economic system of the middle and late 1930s had departed from the administrative-command model.

We do not know very much about the discussions and pressures within the economic and political apparatus which resulted in these major changes. But it is clear that the industrial administrators and specialists provided a significant input to some of these reforms. Some members of the staff of the People's Commissariat for Heavy Industry called for far-reaching economic reforms in 1932–33, involving an increased role for the market.[68] Their proposals were rejected but had some influence on subsequent developments within industry. A national cost-reduction campaign was followed by an industrial price reform on April 1, 1936, and most industrial subsidies were abolished. A few years later, in the summer of 1940, the discussion about enterprise rights was renewed, only to be aborted by the approach of war.[69] But even without these further changes toward enterprise autonomy, the Soviet economic system had undergone substantial modifications as compared with the concept of a planned economy which predominated in the early 1930s. Perhaps the trend within the party referred to by Burlatsky in his article on Khrushchev did not merely fail to die; it was also to a certain extent incorporated within the Stalinist administrative system.

Administrative commands from above were certainly the crucial feature of the industrial system in the 1930s. In the late 1930s, industry, like the rest of the economy, was ultimately subject to the personal orders of Stalin. If Stalin regarded it as necessary, he could order the arrest or even the execution of any of his subordinates. But the industrial system was not merely an "administrative-command system of party-state management." At least three modifications, or groups of modifications, must be made to this simple model.

First, as the work of Berliner, Granick, Lampert, and others has shown, managers and specialists were not simply *vintiki* or cogs in the machine. If they were to carry out their duties to the state and the plan, factory managers, supported by the factory administration and the specialists, had to be quasi entrepreneurial. They systematically broke the official rules, assisted by a vigorous stratum of "pushers" *(tolkachi)*. Likhachev, the engagingly cunning director of the Moscow vehicle works over many years, was almost openly admired as an example of how to get away with it. On the other hand, the system also inhibited enthusiasm and conscientiousness. The penalties incurred for failing to carry out orders from above led many specialists and officials to avoid risk and innovation. Engineers in administrative positions within the factories, required to impose production discipline on the workers, found that their powers were limited, partly by the social prestige which still attached to the industrial working class, partly as a result of the shortages of labor endemic in the system, which enabled workers to exercise a certain independence. In consequence, many specialists sought to avoid the factory floor or even to avoid factories altogether.

Second, many industrial administrators and technical specialists did not passively receive orders from above but actively sought to influence these orders. In the early 1930s both industrial administrators and factory managers strove over several years to secure more realistic plans. This was more than the normal effort of factory managers to reduce the plans they received from their superiors. Fundamentally mistaken conceptions of planning possibilities dominated the Politburo between 1929 and 1932. Resistance to the exaggerated plans played an important part, together with the crisis in the Soviet economy, in changing the approach to planning of Stalin and the party leadership. From the beginning of 1933, plans, though taut, were relatively realistic, and care was taken to consult the specialists in drawing them up.

In the late 1930s both Stalin's power over industry and the influence on it of the NKVD greatly increased. But this did not mean that politicians paid less attention to technologists and industrial administrators. Production plans and new products were directly discussed by the members of the Politburo, the senior staff of the industrial commissariats, and the key factory managers. The industrial administrators and the technologists, in spite of fear of repression, continued to express their professional advice and opinion to the political leaders. On occasion (we do not know how often) they initiated quite wide policy changes and got them accepted.

Third, the incorporation of a quasi market for labor in the Stalinist system and the permanent establishment of the kolkhoz market at free prices also meant that the Stalinist industrial system differed significantly from the administrative-command model.

NOTES

I am most grateful to members of the Conference on Industrialization and Change in Soviet Society for their comments on this paper, and particularly to Stephen Kotkin for his careful suggestions.

1. A. Bek, *Novoe naznachenie* (Frankfurt-on-Main, 1977), published in the USSR in *Znamia*, 1986, nos. 10–11.

2. *Druzhba narodov*, 1987, nos. 4–6. "Riazanov" was based not only on Zaveniagin but also on K. I. Ivanov, Zaveniagin's assistant, who in 1937 became head of the combine (information kindly supplied by S. Kotkin).

3. *Iunost'*, 1987, nos. 3–4.

4. V. Kudriavtsev, in *Nauka i zhizn'*, 1987, no. 12.

5. *Znamia*, 1988, nos. 1–2; no. 1 includes a critical comment by Marshal N. N. Voronov, then in charge of artillery procurement. The previous version, which is not mentioned by *Znamia*, appeared in *Voprosy istorii*, 1968, no. 10, and 1969, no. 1.

6. See comments by A. Latsis in *Izvestiia*, August 17, 1987; by John Barber in *Detente*, 1988, no. 11, pp. 8–11; and by myself in R. Miliband, L. Panitch, and J. Saville, eds., *Socialist Register 1988* (London, 1988), p. 73. Rybakov claimed that "not a single action by Stalin is invented, they are all supported by evidence" (*Literaturnaia gazeta*, August 19, 1987).

7. See also the comments by A. I. Mikoyan's son S. Mikoyan in *Ogonek*, 1987,

no. 50, p. 4. He claims that in the second volume of Mikoyan's autobiography "whole passages were written in for him (for example, against Bukharin), while excluding much that was dear to the author."

8. *Nauka i zhizn'*, 1987, no. 4, pp. 54–65.

9. See T. H. Rigby in R. C. Tucker, ed., *Stalinism: Essays in Historical Interpretation* (New York, 1977), pp. 53–76.

10. *Pravda*, November 3, 1987.

11. Ibid.

12. Ibid.

13. *Literaturnaia gazeta*, February 24, 1988.

14. *Komsomol'skaia pravda*, February 21, 1988. He added, however, that "the 'democratic discussion' was immediately broken off," and the posts were reshuffled a few months later without referring the matter to the Politburo; Beria got the job and Kartvelishvili was posted elsewhere.

15. A. Afanasev in *Komsomol'skaia pravda*, January 15, 1988 (Afanasev is a senior journalist on the newspaper staff).

16. J. Haslam, *Soviet Foreign Policy, 1930–33: The Impact of the Depression* (London, 1983), and *The Soviet Union and the Struggle for Collective Security in Europe, 1933–39* (London, 1984).

17. See Haslam, *Soviet Foreign Policy*, pp. 121–22.

18. Engineers Shauer and Rappoport are named as the initiators of the *nepreryvka* proposals (see *Ekonomicheskaia zhizn'*, June 4–6, July 5, 1929).

19. *Promyshlennost': Sbornik statei*, ed. A. P. Rozengolts (Moscow, 1930), p. 25; *Byli industrial'nye: Ocherki i vospominaniia* (Moscow, 1970), pp. 186–87; and see Sheila Fitzpatrick, "Ordzhonikidze's Takeover of Vesenkha: A Case Study in Soviet Bureaucratic Politics," *Soviet Studies* 37, 1985, pp. 158–60.

20. There are many examples of this assessment in the files of American Engineers in Russia held at the Hoover Institution, and many complaints about this attitude of foreign specialists appeared in the Soviet press at the time (see, for example, the report about Iugostal in *Za industrializatsiiu*, January 1, 1930).

21. *Torgovo-promyshlennaia gazeta*, December 15, 1929.

22. *Pravda*, March 9, 1930.

23. *Izvestiia*, May 20, 1930.

24. *XVI s'ezd: Stenograficheskii otchet* (Moscow, 1931), pp. 300–301.

25. I. P. Bardin, *Rozhdenie zavoda: Vospominaniia inzhenera* (Novosibirsk, 1936), p. 7.

26. S. Syrtsov, *K novomu khoziaistvennomu godu* (Moscow, 1930).

27. See, for example, *Pravda*, August 26, 1930; *Za industrializatsiiu*, October 21, 1930; *Bol'shevik*, 1930, nos. 15–16, p. 4.

28. See A. Khavin, *U rulia industrii (dokumental'nye ocherki)* (Moscow, 1968, p. 78.

29. A. Barmine, *Memoirs of a Soviet Diplomat* (London 1938), pp. 234–35; Barmine claimed that Serebrovskii, head of the industry, while publicly defending this plan, knew perfectly well that it could not be achieved. Production did not exceed 150,000 tons until 1940.

30. *Za industrializatsiiu*, January 4, 1931 (S. Lobov).

31. TsGANKh, f. 3429, op. 1, del. 5242, pp. 45–46 (report to sitting of June 28, 1931).

32. *Finansovye problemy*, 1931, nos. 3–4, p. 21. See also V. V. Kuibyshev, *Stat'i i rechi*, vol. v, *1930–1935* (Moscow, 1937), pp. 118, 122–23.

33. *Za industrializatsiiu*, July 3, 1930.

34. S. Abramov in *Za industrializatsiiu*, September 1, 1932. The article was strongly criticized in subsequent discussion—see, for example, P. Zhigalko in *Za industrializatsiiu*, November 3, 1932.

35. *Za industrializatsiiu*, September 1, 1932.

36. I. V. Stalin, *Sochineniia* (Moscow, 1951), vol. xiii, pp. 185–86.

37. *Byli industrial'nye,* pp. 186–88; this chapter, by the journalist A. Peshkin, was apparently based on a talk given by Tochinskii in 1967, on the occasion of the eightieth anniversary of Ordzhonikidze's birth. This incident was first described in English in Kendall E. Bailes, *Technology and Society under Lenin and Stalin* (Princeton, 1978), pp. 272–73.

38. V. I. Kuzmin, *V bor'be za sotsialisticheskuiu rekonstruktsiiu, 1926–1937* (Moscow, 1976), p. 188, citing party archives.

39. *Industrializatsiia SSSR, 1929–1932gg.: Dokumenty i materialy* (Moscow, 1970), p. 606; for the ten-million-ton target, see, for example, A. Gurevich, *Zadachi chernoi metallurgii v 1932 g.* (Moscow, 1932).

40. See Bailes, p. 278.

41. S. Gershberg, *Rabota u nas takaia* (Moscow, 1971), pp. 199–200.

42. Cited in indirect speech by Ordzhonikidze in September 1932 (S. Ordzhonikidze, *Stat'i i rechi* (Moscow, 1957), vol. ii, p. 427.

43. Ibid.

44. Stalin, *Sochineniia,* vol. xiii, pp. 185–86.

45. Gershberg, p. 197.

46. Other influences were certainly also present. In November 1932 Trotsky published his article "The Soviet Economy in Danger," in which he argued that 1933 should be a "buffer year" between five-year plans, in which resources in industry should be concentrated on first-priority investment, on putting factories into order, and on supplying food, clothes, and housing to the workers; inflation should be halted; and capital investment should be boldly reduced (*Biulleten' oppozitsii,* Berlin, 1932, no. 31, pp. 3–13). At the January plenum Trotsky was bitterly criticized, but industrial policy in 1933 to a considerable extent conformed to this approach.

47. Ordzhonikidze, *Stat'i i rechi,* vol. ii, pp. 417–19; this report was published for the first time in 1957.

48. See E. Zaleski, *Stalinist Planning for Economic Growth, 1933–1952* (Chapel Hill, 1980), pp. 129–33; little is known about the adoption of higher growth rates for industry in the course of preparing the Second Five-Year Plan in 1933.

49. *Znamia,* 1988, no. 1, p. 140.

50. *Znamia,* 1988, no. 2, p. 136.

51. *Znamia,* 1988, no. 1, p. 149.

52. Ibid., pp. 144, 149.

53. *Znamia,* 1988, no. 2, pp. 148–49.

54. Ibid., pp. 154–55. After a pause, Stalin said "grain is gold—we must think again," but Vannikov convinced him that no gold would be able to buy them if they were not acquired before war broke out.

55. *Znamia,* 1988, no. 1, pp. 159–60.

56. Ibid., pp. 137–39.

57. An enthusiastic article on Zinoviev, previously universally denigrated both in the West and in the Soviet Union, appeared in 1988: see I. Lisochkin, "Revolutionary, Theoretician and Publicist," *Leningradskaia pravda,* June 21, 1988.

58. A. Iakovlev, *Tsel' zhizni* (Moscow, 1967), pp. 198–200.

59. Emelianov memoirs, in *Novyi mir,* 1967, no. 2, pp. 87–94.

60. Ibid., pp. 103–7.

61. *Znamia,* 1988, no. 1, pp. 131–32.

62. *Nauka i zhizn',* 1987, no. 12, pp. 23–32.

63. Iakovlev, pp. 452–54.

64. His detailed account appears in *Oktiabr',* 1973, nos. 10–12. It is distinguished by the care with which it establishes that the technologically most advanced weapon is not necessarily the best in terms of military need or industrial possibilities. These

reminiscences appeared at a time when criticism of Stalin in the press was muted, and frank references to repression had almost ceased; perhaps we shall soon get a new version.

65. *Znamia*, 1988, no. 1, p. 133.

66. Iakovlev, pp. 447–57.

67. *Znamia*, 1988, no. 1, pp. 143–49.

68. See my article in *Slavic Review* 42, 1984, pp. 201–23.

69. See the article on the background to the eighteenth party conference of February 1941 by O. Khlebniuk in *Kommunist,* 1988, no. 1.

VI

THE SCOPE, AUTHORITY, AND PERSONNEL OF THE NEW INDUSTRIAL COMMISSARIATS IN HISTORICAL CONTEXT

Don K. Rowney

In the history of large organizations things rarely "begin" without precedent. All organizations seem to have their origins, in the sense of a kind of genetic endowment, from predecessors. If we look, for example, at the administrative institutions of postrevolutionary Russia, "the first socialist society,"[1] we find that new organizations which were founded in the 1920s often, apparently, copied organizational structures and objectives from institutions which existed under the tsars.

On January 5, 1932, the Central Committee issued its decree "Ob organizatsii novykh narkomatov promyshlennosti," by which the "new industrial commissariats" were created.[2] These included the People's Commissariat of Heavy Industry (NKTP), the People's Commissariat of Light Industry (NKLP), and the People's Commissariat of the Timber Industry (NKLes).

Many more such agencies were to follow. During the Third Five-Year Plan in particular, a raft of new commissariats specializing in industrial management was created.[3] These commissariats included such narrowly defined organizations as building materials, medium machine building, heavy machine building, shipbuilding, aviation industry, chemical industry, nonferrous metallurgy, and ferrous metallurgy. But it was the first three, the heavy, light, and timber industries, that appear to have been the founding, or model, structures in what would become an enduring industrial administrative and management system of the USSR.

It is thus historically important to ask what was the nature of the "standard" and whence came the standard. Given the centrality of the national economy and its organization to Bolshevik thinking, one might even argue that an evaluation of the industrial management model is a way of charting the progress, extension, and intensity of the Revolution of 1917. This would seem to be particularly the case if the characteristics of span of authority and of personnel are set into a somewhat broader historical context, enabling us to say how and to what extent they represented departures from the past.

The purpose of this short study, then, is to sketch the extent of state control of industry early in the Five-Year Plan era, to outline the nature of that control—largely by dwelling on who was in charge—and to evaluate these characteristics within a broader context of Russian administrative history.

The reader will quickly perceive that "broader context" here does not mean anecdotal or descriptive material; instead, it means comparable events occurring at different times (and, possibly, places) systematically compared. This study, then, will do its best to establish an appropriate range within which the administrative changes of the late 1920s and early 1930s can be understood within the limits inherent in this schematic format. In certain respects, we propose to retrace a portion of the analytic steps taken by V. Z. Drobizhev some twenty years ago. It is hoped that the reprise will be worthy of the reader's interest, since this study sets the relevant data into a somewhat different context than that used by Drobizhev.[4]

Crossing the Revolutionary Divide

Thought of in terms of its origins, the process of postrevolutionary administrative formation in Russia took one of perhaps four different forms. First, and quite possibly most important, comparatively informal and spontaneously emergent organizations acquired formal, institutional status. Certainly the soviets fell into this category.[5] One might argue, moreover, that in its early days, Rabkrin was the product of an effort to institutionalize numerous emergent worker and peasant control organizations.

Second, and at the opposite extreme, there were cases of comparatively direct transfer of institutions from within the prerevolutionary state apparatus to the postrevolutionary. These were cases of more or less direct transrevolutionary copying. The ministries or commissariats of foreign affairs, finances, ways of communication, and posts-telegraphs provide illustrations of such copying. Sometimes in these cases while offices were copied extensively, personnel were changed; in other instances even the personnel managed to cross over the revolutionary divide.[6]

Third, the revolutionary transformation of institutions sometimes occurred through subdivision. This was the case with the numerous functions of the Ministry of Internal Affairs. This organization was subdivided, beginning early in 1917, into police, health, welfare, statistical, and territorial administrative units which were both more technically specialized and more thoroughly professionalized.[7]

Fourth, the process of revolutionary transformation sometimes involved consolidation. The new commissariats of health and education, for example, derived substantial portions of their institutional structure by gathering agencies from several different prerevolutionary ministries.[8] The reader will, of course, recognize that the third and fourth types of transformation were not mutually exclusive. Indeed, consolidation of functions into one agency might well depend on subdivision of others. The commissariats of education and health, and the Supreme Council of the National Economy (VSNKh) itself, were products of this combined process of subdivision of large, generalist tsarist ministries and consolidation of like functions under one administrative authority.

Background to the Emergence of NKTP, NKLP, and NKLes

Industrial management in the new, postrevolutionary government, as represented by VSNKh, was the product of a special—in some ways unique—process of subdivision of old administrative functions and their consolidation into a new organization. This quasi-commissarial organization took over some operations of the tsarist ministries of trade and industry, finances, and transport, but the resulting administrative structure was different from the specialist commissariats (such as health, education, VChKa, and internal affairs) which were created in the early postrevolutionary era. First, VSNKh was multifunctional, since it was responsible for management of many different commercial and manufacturing branches of the economy. Also, it subsumed the operations of nongovernmental or semi-governmental organizations which had previously managed some manufacturing and commercial operations. Such organizations had also controlled the allocation of some capital, markets, and, to a degree, labor itself. As Alec Nove writes,

> the various glavki [chief administrative subdivisions of VSNKh] (Tsentrotextil' Glavspichki, and the rest) corresponded closely with the analogous syndicates set up by private business before the war, and used for purposes of control by previous governments during the war. The offices and much of their staff were the same.[9]

In the case of industrial management as well as of other institutions, we are not witnessing here a mere transfer of offices and operations; there was also a transrevolutionary survival of political and organizational objectives. Government control of manufacturing and commercial activities and of labor and capital allocation was evident in both pre- and postrevolutionary

Russia. In my view this tradition may have been more important to the emergent structure of industrial management in the USSR than we generally assume it was.

The tendency toward direct government involvement in industrial operations in Russia was very old. As large-scale manufacturing enterprises developed in the later nineteenth century, then, it comes as no surprise that in spite of their size and private ownership, these organizations were influenced, nurtured, and even controlled by the state. As Rieber, Von Laue, Rimlinger, and McKay have shown, the imperial ministries of ways of communication, finances, and even internal affairs influenced industrial development for various purposes in the second half of the nineteenth century.[10]

The Ministry of Trade and Industry, whose legal brief was grounded on an apparent need for coordination by the state, was a twentieth-century foundation, but its origins in principle went well back into the previous century.[11] The creation of trade or marketing syndicates in the 1880s and 1890s carried with it more than a hint of government involvement in industrial coordination and even control, although these institutions were ostensibly private. Early examples of syndicates included the nail and wire manufacturers' syndicate (1886), the sugar industry syndicate (1887), and the petroleum syndicate (1892). As Liashchenko suggests, it was common for these organizations to emerge and flourish with support from and through the cooperation of the state.[12]

One concrete measure of the relative increase of government interest in manufacturing and commerce is the tendency over time for direct state expenditures on economic enterprises to increase or decrease relative to other expenditures. According to data I have taken from Gregory (see table 6.1), between 1885 and 1913 aggregate government expenditures on state enterprises, including state railways but excluding defense, increased more than twentyfold. Expenditures for state railways alone expanded by less than threefold in the same period, suggesting that a substantial share of the increase was accounted for by other state interests in commerce and manufacturing. For additional comparison we may note that although there were many ups and downs throughout the period, expenditures for education and health increased almost sevenfold, from 23 million to 154 million rubles; outlays for administration increased a little less than threefold, from 194 million to 583 million rubles; and those for defense increased almost fourfold, from 240 million to 970 million rubles.

A more direct way of comparatively evaluating the enlarging interest of the state in enterprise is to look at the changing proportion of such expenditures in the annual total of major expenditure categories for the 1885–1913 period.[13] As table 6.2 shows, expenditures on government enterprises rose from 3.7 percent of the total in 1885 to a high of 27.6 percent just before the Russo-Japanese War. Although they declined as a proportion of major expense items after the Russo-Japanese War, ex-

Table 6.1. Tsarist Government Expenditures on State Enterprises Compared with Other Items, Budget Years 1885–1913 (In Millions of Current Rubles)

Category	1885	1894	1903	1913
State enterprises	49	150	818	1,064
Defense	240	331	436	970
Education and health	23	30	52	154
Total of major items*	1,323	1,995	2,961	5,090

Source: Gregory, *Russian National Income,* table F.1, p. 252.
*Totals in the original appear to be incorrect.

penditures on government enterprises still consumed one-fifth of the total by 1913.

It is interesting and, I suggest, enlightening to compare the data in table 6.2 with those presented by Carr and Davies for "net expenditure of state budget" in 1925–26.[14] The budget categories used by Gregory and by Carr and Davies are not identical, and comparison is in any case somewhat risky

Table 6.2. Percentage of Tsarist Government Expenditures on State Enterprises Compared with other Major Catgeories, 1885–1913

Category	1885	1891	1896	1903	1907	1913
Administration	14.7	15.9	12.6	13.2	12.4	11.5
Education and health	1.7	1.7	1.3	1.8	1.6	3.0
Defense	18.1	19.1	14.9	14.7	16.3	19.1
Final consumption	34.5	36.7	28.8	29.7	29.9	33.5
Interest and principal	23.4	16.6	24.4	9.7	12.6	8.3
Government enterprises	3.7	6.5	15.5	27.6	23.1	20.9
Subsidies	3.8	3.6	2.5	3.3	4.1	3.7
Total (in millions of rubles)	1,323	1,552	2,334	2,961	3,574	5,090

Source: Calculated from Gregory, *Russian National Income,* table F. 1, p. 252.

because even like budgetary items may well have been put to quite different uses. Nevertheless, we can derive some perspective on the degree of state intervention in national economic affairs by recognizing that of the 2.6 billion rubles accounted for in 1925–26, some 700 million, or 26 percent, were devoted to the "national economy." Of the additional categories presented by Carr and Davies, "social and cultural measures" consumed 11 percent, "defence" 24 percent, "administration" 10 percent, "transfers to local budgets" 25 percent, and "other expenditures" 3.8 percent. Expenditures for debt service were excluded. To my mind this argues that, from a budgetary point of view in the early twentieth century, the tsarist government was approximately as involved with commerce and manufacturing as the socialist New Economic Policy state in the mid-1920s. Even in 1926–27 the national economy category accounted for as little as 1.2 billion rubles out of a total of 4 billion (33 percent). Worker control and War Communism may have seemed to be the dawn of a revolutionary era in the Russian national economy, but if the NEP era seemed "revolutionary" it is hard to believe that this was principally because of state intervention in the economy. We should probably note, moreover, that whether one thinks of the state presence in either the pre- or the postrevolutionary economy as "large" is likely to be a function of one's tolerance for the state as an operative in the national economy. Our point, rather, is that in this respect there was little difference between pre- and postrevolutionary state economic administrations. Undoubtedly, the radical or revolutionary quality of the post-1917 apparatus had more to do with the political rhetoric and the established political objectives of the day than with concrete achievements, such as budget allocations and their management.

In particular the remarkably bold ambition to assert comprehensive control over the economy—whether through a central plan or by some other means—marks these objectives as unique. Even here, however, we should note that during the Russo-Japanese War and especially World War I, coordination of various phases of manufacturing, trade, capital, and labor supply by the state expanded, as did the tendency for direct state intervention in industrial management and labor control. This was an extension of state authority that Liashchenko calls the "militarization of industry."[15] And even if these programs were not especially successful in the sense that they provided the necessary material supplies to Russia's armed forces, they nonetheless served as a base of experience for such civil servants as economists, statisticians, accountants, lawyers, and bankers as well as for managers and engineers themselves in centralized control of the economy. It must be recognized, nevertheless, that this is not the same thing as the creation of a comprehensive centralized plan or as the establishment of mechanisms for enforcing worker control. These programs appear to have been unique to the Bolshevik era.

At the conclusion of his study of the emergent technological elite in the Stalin era, Kendall E. Bailes offers data on the careers of the early Soviet managerial-technical elite. Within this sample, which Bailes describes as "an elite within an elite," he distinguishes two roughly contemporary groups. One group had successful but predominantly political and administrative careers; the other had predominantly scientific and technical careers, also successful. Bailes finds numerous differences between the two groups: the politicians were younger, less educated, more likely to have been party members, and overwhelmingly more likely to have been products of worker or peasant families than their technologist peers.

For our purposes here, it is significant that the politicians in Bailes's sample were far more likely than the technologists to have been educated after the Revolution of 1917 than before. Although the careers of representatives of each group were singled out for recognition at approximately the same time by Soviet authorities, more than 40 percent of the technologist group were educated significantly earlier than the politicians. That is, the technologists earned their diplomas before 1917, before the era of Bolshevism, and carried with them into the revolutionary era whatever ideas and experiences about industrial organization and management they had learned under the tsars.[16] In spite of manifest class differences—and, by implication, political differences—we can think of all these people as both prototypes and candidates for the roles of state economic managers of the 1920s.

Thus if we simply look at the antecedents to VSNKh, it is clear that the range of Bolshevik and other postrevolutionary concepts of nationalization and state control of manufacturing, commerce, capital, and labor supply was not particularly revolutionary in itself. Whether we focus on the relatively intense period of nationalized and centralized economic management, War Communism, or on the era of mixed state-private management, NEP, many of the concepts and forms of control had their antecedents in the tsarist era.

VSNKh itself, as an administrative structure, and especially considered in conjunction with mechanisms for worker and party control, did represent a radical new step in the effort to consolidate industrial management. But in this respect VSNKh was not unique in post-1917 administration. Several other commissariats emerged as products of this pattern at approximately the same time. One concludes that what was extraordinary, or potentially revolutionary, were the degrees of control, the way in which control was to be achieved, and, of course, who was in control. As Bailes observes, in 1917 and 1918 "workers' control, in particular, seems to have been anathema to most, if not all, technologists,"[17] and we are thus justified in thinking of this element as the focus of revolution in industrial management.

In the central section of this study we shall focus our attention on measures of these characteristics of control, with respect first to VSNKh and then to the three industrial management commissariats which succeeded VSNKh in 1932, the commissariats of heavy, light, and timber industries.

We shall address the question of who was in control by looking at the degree to which the senior administration of state industrial management agencies had fallen into "alien" hands, i.e., the hands of members of the working class and of women. We thus examine the available data for evidence of working-class background and the presence of women among senior administrators. Both of these should provide some indication of the degree of displacement of traditional managerial elites, who were overwhelmingly middle or upper class and male.[18] We shall also address the question of intensity and effectiveness of control. We look at two measures of control among personnel. First, in principle, did they know what they were doing? In order to answer yes we have to show at a minimum that they possessed some formal education, and so we focus on the education variable. Second, were they sufficiently pliant? That is, were their values those of the revolutionary political leadership, or were they those of the preceding generation or of some competing revolutionary group? For this purpose, we focus on the extent to which administrators were party members. Finally, for evidence of changing spans of authority, we can look at the kind and number of institutions which were subordinated to the management commissariats.

Personnel and Structure

The question of who controlled was settled in principle with the Bolshevik accession to power—it was to be the working class. But in fact, the problem of the social origins of industrial managers continued to be of such great interest to survey researchers and politicians that even if we did not have a huge body of recorded public debates on the issue during the 1920s, we would be justified in assuming that the Bolsheviks did not regard the question of control as settled.

Tables 6.3 and 6.4 show the varying presence of senior administrators who, in effect by birth, were departures from the Russian administrative tradition: workers "by social condition" and women. Of the three sample years, 1921 is the most problematic from the viewpoint of interpretation. Not only is the size of the surveyed group small but also the editors of the survey and the substance of the survey itself offer several indications that it is fragmentary.[19] Still, it is useful to compare the "early" VSNKh with its later form and with its successor agencies.

What is interesting about the data in table 6.3 is the comparatively limited presence—never greater than 19.4 percent—of individuals from working-class backgrounds (and probably from lower-class backgrounds, although we do not consider here the problem of peasant entrance into these administrative ranks) through the early period of Soviet industrial management. The reader should keep in mind that these are senior administrative positions requiring, no doubt, some technical expertise but,

Table 6.3. Class Background of Senior Administrators, Central Apparatus of the USSR Supreme Council of the National Economy (VSNKh) and Successor Agencies, 1921–33

Background	Percentage				
	VSNKh 1921 (n = c.150)	VSNKh 1929 (n = 1,442)	NKTP 1933 (n = 573)	NKLP 1933 (n = 419)	NKLes 1933 (n = 155)
Worker	19.4	9.4	6.3	11.9	13.5
Other	80.6	90.6	93.7	88.1	86.5

Sources: For 1921, VSNKh, *Struktura i sostav*, p. 29. For 1929, Ia. Bineman and S. Kheinman, *Kadry*, table II. For 1933, "Tsentral'noe upravlenie narodnokhoziaistvennogo ucheta GOSPLANa SSSR," *Sostav rukovodiashchikh rabotnikov i spetsialistov soiuza SSR* (Moscow: Soiuzorguchet, 1936), NKTP table 20, p. 38; NKLP table 24, p. 42; NKLes table 28, p. 46.

perhaps more important, the managerial skills which are rarely learned in school and could well be acquired in the army, in party work, or in work with soviets, cooperatives, and similar organizations. My point is that even if workers' lack of technical education should have been a hindrance, we need not necessarily assume that they couldn't *manage* at middle and high levels of control. Nevertheless, their numbers are limited.

One way of deciding whether this proportion of workers is "a lot" is to compare it with the proportion present in other state administrations in the USSR at the same time. The major survey of Bineman and Kheinman of the 1929 civil service and cooperative administrations in the USSR and the data which we have already used for 1933 allow us to do this. If, for example, we take a relatively nonpolitical, "benign" organization such as the Commissariat of Posts and Telegraphs, later renamed the Commissariat of Communications (NKSv), do we find a substantially greater or smaller proportion of senior administrators of working-class background? In fact, the figures are very similar. In 1929, according to the Bineman-Kheinman survey, this commissariat had ninety-eight officials of working-class background out of a total of 1,091, that is, 9 percent.[20] In 1933 the figure had increased to about 14 percent, an estimated 690 individuals out of 4,795.[21] Again we are tempted to conclude that this is not a very revolutionary working-class toehold in the Soviet bureaucracy.

On the other hand, if we were to compare these data with class background data for senior state officials in other European countries, I am reasonably confident that we would conclude that these data are at least "acceptably" revolutionary. Ezra N. Suleiman presents data drawn from a later generation for similar categories of French administrators. In six sample years between 1953 and 1969—well after the French national administrative reforms of 1945—only thirty-seven (8.9 percent) of 415 candidates from industrial employees and workers social categories succeeded in gaining entrance to the École Nationale d'Administration, for example.[22] Suleiman comments:

> The reform of 1945 has notably failed in what was considered at the Liberation its most important single feature: democratization of the higher civil service. [The data show] the extent to which higher civil servants are recruited from the upper-middle classes.[23]

Table 6.4, which focuses on the gender of senior officials, offers us the same ambivalent picture as table 6.3. On one hand, the data are in no sense a picture of revolutionary society if we merely compare them with the gross presence of women in the population. Even the VSNKh of 1929, with a senior cohort of women amounting to nearly 40 percent, could still be faulted as laggardly—particularly if we were to look precisely at individual positions. Throughout the 1920s, the urban directory which lists the names of heads and deputy heads of major administrations in the government, *Vsia Moskva*, gives proportions of women which are lower than those given by the 1929 survey.[24] To me this suggests not that the survey is in error—gender is a much harder variable to distort than, say, class—but that women, while holding positions in the senior administration, did not hold top positions in proportion to their numbers.

An even harsher conclusion would apply to the Commissariat of Posts and Telegraphs in 1929, judging from the data presented by Bineman and Kheinman. These data show a commissariat which, in its senior administration, employed only 175 women (16 percent) out of a total of 1,091 senior officials.[25]

On the other hand, if we look at other industrial societies in the same period, it is clear that the transfer of administrative authority to nontraditional elites in the USSR had gone forward comparatively quickly. While VSNKh counted 39 percent of its senior administrators as female in 1929, the entire United States white-collar work force was only 33 percent female.[26]

Table 6.4. Gender of Senior Administrators, Central Apparatus of The USSR Supreme Council of the National Economy (VSNKh) and Successor Agencies, 1921–33

Gender	Percentage				
	VSNKh 1921 (n = n.a.)	VSNKh 1929 (n = 1,442)	NKTP 1933 (n = 573)	NKLP 1933 (n = 419)	NKLes 1933 (n = 155)
Women	n.a.	39.4	16.4	18.6	11.0
Men	n.a.	60.6	83.6	81.4	89.0

Sources: See table 6.3.

Far more important, it is clear from the data that those women who were in the U.S. work force tended to be excluded from managerial (i.e., "managers, officials, and proprietors") status. In 1930 the proportion of American women in this category was 11 percent—much lower than that in VSNKh in 1929, lower even than the figure for Posts and Telegraphs, and significantly lower than the proportions for two of the three industrial management commissariats in 1933. I will leave the reader to speculate about why the administration of lumberjacks might have been an unwelcome role even for the new Soviet woman in 1933.

In my view Soviet industial management *was* socially revolutionary, provided we understand that "revolution" in this context requires modest interpretation. These senior administrations were far more hospitable to products of the working class than imperial senior administrations were, and they were far more feminized than any pre-1917 higher civil service. Moreover, by comparison with other industrial or European societies, one may easily argue that industrial administration in the USSR was relatively proletarianized and feminized throughout the early postrevolutionary era.

The Structure of VSNKh and Its Successors: Authority and Control

The degree of state administrative control over industry varied as a matter of policy between 1917 and 1932. This history has been written by several Soviet historians and, in English, by Carr, Carr and Davies, and Bailes.[27] We shall summarize it here very briefly simply to introduce terms and chronology.

Between the moment of the Bolshevik seizure of power and early spring 1921, War Communism gave VSNKh and its subordinate chief administrations, the *glavki*, enormous authority. But as had happened so many times during the tsarist era, authority did not translate into all of the objectives for which it had been granted. In particular, it did not translate into the power necessary for a successful economic restoration; partly in consequence, the extraordinary writ with which VSNKh had begun its existence in 1918 was revised and weakened in 1921 and 1922.

This moment of reorganization of VSNKh coincides with the introduction of the mixed economy which we know as NEP. The span or scope of VSNKh's authority was drastically reduced in the sense that significant portions of economic activity were returned to private hands and also in the sense that VSNKh's control over enterprises which remained subordinate to it was reduced. That is, the authority of VSNKh's subordinate chief administrations, the glavki, was sharply reduced. Within that segment of the economy that continued to operate directly under state control, competing authorities, such as manufacturing trusts and commercial syndicates, were created or were given enhanced responsibilities. The result was that these organizations as well as the more powerful enterprises themselves competed with VSNKh for managerial control.[28]

With the introduction of the First Five-Year Plan in 1928, much of its earlier authority was restored to VSNKh.[29] New and comprehensive grants of *authority* were clearly not the same thing as the *power* to control events throughout the economy either in general or in detail; it is evident, nevertheless, that the ambition to amass such power at the center was now becoming dominant. Planning, which was the responsibility of the State Planning Commission, or Gosplan, became far more prescriptive than previously—meaning that Gosplan in a sense exercised strategic managerial authority. Detailed industrial management, VSNKh's brief, was relatively centralized once more. Control over the application of new capital to the development of individual facilities now came under VSNKh's control. As Carr and Davies note,

> The most obvious respect in which the glavki [of the late 1920s] quickly acquired greater powers than their predecessors was in the control of capital construction. Measures to enforce control were adopted as early as the summer of 1926. They established the principle that the Vesenkha of the USSR should approve individually all capital construction projects in industry for which the estimated cost exceeded a fixed ceiling. . . .[30]

With the creation of more narrowly structured industrial management commissariats in 1932, administrative structure went through another, characteristically Soviet, stage of subdivision and consolidation. The trunk-and-branch commissarial system of industrial management of the early 1930s, though it seems "rational" in the sense of creating functionally homogeneous agencies, in fact paralleled the specialist commissariats which had been created in the social services and domestic control areas fifteen years before, e.g., education, health, VChKa, internal affairs, and even the independent statistical administration. These had been carved out of the functions of larger conglomerate tsarist ministries shortly after the Revolution.

The issue of relative organizational size is as interesting and important as that of specialization. Sergo Ordzhonikidze, the last director of VSNKh and the first commissar of heavy industry, was compelled to accept control over an organization that was a fraction of the size of VSNKh. Although it is customary to think and speak of these new organizations as a retreat from "gigantomania,"[31] it is probably more accurate to think of them simply as specialized administrations. By any standards, they were bureaucracies of vast proportions. Moreover, as T. P. Korzhikhina has shown, after reorganization the size and power of the commissariats were considerably enhanced. According to Korzhikhina, the seventeen glavki allocated to the original Commissariat of Heavy Industry in 1932 had expanded to a total of twenty-nine by 1934.[32] (The original number would double by 1935.)

In 1935 the Commissariat of Heavy Industry published a directory to its far-flung and ramshackle structure.[33] The directory identifies some seventeen trusts or syndicates—large combinations of enterprises—which were immediately responsible to NKTP. In addition to these there were some thirty-four glavki which oversaw, directly and literally, hundreds of enterprises or groups of enterprises throughout the USSR. Moreover, there were a half-a-dozen major "functional" and staff organizations, responsible for transport, bookeeping, labor, and the like.

Was this an exceptionally large organization by then-applicable international standards of organization? There were of course no government agencies of comparable size and responsibility in major Western countries in the 1930s. This is certainly one of the facts that made the Communist claim to revolutionary distinction valid. In the United States, at any rate, the operational equivalent would have been giant semi-trusts such as the Ford Motor Company in the declining years of Henry Ford's career, General Motors, and the Metropolitan Life Insurance Company in its precomputer, labor-intensive days.

Detailed comparisons with Western industrial management organizations would help us in our effort to achieve perspective on the Soviet organizations, but they would also take us too far afield in the present study. It is, however, worthwhile to recall John Kenneth Galbraith's evaluation of the reasons behind the American industrial equivalent of the huge Soviet commissariats in the era from the 1930s to the late 1960s. After noting that General Motors, in terms of physical structure and income, was of a scale to be worthy of comparison with the U.S. federal government, Galbraith wrote:

> Economists have anciently quarreled over the reasons for the great size of the modern corporation. Is it because size is essential in order to reap the economies of modern large scale production? Is it, more insidiously, because the big firm wishes to exercise monopoly power in its markets? The present analysis allows both parties to the dispute to be partly right. . . . General Motors is not only large enough to afford the best size of automobile plant but is large enough to afford a dozen or more of the best size; . . . it is large enough to produce things as diverse as aircraft engines and refrigerators; . . . it is large enough to have the market power associated with monopoly. . . . The size of General Motors is in the service not of monopoly or the economies of scale but of planning. And for this planning—control of supply, control of demand, provision of capital, minimization of risk—there is no clear upper limit to the desirable size. It could be that the bigger the better. The corporate form accommodates to this need. Quite clearly it allows the firm to be very, very large.[34]

Power to Control: Education and Party
Affiliation, 1921–33

Apart from size, another way of addressing the question of power and control is to inquire whether the senior staff was sufficiently well educated and politically pliant to carry out objectives upon which they decided as a group or which were handed down from above. While they are not, by any means, all that we might wish, the major surveys of the 1920s and early 1930s do address this issue partially. From table 6.5 we can derive a sense of the availability and distribution of individuals who possessed formal educational credentials in the early days of both VSNKh and the industrial management commissariats.

Interesting, of course, is the fact that the VSNKh of 1929 had lost a high proportion of its best-educated senior administrators but that NKTP appears to have regained them—or replacements for them—by 1933. The data give us no basis for a satisfactory, sound explanation for this phenomenon. It may be related to the administrative purge which, by the time of the Bineman and Kheinman survey, was well under way. But this would still not explain the influx of senior administrators possessing higher education diplomas by 1933—unless higher education had been redefined in the interval to include educational experiences which would previously not have met established standards or unless the new industrial commissariats were granted privileges denied to the now-abolished VSNKh.

Fitzpatrick suggests that both these explanations are valid. She notes with respect to Soviet education that precisely at the time under consideration here, i.e., during the First Five-Year Plan,

Table 6.5. Education of Senior Administrators, Central Apparatus of the USSR Supreme Council of the National Economy (VSNKh) and Successor Agencies, 1921–33

Educational Status	Percentage				
	VSNKh 1921 (n = 1,862)	VSNKh 1929 (n = 1,442)	NKTP 1933 (n = 573)	NKLP 1933 (n = 419)	NKLes 1933 (n = 155)
Higher	54.3	22.1	54.6	32.0	46.5
Middle	34.0	47.8	11.2	5.5	8.4
Praktiki	11.7	30.1	34.2	62.5	45.2

Sources: For 1921, *Struktura i sostav*, p. 29. For 1929, Bineman and Kheinman, *Kadry*, table II. For 1933, *Sostav rukovodiashchikh rabotnikov*, NKTP table 20, p. 38, NKLP table 24, p. 42, NKLes table 28, p. 46.

colleges and technical schools were required to admit as students large numbers of young workers from the factories and Communists from low-level administrative jobs (most of them without completed secondary education) and turn them in the shortest possible time into engineers, economists, argonomists [sic], and so on.[35]

Elsewhere Fitzpatrick notes that owing to his aggressiveness and skill as a bureaucratic infighter, Ordzhonikidze, the commissar of heavy industry, was often able to reward what he considered to be desirable behavior of individuals regardless of their class background or party status.[36] William Chase and J. Arch Getty came to a similar but more detailed conclusion based on data drawn from the Soviet Data Bank.

When Ordzhonikidze assumed the positions of people's commissar of Rabkrin and chairman of the TSKK, it appears that he brought no one with him from the Transcaucasian party committee, his former post. But in 1930, when he became chairman of VSNKh, he took nineteen members of the Rabkrin and TSKK staffs with him. Thirteen had worked only in Rabkrin, five had worked in both Rabkrin and the TSKK, and one had worked only in the TSKK.

Following detailed evaluation of individual appointments made by Ordzhonikidze, Chase and Getty conclude:

> When VSNKh was dismantled and Ordzhonikidze became the People's Commissar of NKTP, we know that he took to NKTP ten of the nineteen people who comprised his earlier "family circle." Once again, those trusted comrades with proven executive ability assumed power positions within NKTP.[37]

In any case, still focusing on the question of apparent managerial quality, we can make a direct comparison between the VSNKh-NKTP data and those for the Commissariat of Posts and Telegraphs in the years 1924, 1927, 1929, and 1933. The finding is relatively flattering by Soviet standards to the capacity of industrial management to attract well-educated administrators. The highest proportion of senior administrators with advanced education in Posts-Telegraphs is found in 1927 (19.5 percent of a cohort of 482). For 1924 the figure is only 10 percent, while in 1929 and 1933 it was merely 3.6 percent and 3.8 percent.[38] In more junior positions of Posts-Telegraphs and in provincial administrations, the proportions were correspondingly lower.[39]

So far as party membership was concerned, the data seem more directly or intuitively understandable (see table 6.6). The admittedly faulty survey of 1921 shows the highest proportion of Communists for the entire period. But it should be noted that this figure does not correspond closely with that given by Drobizhev for the VSNKh of 1918 (21.6 percent) or 1922 (5.3 percent).[40] On the other hand, the 1929 and 1933 cohorts of VSNKh and the industrial commissariats are roughly comparable to one another.

Table 6.6. Communist Party Membership among Senior Administrators, Central Apparatus of the USSR Supreme Council of the National Economy (VSNKh) and Successor Agencies, 1921–33

Membership	Percentage				
	VSNKh 1921 (n = n.a.)	VSNKh 1929 (n = 1,442)	NKTP 1933 (n = 573)	NKLP 1933 (n = 419)	NKLes 1933 (n = 155)
Communist	50.0	26.4	26.2	34.8	37.4
VLKSM	n.a.	5.5	0.7	1.7	0
Other	50.0	68.0	73.1	63.5	62.6

Source: See table 6.5

Tables 6.7, 6.8, and 6.9 compare different segments of the 1933 industrial commissariats across the four variables of education, party, gender, and class. Although this method of presentation involves repeating the data for the three commissariats at the most senior (Moscow) administrative level, perhaps the reader will agree that the exercise is worthwhile because of the resulting direct juxtaposition of specific characteristics of personnel throughout the entire administrative apparatus.

Briefly, it may be noted that at every level of organization in 1933 three specific characteristics of personnel are evident. First, the presence of persons with working-class background who were women, even Communists—the "alien" hands, in short—is limited. Nowhere are such people in the majority; nowhere are they close to a majority. Revolutions, whether from above or below, are hard to make.[41]

Second, there is a direct relationship between class and education which was evident in the 1920s but which has, at least up to 1933, survived the crash education programs described by Fitzpatrick and others.[42] Not only do we see that well-educated workers and women are scarce at the most elite levels of these organizations, they are rare throughout.[43]

Third, the data show a pattern of difference between NKTP—the heir par excellence of VSNKh, Ordzhonikidze's commissariat—and NKLP and NKLes. To put matters bluntly, NKTP was comparatively more conservatively staffed than the other two. Its staff was better educated, it is true, but going along with that is the fact that at every level it was less communized and less proletarianized.[44] The NKTP staff would probably also show consistently less feminization but for the fact that NKLes was engaged in what was probably an intensely male occupation.[45] A comparative evaluation, in other words, argues that heavy industry, while not exempt from proletarianization and communization, was for some reason

**Table 6.7. Characteristics of Industrial Commissariat
Personnel, All-Union (Moscow), 1933**

	Percentage		
Characteristic	NKTP (n = 573)	NKLP (n = 419)	NKLes (n = 155)
Education			
Higher	54.6	32.0	46.5
Middle	11.2	5.5	8.4
Praktiki	34.2	62.5	45.2
Party			
Communist	26.2	34.8	37.4
VLKSM	0.7	1.7	0.0
Nonparty	73.1	63.5	62.6
Gender			
Women	16.4	18.6	11.0
Men	83.6	81.4	89.0
Class			
Worker	6.3	11.9	13.5
Nonworker	93.7	88.1	86.5

Source: *Sostav rukovodiashchikh rabotnikov i spetsialistov soiuza SSR* (Moscow 1936); NKTP table 20, p. 38, NKLP table 24, p. 42, NKLes table 28, p. 46.

allowed more flexibility than the other organizations. Undoubtedly this fact was related to the high priority which was assigned to NKTP as the engine to drive the economy forward.

But perhaps it was related to another, political factor. Fitzpatrick has observed that Ordzhonikidze, when he assumed control of VSNKh, immediately proceeded to "implement the new conciliatory policy in industry by bringing back experts who had been in disgrace and appointing them to responsible posts; and his activity in this regard is gratefully remembered in the memoirs of Soviet industrialists."[46] Fitzpatrick goes on:

> When he later came to head the country's most powerful economic bureaucracy, Ordzhonikidze found himself on the other side of the fence, and therefore adopted a completely different attitude to vigilante intrusions by party, security and control agencies than the one he had shown at Rabkrin/ TsKK. As head of the Commissariat of Heavy Industry in the 1930s Ordzhonikidze became a staunch defender of the industrial bureaucracy's turf and prerogatives. He was known for his strong negative reactions to pressures from "outsiders" like regional party secretaries. . . . Secret police intrusion was similarly unwelcome.[47]

Table 6.8. Characteristics of Commissarial Senior
Administrators to Oblast Level, 1933

	Percentage		
Characteristic	NKTP (n = 1,988)	NKLP (n = 1,701)	NKLes (n = 405)
Education			
Higher	50.6	38.2	44.7
Middle	13.2	15.0	9.6
Praktiki	36.3	46.7	45.7
Party			
Communist	25.0	28.2	33.1
VLKSM	2.3	2.4	3.0
Nonparty	72.7	69.5	64.0
Gender			
Women	12.9	15.3	9.1
Men	87.1	84.7	90.9
Class			
Worker	9.3	15.3	13.6
Nonworker	90.7	84.7	86.4

Source: See table 6.7

Similarly, Chase and Getty cite Victor Kravchenko's memoir and write that "his colleagues and subordinates noted Sergo Ordzhonikidze's new management style: conciliatory dealings with factory managers and frequent personal visits to shop floors were the marks of his leadership."[48]

How can we characterize, in summary, the "revolutionary" quality of industrial control in post-1917 Russia? First, we can note that the concept of state control or management was not new and that during the NEP era at any rate, the degree of direct state control of commerce and manufacturing—as measured by budgetary outlays, at least—was approximately comparable to that of the last prerevolutionary years.

The political commitment to form a unified, central administrative apparatus for industrial control, however, was new, as was the vaulting ambition of those politicians and economists who wanted to submit the entire matrix of economic activity to a unified plan. VSNKh, the bureaucratic product of the commitment to unified control, gathered together the prerevolutionary loose ends of manufacturing and commercial control from both governmental and quasi-governmental sources. It may well be that VSNKh was initially seen as of a piece with the specialist commissariats which began

Table 6.9. Characteristics of Entire Apparatus Personnel,
Including Glavki and Trusts but Excluding Enterprises and
Educational Institutions, 1933

	Percentage		
Characteristic	NKTP (n = 23,909)	NKLP (n = 7,165)	NKLes (n = 4,236)
Education			
Higher	43.6	33.9	30.2
Middle	16.3	17.8	24.5
Praktiki	40.1	48.3	45.2
Party			
Communist	20.1	24.0	23.5
VLKSM	2.1	1.9	2.4
Nonparty	77.8	74.1	74.2
Gender			
Women	9.4	13.2	7.7
Men	90.6	86.8	92.3
Class			
Worker	12.9	16.7	12.0
Nonworker	87.1	83.3	88.0

Source: See table 6.7

to emerge after 1917 in the social services and social control areas of government operation. Just as the new health commissariat, run by physicians, monopolized health care and the new education commissariat, run by educators and intellectuals, attempted to monopolize education, so VSNKh may have been genuinely conceived as industrial management in the hands of economic and technical specialists. It was Lenin, after all, who wrote of the "very happy era, when people will speak of politics more rarely and at less length, and when engineers and agronomists will do most of the talking."[49] In the event, however, VSNKh was so large, its operations so broad (and, one might add, so political), that the organizational shell which evolved had more in common with the multiple-function ministries of the late tsarist era (such as internal affairs) than with the specialist commissariats of the postrevolutionary period.

   In the final stage of its structural transformation, beginning in 1932, state industrial control became more and more specialized, with increasing numbers of commissariats focusing on ever narrower sectors of manufacturing and trade. Industrial control thus began to take on more of the characteristics common to the specialist social service and social control commissariats, although whether this meant that the new industrial administrations were typically dominated by individuals with specialist training in the early days seems unlikely. In any event, the structural "model" for branch industrial administration was not new in the USSR in 1932. It was a bureaucratic structure which had already been in use for more than a decade.

It remains, then, that the most radical departure from the past which state industrial control represented was with respect to who was in control. As we have seen, the data which document how much administrative control had fallen into alien (by tsarist standards) hands are not, in themselves, startling. Not only are the proportions of workers and women in senior administration modest, but even party membership was not overwhelming or universal. It is understandable that these data gave political leadership chronic cause for concern and complaint throughout the NEP and early plan era. Still, if we look at these data in historical perspective, as measured by the standards of the past—or even as measured by the standards of other contemporary, more industrialized countries—the achievement of the first generation of Soviet power is impressive. No matter what may have happened in the later plan era, between 1917 and 1933 the USSR was a genuine land of opportunity for many who, before the Revolution, could have seen little on their life horizons, whatever the scale of their ambition.

NOTES

1. Geoffrey Hosking, *The First Socialist Society: A History of the Soviet Union from Within* (Cambridge, 1985).

2. *Resheniia partii i pravitel'stva po khoziaistvennym voprosam 1917–1967*, vol. 2 (Moscow, 1967), p. 370.

3. Most were created in 1939, either as a result of subdivision of existing organizations or "de novo." Cf. T. P. Korzhikhina, *Istoriia gosudarstvennykh uchrezhdenii SSSR* (Moscow, 1986), pp. 189–230.

4. V. Z. Drobizhev, *Glavnyi shtab sotsialisticheskoi promyshlennosti* (Moscow, 1966).

5. Oskar Anweiler, *The Soviets: The Russian Workers, Peasants, and Soldiers Councils, 1905–1921*, trans. Ruth Hein (New York, 1974). See the author's comment that "a clear-cut distinction between strike committee and soviet cannot be made for the early phase of the council movement in 1905 . . . as the genesis of various soviets will show" (p. 39). See also S. A. Smith, "The Economic Crisis and the Fate of Workers' Control: October 1917 to June 1918," *Red Petrograd: Revolution in the Factories, 1917–18* (London, 1983), pp. 230–65.

6. Stephen Sternheimer, "Administration for Development: The Emerging Bureaucratic Elite, 1920–1930," in W. M. Pintner and D. K. Rowney (eds.), *Russian Officialdom: The Bureaucratization of Russian Society from the Seventeenth to the Twentieth Century* (Chapel Hill, 1980), pp. 317–54; see also Don K. Rowney, *Transition to Technocracy: The Structural Foundations of the Soviet Administrative State* (Ithaca, 1989), pp. 67–81.

7. Rowney, *Transition to Technocracy*, chap. 3.

8. See, for example, G. Karanovich, "Etapy razvitiia mestnykh organov zdra-vookhraneniia," *Biulletin NARKOMZDRAVa RSFSR*, 20 October 1927, pp. 16–17.

9. Alec Nove, *An Economic History of the U.S.S.R.* (New York, 1972), p. 52.

10. Alfred J. Rieber, *Merchants and Entrepreneurs in Imperial Russia* (Chapel Hill, 1982); Theodore H. Von Laue, *Sergei Witte and the Industrialization of Russia* (New York, 1969); Gaston V. Rimlinger, "Autocracy and the Factory Order in Early Russian Industrialization," *Journal of Economic History* 20, no. 1 (March 1960), pp. 67–92; John McKay, *Pioneers for Profit: Foreign Entrepreneurs and Russian Industrialization, 1885–1913* (Chicago, 1970).

11. See, for example, the discussions of responsibilities of the Chief Administration of Posts and Telegraphs in *Uchrezhdenie ministerstv*, 1892 ed. (St. Petersburg, 1907), vol. 1, pt. 2. For a discussion of the creation of the ministry, see N. P. Eroshikin, *Istoriia gosudarstvennykh uchrezhdenii dorevoliutsionnoi Rossii* (Moscow, 1983), pp. 281–82.

12. Peter I. Liashchenko, *History of the National Economy of Russia to the 1917 Revolution* (New York, 1970), pp. 675–86.

13. Calculated from data in Paul R. Gregory, *Russian National Income, 1885–1913* (New York, 1982), table F.1, p. 252.

14. Edward Hallett Carr and R. W. Davies, *A History of Soviet Russia: Foundations of a Planned Economy, 1926–1929*, vol. 1, pt. 2 (New York, 1969), p. 974. The data originally came from R. W. Davies, *The Development of the Soviet Budgetary System* (Cambridge, 1958), pp. 83 and 296.

15. Liashchenko, *History of the National Economy of Russia*, pp. 758–60.

16. See the appendix, "Computer Study of the Soviet Technical Intelligentsia," in Kendall E. Bailes, *Technology and Society under Lenin and Stalin* (Princeton, 1979), pp. 431–41.

17. Bailes, *Technology and Society*, p. 23.

18. For class backgrounds, see A. P. Korelin, *Dvorianstvo v poreformennoi Rossii, 1861–1904 gg.* (Moscow, 1979), chap. 4; P. A. Zaionchkovskii, *Pravitel'stvennyi apparat samoderzhavnoi Rossii v XIX v.* (Moscow, 1978); and Seymour Becker, *Nobility and Privilege in Late Imperial Russia* (DeKalb, 1985), chaps. 6 and 7. So far as gender is concerned the presence of women in the corps of Russian officialdom was so rare that the literature generally ignores the variable. For the skeptical reader, a perusal of *Adres-Kalendar': Obshchaia rospis' nachal'stvyiushchikh i prochikh dolzhnostnykh lits po vsem upravleniiam v Rossiiskoi Imperii* (St. Petersburg, annually) for any given year should offer satisfactory evidence.

19. See commentary, passim, on the widely varying number of agencies responding to survey questionnaires in "Vysshii sovet narodnogo khoziaistva: Tsentral'noe upravleniie ucheta i statistiki," *Struktura i sostav organov VSNKh v tsentre i na mestakh v 1921 g.*, (Moscow: VSNKh, 1922). So far as I know, V. Z. Drobizhev was the first scholar in recent times to call attention to the existence of the corpus of survey data of which this VSNKh publication is a part. See his *Glavnyi shtab sotsialisticheskoi promyshlennosti* (Moscow, 1966), p. 215.

20. Ia. Bineman and S. Kheinman, *Kadry*, table 2, Posts-Telegraphs.

21. *Sostav rukovodiashchikh rabotnikov i spetsialistov*, Table 44, Posts-Telegraphs.

22. Ezra N. Suleiman, *Politics, Power and Bureaucracy in France: The Administrative Elite* (Princeton, 1974), tables 2.6 and 2.7.

23. Suleiman, *Politics, Power and Bureaucracy*, p. 55.

24. See, for example, *Vsia Moskva na 1923 g.: Otdel I, Tsentral'nye uchrezhdeniia RSFSR* (Moscow, 1924) and *Vsia Moskva na 1927 g.: Tsentral'nye pravitel'stvennye uchrezhedeniia Soiuza SSR* (Moscow, 1928).

25. Bineman and Kheinman, *Kadry*, table 2, Posts-Telegraphs.

26. *Historical Statistics of the United States: Colonial Times to 1970* (Washington, D.C.

1975), pt. 1, ser. D, pp. 182–232; "Major Occupation Group of the Experienced Civilian Labor Force, by Sex: 1990–1970," pp. 139–40.

27. The best Soviet treatment is in Drobizhev, *Glavnyi shtab*, esp. chap. 3. See also E. H. Carr and Robert W. Davies, *Foundations of a Planned Economy, 1926–1929*, (New York, 1969), vol. 1, chaps. 12–16. For the changing relation between technical elites and state and party institutions, see Bailes, *Technology and Society*, chaps. 2 and 3.

28. Carr and Davies, *Foundations*, pp. 351–60. See also Sheila Fitzpatrick, "Ordzhonikidze's Takeover of VESENKHA: A Case Study in Soviet Bureaucratic Politics," *Soviet Studies* 37, no. 2 (April 1985), pp. 153–72.

29. Fitzpatrick, "Ordzhonikidze," pp. 162–65. For a summary of the legal structural changes, see T. P. Korzhikhina, *Istoriia gosudarstvennykh uchrezhdenii SSSR* (Moscow, 1986), chap. 2.

30. Carr and Davies, *Foundations*, p. 356.

31. Korzhikhina, *Istoriia gosudarstvennykh uchrezhdenii*, pp. 72–74.

32. Ibid., p. 74.

33. "Narkomtiazhprom: Kontora spravochnikov i katalogov," *Predpriiatiia khozorgany i uchrezhdeniia Narodnogo Komissariata Tiazheloi Promyshlennosti* (Moscow-Leningrad, 1935).

34. John Kenneth Galbraith, *The New Industrial State* (Boston, 1967), p. 76.

35. Sheila Fitzpatrick, "The Russian Revolution and Social Mobility: A Reexamination of the Question of Social Support for the Soviet Regime in the 1920s and 1930s," *Politics and Society* 13, no. 2 (1984), p. 134; also the same author's *Education and Social Mobility in the Soviet Union, 1921–1934* (Cambridge, 1979), pp. 127–205.

36. Sheila Fitzpatrick, "Stalin and the Making of a New Elite, 1928–1939," *Slavic Review* 38, no. 3 (1979), p. 391; also Fitzpatrick, "Ordzhonikidze."

37. William Chase and J. Arch Getty, "Industrial and Economic Personnel in the 1930s: A Communication Presented to the National Seminar on Russian and Soviet Social History," manuscript, p. 13.

38. "Narodnyi komissariat pocht i telegrafov SSSR," *Perepis' sviazi 27 ianvaria 1927 goda* (Moscow, 1929), table 7, p. 27.

39. *Perepis' sviazi*, table 8, p. 26 and tables 5 and 6, pp. 50, 51.

40. Drobizhev, *Glavnyi shtab*, tables 18 and 22, pp. 225 and 231.

41. Chase and Getty have made what I take to be a comparable preliminary finding after studying the Soviet Data Bank: "Based on an analysis of social origins . . . education, age and party background, it is fair to say that from 1931 the influx of "new men" into the economic apparatus became notable, although the degree to which these people penetrated the higher echelons of these two agencies [i.e., VSNKh and NTPT] was limited." "Industrial and Economic Personnel in the 1930s," p. 17.

42. Fitzpatrick, *Education and Social Mobility*, pt. 2.

43. In *Sostav rukovodiashchikh rabotnikov*, tables 20–28, one finds party members and principal education categories broken out for detailed cross-classification. My analysis of these data leads to conclusions no different from those which I have already offered here.

44. This in spite of what Drobizhev, at any rate, sees as Ordzhonikidze's special commitment to *partiinost'*; see *Glavnyi shtab*, p. 268.

45. See, however, Fitzpatrick's comment that during the 1930s the female role model was changing from the comparatively feminist standards established within the Bolshevik Party and in society more broadly during the 1920s; "The Russian Revolution and Social Mobility," p. 137.

46. Fitzpatrick, "Ordzhonikidze," p. 165.

47. Fitzpatrick, "Ordzhonikidze," p. 166.

48. Chase and Getty, "Industrial and Economic Personnel in the 1930s," p. 15.

49. V. I. Lenin, *Polnoe sobranie sochinenii* (Moscow, 1963), vol. 53, p. 156.

VII

THE COMMANDER AND THE RANK AND FILE

MANAGING THE SOVIET COAL-MINING INDUSTRY, 1928–33

Hiroaki Kuromiya

The coal-mining industry was a trouble spot par excellence in the Soviet industrialization drive. Two factors contributed to difficulties within the industry. First, rapid mechanization of production was imposed upon a mobile and inexperienced labor force. The coal-mining industry, more than any other, attempted to make a great leap forward from manual to machine labor in a matter of a few years. Workers resisted stubbornly, and machines broke down frequently. As a result, mechanization failed to achieve the expected levels of production and productivity as quickly as had been planned. Second, the peculiarity of underground mining made the supervision of labor particularly difficult. The difficulty was aggravated by the inclination of supervisory personnel to avoid underground work, which involved much discomfort and danger. Labor discipline was lax, and speeding up was hard to implement. In the period of rapid industrialization, the problems of an inexperienced labor force and weak supervision were common to all industries to one extent or another. What distinguished the coal-mining industry was that these problems manifested themselves in a particularly acute form.

The coal-mining industry supplied 60.5 percent of the country's fuel in 1927–28 and 70.5 percent in 1937.[1] Its troubles affected other industries— metallurgy, electric power, transport—that depended on coal, and invited political intervention from above. Two important events in the history of Soviet industrialization, the Shakhty affair of 1928 (which unleashed the violent attack on "bourgeois" specialists) and the Stakhanovite movement of 1935 (which led to the massive purge of Soviet industrial managers),

both originated in the Donbass coal-mining area.[2] The coal-mining industry became a hotbed of the political violence that characterized Stalin's
industrialization drive.

The present essay examines the development of violence in the c al-
mining industry by focusing on the problems of supervising a mobile and
inexperienced labor force and managing rapidly mechanized production.
This study, based largely on the case of the Donbass, discusses how in the
first half of the 1930s the main target of political attack shifted from the
"class enemy" to the class-neutral "commander," or boss. The ideology and
the rhetoric of class war were not discarded, but this shift provided an
important background to the violent events in the latter half of the 1930s.

Mobile Labor

Miners had long been notorious for their poor work attendance. Their
absenteeism was in fact by far the highest of all industrial workers. In 1924,
for instance, the average number of days absent without permission was
35.20 among the colliers, or four times the overall industrial average of
8.80. As administrative pressures mounted, absenteeism declined to 24.06
and 5.72 days in 1928 and 13.78 and 4.4 days in 1930 in the coal-mining
industry and industry as a whole respectively.[3] The high absenteeism,
which increased on Saturdays and Mondays and declined in midweek,
often disrupted production. In 1930 the deputy commissar of labor, I. A.
Kraval, frustrated over the disorder in the Donbass, declared emphatically
that it was "impossible to work when 12 percent of workers don't show
up."[4] The absenteeism of colliers was subsequently reduced by tightened
administrative controls to 13.32 days in 1931, to 10.52 days in 1932, and
owing to the draconian law of November 1932, dramatically to 1.93 days in
1933 and 1.33 days in 1934, whereas the industrial average increased
slightly to 5.96 days in both 1931 and 1932 and dropped sharply to 0.93
and 0.67 days in 1933 and 1934 respectively.[5] Yet the coal miners were still
twice as likely to be truant as the average industrial workers.

High absenteeism was accompanied by high labor turnover. In the coal-
mining industry, the rate of workers discharged to the annual average
work force was 139.3 percent in 1924, 132 percent in 1928, 295.2 percent
in 1930, 205.2 percent in 1931, and 187.9 percent in 1932, whereas the
overall industrial average was much lower: 98.5 percent in 1924, 92.4
percent in 1928, 152.4 percent in 1930, 136.8 percent in 1931, and 135.3
percent in 1932. Harsh administrative controls managed to force down the
turnover rate in the coal-mining industry to 120.7 percent in 1933 and 95.4
percent in 1934, rates lower than the industrial average of 122.4 percent
and 96.7 percent in the respective years. From 1935 onward, however, the
turnover among the colliers began to outstrip the industrial average by a
wide margin: 99.1 percent to 86.1 percent in 1935 and 112.7 percent to

87.5 percent in 1936.[6] The all-time high of 295.2 percent in 1930 meant that on average every collier changed jobs three times a year. Certainly this did not imply that all miners did so. According to a Soviet study, in 1932 "permanent" workers accounted for under one-third of the Donbass miners, the remainder changing their jobs five times a year.[7] The miners as a whole were a highly mobile and unstable work force.

These characteristics were attributed to the miners' peasant backgrounds. In fact, a very large number of Donbass miners were peasants from the Central Black Earth region and the Left Bank Ukraine who annually migrated to work in the Donbass between *pokrov* (1 October, O.S.) and Easter.[8] Their behaviors and customs often baffled urban observers. For example, fistfighting *(stenki),* which Daniel R. Brower has eloquently described as nineteenth-century entertainment among workers,[9] was still frequently observed in the late 1920s among Donbass colliers: barracks fought against barracks, Riazaners against Orelians, etc. On one occasion, five miners were killed in the game. The attempt of a local resident to stop the fighting resulted in his own death. In March 1929 the organ of the Central Committee of the party, *Rabochaia gazeta,* reported with embarrassment and indignation that "mug-beating and 'fistfighting' are entrenched in the everyday life of miners."[10]

To some extent, high absenteeism and violent entertainment were attributable to the nature of mining labor itself. It was "a cripplingly fatiguing task," and there was "in any case an extremely powerful social inertia surrounding traditional rest days." Recreation was therefore ·"of enormous importance to mining communities."[11] However, the contemporary discussion almost invariably blamed colliers' peasant backgrounds.

According to the April–May 1929 trade-union census, 27.8 percent of the Donbass miners held land, and 32.2 percent of the land-holding miners, or 9.5 percent of all miners, had actually engaged in agricultural labor in 1928.[12] This census alone does not show that the miners had exceptionally strong ties to the countryside compared with other industrial workers. For example, 18.8 percent of metal workers (workers in the engineering and metalworking industry) held land, according to the census, but as many as 62.1 percent of these workers, or 11.7 percent of all metal workers, had engaged in agricultural labor in 1928, a rate higher than that of colliers.[13] As the compilers of the census warned, these figures underestimated the degree of miners' ties to the countryside because a large number of miners had already left for the countryside by the time of the census.

Whatever the case, seasonal exoduses had long been particularly characteristic of the mining labor force.[14] In 1922, for example, the number of Donbass miners declined from 116,662 at the beginning of the year to 82,249 on 1 September, a 29.5 percent drop; the number of coal hewers, the most important of all colliers, plummeted by 52.7 percent, from 14,498 to 6,863, in the same period.[15] A year of famine, 1922 may have been exceptional, but similar patterns were repeated periodically: in 1930, when the collectivization drive prompted a large number of miners back to the countryside, and in 1932, when the famine (which took the lives of millions of people) compounded the seasonal fluctuations. Thus from March to August 1930 the number of coal miners fell by 27.1 percent, from 256,934 to 187,440.[16] The numbers of workers in July and August 1930 (202,267 and 183,440) were lower than in the same months of the previous year (212,645 and 209,011). To allow for new recruits, the actual departures were much greater than these figures suggest. The exodus of hewers was said to be more dramatic than that of other colliers.[17] In July and August alone, nearly 10,000 hewers left the Donbass.[18] This flight curtailed the monthly output of coal by 37 percent, from 4,627,900 tons in March to 2,915,200 tons in August.[19]

The movement in the summer of 1932 was somewhat more limited, but the number of miners in the industry dropped by 17.3 percent from January to September:[20]

1 January	407,400
1 February	403,600
1 March	401,400
1 April	391,000
1 May	387,500
1 June	380,600
1 July	375,200
1 August	353,800
1 September	337,700
1 October	341,000
1 November	350,700
1 December	369,700

(In the Ukrainian part of the Donbass, which was hard hit by the famine, the decrease was even sharper: 27.0 percent.[21]) Accordingly, the average daily output of coal in the country fell by 22.4 percent, from 199,000 tons to 154,400 tons, in the same period.[22]

Massive recruitments of labor, to which managers were forced to resort, did not improve the problem. Certainly, as in other industries, the rapid expansion of coal mining induced a rapid influx of workers: despite the seasonal ebbs, the average annual number of colliers (including apprentices) consistently increased from 253,000 in 1928 to 447,500 in 1932, a 76.9 percent rise.[23] Yet an overwhelming majority of the increases were due to new arrivals from the countryside,[24] who were at least as mobile as their older cohorts. Of the 82,000 who first entered industrial labor in the Donbass in 1930, for example, only 53.6 percent remained to work in the mines.[25]

Nor did the attempt at "organized recruitments" through contracts with collective farms bring about the expected results. In the first six months of

1932, for instance, 93.7 percent of newly employed miners came to the Donbass *samotekom,* or spontaneously.[26] In August 1933 the Procuracy of the USSR issued an order to punish according to the criminal code those contractually employed workers who left their jobs without authorization. Yet as far as the coal miners were concerned, the majority were noncontractual workers. The effect of the order was therefore limited, and the abuse of it widespread.[27]

A large proportion of miners thus continued to migrate between town and village. A major railway station in Iasynuvata (Iasinovataia) near Stalino served as an "All-Donbass Labor Exchange," which resembled a "southern marketplace" filled with mobs of people. According to a contemporary observer, these mobile workers were undetermined between collective farms and mines. They drifted spontaneously to the Donbass, "searched around for a better life, went back to the village, and often drifted back to the Donbass. Except for the two–three months in the summer, this movement continued all the year round."[28] The Donbass mines appeared at the mercy of the drifting labor force.

Rapid Mechanization

In the period of the First Five-Year Plan the collieries were at once flooded with new mobile arrivals from the countryside and mechanized rapidly by modern technology. Even though the industry did not stand high on the list of investment priority, the number of heavy coal cutters, for example, increased from 459 in 1928 to 1,473 in 1932 and 1,906 in 1935. The number of coal drills (picks) skyrocketed much more spectacularly, from 71 to 9,020 to 13,501 in the same periods.[29] Thus, where merely 15.7 percent had been cut mechanically in 1927–28, the proportion jumped to 63.6 percent in 1932 and 77.3 percent in 1935.[30] Similarly, conveyors and other machines rapidly replaced manual labor. In 1927–28 mechanized conveying accounted for only 25.9 percent of total output, but in 1932 the ratio rose to 72.8 percent and in 1935 to 79.9 percent.[31]

The old underground order was rapidly encroached upon by mechanization. The "aristocratic" and therefore highly paid trade of coal hewer was hit hardest. Many hewers were forced to go elsewhere or were demoted to horse hands.[32] The conservatism of colliers caused stubborn and sometimes violent resistance. In the Kuzbass coal mines, workers were reported to raise "artisan rebellions against machines."[33] In the Donbass the sabotage of machines by cutting the electric cables and air hoses was said to be "a daily event." When the first coal cutter was introduced into the Valentinovka Mine in 1930, "kulaks and NEPmen started a canard that it would replace fifty hewers and redundant workers would be sacked." The following morning the machine was found smashed.[34] In the Violin Mine, conveyors ("iron horses") and coal cutters were seen as enemies who had descended into the pits to "replace human labor and lower the wages." The managers and party and trade-union leaders could not cool down workers' "boiling hatred" of machines. On 25 February 1930 the conveyor of Long Wall 10 was put out of commission by a bolt thrown into it. The angry miners refused to work:

> "To the pit? No, we don't go to the pit. . . . Let others go to the pit, those who have messed up the mines. . . ." Fedor Godov, a pony driver, leapt up and, growing pale out of anger, vilely cursed the mine manager, the technicians, and the mechanic for a long time: "These guys, let these guys go to the pit!"[35]

The more compliant colliers, however, were often technically inadequate. Many had never used or seen machines at all. Even the new, trained machine operators lacked experienced:

> [In 1930 there were] tens and hundreds of small and minute troubles, damages, and breakages. Here a bolt fell out, there a plug, and in yet another place some part of a machine failed to work. The qualification of the great majority of machine operators was limited to the most elementary skills: the ability to turn on a machine, set it in motion, and stop it. On the first occasion of the smallest trouble, which an experienced operator would have fixed while the machine was in motion, an inexperienced operator (which the overwhelming majority were) would turn the machine off.[36]

The inadequately trained would neither clean nor oil coal cutters, which therefore frequently broke down.[37] Technical illiteracy, aided by the chronic shortage of spare parts, caused such absurdities as the removal of parts from new machines for the repair of old ones.[38] According to a survey conducted in 1933, of 9,000 machinists in the North Caucasus coal mines, only 2,300 knew how to handle machines; the remainder were said to be "utterly illiterate" in technical matters.[39] To be sure, considerable improvements in technical training had been made in the early 1930s. Yet many machinists and other trained miners, like their counterparts in the countryside, were lured to more attractive industries.[40]

Frequent interruptions of production owing to mechanical troubles reduced the wages of piece-rate workers. Worse still, defective machines sometimes electrocuted workers. Many therefore refused to work in the mechanized long-wall face. The shrewder miners went down with coal drills and worked in the pit with their familiar manual picks.[41] Consequently, machine utilization was very low. Even according to official data, one-third of the available equipment lay idle in 1931.[42] Three years later, a census of the equipment of the coal-mining industry found that 26 percent of heavy coal cutters and 35.3 percent of pneumatic drills were in disuse.[43]

Mechanization, moreover, did not reduce but increased the labor force required in the pits. The premechanized face had only two central figures, hewer and carrier (*sanochnik*). In the mechanized long-wall face, a host of new trades were at work: machinist, assistant machinist, driller, exploder, loader, timberer, conveyor shifter, fitter, electrician, adjuster, etc.[44] It was envisaged initially that economies of scale would not lead the division of labor to increase the number of workers. The wide disparity in the mechanization of different production processes, however, contributed to the vast expansion of the work force. Emphasis on cutting and conveying neglected the mechanization of hauling. In 1930 only 6.4 percent of the coal was mechanically hauled to the surface. The proportion rose to 19.6 percent in 1932 and to 39.9 percent in 1935,[45] but as late as 1932, other works, such as the loading of coal into conveyors, were not mechanized at all.[46] To ensure smooth flows of production, a large number of manual laborers were put into the pits.[47]

As a result, in the early 1930s, the mechanization of mining did not increase but decreased the productivity of labor. According to official data, average output per worker-year fell from 207.3 tons in 1930 to 197 tons in 1931 and 193 tons in 1932. It then rose to 206.8 tons in 1933, still lower than in 1930, and to 237 tons in 1934. The Donbass mines, with a higher degree of mechanization than elsewhere, fared even worse: the corresponding index declined from 200 in 1930 to 187.5 in 1933, then rose to 217.8 in 1934.[48]

This problem was not necessarily unique to the Soviet Union, because mechanization did not result immediately in sharp rises in productivity in other countries, either. Britain, for example, raised the proportion of mechanically cut coal from 8 percent in 1914 to 23 percent in 1927 and 61 percent in 1938. As in the Soviet Union, however, the mechanization of haulage had been neglected, with the result that the productivity of labor (output per manshift) increased only 8.9 percent between 1929 and 1938.[49] Yet, like all competitive capitalists, the British coal-mining industry managed to prevent production costs from rising.[50]

In the Soviet Union, rather safely insulated from the Depression in the West, the declines in productivity were accompanied by sharp rises in output costs: 1.6 percent in 1929–30, 32.4 percent in 1931, 31.3 percent in 1932, and 3.6 percent in 1933.[51] As a result, in 1929–33 the costs of coal mining were considerably higher than the sale prices, and the industry was run at heavy losses. The Stalino Coal Trust, for example, lost 6,340,000 rubles in the first eight months of 1933 alone. Of the debt, 2,900,000 rubles were met by the People's Commissariat of Heavy Industry, but the trust still could not pay wages. In the latter half of August the trust was in arrears, with wages amounting to 1,000,000 rubles. How workers responded was not reported.[52]

The quantitative performance of coal mining also lagged considerably behind the plans. In 1929–30 the industry produced 47,780,000 metric tons of coal, or 92.6 percent of the annual plan. In later years, annual output continued to rise, but the rate of plan fulfillment sharply declined to 62.5 percent in the special quarter (October–December) of 1930, to rise gradually to 67.8 percent in 1931, 71.1 percent in 1932, 90.7 percent in

1933, and 97.3 percent in 1934.[53] From 1930 to 1933 output of coal increased by 54.6 percent in physical terms, but the rise was almost entirely due to the expansion of the labor force.[54]

Weak Management

The problems of a mobile labor force and rapid mechanization would have been much less formidable had management been powerful. These problems were in fact to a large extent reflections of weak management. Before 1933 almost no firm managerial authority was exercised and almost no technical instruction was given in the pits. Both machine and labor were left to themselves.

This was to some extent a legacy of the past. In the premachine era, colliers worked free from direct supervision most of the time. Underground work was controlled either collectively by artels[55] and similar gangs, or individually by lone wolves. The pit was workers' territory largely impervious to managerial control. The strong work autonomy, which distinguished mining labor from other industrial labor, was often matched by intimidation and use of brute force on the part of management.

After the Revolution such practices diminished, but the absence of direct and continuous supervision signified not harmonious labor-management relations but mutual ill will and distrust. Managers suspected miners of idling and cheating in the workplace.[56] The latter, in turn, suspected the former of cheating in weighing the coal produced and determining their wages. As late as 1932–33 neither supervisors nor workers carried watches. Workers gathered the time by the amount of work done.[57] Often there were no scales on which to weigh the coal produced. At a mine in the North Caucasus, the weigher had to mark "two tons" on all wagons for want of a scale.[58] Many supervisors, who determined workers' wages, were said to be ignorant of fractions, in any case.[59]

Other problems added to mutual suspicion. The size of output and therefore wages was greatly affected by such geological factors as the hardness and thickness of seams. So the allocation of workplaces was an important source of conflict not only between labor and management but also among workers. Mutual distrust was aggravated by underground intrigues, such as the hijacking of wagons full of coal on the way to the surface.[60]

The prerevolutionary domination of foreign capital in the coal-mining industry, particularly in the Donbass,[61] also seems to have left the legacy of bitter labor-management relations. Miners had been notorious for their antispecialist activities in the 1920s,[62] a factor that made the management of the Soviet coal-mining industry all the more difficult.

The Shakhty affair of 1928 almost eliminated managerial authority from the pits. Donbass colliers were said to have greeted the Shakhty trial by

inscribing on trolleys "Long Live the GPU!"[63] A leader of the miners'
union openly declared in April 1928: "If a technician treats workers rude-
ly, [should we] beat him in the mug? Yes, beat [him] in the mug."[64]
Engineers and technicians were in fact branded as members of the "Shakhty clique" and subjected to verbal and physical harassments.[65] Many were
put on trial. By mid-1931, when Stalin declared the rehabilitation of old
("bourgeois") specialists, half of the Donbass engineers and technicians had
been arrested.[66] The number of engineering and technical personnel in
the coal-mining industry thus dropped from 10,800 in 1928 to 8,000 in
1929 and 5,900 in 1930.[67]

The influx of new, Soviet-trained engineers and technicians subsequently raised the number to 8,500 in 1931, 12,600 in 1932, 13,900 in
1933, 19,100 in 1934, and 22,300 in 1935.[68] It was difficult, however, to
manage the mines after all the violent onslaughts on technical experts, few
of whom dared go into the pits. Much of the task had fallen on the
shoulders of the overman (desiatnik), the equivalent of the factory assistant
foreman. This "commander," who had to deal with fifteen to sixty workers,
was said to "have almost no rights." Like the factory foreman, the overman
had no power to dismiss workers for lack of labor discipline. Nor did he
have the authorization to set the output norms of his men, for it was feared
that the "commander" would otherwise have been outmaneuvered by
workers.[69] The wages of overmen were fixed, often falling below those of
skilled workers engaged in piecework.[70] So unpopular were the positions
that they once had to be advertised: "Whoever wants to become an overman is requested to sign up."[71] As a result, it was said that "there is not a
trace of one-man management" in the pits.[72] The commanders issued
scores of orders, which "no one carries out and the execution of which no
one demands."[73]

The disastrous performance of the industry in the summer of 1932
brought the issue of underground authority on the agenda of the political
leadership.[74] In dealing with it, Stalin and his close associates eventually
circumvented the People's Commissariat of Heavy Industry, which was in
charge of the coal-mining industry.[75] After thrice rejecting the commissariat's working proposals, Stalin was said to have brought some colliers
and "ordinary trade-union and managerial workers" from the Donbass to
Moscow and discussed with them for three days what the organizational
structure of mines was like, how the wages were determined, and how the
managers commanded the mines before the Revolution.[76] The details of
neither the proposals nor the discussion are known, but Pravda reported an
exchange between L. M. Kaganovich, who in April 1933 attended a meeting of Donbass shock workers, and a miner by the name of Kolesnikov.

Kolesnikov: Our overmen are young and inexperienced. People don't want to
listen to them. Old, experienced workers don't want to become overmen.
They say, "I don't want to be a spitoon for all."

Kaganovich: What does it mean "to be a spitoon"?

Kolesnikov: I'll tell you right now. Nobody listens to the overman. Even if he isn't to blame for some bad job, it isn't investigated, and he is spattered with mud from all sides. Now it turns out that he serves as a spitoon: everyone spits as he wishes. . . . Why does the overman know nothing [about coal mining]? Because he is lazy, doesn't want to work, and becomes an overman to play the fool.

Kaganovich: Well, what if we give him more rights?

Kolesnikov: If we give him more rights, we also have to put more into his brain. *(Applause.)*

Kaganovich: What if we give more rights to older cadres who have more in the brain?

Kolesnikov: They won't become overmen. No, they say, [when you] work in the coal face . . . nobody spits at you, curses you. You work honestly and are free.

Kaganovich: Well, for instance, people say that in olden times the shop overmen were true masters in their workshops. . . . Please tell us how things should be.

Kolesnikov: In olden times, when I was quite young, we used to stand at salute when overmen passed by. *(Laughter.)*

Kaganovich: Sure, we don't demand a salute now.

Kolesnikov: We used to ask the overman [for help and advice], but now there goes some kid only eighteen years old. Imagine what kind of overman he really is. . . .

Kaganovich: Please tell us how to make things better. Let's assume this: under what conditions would you become an overman?

Kolesnikov: We have to give the overman the most complete rights so that he will be responsible for everything, so that workers will obey him, so that we will also be able to hold him responsible. . . .[77]

Kolesnikov complained that there was neither authority nor assistance nor advice in the pits on the part of management. In 1933 the overmen were given greater (if not the most complete) powers, including the right to dismiss workers according to the mine regulations.[78]

Simultaneously the party leadership sought to strengthen underground order by sending down technically qualified cadres. The mechanization of mining had rapidly changed the nature of underground work. Machine mining not only intensified the need for on-the-site technical instruction and assistance (which had virtually been absent before 1933).[79] It also eroded the traditional work autonomy of colliers and created the need for direct and continuous supervision: different trades and different stages of mechanized work became increasingly interdependent, and their coordination essential to smooth work flows, a task that required considerable technical and organizational expertise. The notorious reluctance of engineering and technical personnel to go into the pits as overmen and section chiefs (the equivalent of factory foremen) was said to have created a supervisory vacuum.

The so-called functional organization of management, introduced during the First Five-Year Plan, appeared to the party leadership as a mere pretext for engineers and technicians to avoid underground work and sit in the offices. Mines had created over twenty administrative and technical positions or departments: director, chief engineer, director of mining matters, director of capital work, director of rationalization, director of technical normsetting, director of production planning, director of the wage-rating and economic sector, director of the planning department, director of technical safety, director of mechanization, director of the surveying bureau, director of concentration, director of technical propaganda, director of ventilation, director of traffic, director of finance, chief accountant, director of economy, director of storage, etc.[80] This elaborate division of management, modeled to some extent on Taylorist schemes, was intended to increase managerial efficiency,[81] but it instead caused enormous confusion and conflict by cutting single managerial command.[82]

Moscow had long been deeply frustrated: enormous investments seemed to yield few tangible results. "The more machines," it appeared, "the less coal."[83] The 1932 famine crisis had prompted the first deputy chairman of the OGPU, I. A. Akulov, to go to the Donbass, but in January 1933 the output of coal still failed to reach the level of the previous year (see the accompanying figure). In the early months of 1933 five Politburo members, A. A. Andreev, K. E. Voroshilov, G. K. Ordzhonikidze, V. M. Molotov, and L. M. Kaganovich, were dispatched to the Donbass as troubleshooters.[84] Many managers, engineers, and technicians were openly assailed as "antimechanizers";[85] functional management was abandoned in favor of rather traditional line management to ensure single managerial command; and a vigorous campaign ensued to send engineers and technicians underground.

The campaign was said to have met fierce resistance, because engineers and technicians considered it an "affront to their status."[86] The traditional order of status, symbolically divided by the ground, died hard. Communist managers were also said to be sympathetic with their poor colleagues. The deputy director of the Lugansk Coal Trust, Rybalchenko, for example, responded to the campaign with the following remark: "If we transfer 15 percent of engineering and technical personnel from the trust to the mines, then we will be able neither to answer the inquiries of the higher organs, nor to send down scientifically sound directives to the mines."[87] Rybalchenko and the trust director, Egorov, were removed from their positions and expelled from the party as "saboteurs with a party membership card in their pockets."[88]

Whatever the rhetoric, at the time of the famine crisis many managers and party members became increasingly critical of Moscow's policy. They felt that the center merely shifted the blame onto them when in their view it was the famine that undermined production. Indeed, this was a dangerously critical time for Stalin, whose violent attack on the countryside caused

Average Daily Output of Coal in the USSR, 1928-33

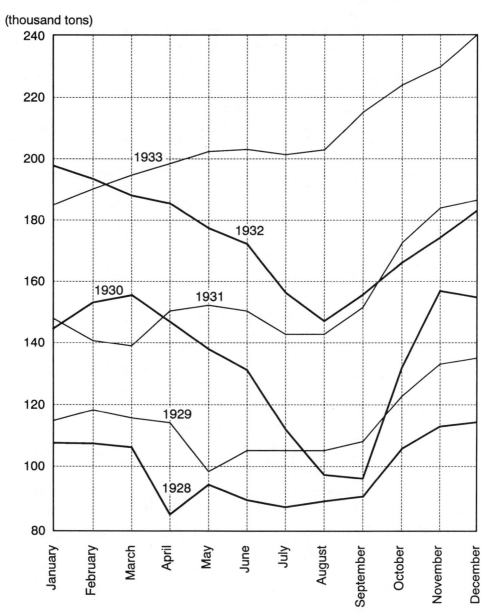

Source: *Pravda*, 6 July 1933, p. 2, and *Itogi perepisi zaboev i oborudovaniia ugol'noi promyshlennosti* (Moscow, 1936), p. 44.

some important party officials (among others M. N. Riutin) to challenge his political leadership.[89] Such critical sentiments were also widespread among Donbass managers and Communists.[90]

Moscow responded with unprecedented severity, which presaged the events of 1936–38.[91] On 1 June 1933 Stalin, Molotov, and Kaganovich sent a telegram urging the Donbass party committee and I. Kosior, N. M. Shvernik, and others dispatched from Moscow to "unconditionally punish all those who smell remotely of sabotage."[92] The deputy director of the North Caucasus Coal Trust, Burykin; the coalfield directors, Gorbachev and Pianov, and the mine director Borozdin, were also removed from their posts and expelled from the party.[93] In August the removal of sixteen Donbass mine directors was announced with much publicity.[94]

These high-handed measures forced many engineers and technicians down the pits. In April 1933 only 390 engineers and technicians were engaged in underground work in the Donbass coal mines, but by October 1933 the number had shot up to about 1,100. In the same period the proportion of Communists working underground increased from around 50 percent to about two-thirds.[95] In the pits, of 7,562 Donbass overmen, 1,408 (18.6 percent) had been demoted or removed by September 1934, and 441 former section chiefs and assistant section chiefs and 891 promotees were placed in their stead.[96] These transfers strengthened underground order to some extent, a factor that may have contributed to the overall improvement in the performance of the industry in 1934.[97]

However, it proved difficult to consolidate managerial authority, even after the severe 1932–33 famine was overcome. In 1935 both labor turnover and absenteeism began to rise,[98] and the division of the pit and the office began to widen. From 1933 to 1937, according to Gosplan data, the number of engineers working underground did not increase, whereas those in the offices rose by 304. In the same period, the number of technicians working in the pits increased by 100, but the offices had attracted many more, 786.[99] In 1940, of 3,095 engineers in the Donbass coal-mining industry, only 320 were working underground.[100]

The troubles of the coal-mining industry were not unique. Other industries, particularly the metallurgical industry, suffered from the same problems of supervising a new, unstable labor force and managing rapidly mechanized production. Yet the troubles seemed especially intense in the coal-mining industry. The task was unenviably difficult; as a 1932 Gosplan report put it, "We have only five years of experience with the mechanization of coal, whereas America has forty years and England thirty years."[101]

What happened during the First Five-Year Plan was a massive injection of machine and labor into the pits without exercising managerial control and supervision. The result was that the underground and the surface were disjointed, actually and symbolically, or at least it so appeared: "The pit lived on its own, and so did the office."[102] The labor force as a whole was relatively new, inexperienced, and mobile, but management appeared to care little about underground discipline or technical assistance and advice. Workers were coming and going, machines kept breaking down, managers and engineers sat in the office, and production went up and down.

The attack against the mining managers, engineers, and technicians that ensued marked an important change in Stalinist politics. Certainly between 1928 and 1931 the managers were far from free of harsh criticism, but the brunt of violence was borne by the alleged class enemies. Yet by 1933 the target of attack has shifted from "class enemies" to class-neutral "commanders"—managers, engineers, and technicians. What mattered seemed to be not their social origins (many were Communists or former workers) but their work and political loyalty. Managerial and technical cadres came to be attacked not as "class enemies," not merely as incompetent or inept bureaucrats, but as "antimechanizers," "saboteurs," "enemies of the party," and "counterrevolutionary" elements.[103]

This onslaught may have been more rhetorical than substantial in scale, but its political impact was more significant than it appeared at that time: workers were explicitly told that their bosses were "saboteurs" and "enemies," and witnessed them expelled from the party. It created a political environment in which workers came to attribute technical and organizational problems to the sabotage of their bosses.[104]

The Donbass affair was also significant in its impact on the overall reorganization of industrial management: in other industries too, "functional management" was to be abolished, and engineers and technicians were to be hounded out of the office to the shop floor.[105]

The real significance of the case of coal mining lay not so much in that its troubles represented the problems of industry as a whole in a particularly acute form as in the way they were dealt with by Stalin. In his concluding speech to the February–March 1937 plenum of the Central Committee, which triggered a massive purge of Communist managers, Stalin proudly referred to his handling of the case. Stalin contended that "the masses," unlike leaders such as himself, "see things, events, and people from the other side, I would say, from below." Their field of vision is "somewhat limited," he continued, but only by combining the views of the leaders and the masses would it be possible to solve problems. As an example, Stalin specifically cited the Donbass case:

> Several years ago . . . we, members of the Central Committee, discussed the problem of improving the situation in the Donbass. The draft of measures submitted by the People's Commissariat of Heavy Industry was manifestly unsatisfactory. Three times we returned the draft to the commissariat. Three times we received different drafts from it. Yet it was still impossible to consider them satisfactory. Finally, we decided to invite some miners and rank-and-file managerial and trade-union workers from the Donbass. For

three days we conversed with them. And all of us, members of the Central Committee, had to acknowledge that only they, only these ordinary people, these "humble folk [*malen'kie liudi*]," were able to suggest the right solution.

Stalin then contended that "ordinary people" sometimes proved "way closer to the truth than some higher institutions," and he said he could cite "tens and hundreds" of such cases.[106] In Stalin's view, the Donbass affair of 1933 was a model case, and the implication was that industrial commanders were in for trouble. The Donbass mines, with their sharp division into the pits and offices, also presented a fine symbolic image of the contrast Stalin made between "humble folk" and "some higher institutions."

NOTES

1. *Itogi vypolneniia pervogo piatiletnego plana razvitiia narodnogo khoziaistva Soiuza SSR* (Moscow, 1933), p. 95, and *Industrializatsiia SSSR: 1933–1937 gg.* (Moscow, 1971), p. 323.

2. The Donbass was a major coal-mining area located in the Donets region of the Ukrainian Republic and the Northern Caucasus region of the Russian Republic. It accounted for 77.3 percent of the country's coal production in 1929 and 60.8 percent in 1938. *Sotsialisticheskoe stroitel'stvo Soiuza SSR (1933–1938 gg.): Statisticheskii sbornik* (Moscow, 1939), p. 47.

3. *Trud v SSSR: Statisticheskii spravochnik* (Moscow, 1936), pp. 96 and 110. For comparison with other industries, see *Trud v SSSR: Spravochnik, 1926–1930 gg.* (Moscow, 1930), pp. 18–19.

4. *Za industrializatsiiu*, 12 November 1930.

5. *Trud v SSSR* (1936), pp. 96 and 110. The famous November 1932 law obliged the managers to dismiss workers for even a single day's unjustified absence.

6. Ibid., pp. 95 and 109, and *Plan*, 1937, no. 9, pp. 21–22.

7. Z. G. Likholobova, "Istochniki popolneniia i rost chislennosti rabochikh Donbassa v period sotsialisticheskoi rekonstruktsii narodnogo khoziaistva (1926–1937 gg.)," *Istoriia SSSR*, 1973, no. 2, p. 133.

8. V. P. Danilov, "Krest'ianskii otkhod na promysly v 1920-kh godakh," *Istoricheskie zapiski*, 1974, no. 94, p. 94.

9. Daniel R. Brower, "Labor Violence in Russia in Late Nineteenth Century," *Slavic Review* 41, Fall 1982, no. 3.

10. *Rabochaia gazeta*, 2 March 1929, p. 2. Fistfighting was seen among southern metallurgical workers as well. (See Hiroaki Kuromiya, "The Crisis of Proletarian Identity in the Soviet Factory, 1928," *Slavic Review* 44, Summer 1985, no. 2, p. 286.) Before the Revolution, Donbass miners were active participants in pogroms. (See *Khrushchev Remembers*, tr. and ed. Strobe Talbott [Boston, 1970], pp. 266–67, and Theodore H. Friedgut, "Labor Violence and Regime Brutality in Tsarist Russia: The Iuzovka Cholera Riots of 1882," *Slavic Review* 46, Summer 1987, no. 2, pp. 255, 259–60.)

11. See the case of British colliers in Barry Supple, *The History of the British Coal Industry, Vol. 4: 1913, The Political Economy of Decline* (Oxford University Press, 1987), pp. 58–59.

12. I. N. Dubinskaia, *Rabochie kadry kamennougol'noi promyshlennosti Donbassa: Itogi perepisi 1929 g.* (Kharkov, 1930), pp. 21 and 24.

13. *Perepis' rabochikh i sluzhashchikh 1929 goda, Tom 1: Metallisty SSSR* (Moscow, 1930), pp. 26 and 39.

14. In the mid-1880s, "60 percent of the miners in Bakhmut *uezd* [in the Donbass] returned each summer to their home villages," and coal production dropped accordingly. Friedgut, op. cit., pp. 248 and 261.

15. L. Liberman, *Trud i byt gorniakov Donbassa, prezhde i teper'* (Moscow, 1929), p. 89. For slightly different figures, see *Khoziaistvo Donbassa*, nos. 38–39, October 1923, p. 19. The year 1921 also brought food shortages, which decreased the number of Donbass hewers by 47.2 percent from February to September. See *Donbass v 1921 godu. Otchet tsentral'nogo upravleniia kamennougol'noi promyshlennosti Donbassa* ([Bakhmut], [1922?]), p. 205.

16. *Ezhemesiachnyi statisticheskii biulleten'*, no. 10 (1930), pp. 2–3. These data refer to the number of workers at the end of each month. Reliable data for the remainder of the year have been unavailable.

17. *Industrializatsiia SSSR. 1929–1932 gg.* (Moscow, 1970), p. 376. According to a February 1930 account, each year 14 percent to 20 percent of the hewers left the Donbass for the countryside. (*Pravda*, 7 February 1930). V. P. Renke and P. A. Shirai, *Zaboishchitskie kadry v rudoupravleniiakh Donuglia: Po materialam perepisei 1923 i 1929 gg.* (Kharkov, 1929), p. 91, cite 15 percent to 16 percent. The movement of 1930 almost certainly surpassed these usual exodus rates.

18. S. V. Kosior, *Vybrani statti i promovy* (Kiev, 1968), p. 389. During the entire summer of 1930, 12,000 hewers left the Donbass, according to a Soviet study. Z. G. Likholobova, *Rabochie Donbassa v gody pervykh piatiletok (1928–1937 gg.)* (Donetsk, 1973), p. 25.

19. *Ezhemesiachnyi statisticheskii biulleten'*, 1930, no. 10, p. 18. See also the attached figure.

20. *Trud v SSSR* (1936), p. 107 (apprentices not included). A vivid description of the "wild exodus" is in Semen Gershberg, *Rabota u nas takaia: Zapiski zhurnalista-dista tridtsatykh godov* (Moscow, 1971), pp. 99–100. The famine continued well into 1933, but its impact on the labor force was mitigated by "extraordinary measures," which included a suspension of workers' leaves and a recall of mining school apprentices from leave to work in the mines. See *Za industrializatsiiu*, 14 February 1934.

21. *Za industrializatsiiu*, 8 October 1933.

22. *Itogi perepisi zaboev i oborudovaniia ugol'noi promyshlennosti* (Moscow, 1936), p. 44. See also the attached figure.

23. *Trud v SSSR* (1936), p. 94. During the Second Five-Year Plan (1933–37), the increase was halted by a variety of productivity campaigns.

24. No comprehensive data are available, but 73.2 percent of the 1928 new cohort and 79.4 percent of those who first entered the industry in 1930 and the first quarter of 1931 in the Donbass came from the countryside. *Narodnoe khoziaistvo SSSR*, 1932, nos. 1–2, March–April, p. 129 (apprentices not included).

25. Likholobova, *Rabochie Donbassa v gody piatiletok*, p. 26.

26. *Bol'shevik*, 1932, no. 16, p. 52.

27. *Spravochnik po trudu dlia rabotnikov ugol'noi promyshlennosti SSSR* (Moscow-Leningrad, 1936), pp. 241–42.

28. Gershberg, op. cit., p. 55, and *Za industrializatsiiu*, 2 February 1935 (description of 1932–33).

29. *Itogi perepisi zaboev i oborudovaniia ugol'noi promyshlennosti*, pp. 124 and 131.

30. Ibid., p. 46, and *Itogi vypolneniia piatiletnego plana razvitiia narodnogo khoziaist-va Soiuza SSR*, p. 262. The first source lists 62.6 percent for 1932.

31. *Itogi perepisi zaboev i oborudovaniia ugol'noi promyshlennosti*, p. 46. The 1927–28 figure refers to the Donbass coal mines and is almost certainly higher than the national average (which is unavailable).

32. See, for example, *Visti VUTsVK,* 29 March and 12 April 1931. The flight of hewers in the summer of 1930 was aggravated by this encroachment.

33. R. I. Eikhe, *Novyi etap i zadachi Sibpartorganizatsii: Doklad i zakliuchitel'noe slovo na V Sibpartorganizatsii* (Novosibirsk, 1930), p. 42.

34. V. Turov, *Na shturm uglia* (Moscow, 1931), p. 9.

35. B. Galin, *Perekhod: Kniga ocherkov (1929–1930)* (Moscow, 1930), pp. 53, 57, 60–61.

36. A. F. Khavin, *Kratkii ocherk istorii industrializatsii SSSR* (Moscow, 1962), p. 178. The author was a journalist who had closely covered the Donbass problem in the 1930s. For similar descriptions, see *Sovetskaia Sibir',* 17 February 1932, and *Pravda,* 16 August 1932.

37. Turov, op. cit., p. 19.

38. See *XVII konferentsiia VKP(b). Sten. otchet* (Moscow, 1932), p. 100.

39. A. A. Zvorykin, *Rekonstruktsiia kamennougol'noi promyshlennosti* (Moscow, 1934), p. 137.

40. Ibid.

41. See the case of Kuzbass colliers in *Vtoraia ugol'naia baza SSSR: Kuzbass,* vol. 2, pt. 2 (Novosibirsk, 1936), p. 34. See also Gershberg, op. cit., p. 115.

42. *Industrializatsiia SSSR: 1929–1932,* p. 270.

43. *Itogi perepisi zaboev i oborudovaniia ugol'noi promyshlennosti,* pp. 130 and 131. According to G. K. Ordzhonikidze, *Stat'i i rechi,* vol. 2 (Moscow, 1957), p. 619, 49 percent of pneumatic drills were idle.

44. See, for example, *Pravda,* 16 August 1932.

45. *Tiazhelaia promyshlennost' SSSR za 1931–1934: Materialy k dokladu N.K.T.P. S. Ordzhonikidze VII s"ezdu Sovetov SSSR* (Moscow, 1935), p. 29, and *Itogi perepisi zaboev i oborudovaniia ugol'noi promyshlennosti,* p. 46.

46. *Ratsionalizatsiia proizvodstva,* 1933, nos. 2–3, p. 22, and *Bol'shevik,* 1932, no. 16, pp. 53–54.

47. *XVII konferentsiia VKP(b),* p. 99.

48. *Tiazhelaia promyshlennost' SSSR za 1931–1934,* pp. 25 and 136.

49. Supple, op. cit., pp. 32, 315–19, 384–85, 616.

50. International Labour Office, *The World Coal-Mining Industry* (Geneva, 1938), vol. 1, p. 208.

51. *Industrializatsiia SSSR: 1929–1932,* p. 347, and *Tiazhelaia promvshlennost' SSSR za 1931–1934,* p. 149. The industrial average was −7.1, 5.9, 13.3, and −1.1 percent in the respective years. In 1931 the costs of mechanized mining in the Donbass was 3.5 percent higher than those of manual mining. *Ratsionalizatsiia proizvodstva,* 1933, nos. 2–3, p. 22. See also G. I. Lomov, *K zadacham rekonstruktsii kamenno-ugol'noi promyshlennosti Donetskogo basseina (tezisy)* (Kharkov, 1930), p. 28, where it is stated that machine labor was less effective than manual labor.

52. *V plenum Donetskogo obkoma KP(b)U. Materialy* (Stalino, 1933), pp. 23–24. In August 1933 the chairman of the Council of Labor and Defense, V. M. Molotov, proposed that the Procuracy immediately prosecute managers for arrears of wage payments. (See *Prikaz po narodnomu komissariatu tiazheloi promyshlennosti: Prilozhenie k prikazu No. 715 ot 11 avgusta 1933 g.*)

53. Eugene Zaleski, *Planning for Economic Growth in the Soviet Union, 1918–1932,* tr. and ed. Marie-Christine MacAndrew and G. Warren Nutter (University of North Carolina Press, 1971), pp. 330–31, and *Stalinist Planning for Economic Growth, 1933–1952,* tr. and ed. Marie-Christine MacAndrew and John H. Moore (University of North Carolina Press, 1980), pp. 550–51.

54. See *Tiazhelaia promyshlennost' SSSR za 1931–1934,* p. 139.

55. See Hiroaki Kuromiya, "Workers' Artels and Soviet Production Relations," in *Russia in the Era of NEP: Explorations in Soviet Society and Culture* (Indiana University Press, 1991).

56. Some colliers worked for twelve to eighteen hours to overfulfill the norms by several times and reported the work done in the prescribed six hours. See, for example, *Trud,* 11 April 1933.

57. See, for example, *Gornorabochii,* no. 21 (8 June 1930), *Molot,* 21 July 1933, and Gershberg, op. cit., p. 108.

58. *Molot,* 5 September 1934.

59. Ibid., 21 July 1933.

60. Ibid., 20 October 1933.

61. In 1912 twenty-four foreign (mainly French and Belgian) joint-stock companies accounted for over 70 percent of all coal production in the Donbass. G. D. Bakulev, *Razvitie ugol'noi promyshlennosti Donetskogo basseina* (Moscow, 1955), p. 153.

62. See, for example, *Otchet Vseukrainskogo soveta profsoiuzov k 3-mu s"ezdu profsoiuzov Ukrainy* (Kharkov, 1926), pp. 209–10; *Gornorabochii,* no. 7 (25 February 1927), p. 1; and L. I. Pystina, "Shakhtinskie sobytiia i inzhenerno-tekhnicheskie sektsii Zapadnoi Sibiri," *Bakhrushinskie chteniia,* 1973, p. 57.

63. Hiroaki Kuromiya, *Stalin's Industrial Revolution: Politics and Workers, 1928–1932* (Cambridge University Press, 1988), p. 27.

64. Ibid., p. 106.

65. *Drukha konferentsiia Komunistychnoi partii (bil'shovykiv) Ukrainy, 9–14 kvitnia 1929 r. Sten. zvit* (Kharkov, 1929), p. 17. See also I. V. Paramonov's firsthand account in his *Puti proidennye,* 2d ed. (Moscow, 1970), pp. 203–4.

66. See Kendall E. Bailes, *Technology and Society under Lenin and Stalin: Origins of the Soviet Technical Intelligentsia, 1917–1941* (Princeton University Press, 1978), p. 150, and Nicholas Lampert, *The Technical Intelligentsia and the Soviet State: A Study of Soviet Managers and Technicians, 1928–1935* (London, 1979), p. 92.

67. *Trud v SSSR* (1936), p. 106 (data on 1 January of each year).

68. Ibid. The increases in 1934 and 1935 were due in part to the inclusion of mining foremen *(gornye mastera)* and overmen *(desiatniki).*

69. See the remark of the people's commissar of labor, A. M. Tsikhon, in *XVII konferentsiia VKP(b),* p. 29.

70. *Bol'shevik,* 1931, no. 17, p. 57.

71. *Gornorabochii,* no. 43 (November 1930), p. 17.

72. See, for example, *Za industrializatsiiu,* 25 January 1930.

73. *Pravda,* 21 April 1933.

74. See the Central Committee resolution of 16 September 1932, "O rabote ugol'noi promyshlennosti," *Spravochnik partiinogo rabotnika,* vyp. 8 (Moscow, 1934), p. 478.

75. Published documents do not suggest that Commissar Ordzhonikidze was particularly concerned about the problems of the coal-mining industry. See, however, n. 91.

76. I. V. Stalin, *Sochineniia,* ed. Robert H. McNeal, vol. 1 (14) (Stanford, 1967), pp. 239–40; *XVII s'ezd VKP(b): 26 ianvaria–10 fevralia 1934 g. Sten. otchet* (Moscow, 1934), pp. 540, 549, and 563; and L. M. Kaganovich, *Ot XVI k XVII s"ezdu partii: Doklad o rabote TsK VKP(b) na Moskovskoi ob"edinennoi IV oblastnoi i III gorodskoi partiinoi konferentsii 17 ianvaria 1934 g.* (Moscow, 1934), p. 29.

77. *Pravda,* 14 April 1933.

78. *Sobranie zakonov i rasporiazhenii raboche-krest'ianskogo pravitel'stva SSSR,* 1933 (pt. 1), 31:182.

79. When drills broke down, managers and technicians would order them to the surface. Their behavior reminded a *Pravda* reporter of Gothamites who sought to put their cattle up on the roof to graze grass growing on it. Gershberg, op. cit., p. 120.

80. *KPSS v rezoliutsiiakh i resheniiakh s"ezdov, konferentsii i plenumov TsK,* 8th ed., vol. 5 (Moscow, 1971), p. 94.

81. The rationale behind "functionalism" was that even well-trained and experienced people were believed incapable of managing complex modern factories in traditional fashion. All the truer, it appeared, given the acute shortage of such cadres in the Soviet Union. Later it was alleged that functionalism had been used to justify the inadequate expertise of managers and technicians.

82. See, for example, I. V. Paramonov, *Uchit'sia upravliat': Mysli i opyt starogo khoziaistvennika*, 2d ed. (Moscow, 1970), pp. 149–50.

83. L. M. Kaganovich's remark in *Pravda*, 15 April 1933.

84. *Gody geroicheskogo truda* (Stalino, 1961), p. 28, and *Khrushchev Remembers*, p. 65. For the 1933 managerial reorganization in the Donbass, see an important work by Nobuaki Shiokawa, "Donbasu tankō no kiki to saihen," in *Sobeto seifu chitsujo no keisei katei*, ed Yuzuru Taniuchi (Tokyo, 1984).

85. The director of the Stalino Coal Trust, E. T. Abakumov, for instance, was removed from his post as an "antimechanizer." However, a colleague of his subsequently maintained: "I know few managers who would have done more than Abakumov did for the mechanization of the coal industry." Paramonov, *Puti proidennye*, p. 374.

86. See, for example, *Trud*, 26 May 1933.

87. Quoted in *Pravda*, 14 April 1933.

88. *Sotsialisticheskii Donbass*, 23 and 26 May 1933, and *Planovoe khoziaistvo*, 1933, no. 4, p. 51. According to *Pravda*, 23 May 1933, Rybalchenko and another person were sent to the court.

89. For Riutin, see, for instance, "K politicheskomu portretu: M. N. Riutin," *Izvestiia TsK KPSS*, 1990, no. 3.

90. This point is examined in detail based on archival sources in a book I am writing on the Donbass.

91. Evidently, in early 1933 industrial managers, like their counterparts in the countryside, were threatened with harsh punishments. Addressing the joint plenum of the Central Committee and the Central Control Commission on 10 January 1933, Ordzhonikidze declared: "I don't think that industrial managers and personnel want the party to enforce discipline in industry in the way we now have to among the directors of state farms. Nor do I think that any factory director would become envious of the state-farm director whom we have to expel from the party, remove from the occupied position, and put in jail." (Ordzhonikidze, op. cit., p. 443.) Three weeks later, Ordzhonikidze, using the threat of imprisonment, harshly attacked the managers of the Donbass metallurgical industry, which was also in crisis at that time. (See ibid., pp. 446–60.)

92. *Sotsialisticheskii Donbass*, 4 June 1933, and *XII z'izd Komunistychnoi partii (bil'shovykiv) Ukrainy. 18–23 sichnia 1934 r. Stenohrafichnyi zvit* (Kharkov, 1934), p. 401.

93. *Planovoe khoziaistvo*, 1933, no. 4, p. 51.

94. *Molot*, 9 August 1933. See also *Za industrializatsiiu*, 5 August 1933.

95. *Promyshlennost' i rabochii klass Ukrainskoi SSR: 1933–1941*, vol. 1 (Kiev, 1977), p. 176. According to another source, in April 1933 there were only sixty-eight engineers and technicians working as section chiefs. In September 1934 there were about 1,200. *Za polnuiu pobedu na ugol'nom fronte: Materialy III sleta udarnikov peredovykh shakht Donbassa 15–16 sent. 1934 g.* (Stalino, 1934), p. 26.

96. *Za polnuiu pobedu na ugol'nom fronte*, pp. 23–24; 110 overmen were sacked as "saboteurs."

97. See n. 48.

98. See n. 6 and *Trud v SSSR* (1936), p. 110.

99. *Industrializatsiia SSSR: 1933–1937*, p. 335. See also *Promyshlennost' i rabochii klass Ukrainskoi SSR*, p. 446.

100. *Industrializatsiia SSSR: 1938–1941 gg.* (Moscow, 1973), p. 110.

101. *Industrializatsiia SSSR: 1929–1932*, p. 181.

102. See Nikita Izotov, *Moia zhizn' moia rabota* (Kharkov, 1934), p. 56.

103. See *XVII s"ezd VKP(b)*, pp. 56, 286, and 574, and *Sotsialisticheskii Donbass*, 1933, passim. For attacks on managers in general in 1934–35, see also Hiroaki Kuromiya, "Edinonachalie and the Soviet Industrial Manager, 1929–1937," *Soviet Studies* 36, April 1984, no. 2, and Gabor T. Rittersporn, "Héros du travail et commandants de la production: La campagne stakhanoviste et les stratégies fractionnelles en URSS (1935–36)," *Recherches*, 1978, nos. 32–33.

104. Note particularly Aleksei Stakhanov, *Rasskaz o moei zhizni* (Moscow, 1938).

105. Note particularly L. M. Kaganovich's report in *XVII s"ezd VKP(b)*, pp. 533–47, and *Soveshchanie khoziaistvennikov, inzhenerov, tekhnikov, partiinykh i profsoiuznykh rabotnikov tiazheloi promyshlennosti: 20–22 sentiabria 1934 g. Sten. otchet* (Moscow-Leningrad, 1935).

106. Stalin, op. cit., pp. 239–41.

VIII

MASTERS OF THE SHOP FLOOR
FOREMEN AND SOVIET INDUSTRIALIZATION

Lewis H. Siegelbaum

Addressing the Eighth Congress of Trade Unions in December 1928, M. I. Tomskii, the soon-to-be-ousted chairman of the trade unions' central council, referred to a recent incident at the Leningrad Skorokhod shoe factory. There, a foreman had been shot and killed by a worker. This act, he said, might be attributed to the "abnormal" and "hooligan" nature of the worker, but such an explanation was too simplistic and clichéd. In his view, what was responsible for this and similar "unhealthy and shameful" occurrences of recent times was the "uncultured" and "rude" behavior of foremen and the unions' failure to intervene in relations between foremen and workers.[1]

Tomskii's interpretation appears well founded. Over the previous few years, the press had reported numerous instances of foremen establishing or perpetuating "old regime" relations with workers. They demanded bribes in the form of money, vodka, and sexual favors in return for preferential job assignments; they compelled workers to work on the side for them, using the factory's equipment; they placed their unqualified relatives in high wage-skill categories; they threatened workers with demotion or dismissal if the latter complained or in other ways challenged their authority, and in several cases, made good on their threats. Far from attempting to put a stop to these outrageous acts, some factory and shop committee chairmen willingly served as accomplices.[2] Some workers were moved to respond in kind. The incident at Skorokhod was only one of several reported by the press.[3]

At the same time, however, the press had been critical of other actions by foremen, actions that belie their image as the tyrants of the shop floor. From Kolomna it was reported that before Easter and other holidays, foremen assigned workers to better paying and easier tasks, that being "insufficiently independent in their relations with workers," they were indulgent with them and were thus guilty of "tailism."[4] At Krasnoe Sormovo, foremen were said to be too lenient with absentees, compensating them with overtime work, while at Krasnaia Oborona in Moscow, they took a "conciliatory" attitude toward drunkenness among workers.[5] Workers in their turn could be indulgent toward foremen. At a production conference in the Stenka Razin glassworks (Nizhnii Novgorod *guberniia*), workers argued that it was not the foremen but the higher administration that was responsible for the high proportion of defective goods.[6] And in a letter to *Trud,* a worker from Krasnoe Sormovo defended a foreman against the charge of carelessness, claiming that all the sins of the administration were wrongly placed on him.[7]

How are we to reconcile these two diametrically opposed images of foremen? If it was not merely a function of different personality types, we must seek to explain why foremen were brutes toward workers in certain circumstances and their allies in others. To do this, we first need to appreciate the intermediate position that foremen occupied in the Soviet industrial hierarchy.

Like their counterparts in the capitalist world and in Russia before 1917, Soviet foremen were Marx's "sergeants of an industrial army." They were the "non-coms" who partially bridged the gap between management and rank-and-file workers, between "the demands for maximum output and the need to maintain social relations with those under [them], between accumulation and legitimation."[8] From the dawn of the factory age, which in Russia's case can be dated from the 1880s, foremen both facilitated the formal subjection of labor to capital and made difficult management's real control over the labor process. Only with the managerial revolution of the late nineteenth and early twentieth centuries could supervision be placed on a more rational basis. Instead of foremen's determination of job tasks, skill levels, and appropriate pay, "the skilled engineer was now actively involved—as pacemaker and technical supervisor—in the work of management."[9]

This revolution did not triumph everywhere or soon. Worker resistance, both active and passive, slowed it down, as did the costs involved in expanding the white-collar work force. Yet, from employers' point of view, the advantages of adopting bureaucratic and technical forms of control increasingly outweighed their problems. Those firms that adopted rationalization measures often gained a competitive edge that spurred on others to imitate and experiment with their own. All the while, the functions, flexibility, and authority of foremen in the Western industrial nations were being reduced. They too became subjected to a division of labor that parcelized their responsibilities at the same time as it narrowed the interstices between management and labor.

Explaining why no such fate befell Soviet foremen in the interwar period is the central problematic of this essay. That Soviet industrialization deviated from capitalist experience in this respect may seem surprising, given the extensive borrowing of Western models of management and technology. Not for lack of trying did Soviet authorities fail to put foremen and their relations with workers on a more "modern" footing. Like their Western counterparts, Soviet foremen found themselves, at least in the early stages of industrialization, "between Taylorism and technocracy."[10] They, and the workers they supervised, also were subjected to the political imperatives demarcated by the Communist Party. The survival of foremen's traditional powers therefore suggests that what Michael Burawoy has called "the politics of production" not only had a different outcome in the USSR but were played by different rules.[11]

The Foreman's Empire Challenged

Foreman is a notoriously difficult term to define, mainly because the difference in function between those bearing the title and other supervisory personnel is often purely semantic. The problem of definition is compounded by the existence of different degrees of hierarchy within separate branches of industry, or, depending on the size of an enterprise and its constituent shops, within the same industry. Thus a shop foreman in one enterprise could be referred to as a shop supervisor in another; a gang boss in construction or mining might be an overseer or assistant foreman in a larger metalworks shop, whereas in small establishments, a less elaborate hierarchy may not permit such intervening categories between foremen and manual workers.[12]

While by no means peculiar to Soviet Russia, the terminological confusion in that country has certain unique features owing to the survival of indigenous precapitalist or at least preindustrial terms ("elder," *nadsmotr-shchik, desiatnik, prorab*), those borrowed from other languages *(master, ober-master, instruktor)*, and certain generic and syncretic terms, usually of military provenance, which took on peculiar meanings in the Soviet industrial context *(brigadir, podmaster, kadr spetsialist, malyi komandir,* even *srednyi admi-nistrativno-tekhnicheskii personal)*. The coexistence of all these terms, all with their own specificities and nuances, reflected the multitude of organizational patterns, managerial strategies, and ideological constructs that bore on both the formal definition of foremen's responsibilities and their real power on the shop floor. It is also worth noting that terminology had an important relational dimension. For example, whether foremen were to be classified among engineering-technical personnel (ITR) seems to have depended on the referent group. If it was only technicians and engineers, then foremen were excluded; but in distinguishing them from manual workers, foremen were often included among these "specialists."

At the risk of overgeneralizing, it can be said that as of the mid-1920s, foremen occupied the lowest rung on the managerial hierarchy, being subordinate to shop supervisors *(nachal'niki tsekha)* and exercising full *(pol-*

nopravnye) powers of supervision over manual workers. This arrangement formally owed its existence to the "Bolshevik" principle of *edinonachalie* (one-man management), but in fact was little different from the prerevolutionary factory regime.[13] Even if foremen typically were nominated by the trade unions' factory committees, the qualities of a good foreman in a Soviet enterprise were identical to those that comprised competence before the Revolution.

Essentially, he—there were very few forewomen even in industries with a predominantly female work force—had to match job tasks *(nariady)* to available workers; ensure that the appropriate equipment was in working order and that supplies of power, tools, spare parts, and raw and semi-finished materials were adequate; understand technical processes sufficient to be able to impart his knowledge to new workers or trainees and evaluate the performance of his charges; and mete out sanctions to workers who violated labor discipline and rewards to those who overfulfilled their quotas. Notwithstanding the creation of planning departments, labor economics sections, and rates and norm bureaus within some Soviet enterprises, the overwhelming majority of foremen were expected to fulfill all of these tasks.

In doing so, they could rely on intermediaries who combined manual labor with supervision and usually received some compensation over and above their normal wage. Traditionally known in manufacturing industry as *masterovye,* these skilled or senior workers took the title of *brigadiry,* a term that is probably of Civil War vintage. In mineral and peat extraction as well as the construction industry, where the labor force was more fluid and seasonal, the prerevolutionary term *starshii* (elder) persisted, as did the group of workers, the artel, over which the elder presided. Agreements between foremen and elders were commonly on a task rather than time basis, the task being known as *akkordnaia rabota.* Wages were paid to the artel and distributed by the elder out of the common "pot."[14]

Although foremen enjoyed broad discretion and in the eyes of many workers appeared to be a law unto themselves, they were in fact restrained by rules and procedures to a degree that was unknown before the Revolution. For a start, there was the enterprise triangle, consisting of management, the party cell, and the trade union committee. One function of the latter two was to head off trouble between workers and line supervisors by inviting and investigating complaints and sponsoring production conferences at which grievances could be aired. While many a party organizer and trade union committee chair colluded with management, this was not always the case. Mention should also be made of the enterprise Rates and Conflict Commissions (RKK) and arbitration boards, which routinely took up alleged violations of collective agreements, and of worker-correspondents who shed the light of publicity on the misconduct of foremen and other shop-floor personnel.[15]

Even more of a constraint were the bureaucratic procedures that foremen had to follow in carrying out their daily functions—confirming the list of workers reporting for work, recording on the work order the amount of work done and the time it required, and assigning skill levels (*razriady*) to workers and tasks in accordance with industrywide manuals. Of course, the latitude for circumventing such procedures and doctoring the records could be considerable. But from the mid-1920s, Soviet foremen were confronted with a still more serious challenge to their autonomy and status. This was scientific management, or in its Soviet version, NOT, the scientific organization of labor.

Typically, NOT has been regarded by Western scholars as a means of increasing pressure on workers to speed up their pace of production, which correspondingly provoked intense opposition among the older, highly skilled stratum. This was the case, but NOT had a broader agenda and its opponents were not exclusively skilled workers. Most closely identified with Alexei Gastev and the Central Institute of Labor (TsIT) over which he presided, NOT actually encompassed a range of principles and procedures that extended far beyond the activities of that body and its provincial affiliates. As Samuel Lieberstein noted over a decade ago, NOT seemed to provide a pragmatic recipe for overcoming Russian backwardness, a relatively painless way of catching up to and overtaking the advanced capitalist countries.[16] As such, it was embraced by many engineers and the planning establishment with a passion reminiscent of a cult or religion. Its totems—precision of measurement and technique, standardization, and specialization—were the constituent elements of a productivist utopia that was the very antithesis of Soviet reality.

Instead of relying on rule-of-thumb methods to determine how machines should be used and what could be gotten out of them, NOT offered the "passport," a card attached to each machine on which was written its specifications, optimal speed of operation, and so forth. Instead of basing output norms on approximations of workers' everyday performance (or worse still, what was needed for workers on piece rates to exceed the wages of those paid on an hourly or shift basis), it introduced and celebrated time-and-motion analysis via the stopwatch and camera. And in place of on-the-job training or that offered by the factory apprentice schools, it redefined and simplified occupations such that they could be learned in two-month courses run by the Central Institute of Labor.

NOT, then, constituted an ambitious program that entailed the reorganization not only of labor but of management as well. Indeed, the latter was a prerequisite for the former and nowhere more so than at its lower levels. It was, after all, foremen who had employed rule-of-thumb methods in determining how machines should be used, what constituted appropriate output norms, and how workers should be trained. Consequently, it was foremen whose job profile was to be radically redefined.

Instruktazh and Ustanovka

To take up the matter of training first, Gastev was fond of quoting from his spiritual mentors, Taylor and Gilbreth, to the effect that "the main difficulty in applying the scientific organization of labor consists in the struggle against old methods of training." Writing in early 1924, he recalled that "when Taylor began to apply his ideas of organizing a functional system of management, he immediately came up against the lack of appropriately trained foremen. . . . He himself began to prepare and teach foremen who could work according to his plan."[17] If Taylor and his disciples found American foremen lacking in this respect, their Soviet counterparts were still more "backward." Gastev repeatedly railed against the "harsh bellowing," "overbearing" attitude, and "boasting" of foremen, which, he claimed, masked their lack of talent.[18] What was required was to train foremen in the art of instruction—*instruktazh*—the key to which was the correct positioning *(ustanovka)* of workers.

These terms were a kind of incantation for Gastev. No aspect of TsIT's work consumed as much of his attention as the production of instructional cards to be used by "instructors" in training workers. By employing such cards, Gastev insisted, what would otherwise have taken five to seven years of traditional apprenticeship or at least a year in a factory apprentice school could be accomplished in a few months and at a fraction of the cost.[19] The argument was sufficiently convincing to garner for the institute's share company (incidentally, named "Ustanovka") contracts from the Commissariat of Labor and several unions for the training of some 10,000 unemployed workers in the metal trades. By the early 1930s, TsIT's instructional cards or those based on its methods had become an important feature of the Soviet industrial scene. Summing up fifteen years of the institute's activities, Gastev could claim (in 1936) that some 20,000 instructors, controllers, and consultants had used the cards to train over 500,000 skilled workers in more than 200 occupations.[20] Unquestionably, many of these "instructors" were foremen who themselves had been trained at TsIT "bases." But not only foremen were encouraged to administer instruktazh. Brigade leaders were as well, and, in the guise of *sheftsvo* (patronage) and Izotovite schools, so too were skilled workers.[21]

The standardization and democratization of vocational training, based on engineers' appropriation of technical specifications and job profiles, constituted a potential threat to foremen's empire. That the threat was never actualized can be explained by several factors. First, instruktazh was administered selectively, concentrating on semi-skilled assembly-line work in the metal trades, certain occupations in the textiles industry, and construction work. Even in these occupations, the turnover of workers was so great that training was done, as it were, on the run. Second, there was a great deal of confusion over what the appropriate specifications for new—

often imported—machines should be and a dearth of competent technical personnel to interpret and enforce them. As new technologies were introduced, debates about the appropriate division of labor erupted. This was particularly the case in the mining industry, where, as I have discussed elsewhere, engineers and administrators went back and forth on the question of subdividing or combining occupations. Some argued that the decomposition of the miner's craft made it easier to train newcomers; others insisted that when workers combined several tasks, stoppage time was reduced.[22]

But perhaps most important of all, instruktazh failed to take hold because it presupposed the cooperation of foremen in the stripping of their powers. They simply had nothing to gain by conveying standardized instructions to workers, especially as those instructions often did not reflect the (chaotic) reality of the shop floor. In any case, loss of control over the training of new workers jeopardized the standing of foremen with respect to all their charges. Pressed from above by the technical rationality of engineers and from below by "upstart" brigade leaders and shock workers, foremen did their best to keep both at bay.

That they enjoyed a measure of success is evident in the revision of vocational training programs in the 1930s. The narrowing and shortening of the factory apprentice school curriculum in 1933 and the even more abbreviated technical minimum courses that were introduced in the same year reflected official impatience with *both* traditional apprenticeship and TsIT's methods. In the event, the new courses actually strengthened the hand of foremen.[23] The scheme for technical minimum courses was devised by the Council on Labor and Defense and monitored on the national level by the industrial commissariats. But it was individual enterprises that ran the courses (or in some cases "circles") and foremen who taught them.[24] When, in 1935, state technical examinations were administered to over 800,000 workers employed in 255 "leading occupations," foremen comprised the main group within the skills commissions that devised the examinations and assessed workers' performance.[25] Similarly, with respect to the craft, railroad, and factory training schools that were set up in 1940 to train labor reservists, the curriculum was almost entirely practical, and, appropriately enough, foremen comprised 86 percent of the staff.[26]

The survival of apprenticeship, even in its truncated and bureaucratized form, meant that foremen remained arbiters of workers' advancement through the ranks (*razriady*). They had primary responsibility for determining who qualified for each skill level and, indeed, for interpreting what constituted skill. They retained this power not despite the multiple social and economic dislocations accompanying industrialization but because, in such circumstances, someone had to give instructions to workers and grade their performance. Since, in Kendall Bailes's piquant phrase, engineers "fled from production," trade unions no longer could impose their own rules, and workers' own traditional networks had been sundered or driven underground, it was left to foremen to mediate between the utopian targets and behavior prescribed by higher authorities and the existing work culture. The implications of this relationship for the determination of output norms and the enforcement of labor discipline were profound. But before turning to these matters, we might consider what it took to become a foreman during these years and who served in this capacity.

Trajectories of Soviet Foremen

No category of industrial personnel grew as fast in the early 1930s as did foremen (see table 8.1). While the number of workers in large-scale industry nearly doubled between 1929 and 1934, there were still relatively twice as many foremen supervising them at the end of this period as at its outset.[27] Despite the attention that Soviet and Western historians have given to questions of social background and mobility, it is difficult to be precise about the process by which foremen were recruited. At best, we can trace three trajectories.

One was via formal education in which the rabfaks and industrial technicums played the major role. That is, some of the workers who had been selected for promotion via education as well as students from other social backgrounds left these institutions or graduated to become foremen rather than proceeding on to VTUZy and an engineering degree.

A second path was charted by a decree of September 1933 stipulating that graduates of higher and secondary technical institutions "must pass through the school of lower administrative-technical personnel (foreman, subforeman, shift engineer, etc.)."[28] Intended to give young engineers

Table 8.1. Managerial and Engineering-Technical Personnel in the USSR, 1929–33

Personnel	October 1929 No.	%	April 1930 No.	%	November 1933 No.	%	% 1933/30
Directors and assistants	—	—	8,507	9.5	16,926	5.4	198.9
Admin./prod. specialists	—	—	56,835	63.2	197,569	63.3	347.6
Scientific-lab.	—	—	4,605	5.1	13,714	4.4	297.8
Foremen	18,695	22.6	20,814	23.1	83,846	26.9	402.8
Total	82,689		89,911		312,055		347.1

Source: A. E. Beilin, *Kadry spetsialistov SSSR. ikh formirovanie i rost* (Moscow, 1935), pp. 122, 216.

some supervisory experience as well as to professionalize foremanship, this decree proved difficult to enforce and does not appear to have been widely observed. "I at least have not seen such foremen," reported a construction trust official, who attributed their absence to young engineers' preference for planning departments and their reluctance to "dig around in the earth in primitive conditions."[29] As late as June 1941, the cadre department of the Commissariat of Heavy Machine Construction regarded the appointment of engineers and technicians to foreman's responsibilities as "insufficient in the extreme."[30]

As is evident from table 8.2, the vast majority of foremen did not become so as a result of formal specialized education but rather were *praktiki*. Three out of four foremen in November 1933 had been workers, 54 percent of whom were promoted from the bench during the First Five-Year Plan.[31] Scattered data suggest that most had considerable production experience, primarily in the skilled trades. Thus only 11 percent of foremen surveyed in Moscow had less than seven years of production experience, as contrasted with nearly 40 percent of workers nationwide who had less than two years' experience as of 1933.[32] At the Ilich Metallurgical Factory in Mariupol, only one of ninety-five foremen had less than five years' experience as of 1932, whereas fifty-eight had more than ten, most of it as workers in the same factory.[33] Another study, from 1934, found that the proportion of foremen who were under twenty-three years of age ranged between 4.2 percent and 11.1 percent, compared to 5–6 percent for engineers, 15 percent for economists, and 35 percent for technicians. The corresponding proportion of workers was 41 percent.[34] In other words, to the extent that respect on the shop floor was a function of skill, experience, and age, many foremen were in a position to demand it.

During 1935 thousands of workers who had received a grade of "excellent" on the state technical examinations were promoted to foremen. Thereafter Stakhanovites constituted the main pool of recruits. What training these workers received either before or after their promotion consisted of either TsIT's short-term courses or, from 1936, the more elaborate master of socialist labor course. The latter entailed two years of study and was specifically designed to "raise the cultural-technical level of workers to that of ITR [engineering-technical personnel]."[35] While in terms of specialized education the course was said to approximate what was offered in the technicums, the narrowness of its curriculum did not permit those who completed it to enter a secondary educational institution without additional study.

It did, however, enable foremen to become shift engineers and shop supervisors. For, just as thousands of Stakhanovites were promoted to the ranks of foremen, many who had preceded them to this position moved higher up the industrial hierarchy, partly as a result of the Great Purge and partly through "natural" attrition. This ratchet effect may explain why by 1941 the production *stazh* (and probably the age) of foremen was consider-

Table 8.2. Educational Background of Foremen in the USSR, 1929–41

Date	No. of Foremen	Higher Education		Secondary Technical		Praktiki (%)
		Complete (%)	Incomplete (%)	Complete (%)	Incomplete (%)	
October 1929	18,695	2.7	1.2	6.2	1.8	88.1
April 1930	20,814	3.4*		7.8*		88.8
November 1933	83,846	1.2*		4.9*		93.9
November 1939	212,613	1.7*		9.4*		88.9
January 1941	138,363	3.0	0.7	7.5*		88.8

Sources: For 1929, M. Firin, "K voprosu o probleme kadrov," *Ratsionalizatsiia proizvodstva*, nos. 9–10 (1930), pp. 48–50; for 1930 and 1933, Beilin, *Kadry spetsialistov*, pp. 216, 222; for 1939 and 1941, *Industrializatsiia USSR. 1938–1941 gg., Dokumenty i materialy* (Moscow, 1973), pp. 218, 276.
*Data do not distinguish between "complete" and "incomplete."

Table 8.3. Social Background, Party Saturation, and Gender of Foremen in the USSR, 1929–41

Date	No. of Foremen	Party Members and Candidates (%)	Komsomolites (%)	Workers (%)	Women (%)
October 1929	18,695	33.5	—	72.1	—
November 1933	83,846	34.8	—	76.8	1.7
January 1941	138,363	29.8	8.2	—	10.3

Source: For 1929 and 1933, Beilin, *Kadry spetsialistov*, pp. 222, 237; for 1941, *Industrializatsiia SSSR, 1938–41*, pp. 277–78.

ably less than what it had been in the mid-1930s. Whereas by the latter date those with ten or more years of production experience comprised 35.7 percent of foremen, almost exactly the same proportion (35.8 percent) had less than five years' experience.[36] It also would tend to account for the increased presence of women in the profession (see Table 8.3). Here, though, the critical factor was not so much the Great Purge as the feminization of the industrial working class, a process that was intensified in the late 1930s and early 1940s by the buildup of the Red Army.

In sum, the foremen of the 1930s were mainly "yesterday's workers," in many cases quite literally so. More specifically, and not unlike their counterparts in the industrialized West, they were drawn overwhelmingly from the working class, lacked formal technical education, and were predominantly male. Whether in other respects a particular strategy was pursued in selecting foremen, for example, on the basis of their nationality or party membership is impossible to say with any degree of certitude. While the proportion of foremen who were party members was approximately twice that of workers in general, the lack of systematic data on party membership among the strata from which foremen were recruited (e.g., brigade leaders, shock workers, those in the higher skill grades, Stakhanovites) make any correlations on this score speculative. Certainly among Stakhanovites, who were not necessarily in the top *razriady* but appear to have constituted the main pool of recruits for foremanship in the late 1930s, party saturation did not come close to what it was among foremen.[37]

In contrast to contemporary and even earlier Western experience, foremanship in the USSR tended not to be a terminal appointment. The barrier between foremen and high echelons of the industrial hierarchy remained bridgeable in the 1930s, making foremanship a way station on the path of upward mobility. This would explain in part the continued predominance of praktiki among shift and shop supervisors, shop technicians, and even enterprise directors.[38]

Can we therefore conclude that by promoting workers who had already displayed a degree of reliability (by joining the party, rate-busting, sharing the "secrets" of their trade, serving as worker-correspondents or trade union activists), the party was shoring up its and management's authority on the shop floor? The simple answer is that it seems likely. But what kind of authority did foremen have and how did they use it? What countervailing pressures existed to complicate the strict line of authority from the director's office down to the work bench? These are the questions to which we must now turn, focusing on the two most conflictual aspects of shop-floor relations, output norm determination and labor discipline.

"Science" vs. Foremen

Earlier it was argued that the threat to foremen posed by NOT was more apparent than real with respect to vocational training. There was, however, another aspect of the scientific organization of labor that most definitely challenged foremen's power. This was the determination of output norms based on the technical capacities of machines and time-and-motion study of individual workers. Introduced in the mid-1920s in connection with the rationalization campaign, technical norm determination had the double purpose of revealing potential output and, because norms were linked with wages via the piece-rate system, of stimulating workers and management to reach that potential.

The role of TsIT in promoting technical norm determination was clearly important. It organized conferences to discuss and advertise the use of chronometry, analyzed procedures pioneered in the West, conducted its own laboratory experiments, and provided training for norm setters. And when, in 1927, a Central Council on Technical Norm Determination was formed, its bureau included Gastev, Ia. M. Punskii, and other leading lights from TsIT.[39]

But within industrial enterprises, the main burden of formulating and defending such norms fell to the Technical Norm Bureaus, or TNBs, and their diminutive staff of norm setters. These were the organs, clothed in the mantle of "science," that were supposed to eventually eliminate the notional targets established by foremen on the basis of past experience, negotiation with artel or brigade leaders, or simple observation (*glazomer*). These were the organs, therefore, that threatened to expropriate what had become a traditional function of foremanship, depriving foremen of a great deal of their maneuverability.

Labor economists, trade union officials, and other advocates of technically based norms repeatedly asserted that foremen had a vital role to play in the process. They would serve, so the argment ran, as consultants to the TNBs and instructors of new production methods revealed by the TNBs to be more efficient. They, no less than norm setters and workers themselves, had a stake in discovering the "correct," scientifically determined norm for each job.[40]

For their part, foremen were under no illusions about what the new organs meant. Norms coming down from an office that was not party to informal negotiation with workers were bound to be higher than those set by foremen. Since foremen had to see to it that norms were fulfilled—no matter what their origin or method of determination—it was in their interest to create a "reserve" in case of unforeseen shortages of materials, breakdowns, and stoppages. Moreover, "tight" (zhestkie) norms exacerbated tensions and disgruntlement on the shop floor. This is why foremen took a characteristically uncooperative attitude toward technical norm determination and the TNBs or, to cite one of many euphemisms that were employed in the press, "fail[ed] to appreciate their importance."[41]

Not surprisingly, workers were mistrustful of TNBs and their work. "The chronometrist must approach the worker tactfully so as not to make him nervous and intentionally or unintentionally distort the production process," advised Trud.[42] The problem, however, was not the behavior of chronometrists but the close association of their work with increased output norms. When time studies were conducted openly, workers intentionally slowed down; when attempts were made to conceal such monitoring of work methods, "disturbances" (volnenie) occurred.[43] Gastev's recommendation that output norms should be based on not only the best worker but the "super-best" (sverkh-luchshii) and that other workers should be trained so that they eventually would be able to fulfill such norms could not have helped.[44]

A curious alliance was thus forged between foremen and a substantial part of the industrial work force over the issue of norms. Curious, because the arbitrariness and favoritism displayed by foremen in setting norms and assigning them to individual workers had been—and would continue to be—a common complaint among workers. But the contradiction is probably more apparent than real. Workers favored by foremen were not alone in feeling threatened by the new system. As agitated as many workers were about foremen's license, the prospect of norms being determined and periodically revised upward by TNB "bureaucrats" was still more objectionable. The arguments used in defense of TNBs, that they were completely impartial, that they concerned themselves "not with the individual worker—Ivanov, Petrov, Sidorov—but workers in general," and that their decisions were based on scientific principles, would hardly have satisfied workers.[45] Foremen were generally accessible to workers; norm setters were not. While, as we have seen, foremen were overwhelmingly male and had their roots in the working class, the social origins and sexual composition of norm setters were more mixed and their authoritativeness was therefore more questionable. Even if foremen were prone to dish out abuse in the form of curses and fists, it was a menu with which workers were familiar. That of norm setters was mystifying and therefore less palatable. Associated with the upward pressure on norms and the downward pressure on rates and living conditions, norm setters were frequent targets of *spets* baiting in the late 1920s.

This is neither to idealize foremen-worker relations nor to deny that in certain instances workers could forge alliances with engineering staff against foremen's arbitrariness.[46] It is rather to suggest that for many workers, foremen's manipulation of norms was the lesser of two evils. For a brief period during the First Five-Year Plan, some workers seized the opportunity to avoid both. Organizing themselves as production collectives and communes, workers, primarily in the metalworks and textile industries, were able to institute self-management, which included—at least in some cases—the self-determination of rates and norms. It may well have been the assumption of these functions by the Baltic Shipyards' Bakunin commune that induced one of its members to boast that "now, brother, we don't toady. Nobody sucks up to the foreman."[47] By the same token, such syndicalist tendencies weighed against the collectives and communes in the eyes of higher authorities, and explain in part why they were disbanded in 1931–32.

As it turned out, the technically based norms of the TNBs did not manage to displace those based on foremen's estimations. For this, there were many reasons: the incompetence of norm setters who by and large were *praktiki*, the vast number of norms to be revised (several tens of thousands in large enterprises), the addition of "laid-on" *(nakladnoe)* time to take account of the unfamiliarity of equipment and problems in intraenterprise routing, intimidation by workers, and, especially during the First Five-Year Plan years, interenterprise competition for skilled workers.

But even where such norms were applied, foremen were able to mitigate their effects. For example, they employed the "pencil," that is, the registration of nonexistent work, which in some railroad repair shops could represent a quarter of workers' wages.[48] More commonly, they arbitrarily raised rates for particular jobs. "Let's say one piece of repair work costs ten rubles," recalled an informant of the Harvard Interview Project. "I would raise it to fifteen by adding some artificial cost to the transport of goods which they could not check up on. And so the worker would overfulfill [sic] his norm by 150 percent."[49] For workers in the highest skill categories, these additional earnings *(prirabotki)* could amount to as much as 180 percent of their base rate as established in collective wage agreements.[50] The same effect could be achieved by ascribing work performed on an overtime basis to the normal shift or paying out bonuses to workers even when they did not fulfill their norms.[51] Finally, by juggling work assignments so that all workers occasionally performed tasks with "looser" norms or at higher skill levels, foremen could anticipate and preempt workers' complaints. As another informant put it, "I could 'set up' a situation in which a worker could achieve a higher norm than usual by giving her easier work or arranging her material in advance. This was the way it was usually done in all fields."[52]

It is unlikely that foremen could have engaged in such sleights of hand without at least tacit approval from higher management. For, in the context of taut planning and massive labor turnover, not only foremen but also shop supervisors, technical directors, and directors found the TNBs to be millstones around their necks. The reserves of productivity that foremen accumulated relieved some of this pressure, providing enterprise management with a degree of flexibility in its struggle to keep up with periodic revisions in centrally determined plans.[53]

This tug of war between management and commissariat officials over technical norms began to shift in favor of the former in 1933, a year of great crisis and much second thinking by the political leadership. Having earlier been persuaded by Gastev and other NOTists to install a system of management based on functional principles and a minute division of labor in the textile and construction industries, the commissariats found that the former encouraged the avoidance of personal responsibility (*obezlichka,* one of the cardinal sins discussed by Stalin in his "New Conditions, New Tasks" speech of June 1931) and the latter bred chaos. When enterprises were ordered to phase out certain functional departments (rationalization bureaus, planning sections, and where appropriate, capital construction offices) and trim the staff of others, directors seized the opportunity to reduce the size of their TNBs and their capacity to formulate technically based norms.[54]

Although some directors were accused of going too far, as NOT's influence waned, so did official faith in technics and, in particular, technical norm determination. Stalin's abandonment of technology in favor of cadres deciding "everything" marked the culmination of the shift in official attitudes.[55] At an industrial conference in May 1935—the same month in which Stalin exchanged formulas—Ordzhonikidze attacked "the technical norm determination to which we are accustomed" as "not fit for the devil," and his deputy, Piatakov, was no less critical.[56]

The victory of enterprise management, however, proved to be short-lived. The eclipse of technically based norms did not give managers a free hand but rather ushered in Stakhanovism, the exemplars of which outdid anything norm setters could have imagined. As I have detailed in my book devoted to the subject, Stakhanovism immensely complicated foremen's lives. Failure to adequately service a Stakhanovite or enable an ambitious worker to become one could have serious consequences, including criminal prosecution. Yet if a foreman chose to protect himself in this manner, he risked creating imbalances in the delivery of supplies, overloading machinery, and neglecting his other duties.[57]

One way of reading Stakhanovism is to see it as an attempt by the party leadership to pry a portion of the working class away from the rest and at the same time to sever its dependence on foremen and other supervisors.

To the extent that such a strategy existed and was successful, the result was doubly ironic. Not only did many Stakhanovites eventually become foremen, but, owing to the peculiar circumstances of the late 1930s and early '40s (to be discussed below), they were vested with powers that strengthened the dependency relationship between them and their subordinates.

Foremen and Labor Discipline

The problem of labor discipline was not peculiar to the 1930s, but the dimensions it assumed during that decade were sufficient to cause much alarm among trade union, state, and party officials. Violations of labor discipline covered a multitude of sins—lateness, absenteeism, frequent job changing, the misuse of equipment, idling on the job, refusal to carry out instructions, attacks on unpopular workers and managerial-technical personnel—and stemmed from a variety of causes.[58] There is no doubt, though, that the shortage of labor, which the key industrial sectors experienced as a chronic phenomenon after 1929, severely hampered efforts to combat such behavior.

Trade union, Komsomol, and party committees developed a number of strategies to improve the standard of labor discipline. The organization of collective responsibility via socialist competition, shock brigades, and cost-accounting brigades was one. Visits to the homes of offenders, production-comrades courts, boards of disgrace *(chernye doski),* and denunciations in factory newspapers was another. A third, aimed at reducing labor turnover, was to offer incentives to workers to sign contracts committing them to remain at their jobs for several years, a scheme that went by the revealing name of *samozakreplenie.* Finally, the provision of special services and goods to outstanding workers was intended at least in part to spur others to emulate their example.

These techniques had some success in socializing the new industrial labor force, but the persistence of "flitting," "sponging," and other forms of "petty bourgeois spontaneity"—by no means limited to new workers—provoked sterner measures. There is no need to rehearse the legislation that was aimed at increasingly restricting workers' mobility and freedom of action within their places of work.[59] For our purposes, it is sufficient to note that the effectiveness of such legislation critically depended on its enforcement by enterprise management. And there was the rub. As managers have discovered the world over, fining, demoting, and dismissing workers have limits beyond which the fragile cooperation and consent of workers becomes jeopardized. But beyond this general rule, the imposition of such punitive measures in circumstances of a chronic labor shortage and super-ambitious production targets threatened to deprive Soviet enterprises of their most vital resource, labor power.[60]

These considerations, perfectly rational from the perspective of individual enterprise directors, in fact vitiated the impact of the coercive legislation. Vesting in enterprise management the power of enforcement, political authorities repeatedly condemned its preference for "the path of least resistance." It is in this context of conflicting pressures and demands with respect to labor discipline that we can analyze the role of foremen.

On January 3, 1933, *Trud* reported that two workers had been arrested for stabbing and seriously wounding a shock worker who had been promoted to foreman at the Sacco and Vanzetti machine construction factory in Stalingrad. The account of this incident was as emblematic as were those from the late 1920s to which reference was made at the outset of this essay. Whereas foremen's rude behavior was cited in those accounts as provocation for attacks on them, in this case the culprits were described as "truants, loafers, and bodgers" (from "class alien" backgrounds, to boot!) who had been dismissed by the exemplary foreman in accordance with the decree of November 15, 1932. That law called for the dismissal, confiscation of ration coupons, and removal from enterprise accommodation of workers who had been absent from work for as little as a single day.

The decree itself and the campaign surrounding it suggest both the desperation and the powerlessness of the regime in its efforts to deprive workers of the leverage they enjoyed on the shop floor. For it is clear that foremen were at best highly selective in enforcing the decree's provisions and that in evading responsibility, had numerous collaborators within the factory administration. This point may be illustrated by citing the procedures used at the Kharkov Locomotive Engine Works and recommended for adoption by other factories. At the beginning of each shift, the timekeeper presented the foreman with a list of absentees. Every three days, the foreman reported to the shop supervisor, who, after investigating the reasons for absences, forwarded the names of those absent without excuse to the factory's service department. The department would then remove the offenders from their apartments and withdraw their ration books.[61]

There were numerous ways of sabotaging this process and all seem to have been employed. Foremen could retroactively inform timekeepers that absences were authorized or simply strike certain names from the list. Shop supervisors could similarly amend the lists they turned over to the service department. Finally, even those workers dismissed from one shop could be rehired by another without losing their entitlement to rations or accommodation.[62]

Simple humanitarianism should not be ruled out as a motivating factor here. Excuses that outside investigators considered illegitimate or questionable, such as the loss of a pass to enter the factory, illness in the family, or difficulty with housing authorities, may have been viewed otherwise by supervisors. But it was not only or necessarily feeling and sentiment that ruled the "informal organization" constructed by foremen and other factory personnel.[63] Charged with the task of keeping production flows moving, they could ill afford the loss of workers whom they had trained and with whom they had developed mutual understandings about effort and reward. By the same token, workers who did not share such understandings probably did not benefit from foremen's indulgence.

In any case, the campaign to combat absenteeism died a quiet death in 1933. Had the regime overreached itself or were its priorities changing? Even while the campaign was in full swing, a new one was emerging. This was to make full use of the work day. The new campaign coresponded to the increased emphasis on the "mastery of technology," which itself reflected the shift to a more intensive strategy of industrial expansion. It included criticism of foremen for concealing stoppages; failing to organize in advance the delivery of blueprints, tools, and spare parts to the shop floor; and allowing workers to wander about the factory, thereby "transforming the shops into boulevards [and] passage ways."[64] One proponent of *uplotnenie* even went so far as to warn that "along with workers who violate labor discipline, it is necessary to hold responsible the foremen who permit the violations."[65]

But it is obvious that the main targets of the campaign were workers and that criticism of foremen was intended to steer them in the direction of becoming true *nachal'niki.* "Without the knowledge of the *desiatnik,* no worker is to be moved," proclaimed a joint Sovnarkom-Central Committee resolution of May 1933 that sought to sort out the mess in the Donbass coal industry. "He attaches *(prikrepliaet)* workers to their places and machines."[66] In the factories, various schemes were developed for keeping workers at their benches. At the Leningrad Bolshevik factory, passes were used; different colored flags could be hoisted over the bays at the Kaganovich Ballbearings Factory in Moscow to alert foremen or mechanics to problems; and at the Marti factory, "S" tokens (for *skvoznoi prokhod*) were distributed to managerial and technical personnel as well as party and union officials, while workers had to obtain ordinary tokens from foremen if they had to relieve themselves or were sent on an errand.[67] Meanwhile, foremen were acquiring the accoutrements of managerial personnel—telephones to connect them with dispatchers, desks, time account clerks, and salaries that were well above the average wages of workers and often higher than what technicians, economists, and other staff personnel earned.[68]

All of this was part of the articulation of a strictly hierarchical factory regime to replace the Taylorite functionalist model that had fallen into disrepute. At its lowest level, the regime now included brigade leaders, who were given formal responsibility for the fulfillment of the production tasks assigned to the brigade and the maintenance of labor discipline among its members. Above them stood section and shift foremen possessing general supervisory, instructional, and punitive powers with respect to all workers in their section or on their shift, and responsibilities for the proper use of all materials and equipment at their disposal. And so it went, to senior foremen, unit and shop supervisors, all laid out in model statutes drafted by a conference of directors, chief engineers, *glavk,* trust and commissariat officials for different branches of heavy industry.[69]

The extent to which such prescriptions improved enterprise administration and labor discipline is difficult to determine. Certainly compared to the primeval chaos of the early 1930s, industry as a whole performed more efficiently. But this undoubtedly had much to do with the settling in of workers, the stabilization of the situation in the countryside, and corresponding improvements in food supply. Moreover, clear-cut lines of authority did not in and of themselves guarantee that "commanders" or workers would observe the rules. Informal shop-floor negotiation achieved what conformity to formal procedures could not, namely, mutual accommodation between workers and their bosses.

This is precisely why Stakhanovism was so threatening and why many foremen and workers at least initially resisted it. Stakhanovism shook up the shop-floor pecking order and the mutual understandings on which it was based. Some workers, resentful of the special treatment given to Stakhanovites and fearful of the consequences their records would have for output norms, sabotaged their work. Others, seeking the material rewards that went along with Stakhanovite status, denounced foremen and other supervisors for not providing the necessary materials and assistance. Stakhanovites, protected by local party officials and access to the press, often exposed foremen's shortcomings.

As we already have seen, the favoritism exercised by foremen was endemic; what Stakhanovism did was not only to raise the ante but also, in an important sense, to turn the tables on foremen by calling into question their competence and status. After all, the vast majority of innovations in work methods were attributed to workers rather than their supposedly more knowledgeable bosses. It (or rather the progressive piece-rate system) also enabled the innovators and many who emulated their example to earn far more than what foremen normally received.

Not surprisingly, foremen often figured among those prosecuted for crimes against the Stakhanovite movement. Of twenty-one people convicted of such crimes by the Ivanovo People's Court up to March 1936, four were foremen and seven were adjusters; among the cases that were referred to the Supreme Court of the RSFSR by district and regional courts in January and February 1936, 20 percent involved brigade leaders or foremen, as compared with only 11.5 percent involving shop supervisors and department personnel.[70] Charges against foremen typically concerned failing to service Stakhanovites, arbitrarily cutting their rates, and "disorganizing production."

Yet it did not take long for Stakhanovism to be tamed, that is, to become routinized and "contaminated" by the very practices it was supposed to overcome. As trade union officials inflated the number of Stakhanovites, Stakhanovite status became devalued; in many enterprises, even occasional overfulfillment of output norms was sufficient for a worker to be considered a Stakhanovite. Stakhanovite periods (*polosi*) inevitably turned into storming sessions and were just as inevitably followed by slumps in activity. Factory directors discovered that they could use Stakhanovites as expediters while at the same time avoiding the general application of Stakhanovite methods.

The failure of Stakhanovism to significantly curtail managerial indiscipline was one of the factors that led to the undoing of many managers during the Great Purge of 1937–38. However, the weight of state repression now fell most heavily on enterprise directors and higher personnel rather than low-level cadres. True, in the context of heightened class vigilance, the class alien backgrounds of some foremen and their past slights against individual workers were sufficient to evoke accusations of wrecking. But, at least in published reports of *aktiv* meetings, foremen were more often among the accusers than the accused.[71]

The Great Purge proved to be a boon to many foremen who became the prime candidates to replace their bosses further up the industrial hierarchy. For those who remained or became foremen, the purge had another and less appealing consequence, namely, the disorganization of production and a serious decline in labor discipline. References to the paralysis of industrial cadres and the fact that "backward" and "unconscious" elements among the workers were taking advantage of it appeared throughout 1937.[72] Aggregate figures on absenteeism provide only a dim reflection of the problem, no doubt because managers were reluctant to record workers as absent. Still, the recorded rate in 1937 was higher than for any year since 1932.[73] The situation seems to have been particularly serious in the mining industry, where directors insisted that if they dismissed workers for lateness and unexcused absences, workers would find employment at neighboring mines. It was an old excuse but probably a valid one. As if the clock had turned back to the early part of the decade, the old scheme of *samozakreplenie* was dusted off, now by the newly appointed commissar of heavy industry, L. M. Kaganovich.[74]

Even when workers were on the job, they were not necessarily at work. If, as was claimed in 1939, Krivoi Rog iron ore miners had become accustomed to working three or four hours per day and no more, then we should not be surprised that figures for the first half of 1938 show them spending only half of their nominal work time productively.[75] Elsewhere, the situation was only marginally better. In the rolling mills of the nation's steel industry, downtime accounted for 23 percent of work time in the last six months of 1937.[76] With war clouds gathering over Europe, the laggardly pace of production in Soviet industry was even more alarming than it otherwise would have been.

This, then, was the context in which the state redoubled its effort to establish strict labor discipline. The best known features of this effort were the decrees of December 1938, which introduced work books and extended the provisions of the 1932 law, and the criminalization of labor truancy via the decree of June 26, 1940. Another that has received comparatively little attention was the campaign to transform the foreman into the "central figure of production."[77] This campaign was initiated in January 1939 by the publication in *Pravda* of a series of letters from foremen complaining about their lack of authority on the shop floor. "In our shop, the foremen are regarded merely as elder comrades," wrote one. "Of course, it is known that they can go to the shop supervisor and demand that someone be fired. . . . But, it is also known that they themselves cannot decide this."[78] Other letters detailed the excessive amount of time foremen spent on paperwork and fetching tools and spare parts, and their low salaries relative to Stakhanovites' wages. In earlier years the fact that many foremen were earning less than some of the workers they supervised occasionally received critical comment in the press.[79] Now it was claimed that this anomaly was hampering the recruitment of foremen among Stakhanovites.

Some of these complaints eventually were met in a joint Sovnarkom–Central Committee resolution issued in May 1940. The resolution, "On Promoting the Role of Foremen," applied only to factories in heavy-machine construction, though it probably was intended to serve as a model for other industries as well. The most significant aspect of the resolution is that it essentially repeated, with slightly greater specificity, the provisions of the model statutes drawn up six years earlier. Just as in 1934, foremen were now given authority to hire and fire workers subject to confirmation by shop supervisors and to assign skill categories to, penalize, and reward workers as they saw fit.[80]

The resolution thus bore approximately the same relation to the repressive laws of December 1938 (and the soon-to-be-decreed edict of June 1940) as the model statutes did with respect to the legislation of November 15, 1932. Both were attempts to extricate the regime from a vicious cycle of its own making. As Donald Filtzer has perceptively noted, "where the policies of the regime threatened to disrupt the functioning of the economy, the rule was either to ignore the law or, if that was impossible, get around it as best one could."[81] The statutes and the 1940 resolution in effect acknowledged that foremen could do just that without too much risk of punishment. In short, by decade's end, foremen were as they had once been—masters of the shop floor.

The second and most egregiously Stalinesque edition of the *Bol'shaia Sovetskaia Entsiklopediia* distinguished foremen in socialist enterprises from their counterparts under capitalism. In the former, the foreman was said to be "the direct organizer of the productive process"; in the latter, "the steward of the proprietor."[82] The distinction obscures as much as it reveals. As Daniel Nelson, David Montgomery, and other American labor historians have pointed out, foremen were powers in their own right in turn-of-the-century factories; workers' hatred of them was at least as much a function of their arbitrariness as it was of their "stewardship" of capital's interests.[83] Indeed, it was their lack of control over foremen that convinced many employers to experiment with scientific management or at least to systematize some aspects of their operations. These thrusts were often parried in the same way that Soviet foremen warded off the impact of NOT. But inexorably, foremen were losing their discretionary power to personnel departments, quality-control inspectors, and feed-and-speed men on one hand and to the maze of seniority and trade union rules enforced by shop stewards, on the other. By midcentury, foremen in the industrialized West were routinely being referred to as the "stepchildren of industry" and "marginal" and "forgotten" men.[84]

Soviet foremen, at least up to the Great Patriotic War, retained most of the power they had had at the outset of industrialization. There are three principal reasons why this was so.

First, the thinning of the ranks of skilled, experienced workers via promotion or mobilization for collectivization and the suppression of traditional mechanisms for adaptation to an industrial environment (e.g., the artel) ensured foremen of a major role in training and otherwise breaking in the mass of new workers. That the regime increasingly opted for on-the-job training—itself a response to the critical shortage of skilled workers—enhanced foremen's position in this respect.

Second, the resistance of enterprise management and workers to external intervention in the setting of output norms left foremen much room for adjusting and evading these procedures to suit the highly fluid circumstances of the shop floor. The absence of effective trade union representation, institutionalized seniority rules, or shop steward advocacy obviously contributed to foremen's ability to juggle workers, playing off some against others and distributing bonuses as favors. This is not to suggest, however, that foremen were dictators who could operate according to whim. What was lacking in terms of formal countervailing forces was to some extent compensated by the prevailing shortage of labor, the survival of informal bonds among workers (about which we need to know a great deal more), and the ever-present possibility of worker resentment being unleashed against bosses in general. This possibility became a reality during the years 1936–38.

Third, foremen retained their power at least to some degree because for both practical and ideological purposes—the two are not easily disentangled—it suited the regime for them to have it. Foremen had several qualities that appealed to the political leadership. They came from the right class. True, many perpetuated the traditions of *masterovshchina*—the extraction of favors, alcoholism, and rudeness. But such forms of behavior were well on their way to becoming endemic to Soviet (male) culture, and in any case could be excused as part of the rough and tumble of shop-floor life.

Obviously, these factors did not weigh equally throughout Soviet industry. Foremen's power varied from one branch of industry to another
depending on the skill, gender, nationality, and age of the work force and
of foremen themselves, as well as differences in technology. Establishing
these correlations for different industries should be high on the agenda of
future research.

But in the final analysis, it was what foremen were not as much as what
they were that secured their position within the industrial hierarchy. They
were not, nor did they have pretentions to be, "bigwigs"; their realm was
contained by the shop floor and their mastery over it did not constitute a
political threat. The coalitions they entered into with workers were of a
purely negative kind and could not be translated into opposition to the
factory regime itself.

All of this may help to explain the extraordinary toast that Stalin made in
October 1937, that is, in the midst of the Great Purges. Addressing a
gathering of factory directors, engineers, foremen, and Stakhanovites
from the metallurgical industry, the old *praktik* characterized the tens of
thousands of "small and middle-level leaders" as "modest people" who "do
not thrust themselves forward" and "are hardly noticed." "But," he went
on, "it would be blindness not to notice them, since on these people
depends the future of production in our entire economy . . . and the fate of
our economic leadership."[85] Indeed it would.

NOTES

An earlier version of this essay appeared in *Stalinism: Its Nature and Aftermath,* ed.
Nick Lampert and Gabor T. Rittersporn (London: Macmillan, 1992; Armonk,
N.Y.: M. E. Sharpe, 1992).

1. *Trud,* December 13, 1928, p. 2.

2. See, for example, *Fabzavkom* (supplement to *Trud*), 1924, no. 2, p. 2; 1924,
nos. 4–5, p. 11; *Trud,* July 15, 1927, p. 3; August 7, 1927, p. 6; March 8, 1928, p. 3;
April 27, 1928, p. 3; April 28, 1927, p. 3; May 11, 1928, p. 3; June 21, 1928, p. 3;
June 29, 1928, p. 6; July 13, 1928, p. 5.

3. *Trud,* September 16, 1927, p. 5; May 10, 1928, p. 3; *Voprosy truda* (hereafter
VT), 1929, no. 1, p. 21.

4. *Trud,* July 15, 1927, p. 3.

5. *Trud,* December 28, 1928, p. 3.

6. *Trud,* July 29, 1927, p. 4.

7. *Trud,* August 7, 1927, p. 6.

8. See respectively Karl Marx, *Capital,* vol. 1 (New York, 1967), p. 424, and
Joseph Melling, " 'Non-Commissioned Officers': British Employers and Their Supervisory Workers, 1880–1920," *Social History* 5, 1980, no. 2, p. 193.

9. John Foster, *Class Struggle and the Industrial Revolution* (London, 1974), p.
227.

10. Reinhard Bendix, *Work and Authority in Industry* (New York, 1963), pp.
206–11; Charles Maier, "Between Taylorism and Technocracy: European Ideolo-

gies and the Vision of Industrial Productivity in the 1920s," *Journal of Contemporary History* 5, 1970, no. 2, pp. 27–61.

11. Michael Burawoy, *The Politics of Production* (London, 1985).

12. Sven Grabe and Paul Silberer, *Selection and Training of Foremen in Europe* (Paris, n.d.), p. 4 refers to a Dutch report listing more than 100 titles given to people performing foremen's functions, whereas in the United Kingdom, the title "foreman" was used on four different levels in industry, from leading hands to superintendents. See National Institute of Industrial Psychology, *The Foreman: A Study of Supervision in British Industry* (London, 1951), pp. 86–98.

13. For foremen's role in prerevolutionary factory life, see inter alia, Reginald Zelnik (ed.), *A Radical Worker in Tsarist Russia: The Autobiography of Semen Ivanovich Kantachikov* (Stanford, 1986), pp. 18–19, 53, 55, 61, 63, 73–74, 88–89; P. Timofeev, "What the Factory Worker Lives By," in Victoria E. Bonnell (ed.), *The Russian Worker, Life and Labor under the Tsarist Regime* (Berkeley, 1983), pp. 85–90, 93–95, 98, 101–8; Rose Glickman, *Russian Factory Women: Workplace and Society, 1880–1914* (Berkeley, 1984), pp. 142–43, 211–12; and Stephen Smith, *Red Petrograd* (Cambridge, 1983), pp. 39–41, 64, 119, 136. The transition from the revolutionary upheaval of 1917–18 when foremen's powers were circumscribed by workers' control to the mid-1920s remains to be explored.

14. On the artel, see Hiroaki Kuromiya, "Workers' Artel and Soviet Production Relations," in Sheila Fitzpatrick Alexander Rabinowitch, and Richard Stites (eds.), *Russia in the Era of NEP: Explorations in Soviet Society and Culture* (Bloomington, 1991), pp. 72–88.

15. A member of the collegium of NKTrud RSFSR counted twenty-three channels through which labor disputes could be handled. See *Trud*, January 14, 1928, p. 2.

16. Samuel Lieberstein, "Technology, Work and Sociology in the USSR: The NOT Movement," *Technology and Culture* 16, 1975, no. 1, p. 49.

17. A. K. Gastev, *Trudovye ustanovki* (Moscow, 1973), pp. 308–9; *Trud*, March 4, 1924, p. 2.

18. *Trud*, February 29, 1924, p. 2; March 6, 1924, p. 2; March 30, 1924, p. 3.

19. *Trud*, April 19, 1928, p. 2. See also *Organizatsiia truda*, 1933, no. 6, pp. 3–4.

20. This was a modest claim, for, according to the commissar of labor, 750,000 workers had been so trained by 1932. See Sheila Fitzpatrick, *Education and Social Mobility in the Soviet Union, 1921–1934* (Cambridge, 1979), p. 200.

21. See, for example, *VT*, 1933, no. 6, pp. 34–36; *Voprosy profdvizheniia* (hereafter *VP*), 1933, no. 11, pp. 57–58.

22. Lewis H. Siegelbaum, *Stakhanovism and the Politics of Productivity in the USSR, 1935–41* (Cambridge, 1988), pp. 58–63. Foremen, who continued to assign workers at each shift's *nariad*, remained oblivious to the issue, that is, until the advent of Stakhanovism, after which they had to pick up the pieces, so to speak. See also Hiroaki Kuromiya's essay in this volume, "The Commander and the Rank and File: Managing the Soviet Coal-Mining Industry, 1928–33."

23. Fitzpatrick, *Education and Social Mobility*, p. 226; Marcel Anstett, *La formation de la main oeuvre qualifée en Union Sovietique de 1917 à 1954* (Paris, 1958), pp. 106–14; *Industrializatsiia SSSR, 1933–1937 gg., Dokumenty i materialy* (Moscow, 1971), pp. 434–36.

24. David Granick, *The Management of the Industrial Firm in the USSR* (New York, 1954) p. 119; *Za promyshlennye kadry*, 1936, no. 2, pp. 7–8; John Scott, *Behind the Urals* (Bloomington, 1972), p. 174.

25. *Industrializatsiia severo-zapadnogo raiona v gody vtoroi i tret'ei piatiletok, 1933–1941 gg., Dokumenty i materialy* (Leningrad, 1969), p. 432; *Za Industrializatsiiu* (hereafter *ZI*), January 4, 1935, p. 4; and *VP*, 1934, no. 3, pp. 12–21, for public technical exams which served as a model for the state technical minimum scheme.

26. *Industrializatsiia SSSR, 1938–1941 gg., Dokumenty i materialy* (Moscow, 1973), p. 263.

27. The proportion of foremen to workers was 2.2 percent, ranging from 1.8 percent in machine construction to 4.0 percent in coal mining. See A. Khavin, "O mastere," *ZI*, January 11, 1935, p. 3.

28. *Sbornik vazhneishikh zakonov i postanovlenii o trude* (Moscow, 1958), p. 123.

29. *Sovet pri narodnom komissare tiazheloi promyshlennosti SSSR, Pervyi plenum, 10–12 maia 1935 g.* (Moscow-Leningrad, 1935), p. 252.

30. *Industrializatsiia SSSR, 1938–41*, p. 281.

31. *ZI*, January 11, 1935, p. 3.

32. Ibid; *Professional'naia perepis', 1932–1933 g.* (Moscow, 1934), p. 17.

33. *VT*, 1933, no. 1, p. 60.

34. *VP*, 1934, no. 12, p. 66; *Professional'naia perepis'*, p. 17.

35. M. Iazvin, "Kursy masterov sotsialisticheskogo truda," *Stakhanovets*, 1939, no. 8, p. 28, and *Industrializatsiia SSSR, 1933–37*, pp. 503–4.

36. *Industrializatsiia SSSR, 1938–41*, p. 274.

37. Siegelbaum, *Stakhanovism and the Politics of Productivity*, pp. 174, 176.

38. The proportion of praktiki among each was respectively 60.6 percent, 58 percent, and 76.5 percent. See *Industrializatsiia SSSR, 1938–41*, p. 276. In the Ruhr already before 1914, "a position as Steiger or Meister represented the ultimate achievement, not the beginning, of a career." E. G. Spencer, "Between Capital and Labor: Supervisory Personnel in Ruhr Heavy Industry before 1914," *Journal of Social History* 9 (1975), p. 181. For career patterns of foremen in other European countries, see Grabe and Silberer, *Selection and Training of Foremen in Europe*, pp. 42–51, and in the United States, Edward S. Cowdrick, "Foreman Training in American Industry," *International Labour Review* 27, 1933, no. 2, pp. 207–19; and Nelson Lichtenstein, "'The Man in the Middle': A Social History of Automobile Industry Foremen," in Nelson Lichtenstein and Stephen Meyer (eds.), *On the Line: Essays in the History of Auto Work* (Urbana and Chicago, 1989), pp. 153–89.

39. See Lewis H. Siegelbaum, "Soviet Norm Determination in Theory and Practice, 1917–1941," *Soviet Studies* 36, 1984, no. 1, pp. 49–50.

40. *Trud*, July 15, 1927, p. 3; April 27, 1928, p. 3; *VT*, 1932, no. 10, pp. 14–16.

41. *Trud*, July 15, 1927, p. 3; January 11, 1929, p. 5; *VT*, 1929, no. 12, p. 63; *VT*, 1931, nos. 3–4, p. 32; *VT*, 1933, no. 6, pp. 73–74; see also *VP*, 1933, no. 11, p. 23, for the injunction that "the foreman and the norm setter must not represent themselves as polar opposites."

42. *Trud*, March 6, 1928, p. 1.

43. P. B. Zilbergleit, *Proizvoditel'nost' truda v kamennougol'noi promyshlennosti* (Kharkov, 1930), pp. 33, 39; *Trud*, March 16, 1928, p. 4. See *Trud*, January 8, 1929, p. 2, wherein it was reported that secret time study had provoked at least thirteen disturbances in 1928.

44. *Trud*, May 15, 1928, p. 1. O. A. Ermanskii, a labor physiologist and advocate of setting norms on the basis of optimal expenditures of energy, characterized Gastev's recommendation as typifying the "capitalist principle." Most trade unionists attending the conference at which these proposals were advanced were critical of both. See *Trud*, May 19, 1928, p. 5.

45. See *Trud*, January 6, 1928, p. 4. These assurances were given in response to a Kolomna factory worker who referred to the TNB as an "eyesore."

46. For evidence of such alliances, see David Shearer's essay in this volume.

47. Lewis H. Siegelbaum, "Production Collectives and Communes and the 'Imperatives' of Industrialization in the USSR, 1929–1931," *Slavic Review* 45, 1986, no. 1, p. 75. For the boast referred to, see the epigraph of the article.

48. *Trud*, April 27, 1928, p. 3. This was also the case among *desiatniki* in the coal-mining industry, according to *Udarnik*, 1932, no. 2, pp. 15–16.

49. Harvard Interview Project on the Soviet Social System, interview no. 99, pp. 8–9. See also no. 456, p. 10.

50. *VT*, 1931, nos. 3–4, p. 32; *VP*, 1934, no. 3, pp. 40–43.

51. *VP*, 1935, nos. 2–3, pp. 57–63; 1935, nos. 5–6, p. 47; Harvard Interview Project, no. 99, pp. 8–9.

52. *VP*, 1934, no. 3, pp. 35–45; 1934, no. 4, p. 47; 1934, no. 10, pp. 59–64; Harvard Interview Project, no. 1106, p. 13.

53. For directors' defense of flexibility, see *Soveschchanie khoziaistvennikov, inzhenerov, tekhnikov, partiinykh i profsoiuznikh rabotnikov tiazheloi promyshlennosti, 20–22 sentiabria 1934 g.* (Moscow, 1935), pp. 223–26.

54. For one such directive to the coal-mining industry, see *Industrializatsiia SSSR, 1933–37*, pp. 245–46. According to the head of the Commissariat of Heavy Industry's Labor Department, the number of norm setters had declined by one-and-a-half times in 1933–34 because directors "misunderstood" the directive. See *Soveshchanie khoziaistvennikov*, p. 227.

55. I. V. Stalin, *Sochineniia*, ed. R. McNeal (Stanford, 1967), vol. 1 [14], pp. 56–64.

56. *Sovet pri narodnom komissare*, pp. 172–74.

57. Siegelbaum, *Stakhanovism and the Politics of Productivity*, pp. 164–68.

58. See V. Andrle, "How Backward Workers Became Soviet: Industrialization of Labour and the Politics of Efficiency under the Second Five-Year Plan, 1933–37," *Social History* 10, 1985, no. 2, pp. 147–69. It is important to stress that "labor discipline" was a discursive category the dimensions of which shifted over time. Hence, what might have been considered initiative could suddenly become an instance of indiscipline, or vice versa.

59. For an excellent treatment of this legislation, see Donald Filtzer, *Soviet Workers and Stalinist Industrialization* (Armonk, 1986), pp. 107–15, 233–53.

60. Filtzer is right to emphasize these circumstances as enabling workers to maintain control of the labor process, even if he exaggerates the degree of control by, among other things, ignoring the role of foremen.

61. *VP*, 1933, no. 4, pp. 45–46.

62. *Trud*, February 10, 1933, p. 3; February 12, 1933, p. 3; *VP*, 1933, no. 5, pp. 45–47; *VT*, 1933, no. 4, pp. 61–64; *VP*, 1933, no. 7, p. 75.

63. For the distinction between formal organization governed by "logic" and informal organization based on "feeling and sentiment," see the seminal article by Fritz J. Roethlisberger, "The Foreman: Master and Victim of Double Talk," *Harvard Business Review* 23, 1945, no. 3, pp. 290–92.

64. *VP*, 1933, no. 3, pp. 31–33; 1933, no. 13, p. 60; and for quote, 1934, no. 7, p. 50.

65. *VP*, 1934, no. 7, p. 50

66. *Trud*, May 22, 1933, p. 1; see also *VP*, 1933, no. 7, pp. 3–11.

67. *VP*, 1933, no. 11, p. 76; 1934, no. 7, pp. 50–51.

68. *VT*, 1933, no. 5, p. 67; *VP*, 1933, no. 11, p. 76; TsUNKhU Gosplana SSSR, *Zarabotnaia plata inzhenerno-tekhnicheskikh rabotnikov, sluzhashchikh i uchenikov v sentiabre-oktiabre 1934 g.* (Moscow, 1936), pp. 6–51.

69. *Soveshchanie khoziaistvennikov*, pp. 343–70.

70. *Sovetskaia zakonnost'*, 1936, no. 3, p. 7; *Sovetskaia iustitsiia*, 1936, no. 8, pp. 4–5.

71. *Pravda*, March 26, 1937, p. 3; *ZI*, April 4, 1937, p. 3; April 10, 1937, p. 2.

72. See *Pravda*, June 24, 1937; *ZI*, May 5, 1937, p. 2; *Stakhanovets*, 1937, no. 8, p. 20.

73. John Barber, "Labour Discipline in Soviet Industry, 1928–1941," paper presented to Twelfth AAASS Convention, Philadelphia, November 1980, table B.

74. *Pravda*, January 4, 1938, p. 2.

75. Filtzer, *Soviet Workers and Stalinist Industrialization*, p. 168; *Planovoe khoziaistvo*, 1938, no. 1, p. 63.

76. *Planovoe khoziaistvo,* 1938, no. 2, p. 63.

77. *Mashinostroenie,* November 2, 1938; *Pravda,* January 8, 1939, p. 2. See also P. A. Morozov, *Master, polnopravnyi rukovoditel' uchastka* (Moscow, 1949).

78. *Pravda,* January 6, 1939, p. 2.

79. See, for example, *ZI,* August 28, 1934, p. 3; October 4, 1936, p. 2.

80. The resolution is in *Industrializatsiia SSSR, 1938–41,* pp. 121–25.

81. Filtzer, *Soviet Workers and Stalinist Industrialization,* p. 246.

82. *BSE,* 2nd ed., XXVI (1954), p. 456.

83. Daniel Nelson, *Managers and Workers* (Madison, 1975), pp. 34–54; David Montgomery, *The Fall of the House of Labor* (Cambridge, 1987), pp. 115, 129–30, 204–5; William H. Lazonick, "Technological Change and the Control of Work: The Development of Capital-Labour Relations in United States Mass Production Industries," in Howard F. Gospel and Craig R. Littler (eds.), *Managerial Strategies and Industrial Relations* (London, 1983), pp. 125–29. It is interesting that whereas United States labor historians tend to stress foreman-worker antagonism around the turn of the century, their British counterparts stress mutual accommodation. For an example of the latter, see Craig Littler, *The Development of the Labor Process in Capitalist Societies* (London, 1982), pp. 86–87.

84. See Roethlisberger, "The Foreman: Master and Victim of Double Talk," p. 284; Thomas H. Patten, Jr., *The Foreman: Forgotten Man of Management* (New York, 1968); Loren Baritz, *The Servants of Power* (Middletown, Conn., 1960), pp. 182–84.

85. *Pravda,* October 31, 1937, p. 1.

IX

FACTORIES WITHIN FACTORIES

CHANGES IN THE STRUCTURE OF WORK AND MANAGEMENT IN SOVIET MACHINE-BUILDING FACTORIES, 1926–34

David Shearer

In the late 1920s the Soviet leadership launched a modernization drive that transformed the manufacturing base of the country's economy. Within a few years, scores of new industrial branches were created while hundreds of new factories were raised from the urban and rural landscapes. Some of these were the largest factories of their kind in the world. They employed thousands of workers each and were equipped with the latest in modern machinery. Old factories were reconstructed and expanded, often changed beyond recognition into new ones. Their old shops were razed or stripped and abandoned as production lines started up in new, often half-completed structures.

Reconstruction and expansion of the country's machine-building industries took first priority in the state's economic modernization program. Soviet leaders believed that creation of a modern industrial manufacturing base would be impossible without first developing an integrated system of machine-manufacturing industries. This was no easy task. Prior to the industrialization drive, Soviet machine-building capacity was limited, and the country relied heavily on foreign imports to supply major industrial producer needs. With some notable exceptions, most metalworking factories were relatively small and served regional markets. Even in the large state-run factories, work was unsystematic and was based largely on artisanal forms of labor and production organization.

In contrast, the state's reconstruction strategy was designed to lay the foundation of a modern, factory-based network of machine manufacture. The state's reconstruction strategy gave priority to the development of large-scale factories using integrated mass-production technologies. The success of this strategy depended on the introduction of strict product specialization, the creation of formalized managerial and work routines, and the application of systematic engineering techniques to control standardized production processes. This was a bold plan to create, nearly out of whole cloth, an indigenous, nationally integrated industrial manufacturing system.

Reconstruction did, indeed, bring about a dramatic transformation in the size, technological structure, and productive capacity of factories. The Soviets made remarkable progress toward the goal of creating a mass-production system of machine manufacture. At the same time, the factory system which emerged in the 1930s did not correspond to that which industrial planners envisioned. Suppressed market forces distorted administrative policies in ways that planners did not anticipate. In addition, traditional characteristics of production and social organization continued or reappeared in the factories to exert a powerful hold. These factors shaped industrial reconstruction in ways the state could neither overcome nor entirely control.

Ironically, reconstruction policies often accentuated what were perceived as backward forms of production and work organization, forms that modernization was supposed to eliminate.[1] Differentiated patterns of technological reconstruction and rapid expansion in factory size, for example, exacerbated problems of production integration between shops. As systematic managerial and engineering techniques began to break down, production control devolved into the hands of increasingly powerful shop administrators and production foremen. As a result, prerevolutionary practices of shop contracting reappeared in the guise of socialist shop competitions. At the same time, machine shops within large works fell increasingly under the control of competing industrial administrative organizations, the *ob"edineniia*. This process exacerbated problems of factory integration despite the legal status of factories as financially autonomous, economically integrated production organizations.

State strategy notwithstanding, what emerged in most factories during the early 1930s was a curious blend of modern technologies and traditional work methods. This was a factory system which German observers characterized as a *grosser Kleinbetrieb*, a "gigantic small shop." "Kleinbetrieb" referred not so much to factory size as to the traditional managerial techniques which were used to run small firms or artisanal workshops. The difference was that these techniques were still being used to operate huge production works equipped with new and complex manufacturing technologies. Rather than an integrated system of specialized production shops, what evolved in most works did not resemble a factory so much as a vast production city, a conglomeration of semi-autonomous shops, a patchwork of factories within factories.

Archive and industrial census records of the period reveal the dimensions of the changes which occurred in factories. These records reveal the intended and unintended consequences of administrative reforms, technological renewal, and reorganization of production. More important, these records reveal the extent to which industrial organization and the character of the state itself were shaped by the very social and economic relations which the state sought to remake.

This essay describes the organization of work and management which evolved in Soviet machine-building factories during the period of reconstruction. It emphasizes the mixed character of that factory system, a constantly evolving system which conflated various historical stages of development into a unique combination of modern and traditional, capitalist and socialist. This was a factory system that defies easy categorization, one that was neither entirely planned nor entirely self-generated. This essay examines the economic, social, and political factors which shaped the Soviet factory system during the crucial years of reconstruction in the late 1920s and early 1930s.

Industrial Reorganization and the Power of the Associations

Administrative reorganization in 1929 was designed to rationalize production and financial operations under conditions of rapid, large-scale industrialization. As specialization of factory production increased, industrial planners abandoned the principle of decentralized administration of factories by geographic proximity. Regional administration of factories by an umbrella trust organization had been the basis of industrial organization in the 1920s. With expansion of the industrial system in the late 1920s, industrialists adopted the administrative logic of centralized management by industrial branch. Factories producing similar types of products, regardless of where in the country they were located, were placed under the single administrative authority of an industrial production association. This association, or cartel, was called an *ob"edinenie*. Obedineniia were created for each branch of machine building: one each for turbine construction, machine-tool manufacture, automobile and tractor production, shipbuilding, etc.

Under the vigorous leadership of Sergo Ordzhonikidze, VSNKh, The Supreme Economic Council, closed regional trust offices. Unlike the old trust offices, which were located in regional urban or industrial centers, obedineniia offices were situated in Moscow.[2] Also unlike the trusts, production associations were invested with powers that had hitherto been dispersed among several middle-level bureaucracies. Associations concentrated in one authority the administrative functions of the old chief administrations, the *glavki*. Glavki had coordinated activities of the various regional trusts within a particular branch of manufacture. Associations were endowed with responsibility for the technical coordination and supply functions that had previously been vested in the old trusts, and they combined the financing and marketing functions of the short-lived industrial syndicates of the late 1920s. Throughout the 1920s, responsibility for commercial and financial activities and for production and planning functions of industry overlapped the administrative boundaries separating the syndicates, trust organizations, and glavki. Their elimination and the creation of the associations streamlined industrial administration, eliminating much of the competition that had previously characterized relations between middle-level bureaucracies during the latter 1920s.[3]

The obedineniia served their function but in so doing created new sets of problems. VSNKh established the cartels as subordinate administrative organs to carry out the economic tasks established by VSNKh and other state planning agencies. Rights and responsibilities of the associations were supposed to be carefully delineated within a series of administrative regulations. But because of the authority and responsibilities vested in them, the obedineniia became powerful institutional entrepreneurs in their own right. Hidden market forces fostered entrepreneurial and administrative competition among associations that defied the ability of state inspectorate and planning organs to regulate. Moreover, competition among associations set up an entrepreneurial dynamic that led the associations to usurp factory administrative authority and to interfere directly in the affairs of factory production and labor organization.

Even though factories were subordinate administratively to their associations, the former were supposed to have a wide scope of independence in controlling production. Indeed, administrative reorganization in 1929–30 was intended to strengthen the factory's autonomy in relation to higher administrative organs such as production trusts and associations. According to the December 5, 1929, decree of the party's Central Committee, the factory constituted the "fundamental link" in the management chain of industry. Its director was to have "a necessary degree of independence" in the technical outfitting of the factory, in the organization of supplies and labor, in the hiring of qualified engineering and administrative personnel, and "generally, in the creation of the most optimal conditions of . . . production."[4] The decree did not spell out the legal regulations on which the factory director's authority was to be founded. But the factory was supposed to operate on the basis of full-cost accountability, *khoziaistvennyi raschet*, which underscored its implied control over production management and circulating capital.[5]

The December 5 decree, never officially superseded, was frequently cited as the legal basis for the autonomy of the factory as the fundamental production and industrial administrative unit. Yet between 1930 and additional reforms in 1932, administrative authority grew more confused rather than clearer. Even the December 5 decree reflected ambiguity in the factory-association relationship. That document defined factories as financially autonomous, financially accountable organizations. But according to that same decree, the association owned all capital, both fixed and working, of the factories.[6] Likewise, associations possessed the authority to plan production and to set quotas for each factory and for the branch as a whole. Trusts also organized all supplies and sales of their factories.[7]

Although the principle of factory autonomy was never repudiated, decrees and laws subsequent to the December 5 ruling increasingly concentrated authority in the hands of association management. A Central Committee decree of December 1931, for example, further defined the economic relationship between factory and obedinenie in a way that clearly favored the latter's authority over the former. Although the factory was supposed to operate on a cost-accountability basis, the enterprise had no profit-and-loss account of its own. Success of the factory was assessed on the basis of the difference between planned and actual costs. In the final analysis, however, the association determined these costs.[8] The associations retained the authority to hire and fire the chief engineering and managerial staff, and although the director's position was subject to nomination and approval by the regional party organization, the association was included in the review process of the nominee. The association controlled the right of audit, for which the factory paid, and by an October 1930 decree of the Council of National Economy, associations came to control up to 80 percent of the supply functions and inventories of the factory, even supplies and inventories at the shop level.[9]

Though never stipulated, in many instances associations came to control the hiring and distribution of personnel, even in the lower echelons of factory administration. At times they also usurped the authority to decide questions of technical reconstruction and to interfere directly in matters of labor and production organization within the shops.[10] Thus despite the legal autonomy of factories as economically and technologically integrated production organizations, production shops within large works fell increasingly under the control of different and competing industrial administrative associations. Competition among associations and their attempts to maintain financial and production discipline in factories and shops under their jurisdiction set up an administrative relationship that often worked against the goals of greater factory specialization and autonomy.

Records of the machine-tool cartel Soiuzstankoinstrument, or SSI, reveal that interference of the associaton in day-to-day factory operations evolved gradually, in an unplanned fashion.[11] Association interference evolved in large part in response to the increasing number and severity of production breakdowns in the association's factories. When a breakdown occurred and persisted for more than a few days, the SSI leadership convened an extraordinary commission of inquiry. Engineering and managerial personnel from the association composed the commission. This group was dispatched to the factory to determine the causes of the breakdown and to make recommendations for reestablishing production.

During the period of inquiry, the line between investigation and management became fuzzy. More often than not the commission would stay on at the factory from two weeks to two or three months, until production lines were again operating on a regular basis. Association departments took over the work and functions of corresponding factory departments. They drew up supply and labor needs based on the recommendations of the commission of inquiry. They also had the authority to allocate extraordinary funds. Normally the commission worked with factory management and engineering staff, but the commission had complete power to reorganize labor, mobilize technical staff, reroute supplies, and alter inventories. The commission also possessed the authority to remove and reorganize machinery and production processes. Often association departments bypassed the production and planning departments of the factory administration, working directly with shop heads. As the frequency and severity of production stoppages increased, the work of these special commissions became institutionalized as a semi-permanent system of crisis management.

In some instances, commissions went so far as to establish quarterly and yearly production quotes. In October 1930, for example, a serious production breakdown at the Krasnyi Proletarii works led the SSI to undertake an assessment of production resources at the factory. An extraordinary commission from the trust's production planning and labor organization departments developed measures for the factory to fulfill the production program for the final quarter of 1929 and worked up a plan for the whole of the 1930 production year. A group from the technical department and from the rationalization sector of the association supervised reorganization of some of the basic and auxiliary production processes at the factory to ensure fulfillment of the plan worked out by the planning commission.[12]

Frequent decrees from higher economic organs, usually VSNKh, delineating new forms of economic and work organization often forced associations to encroach on factory administrative prerogatives. Decrees required factories to provide detailed reports on the state of preparation and implementation of new methods of work organization, such as the seven-hour day, the continuous work week, the campaign to mobilize factory resources, and the attempt to introduce the four-brigade system of work organization. Decrees were typically sent to the obedinenie, which in turn was responsible for ensuring compliance by the factories. Assessing production capabilities was often beyond the capability of the factory staff, and reports on preparation and implementation were often required in "the shortest possible time" (do srochno). Thus in each instance mentioned above, departments of the machine-tool association Soiuzstankoinstrument had to be mobilized and sent to the factories to carry out the accounting and production surveys required by VSNKh authorities. Indeed, between 1930 and 1932 the association was forced to conduct major production surveys and forecasts of its factories almost every quarter.[13] Since the surveys were often associated with reorganization of production in a factory, association departments were actively drawn into detailed management of factory operations.

To ensure their own economic accountability, associations audited factory accounts, sequestered factory funds, and performed other supervisory activities that interfered directly in factory administration. This kind of interference occurred with some frequency in relations between Soiuzstankoinstrument and its factories, especially in relations with poorly administered factories. By mid-1931, for example, the commercial accounting and production planning departments of the SSI had taken over the work of the corresponding departments in the Sverdlov machine-building plant on a near-permanent basis. At times even a well-organized plant like the Krasnyi Proletarii found itself in arrears to the SSI and overwhelmed by accounting tasks. As a result, in the last quarter of 1929 the association moved to sequester and audit the factory's commercial and production account books. Although the factory director protested, the SSI placed its own commission in charge of the factory's commercial accounting department for three months until back payments had been secured.[14] To generate the capital for back payments, however, the commercial department of the SSI was charged to "do everything possible" to speed up the rate of capital turnover for the final quarter of the year.[15] In turn, this charge required the commercial department to monitor closely the time between production output and sale. To shorten the time between finishing and sale of machinery, the commercial department coordinated its activities with the production planning department of the association to intervene in the final stages of production assembly in the factory. Thus the necessity to maintain its own financial accountability led the association step by step to intervene in the daily commercial and production activities of the Krasnyi Proletarii, prerogatives that were supposed to belong to the factory administration.

Numerous other examples exist of association intervention in factory and production operation. In late January 1930, for example, a commission from the SSI accounting department was sent to the Krasnyi Proletarii to investigate a growing discrepancy between the growth in wages and labor productivity. The commission found that the discrepancy reflected a lack of systematic technical and work norming and a lack of control over forms of wage payments. Acting on the commission's recommendation, the appropriate association departments sent representative groups to reorganize the structure of wage dispersal and technical norming in the factory. The latter especially led to "significant" changes in the work organization of the main machine shops. In addition, the labor and economics department of the SSI was advised to survey the factory work force. It was authorized to reorganize work groups; release superfluous workers, especially clerical staff; establish hiring quotas in individual shops; and "create a general methodology of work distribution in both production and auxiliary areas of the factory."[16] The leaders of the SSI struggled hard to maintain financial discipline in their factories. In so doing, the association often bypassed factory administration, becoming increasingly and directly involved in the actual operation and organization of factory production.

Competition among associations, combined with their increasing intervention in shop management, aggrevated problems of production integration and factory cohesion. Indeed, competition among associations helped to maintain the administratively unwieldy and costly system of universal production in factories. Despite official policy to specialize, most machine-building factories continued to manufacture a range of products.[17] Resistance to specialization was especially strong in the two crucial auxiliary activities of metal supply and machine tooling and instrumentation. As of 1932, for example, nearly 37 percent of Soviet machine-building plants continued to maintain their own smelting capabilities. Machine-building factories accounted for 25 percent of all Martin furnace production in the country, and they supplied about 17 percent of their own metal needs.[18] This practice continued despite the state's massive construction efforts in the metallurgical industry and despite stated policy to separate metalwork from metal supply.[19]

Similarly, many machine-building works continued to maintain their own tool- and instrument-making shops. Only 42 percent of Soviet machine-tool needs were satisfied by domestic production in 1930–31 and only 20–21 percent of those machine tools came off production lines of factories within the state machine-tool consortium Soiuzstankoinstrument.[20] Nearly half the domestic production of machine tools in 1931–32 came from factories not under SSI control. A significant proportion of these were made by machine-building factories for their own needs. Indeed, all of the new auto and tractor factories of the period were constructed to supply their own machine tools.[21] Although the SSI was supposed to administer all domestic production and supply of machine tools, other machine-building factories and associations threatened SSI control of that branch.[22]

To standardize production of machine tools along lines dictated by the Soiuzstankoinstrument, the head of the cartel, E. Alperovich, sought successfully to extend SSI control of design and production planning of machine-tool types in factories under the jurisdiction of other obedineniia.[23] Such crossing of association lines was a common practice during the early 1930s. At times, administrative overlap approached the level of bureaucratic comedy. All the major older factories that remained unspecialized suffered under divided administrative authority. These factories included some of the largest machine-building plants in the country: the Krasnoe Sormovo works, the Krasnyi Profintern in Briansk, the Kramatorsk works in southern Russia, and the Krasnyi Putilovets in Leningrad. By 1934 the Krasnyi Putilovets labored under the administrative authority of four specialized production conglomerates: the turbine-building association, Turboostroenie; the auto-tractor conglomerate, Gutap; the obedinenie for specialized machine building, Spetsmashino-stroenie; and the metallurgical production association, Gump.

For factories under the jurisdiction of several associations such a situation could make for chaos. Factory production meetings were attended by inspectors from as many associations as had jurisdiction in the factory. According to the director of the Krasnyi Putilovets, T. Ots, there existed little or no cooperation among these obedineniia. Each year the factory received the various drafts of four separate and often incompatible production plans from each of the associations with jurisdiction over some aspect of production in the works. Each association aimed to use the Krasnyi Putilovets to further its own interests against those of the other associations. Ots complained in particular that the associations used the various shops under their production planning control to compensate for back orders in other factories or to fill "on-the-side" and small-batch orders unrelated to the production profile of the Krasnyi Putilovets.[24]

The Krasnyi Putilovets was an extreme case. Not all factories labored within such a labyrinth of administrative confusion. The Krasnyi Proletarii works in Moscow, for example, fared better because it was specialized for machine-tool production. The Krasnyi Proletarii came under the nearly exclusive jurisdiction of the SSI association. Still, the plant continued to manufacture diesel engines as well as machine tools. It was therefore subject to periodic inspection by the Commissariat of Transport. The NKPS inspector attended factory production meetings periodically. When serious complaints or conflicts arose, usually over low quality or late delivery, he sat in on the meetings of the association board of directors. Exchanges could be rancorous and could often hinder the orderly business of the board.

The pursuit of association interests across administrative boundaries exacerbated structural tensions that threatened the organizational and administrative integrity of the factory. Many major industrial writers referred to the problems which arose as a result of obedinenie competition. The story already related about the Krasnyi Putilovets was only one such story. Administrators in VSNKh expressed concern over the isolation of obedinenie from each other and their tendency to treat factories and shops as feudal fiefdoms.[25] Industrial writers complained bitterly about the "hoarding" of experience resulting from mutual hostility, arguing that the cost in duplicated and wasteful effort was nearly incalculable. One author claimed to have found numerous instances in which practical experience in one shop was withheld from workers and engineers in another shop within the same factory merely because the two shops worked under the authority of different associations.[26] The writer condemned such practice, arguing that it should be treated as a criminal offense. VSNKh and other state economic and judicial organs intervened often to regulate conflict between obedineniia. But despite such intervention, market and administrative competition between associations created an entrepreneurial dynamic that could actively hinder factory production integration and specialization.

Reconstruction and Changes
in Production Organization

Rapid expansion in factory size and the scale of change overall in industry during the period of reconstruction aggravated problems of factory integration. Between 1929 and 1932 nearly two-thirds (62 percent) of existing machine-building factories underwent major reconstruction, that is, 50 percent or more of their machine stocks were replaced. By 1933 less than one-quarter of domestic machine production was carried out in what were designated as unreconstructed works.[27] Reconstruction meant expansion as well as replacement of equipment, and during the First Five-Year Plan the amount of capital stock in individual machine-building works increased anywhere from 150 to 400 percent.[28] Overall in the machine-manufacturing industries, the number of machine stocks doubled, while the total amount of capital stock nearly tripled during the First Five-Year Plan.[29] The average number of machine production shops in machine building plants also tripled during the first five-year plan period, as did the numbers of production and clerical workers in factories. By the end of the period, some factories had fifty to sixty major machine production shops, with attendant auxiliary shops for each.[30] The production and organizational structure of the factories in the early 1930s expanded and changed so rapidly from year to year, and even from month to month, that "more than a few" directors never knew at any one time the number of shops or the names of shop heads in their works. Nor did they know the full range of their factory's production profile.[31] Personnel turnover during this period was also high, and that only added to the confusion caused by rapid reconstruction.

The rapidity and scale of change bewildered many managers. But the increase in size of factories and the rapidity of change did not account for all of the problems associated with industrial reconstruction. Because of the expansion of production capacity, many factories reorganized to specialize and differentiate production processes. Ironically, however, the pattern of work specialization within factories exacerbated problems created by lack of overall specialization of the factory's product range. Although many older factories continued to manufacture a range of goods, reconstruction and reorganization increased the degree of differentiation and specialization of production shops and lines within the works. Previously, machine work had been organized in shops by the similarity of machine operations, regardless of product specialization. By 1932, however, most machines (70 percent) had been regrouped in specialized shops according to the differentiation of manufactured products.[32] In other words, factory managers separated machine work for production of one item from similar work done for another product made by the same factory. Such reorganization had progressed even during the 1920s. By the early 1930s it was as far advanced in older reconstructed factories as in the new highly specialized works.[33]

Reconstruction of the Krasnyi Proletarii works in Moscow was typical of this process. By the end of 1930, as it neared completion of its reconstruction program, the Krasnyi Proletarii works separated its complement of lathes into two separate machining shops, one for machine-tool metalworking and one for the working of parts for production of diesel engines. Originally, all lathe and milling work had been done in one "long shop" regardless of the nature of the work being done or its final destination in the production process. During reconstruction in 1929, the long shop was partially destroyed and reconverted into the machine shop for diesel construction. A new machine shop was constructed on the site of the old foundry, dismantled in 1926, which was then used for the machining of tools and parts for lathe building and other machine-tool construction. These shops had many of the same kinds of tools, and workers performed many of the same kinds of operations. But factory management administered the shops separately.[34]

A similar process of reconstruction and differentiation was carried out in other factories. At the Krasnyi Profintern works in Briansk, separate machine shops were created for areas of the factory concerned with locomotive production and for production of tractors and plows. The same was true of machine work at the Kolomenskaia works on the Moscow River. There, separate machine shops were organized for work on locomotives and for work on river barge and ship construction. Stamping and pressing equipment was also specialized by shop according to the type of product manufactured.

Specialization of machine work according to the type of product manufactured made sense as a means to rationalize production and lower costs.[35] But some critics worried about the consequences of this trend in factory reorganization because it threatened to enhance the administrative autonomy of the individual machine shop. Many managers argued that under conditions of rapid factory expansion, coupled with a consequent lack of strong central factory management, shop specialization and regrouping of machine work by product could undermine the factory as an integrated production organization. Some worried that such specialization would abet interference of the obedinenie in the production process directly at the shop level.[36] One engineer, speaking at a 1929 Moscow conference on industrial management, offered his view of what would happen if the trend continued in factory organization toward shop specialization. Comrade Livait, an engineer in the textile machine-building trust, contended that shop specialization was inimical to the development of mass-production culture. "Specialization should proceed according to the principle of technological work organization *(tekhnicheskaia obrabotka),"* he argued, "not by product."

> The latter type of specialization will only strengthen the shop. We could end up with a situation in which each shop has its own labor bureau, its own planning bureau, etc. This would encourage varying wage politics within a single factory and less production integration and order. We cannot allow different *kombinaty* to operate in a factory, each with its different politics for the same kind of production processes and the same kind of workers. This would only return us to the old artisan way.[37]

As it turned out, engineer Livait gave an uncannily accurate prediction of what in fact came to pass.

Industrial priorities during the First Five-Year Plan favored the concentration of manufacture in large-scale works organized for mass production, that is, for long production runs of standardized machine parts.[38] To make administration of these works manageable, expansion in the size and production capacity of any single factory was supposed to be offset by strict specialization of the product range manufactured in that plant. But although expansion was rapid, strict specialization did not follow. By 1933, 60 percent of all capital stock in the machine-building industry was concentrated in factories engaged in mass production either of finished or semi-finished products. Works organized for continuous flow mass production of single items, however, accounted for only 20.6 percent of capital stocks. By 1933 less than one-third (31.4 percent) of all machine stocks were concentrated in factories specialized for the mass production of one or two items.[39] On the other extreme, less than one-fifth (17 percent) of machine stocks were being used in factories or on lines engaged in small batch or single item production.[40] Between these extremes, over one-half (52 percent) of the machine stocks in machine-building factories were concentrated in works or in shops engaged in mass production but unspecialized in their product range, or in works engaged in long serial runs of a number of products.[41] In other words, a large proportion of works produced goods on a massive scale but without the techniques of specialization and work differentiation which made such production cost-effective and administratively manageable.

From Functionalism to Shop Administration

As factory size expanded and production became more specialized and complex, the functional departments of the central factory administration began to atrophy as active managerial organs. This was not always so, especially in highly specialized works which maintained strong production planning and preparation departments. So too in small or medium sized works with no more than several major production shops, works such as the Krasnyi Proletarii, planning and control departments remained an active part of production management. In large unspecialized factories, however, the central departments became increasingly alienated from the actual operation of production. Factories suffered from a lack of trained clerical staff and engineering personnel, and still more from a lack of attention to the establishment of systematic financial and production accounting methods. As a result, in "all but a very few" enterprises systematic financial accounting methods were never implemented.[42] In factories that maintained staffed accounting departments, outdated financial accounting practices proved inadequate to the task of managing the growing complexity of production. Lack of attention to the expansion and modernization of routing and dispatching systems contributed to the consequent breakdown in production coordination.[43] Labor, financial accounting, and production planning departments continued to keep statistical records, but these were little used for shop-floor operational management. These records were passed on to the several associations with jurisdiction over the factory or were sent to inspectorate organs and sections of the police.[44] Functional departments in the factory became more an adjunct of the state statistical apparatus and less a departmental system of production management.

By 1932 industrial leaders openly discussed a state of crisis, acknowledging that functional departments had lost commercial and production control over their factories.[45] Some authors feared the imminent demise of the factory as an integrated economic production organization.[46] V. Grossman, Presidium member of VSNKh and head of its sector on rationalization and industrial management, articulated the sense of crisis. In 1932 he wrote specifically about the machine-building industries that there existed "no systematic central factory administrative organization that could be called characteristic of the whole of the various industrial branches." According to Grossman, a VSNKh survey showed that inter- and intrashop planning was "different in nearly every factory." In "many" factories such planning "simply did not exist at all."[47] Grossman noted further that in the majority of factories "no central factory control existed over technological processes and equipment, or over labor and wage organization." In many plants second and third shifts worked with no responsible shift engineer. In general, control over production was left "almost entirely" to the shop administration, or worse yet, to no one at all.[48]

In theory, functional departments of the central factory administration were supposed to coordinate all aspects of production. Administered within the chief engineering section of factory management, these departments included the technical norm bureau, the department of rationalization, the labor economics department, the production preparation department and instrument shop, the factory technical laboratory, and the production control department. Each of these departments bore the responsibility to set factory policy in its area of expertise, and each was supposed to coordinate its work with every other department. When the factory received an order for a particular assembly the production preparation department was in charge of establishing the skill level required and the types of materials needed for working each piece of the assembly. The planning department was supposed to establish production quotas and deadlines for each shop as well as organize the flow of work and distribution of materials throughout the factory. Based on data gathered by its personnel, the technical norm bureau, or TNB, was supposed to determine the limits of use for each machine in the factory. Information such as maximum and minimum cutting speeds and types of work which could be done on any particular machine was to be posted on a "passport" card attached to that machine. The rationalization department sought ways to cut time and costs of production, and the labor department was supposed to determine wage scales and bonus percentages based on calculations made by the TNB.

Calculations made by the different departments were to be translated into specific production tasks through an elaborate system of work instruction cards. When the functional system worked properly, departments transmitted work cards to the various shop administrations which, in turn, transmitted instruction cards to production foremen and work brigade leaders on the shop floor. The latter were responsible for ensuring the fulfillment of production orders according to the exact instructions written on the cards. In contrast to the older line form of management, functionalism allowed foremen little or no discretionary authority over production and wage decisions. Under functionalism, the foreman's role was reduced to that of a mere executor of specific production orders sent down from the various functional departments.

The systematic character of functional management appealed to managers for both political and economic reasons. Before functional administration was introduced in the early 1920s, shop managers and foremen possessed a wide range of powers. Shop managers acted as semi-independent contractors, securing work for the shop from factory management. Shop administrators and foremen determined costs in their own shop, including wages, and foremen had the authority to hire, fire, and discipline workers as they saw fit. In turn, foremen earned the hatred of workers as the most immediately obvious representatives of an exploitative capitalist system. Functionalism promised to eliminate the arbitrary power and widely varying policies of shop administrations and individual foremen by placing production decisions in the hands of specialized experts working in the various managerial departments. According to proponents, such a system offered fair and uniform treatment of workers subject to the scrutiny of trade union and party inspectors.[49]

By bringing every aspect of production under systematic managerial control, functionalism also appealed to industrialists increasingly worried about production costs. They saw in functionalism the best way to bring order and financial discipline to the disparate economic and commercial activities of the factory. Thus Soviet managers adopted functionalism in the middle 1920s as a key part of the movement to rationalize industry. The introduction of functional forms of management in factories went hand in hand with the attempt to introduce systematic financial accounting methods, *khoziaistvennyi raschet,* into the whole of the industrial system.[50]

Finally, functionalism appealed to managers concerned about declining skill levels in the work force.[51] Optimistic proponents believed that the introduction of functional methods of management, coupled with the planned reequipment of factories using automated machinery, would greatly reduce the need for highly skilled workers in the production shops. Skilled craft workers would continue to play an important role in the tool and instrument shops and in production design bureaus. But advocates of new management argued that when fully implemented, functional specialization would disperse the various skills required to operate machinery among an array of set-up men, technical normers, and actual machine tenders. Functionalists believed that in most production shops, well-trained machine tenders would be needed who knew their tools and who could follow detailed technical instructions. Such workers would require training and experience but not nearly so much as universally skilled machinists who passed through traditional apprentice programs.[52] Functional forms of management promised to reduce the costs and time needed for training labor recruits, and by reducing the need for skilled workers at the bench, functional specialization of work promised to lower the costs of labor in production.[53]

Functional management was supposed to ensure systematic continuous production operation with a minimum of cost and a maximum of output. The problem with this vision of organization was that it never really worked. Even where functional departments were relatively well established, engineers and technical personnel never found effective managerial mechanisms to translate their calculations into practical work tasks on the shop floor. A dearth of experienced staff, coupled with antiquated routing and dispatching systems, accounted for much of the problem. As often as not, pieces arrived in the shops with no accompanying instructions about what to do with them. Conversely, shops received production orders for pieces with no instructions attached detailing machining specifications or types of metal to be used in making the piece. Foremen complained that when they did receive instructions, work orders were often contradictory, or they received incompatible instructions from different departments.[54] Even if they were technically qualified, and many were not, foremen were often enough unwilling to cooperate in implementing technical regulations established by the functional departments. The foreman's job was task oriented, and as a result, foremen were often forced to ignore regulations and work instructions from functional departments in order to meet their production quotas by specified deadlines. It was common for foremen to argue that if they tried to adhere to all the rules and regulations sent down from the departments they would never get anything accomplished.[55]

Foremen often found themselves in alliance with workers in resisting functional managers. Although little love was lost between workers and foremen, both groups found common ground in a shared resentment of technical norm personnel. Normers were notoriously rude and often unqualified for their tasks. Workers disliked the *normirovshchiki* because whenever they appeared in the shop with their stopwatches and clipboards, piece rates went down and production quotas went up. Foremen disliked normers because their presence in the shop represented the most blatant encroachment of management on traditional prerogatives of the foremen. Foremen often colluded with workers against normers by ignoring infractions of machine use and piece-rate regulations or by tacitly acquiescing in workers' attempts to deceive normers when they appeared in the shop to time work operations.[56]

The loss of systematic engineering and managerial control over production became a prominent theme in production meetings and engineering conferences throughout the early 1930s. At a public discussion in 1930, one engineer, O. Mirskii, described the detrimental effects of poorly established rate and norm work in production shops of the AMO automobile plant in Moscow. Describing a tour of one of the machine shops, Mirskii reported that he saw a large number of workers sitting or standing idly by while a number of machines also stood unused. He noted that workers "did not even start" when he approached with the shop head and a foreman. Mirskii remarked on this phenomenon and asked why the workers were not working. The shop *nachal'nik* replied that this resulted from the norming system. "They work according to the norm set by the TNB," he said. "They have reached their quota for this shift and have gone beyond. Now they have stopped working. That is all there is to it."[57] Interestingly, neither the foreman nor the shop head felt compelled to report to the TNB such a low output quota for that section of the shop.

The exasperation expressed by engineer Mirskii was typical. He complained that in the AMO automobile plant there existed no standardized control of machining speeds. Even when specifications existed, Mirskii declared, there was "no connection between cutting speeds specified in the technical norm bureau and those used in actual practice." Workers admitted that they often set machine speeds "by the pitch of the cutting sound."[58] Speeds were set and reset by workers each in their turn as numerous workers used the same machines. Mirskii as well as other engineers confirmed this practice. One engineer, a certain Vishniak, described his observation of the use of one machine on which tens of different machinists worked pieces within the space of one shift. Workers did not seem to have specified work stations, he reported, and worked on whatever machine was available, regardless of whether the task fit the specifications of the machine or not.[59] Vishniak reminded his colleagues that this practice not only detracted from efficient machine use and labor organization. He pointed out that such practices also wore out machines quickly.

As systematic managerial and engineering techniques broke down, control over work, labor, and wage organization devolved into the hands of increasingly powerful shop administrators and production foremen. By 1932, output quotas, technical norms, and discretionary forms of wage payments were routinely fixed by shop administrators and production foremen instead of by functional departments in the central factory administration.[60] In the Krasnyi Proletarii plant, for example, a new set of regulations issued in April 1931 strengthened the production and economic rights and responsibilities of the foreman "commensurate with his vital place in the production process."[61] The regulations gave foremen wide leeway in setting output quotas and technical norms for machinery and in allocating work tasks and determining the skill levels required to realize those tasks. Foremen were responsible "to ensure proper labor discipline and economic organization of work." They therefore were given the right to hire, fire, and discipline workers with the authority and consent of the shop administration. They were also given discretion over the distribution of bonus wages and "other forms of work encouragement."[62]

Factory management endorsed the new regulations, but according to the memoirs of one of the chief production engineers of the works, staff in the central factory departments resented the new rules.[63] Under functionalism, responsibility for establishing work regulations had fallen within the managerial jurisdiction of central factory departments: the technical norm bureau, the office of labor organization, and the wage rates and norms bureau. The new regulations severely curtailed the authority of the central departments, decentralizing responsibility to the individual shop level. Relations between shop administrations and central factory departments had always been problematic. The new set of regulations added to tensions between occupational groups.

Despite resentment by departmental staff, other factories and production associations made changes in production relations similar to those instituted at the Krasnyi Proletarii. By 1933 production planning, labor recruitment, calculation of wages and financial budgets, and work organization for the separate shops at the Kolomenskaia machine-building works in Moscow was being carried out within the apparatus of the individual shop administrations. In late summer of that year a factory production conference codified the increasing authority of shop administrations over against that of the functional departments of the central factory administration. A detailed set of regulations redefined the structure of economic and technical management in the factory and eliminated a complete layer of technical subdepartments previously administered under the authority of the chief engineering sector. New regulations eliminated that sector altogether and placed the chief engineer in direct subordination to the director as one of the latter's staff members.[64] Similar reorganizations occurred in 1932 and 1933 in other major works such as the Kharkov locomotive plant, the Krasnyi Putilovets complex in Leningrad, and the Gorky automobile plant.[65]

To a large extent, the shop movement of the early 1930s represented a spontaneous response to the breakdown of systematic central factory management. But it gained momentum from the official campaign against functionalism and bureaucratism during the same period. The Kolomenskaia factory regulations, for example, followed on from a decree promulgated August 21, 1933, by Sovnarkom and the party Central Committee. That decree charged that functional forms of management often led to excessive bureaucratization and lack of responsibility (*obezlichka*) in production organization and factory work.[66] Consequently, the Sovnarkom decree demanded that factories set about to eliminate middle layers of managerial bureaucracy between the office of director and the shop administration. The regulations adopted at the Kolomenskaia factory were designed to accomplish just that end.[67]

A similar decree of August 15, 1933, on simplifying factory management decentralized to the shop level many of the functions that originally fell within the purview of central factory departments. The decree especially encouraged factories to eliminate the nest of departments that had grown up around the chief engineering office and to reduce the status of the chief engineer to that of one among several subordinates within the office of director. Other reforms were designed to eliminate managerial overlap. Rationalization and technical norm bureaus, for example, were either eliminated altogether or, in most cases, combined within a single rationalization department.[68] In large factories, reforms went so far as to allow individual shops to open credit accounts with the state bank and to negotiate their own contracts for supplies and materials.[69] In most factories control over stores and inventories was decentralized to the shop level.[70]

Changes in the structure of piece-rate and bonus wage determination enhanced shop autonomy. Throughout the early 1930s, official policy encouraged the increased use of individually and progressively determined piece rates and bonus systems. Economic leaders endorsed these measures in the hope of stimulating productivity and work responsibility among workers, improving the quality of production, and eliminating practices of wage leveling.[71] By 1932, slightly less than two-thirds of all work hours in the machine-building and metal industries were paid under some kind of progressive piece rate and bonus system.[72] By 1934, that figure had reached 70 percent.[73] Piece rates in themselves did not threaten factory authority. In many factories, however, piece-rate and bonus systems were defined as discretionary forms of wage payment. They were not fixed for the factory as a whole through negotiation between central factory administration and trade union officials. More often than not they were negotiated shop by shop.

Indeed, by 1934 the director of the Kuznetsstroi works, B. Butenko, boldly asserted in a production meeting that the task of setting wages and enforcing wage policy belonged primarily to the shop administration. When queried about the function of the central factory labor organization department and that of the rate and norming bureaus, Butenko replied that "their task is to study the labor process, not to set wage policy.... They function at the discretion *(po zadaniiu)* of the shop administrator and production foreman."[74] Thus, as piece rates and bonus systems encompassed an increasingly large proportion of the wage bill—and an increasing proportion of workers—a consequent proportion of the system of wage determination fell within the discretionary power of the individual shop administration.

As central factory management atrophied, shop administrators revived prerevolutionary practices of shop contracting. Shop contracting reappeared in the guise of socialist shop competitions as shop administrators began to contract directly with each other, with factory management, even with sources outside the factory. This they did without immediate consultation through the vertical chain of central factory planning departments. To coordinate supplies and operations with other shops, managers set up production accounting departments *(khozraschetnye proizvodstvennie otdely)* within the shop administrative structure. These departments were supposed to be ad hoc organs subordinate to the functional departments of the central factory administration. In fact, these departments acquired a semi-permanent administrative status. They "clearly usurped and duplicated" the production planning, supply, and even financing work that was supposed to be done by the functional departments of the central factory administration.[75] Under control of the shop administrator, these departments contracted with other shops in the factory for supplies and semi-finished materials, and they often bypassed central administrative factory departments to work directly with production association staff in planning production and supply in and for their shops.[76]

The practice of shop contracting became widespread in the early 1930s. Contracts were drawn up and signed as legally binding documents between the shop administration and a second party: another shop, an outside source of supply, or the central factory administration. In the latter case, these documents stipulated the amounts and prices of materials to be supplied to the shop by the factory administration and the amount of goods and prices for which the shop was responsible to the contracted party to manufacture. The contract was based on a total cost estimation which the shop supplied and the central factory administration could verify. The contract stipulated dates of delivery of materials from the central administration to the shop and of final products from the shop to the central factory administration. Though contracts differed in particulars, questions of wages, labor organization, and hiring and firing were often left specifically to the discretion of the shop administration. Shop accounting departments were expected to incorporate all production costs, overhead costs, and labor costs within the general cost estimate given in the contract.

Shop heads and production foremen enhanced their authority in ways not directly related to production and work organization. As normal commercial and social structures began to break down during the years of rapid industrialization and collectivization, the factory took on an increasingly paternal role. Shop heads quickly realized that supplying the social and material needs of workers had a direct effect on productivity, and they worked hard to wrest these functions from the sphere of trade union and party authority. By 1934 shop administrators at the Kuznetstroi works routinely oversaw housing, food, and even hygiene needs of workers in their shops. Each shop maintained its own cafeteria, to which workers were admitted only with ration cards administered by the corresponding shop. Each shop built and maintained its own baths, and each shop took responsibility for upkeep over barracks that housed laborers from its shop.[77] Shop heads also routinely controlled distribution of shock work awards and bread ration cards which gave workers access to further social and material privileges. This practice stood in contrast to the early days of the shock work movement in 1929 and 1930 when trade union and party organs controlled the allocation of these distinctions.

The better material and social privileges a shop could provide, the better were its chances of drawing a skilled and stable work force. Some shops set up stores, and one enterprising shop administrator even ran a dress shop. In that store, workers or their wives could use the shop's food ration cards as barter currency. Discussion of the social and material well-being of workers engaged considerable amounts of time at production meetings. These discussions provoked heated exchanges when shop heads felt their authority in this area challenged or their efforts diminished by what they considered unfair advantages in other shops. In a 1934 factory production meeting at Kuznetsstroi, one shop *nachal'nik* complained that while money had been allocated from central administration for expanding showers in other shops, he had received inadequate funds for proper expansion in his shop.[78] Another nachalnik reported in outrage that the trade union and party cell functionaries in his shop had somehow gotten hold of shock worker ordinations and bread cards and were distributing them without consent of the shop administration. The nachalnik regarded this action as a direct challenge to his production authority. He demanded that the factory administration and party committee help put a stop to it. Otherwise, he warned, "we nachalniki will lose our influence over the workers."[79]

That a shop administrator could make such a complaint about party interference in 1934 revealed the extent to which production and social relations had changed in the factories since the 1920s. Previously, party and trade union functionaries controlled shock work ordinations, and they had the power to remove shop heads and managerial personnel. By 1934, however, the situation was different. Whether reluctantly or willingly, control over the social welfare aspects of their work force showed the authority that line managers had come to possess over any matter that affected productivity. Upon hearing the lament of the shop head at the

Kuznetsstroi meeting, director Butenko expressed his astonishment that the shop administration had permitted the situation to arise in the first place.[80] Other speakers expressed similar surprise. Butenko made it clear that party functionaries had no business interfering in policies affecting shop productivity. He promised to discover who was responsible and to put a stop to it.

By 1934 it was clear that functional management had collapsed—and that factories had returned to traditional, even prerevolutionary, forms of shop administration. As before the Revolution, shop administrators and foremen in the early 1930s wielded considerable power over methods of work organization and wage policies in their shops. According to director Butenko of the Kuznetsstroi works, the shop nachalnik had become "the undisputed master of his part of the factory."[81] Decentralization of authority to the shop level strengthened the responsibility of those managerial groups most directly involved in the production process. Often, however, it did so at the cost of overall factory production integration and systematic managerial policies. The breakdown of systematic engineering and managerial supervision adversely affected attempts to introduce routinized forms of work organization and standardized manufacturing techniques.

Indeed, the problem of "technical leadership" became acute after the collapse of functional management in the early 1930s.[82] Increasing shop control over wage determination, for example, enhanced shop autonomy, but at a price. Decentralization of wage controls contributed to wide variations in the wage system, and it encouraged increasingly high rates of turnover among workers. At the Kuznetstroi complex director Butenko advocated shop responsibility for determining wage structures. But he complained in a production meeting in October 1934 that wage systems differed erratically from shop to shop. He described a practice in which shop heads and foremen would adjust discretionary wage differentials as a way to steal workers from other shops during shock production campaigns or as a means to reduce the number of workers in their employ during slack production periods.[83]

According to the chief engineer of the Kuznetsstroi factory, Bardin, the unregulated wage politics of shop administrators represented a reversion to "barbarian . . . colonial" attitudes toward labor and production organization. Shop wage policies, he declared, thwarted any attempts at rational organization of labor. He charged that shop administrators purposely varied discretionary wage levels as an easy way to regulate labor. It was easier than firing, Bardin noted, which could bring trouble from trade union officials. In addition, turnover which resulted from wage differentials was registered in labor statistics as a decision by the worker to leave his or her workplace voluntarily. Thus turnover resulting from the practice of wage finagling did not register statistically as poor management of labor. It strengthened the argument that turnover was a problem of poor labor discipline among workers rather than of disorganization on the part of management.[84]

Engineers and other factory officials acknowledged the failures of functional management, but many argued that these were failures of a new system requiring time for adjustment. In any case, supporters of functional management argued that a return to autonomous shop control would only bring chaos to the workplace. One writer, Ia. Ia. Ossovskii, claimed that in Moscow-area metallurgical and machine-building factories, internal shop turnover of workers from one work station to another reached "at least" as high as 5,000 percent in a year. Writing in the journal *Metall* in late 1930, Ossovskii ascribed such high turnover rates to a number of irregularities but mainly to managerial disorganization at the shop level. He claimed that shop administrators and production foremen paid "absolutely no attention" to proper labor and wage organization, let alone to the appropriate technical organization of production.[85] The editorial board of *Metall* attached a lengthy addendum to Ossovskii's article strongly disagreeing with his conclusions about the reasons for such high rates of turnover. Interestingly, though, the editors did not dispute Ossovskii's figure of 5,000 percent.

The collapse of systematic engineering and managerial control accentuated the local character of production and work organization. Despite the pretense to planning, organization of work in most factories came to depend largely on the local labor market and the technological and production structure in the individual shop. Jerry-rigging and cannibalizing machines and their fixtures became commonplace. This resulted in a process of technological evolution that defied standardized operating procedures. A skilled worker entering a shop for the first time required training on machinery in that shop even if that worker had operated similar equipment in another shop or factory.[86] Shops and factories guarded their production secrets jealously, and that accentuated the ad hoc character of work organization.

Because of the often unique character of work organization that evolved in shops, work experience in one locale became as valuable to the maintenance of production lines as either formal skill or engineering knowledge. Successful production strategy became contingent not on the maintenance of formalized managerial structures and standardized engineering techniques but on knowledge of local conditions and on the combined skills and experience of all groups in the factory. Getting things produced became of necessity an heroic rather than a bureaucratic task.

Industrial officials never fully resolved the tension between systematic managerial control and decentralized production authority. Despite official repudiation of functionalism in 1934 by the Seventeeth Party Congress, functional bureaucracies continued to operate within the industrial administrative apparatus. Occupational conflicts continued between central factory authorities and shop administrators over the setting of wage policies, forms of work organization, and output quotas. Resurgent trade union and party activism in the middle 1930s exacerbated these conflicts and the lines of managerial authority. The rise of Stakhanovism and the threat that it posed to managerial authority further complicated and politicized an already ill-defined system of factory management.

If the structure of authority in the factories suffered from a lack of clear definition, so too did the organization of industrial administration at the national level. Officials continued to promulgate reforms in the attempt to regulate relations between factory and higher administrative organizations. Sergo Ordzhonikidze, the head of the Commissariat of Heavy Industry, NKTP, sought continually to institutionalize greater production responsibility at the factory level of administration. In 1932, for example, the NKTP abolished the obedinenie system and dispersed authority between factory administration and middle-level glavki. Within months after disempowerment *(razukrupnenie)* of the obedineniia, the NKTP transferred over 9,000 engineering and managerial personnel into factory positions.[87]

The purposes of the 1932 reforms reestablishing the glavki were in large part the same as those in 1930 which had abolished the regional trusts and created the obedineniia. Industrial planners hoped to decentralize operational control of production to the factory level. Despite disempowerment, however, authority once again tended to concentrate within the middle-level bureaucracies. Administrative and economic pressures that confronted obedineniia leaders also led glavki heads increasingly to usurp planning and operational responsibilities not originally intended to be in their sphere of administrative competence. Whether in the form of obedinenie or glavki, these middle-level bureaucracies formed the most important link in the chain of industrial administration. In response to pressures from above and below, those who sat in leadership positions in these bureaucracies fought aggressively to establish and expand their sphere of authority. Although constrained by the ultimate power of high economic and party organs, obedinenie and glavki leaders took initiative and fashioned creative and adaptive solutions to the problems of the industrial crisis that overtook the country in the early years of the 1930s. These were experienced, competent individuals who actively shaped the industrial system which emerged during the interwar period.

That system defies easy characterization. Industrial reconstruction in the 1930s produced large, often huge, factories in which production was organized on a massive scale. But the different parts of the factory were often not integrated, either administratively or technologically. Traditional forms of administrative and work organization persisted and even revived, concurrent with the most extensive campaign ever undertaken to modernize the technological structure of machine manufacture. Indeed, M. P. Rudakov, VSNKh Presidium member, emphasized that the one process accentuated the other, that the influx of new, sophisticated machinery exacerbated the disproportion between traditional work methods and modern technological processes.[88]

Suppressed market forces and the demands for economic accountability created competitive production relations between factories and associations and encouraged aggressive behavior among association leaders. That behavior transformed the obedineniia from administrative bureaucracies into quasi-entrepreneurial institutions, behavior which state and party officials alternately encouraged and repressed. In his continuing struggle against bureaucratism, Ordzhonikidze exhorted industrial leaders to take more initiative. But the nascent capitalist activities of the associations distorted attempts by higher authorities to plan and administer a socialist economy. In turn, central authorities attempted to correct distortions and to cope with the growing complexity of the economy through constant reorganization. As a result, the industrial administrative apparatus that developed did not conform so much to the rigid structure of a command economy as to that of a constantly changing system. This was a system that evolved, often in an ad hoc manner, through the interaction between planned policies and reaction to the unforeseen consequences of those policies. Reconstruction altered traditional patterns of social and economic organization but did not eliminate them. Indeed, the persistence of traditional methods of work and economic organization shaped industrial strategy and the character of the state as much as did the attempt by state planners to refashion society and economy.

NOTES

1. Moshe Lewin first suggested that given Soviet industrial and social conditions, rapid technological modernization accentuated perceived forms of backwardness associated with traditional work and social relations. See his *Making of the Soviet System* (New York: Pantheon, 1985), p. 37.

2. For small-scale industry a combination of branch and geographic administration was established within the administrative structure of republic and local councils of the national economy.

3. As of 1931 *Vsia Moskva* listed fourteen machine-building associations. For a discussion of these reforms and their economic and administrative motivation, see Iu. K. Avdakov, *Proizvodstvennye ob"edineniia i ikh rol' v organizatsii upravleniia sovetskoi promyshlennosti, 1917–1932* (Moscow, 1973), pp. 216–18.

4. *Resheniia Partii i pravitel'stva po khoziaistvennym voprosam* (Moscow, 1967), vol. 2, p. 136.

5. Ibid.

6. Ibid.

7. Ibid. See also Avdakov, *Proizvodstvennye ob"edineniia*, p. 219.

8. Decree of the Council on Labor and Defense, July 23, 1931. *Resheniia*, vol. 2, p. 343.

9. Avdakov, *Proizvodstvennye ob"edineniia*.

10. At a 1931 conference, Sergo Ordzhonikidze, the head of VSNKh, expressed his concern over the state of affairs that allowed production cartels to usurp functions that were supposed to be within the factory's sphere of authority. He complained that in many factories, directors had "almost no direct participation" in the ordering and distribution of materials and equipment for the factory. This was

done, he argued, by the cartels. "almost to the exclusion of the directors and their staff." *Pervaia vsesoiuznaia konferentsiia rabotnikov sotsialisticheskoi promyshlennosti: Stenograficheski otchet* (Moscow, 1931), p. 11.

11. Protocols, stenographic records, and reports of the SSI and its predecessor, Stankotrest, exist for the whole of the period of their existence, 1929–32. These were some of the hardest and historically most obscure years of the interwar period. For archival materials covering Stankotrest and the SSI, see TsGANKh 7880, op. 1, d. 2, *Materialy i protokoly zasedanii pravlenii Stankotrest i Soiuzstankoinstrument, 1929–1930;* ibid., d. 3, *Materialy i protokoly zasedanii pravlenii Stankotrest i Soiuzstankoinstrument, 1929–1930;* ibid., d. 3, *Materialy i Protokoly zasedanii pravlenii Stankotrest i Soiuzstankoinstrument, 1929–1930;* ibid., d. 41, *Materialy i protokoly zasedanii pravlenii Stankotrest i Soiuzstankoinstrument, 1930–1932.*

12. Protokol no. 3, *Zasedanie pravleniia* a 17.IX.1929. TsGANKh 7880, op. 1, d. 2, 11. 5–7.

13. *Protokoly zasedanii pravlenii Stankotrest i Soiuzstankoinstrument, 1929–1930.* TsGANKh, 7880, op. 1, d. 2. See also *Protokoly zasedanii pravlenii Stankotrest i Soiuzstankoinstrument, 1930–1932.* TsGANKh 7880, op. 1, d. 41.

14. Protokol no. 7, *Zasedanie pravleniia,* 14.X.1929. TsGANKh 7880, op. 1., d. 2, 11. 10–11.

15. Ibid., 1. 10.

16. Unfortunately, no specific information was given as to the nature of those changes. See Protokol no. 11, *Zasedanie pravleniia,* 31.I.1930. TsGANKh 7880, op. 1, d. 2, 11. 20–22a.

17. Although many factories had been reorganized for mass production, by 1933 only 21 percent were specialized for production of just one item. See Ia. Kvasha, "Mashinostroenie i vosproizvodstvo oborudovaniia v narodnom khoziaistve," *Planovoe khoziaistva* nos. 5-6 (1933), pp. 38–39.

18. Dzh. Pepper, "Itogi pervoi piatiletki v oblasti spetsializatsii, kooperirovaniia i kombinirovaniia mashinostroeniia," *Planovoe khoziaistva* no. 3 (1932), pp. 123–24.

19. E. S. Perelman, *Mashinostroenie v SSSR* (Moscow, 1931), p. 91.

20. Kvasha, "Mashinostroenie," pp. 51–52.

21. Ibid. See also Perelman, *Mashinostroenie,* pp. 8–9.

22. E. Alperovich, "Sovetskoe stankostroenie na novom etape," *Planovoe khoziaistva,* no. 7-8 (1933), p. 52.

23. *Postanovlenie,* VSNKh, SSSR, no. 1396, 1930.

24. Reported in Z. Shkundin, "Voprosy upravleniia promyshlennosti na sovremennom etape," *Planovoe khoziaistva,* no. 3 (1934), pp. 85–86, 94. See Ots's original complaints in a letter to *Za industrializatsiiu,* January 14, 1934.

25. Spektor, "Balans oborudovaniia na 1931 god i zadachi mashinostroeniia," *Metall,* nos. 2-3 (1931), p. 4.

26. Ibid. The practice of socialist competition exacerbated the problem of competition and hoarding of experience.

27. Kvasha, "Mashinostroenie," pp. 39–40. Unreconstructed works were designated as those in which less than 50 percent of machinery was replaced.

28. Ia. S. Rozenfeld, *Istoriia mashinostroeniia SSSR* (Moscow, 1961), chart, p. 216. Most of the increase in production capacity was achieved by renewal and expansion of machine stocks in factories. In addition, much of this increase came from the construction and equipping of new works. But despite the priority and publicity given to new factory construction, most of the new machinery that entered Soviet factories went into the reconstruction and expansion of older plants. Only about 37 percent of all new machine installations between 1929 and 1933 were placed in enterprises constructed during the plan period. In contrast, nearly 53 percent went into factories founded before the Revolution. See Kvasha, "Mashinostroenie," pp. 39–40.

29. *Perepis' oborudovaniia promyshlennosti, 1932–1933: Metaloobrabatyvaiushchee oborudovanie SSSR* (Moscow: TsUNKhU, 1933), p. 99. See also *Sotsialisticheskaia stroitel'stvo SSSR* (Moscow: TsUNKhU, 1935), p. 35.

30. Kvasha, "Mashinostroenie," p. 40. See also Shkundin, "Voprosy Upravleniia," p. 85.

31. M. Kaganovich acknowledged this in a speech to the First All-Union Production Planning Conference for the Metal and Electrotechnical Industries, held in Moscow in January 1931. This quote is reported in Shkundin, "Voprosy Upravleniia," p. 85. See also S. M. Kovartsev, "Planirovanie proizvodstva," *Metal,* no. 1, 1931, pp. 3–9, for the most complete summary of the conference. He also quotes Kaganovich to a similar effect, p. 3.

32. *Perepis' oborudovaniia promyshlennosti, 1932–1934: Oborudovanie metalloobrabatyvaiushchei promyshlennosti* (Moscow: TsUNKhU, 1935), vyp. 4, p. 74. Note that grouping of machinery by type was not the same as differentiation by flow arrangement in the production process. Only about 21 percent of machine stocks were organized in flow arrangement. See Ibid.

33. Ibid.

34. For a description of reconstruction at the factory, see *Istoriia zavoda 'Krasnyi Proletarii'.* TsGAOR 7952, op. 3, d. 94, 1.76.

35. On balance, such reorganization produced the desired results of lowering production costs. See O. M. Kuperman, "Mashinostroitel'naia promyshlennost' na putiakh rekonstruktsii," *Puti Industrializatsii,* nos. 11-12 (1930), p. 83.

36. See, for example, the discussion of problems of shop specialization in "Doklad M. P. Rudakov: Funktsional'naia organizatsiia upravleniia promyshlennosti i sotsialisticheskoe sorevnovanie,' 16.VIII.1929," *Protokoly Organizatsii Rabotnikov NOTa.* TsGAOR 5286, op. 1, d. 6, 11. 75–102.

37. Livait made his comments in response to the speech given by M. P. Rudakov on functional management. TsGAOR 5286, op. 1, d. 6, 1. 99. Differentiation of work processes by product and shop had an interesting effect on workers' perceptions of themselves. In factory and party cell meetings workers identified themselves not just by their specific occupation, such as "machinist Shevrev," as they had done when all machine work was done in one shop. Workers increasingly came to identify themselves by the shop they worked in. Identification with and pride in working in a particular shop could be reinforced by such things as official sanction of intrashop socialist work competitions. A worker's identification with his or her shop was also reinforced by the increasing autonomy of shops within the factory administrative structure.

38. Writers of the period distinguished mass production *(massovoe proizvodstvo)* from individual and small-batch production *(individual'noe* and *melkoseriinoe)* and also from machinery and equipment engaged in large serial production *(krupnoseriinoe proizvodstvo).* Within the category of mass production, distinctions were made variously between categories of continuous flow *(massovo-potochnoe),* mechanized continuous flow, and factories engaged in continuous flow of one or several items.

39. Kvasha, "Mashinostroenie," pp. 38–39. The latter included such factories as the newly opened auto and tractor works at Gorky and the Stalingrad tractor works. Manufacture of automobiles, tractors, and electrical supply equipment accounted for most of the investments made in mass-production and in continuous-flow production processes. One observer estimated that if the Stalin tractor plant alone was closed, the share of equipment engaged in continuous-flow mass production would fall from 31 to 28 percent. See *Materialy po kachestvennym pokazateliam raboty promyshlennosti v 1931 g.* (Moscow: TsUNKhU, 1932), p. 7. Factories engaged in mass production accounted for a slightly higher percentage of production than that represented by their capital stock value. While 40 percent of all capital stock was concentrated in factories engaged in mass production, those factories accounted for

48.6 percent of all production in the machine-building industries. In other words, nearly half of all Soviet machine-building production in 1932 was being done under conditions of mass production. Factories with continuous-flow lines accounted for 31.4 percent of all capital stock and turned out just over 35 percent of the machine production in the country. Kvasha, "Mashinostroenie." See also Zolotarev, "Sovetskoe mashinostroenie-vedushchee zveno tekhnicheskoi rekonstruktsii." *Planovoe khoziaistva*, nos. 7-8 (1933), p. 21.

40. Calculated from Kvasha, "Mashinostroenie." chart, p. 40, and from Zolotarev, "Sovetskoe mashinostroenie," p. 21.

41. Calculated from Kvasha, "Mashinostroenie," chart, p. 40. Factories engaged in large-scale serial production accounted for 23 percent of the industry's capital stock by 1932. Thus I arrive at the figure of 52 percent in the following manner: 60 percent of stocks engaged in mass production plus 23 percent of stocks engaged in large-scale serial runs minus 31 percent of stocks concentrated in mass production of one or two items.

42. Ordzhonikidze to a gathering of industrial managers, *Pervaia konferentsiia rabotnikov sotsialisticheskoi promyshlennosti: Stenograficheskii otchet s ianvaria 30 po 5 fevralia 1931* (Moscow, 1931), p. 12. Ordzhonikidze demanded to know from his audience "if any one of you factory directors or shop heads can tell me which of you work on the basis of *khozraschet?*" Replies ranged from "few" to "none" to "on paper." Ordzhonikidze emphasized his point by concluding that the answer was closer to none. See similar criticisms by V. Ia. Grossman in his discussion of *khozraschet* in *Sotsialisticheskaia ratsionalizatsiia promyshlennosti: Itogi i blizhaishie zadachi* (Moscow, 1932), pp. 41–42.

43. See the August 12, 1931, "Postanovlenie prezidiuma VSNKh SSSR o vnutri-zavodskom, mezhtsekhovom i vnutritsekhovom planirovanii" in *Industrializatsiia SSSR, 1929–1932* (Moscow, 1970), pp. 258–60. At a production meeting of the Kuznetsstroi metallurgical and machine-building complex in October 1934, the director, B. Butenko, blamed continuous production stoppages on a "complete lack of central factory organizational and production cost accounting." TsGAOR 7952, op. 5, d. 69, 1. 6.

44. See, for example, the complaint by the management expert Shatunovskii in 1929 that because of RKI and GPU policies, industrial statistics were becoming increasingly difficult to obtain. Shatunovskii complained to an RKI official, M. P. Rudakov: "How can you expect us to correct mistakes if you do not allow us access to the statistics we need to assess trends in industry and labor?" Rudakov replied that Shatunovskii could see conditions for himself without the need for statistics. *Protokoly sobranie Organizatsii Rabotnikov NOTa*, TsGAOR 5286, op. 1, d. 6, 1. 23.

45. This assessment was repeated in the August 12, 1931, "Postanovlenie prezidiuma VSNKh SSSR o vnutrizavodskom: Mezhtsekhovom i vnutritsekhovom planirovanii," in *Industrializatsiia SSSR: 1929–1932* (Moscow, 1970), pp. 258–60.

46. Note that others welcomed this prospect. They argued for a radical specialization of production not by product but along strict lines of technological operations. Finished parts would be sent to plants designated only for assembly. See "Doklad A. A., Gofmana, 'Reorganizatsiia promyshlennosti po priznaku tekhnologicheskikh protsessov,'" *Protokoly i stenogrammy zasedanii Organizatsii Rabotnikov NOTa, 9.XI.1930*. TsGAOR 5286, op. 1., d. 15. See esp. Gofman's suggestion to unit machine shops doing similar kinds of work from ten to twelve different factories under the authority of one technical production obedinenie. Gofman went so far as to suggest that these be physically united under one roof as well as administratively united. Ibid., 1. 21.

47. V. Grossman, *Sotsialisticheskaia ratsionalizatsiia*, pp. 24–25.

48. Ibid., p. 40. Ordzhonikidze made much the same kind of criticism at the January 1931 industrial managers conference. See *Pervaia konferentsia rabotnikov sotsialisticheskoi promyshlennosti*, pp. 17–18.

49. When it was first introduced, many workers supported functional division of management because it curtailed the power of the hated foreman. Even though functional division of management increased managerial intervention in production, in theory it did so in an evenhanded way: through the application of standardized work regulations. Workers did not so much oppose bureaucratization of work as the arbitrary exercise of managerial authority. Functional division of management increased the authority of the chief engineering section of factory management, and in the early years of functional management, during the middle 1920s, it was not uncommon for workers to ally with engineering staff against foremen. See, for example, the memoir of engineer Gildebrand of the Krasnyi Proletarii factory in which he describes several instances where workers sought the help of engineering staff against foremen who continued to show favoritism in the distribution of well-paid piece work. *Istoriia tekhnicheskoi kultury na zavode 'Krasnyi Proletarii'.* TsGAOR 7952, op. 3, d. 94, 11. 74–75. Despite an initial enthusiasm, however, the use of functional management caused serious problems in the organization of production and in its consequences for social conflict in the factory. For an interesting account of pressure from working groups for routinization of work in America, see Walter Licht, *Working for the Railroad: The Organization of Work in the Nineteenth Century* (Princeton: Princeton University Press, 1983).

50. Frederick Taylor, the American efficiency expert, developed the best-known kind of functional management at the Midvale Steel Company in Pennsylvania in the 1890s. Although his system drew much attention and some imitation, it proved impracticable and in America was not widely adopted. In the 1890s and early 1900s Russian industrialists became interested in functional management and other systematic forms of industrial administration then being popularized in Europe and America. Russian industrialists took an interest in systematic forms of management because of the economic depression of the 1890s. They saw in functionalism a way to bring the various production activities of the factory under closer financial scrutiny by higher managerial personnel. It was not until after the 1917 Revolution, however, that functionalism became standard managerial practice.

51. For discussion of the problems associated with an anticipated decline in skill levels of the work force, see the section on labor in *Metallopromyshlennosti za 10 let* (Moscow, 1927).

52. The most extreme proponent of functional labor training methods can be found in Aleksei Gastev. Gastev founded his system of labor training institutes on the idea that all work operations, both mechanical and human, could be systematically analyzed in their component parts and reduced to combinations of several simple motions. He believed that with the increasing use of automated machinery and the full use of functional management methods, workers trained in the several basic skills could adapt quickly to any work situation. Gastev first articulated these views in his book *Kak nado rabotat'* (Moscow, 1922). In the 1920s and 1930s Gastev's system of institutes trained hundreds of thousands of workers in six-month courses in the simple work methods which he developed. Graduates of his institutes, however, were ill prepared for actual work conditions in factories. Industrial managers did not take Gastev seriously and were reluctant to contract with Gastev's institutes to train labor recruits for their factories. Most of Gastev's contracts came from trade union organizations and regional branches of Narkomtrud, the Commissariat of Labor. For this assessment, see the reports by Gastev respectively to Narkomtrud and the central committee of metallists' union. "Stenogramma doklada A. K. Gasteva 'Po podgotovke rabochei sily v periode rekonstruktsii na bazakh Ustanovka TsITa, 1926–1927." TsGAOR 5515, op. 24, d. 81; "Stenogramma doklada A. K. Gasteva 'O rabote TsTITa,' 15.II.1928." TsGAOR 5469, op. 12, d. 545.

53. N. A. Stremlianova, for example, described the effects of technological reconstruction and the introduction of functional management at the Klimovskii

textile machine-building factory in the late 1920s. She claimed that the use of automated machinery and functional specialization of work allowed an overall reduction of skill levels in the factory work force from 5.3 to 3.2 on a scale from 1 to 8. Unfortunately, Stremlianova did not make clear how she was able to identify the specific causes for declines in skill levels. See her *Organizatsiia truda na mashinostroitel'nom zavode: Opyt klimovskogo zavoda* (Moscow, 1931), p. 24. Interestingly, it does not appear that proponents of functional management considered whether the savings in production costs supposedly resulting from reduction in the necessary skill levels of any individual worker would be offset by the increased costs required for the expansion of technical staff which functional management demanded.

54. These problems plagued functional management from the very beginning. See discussion of these problems by foremen at the *Krasnyi Profintern* factory as early as 1926. *Protokol soveshchaniia vydvizhentsev na zavode 'Krasnyi Profintern'*. TsGAOR 7952, op. 6, d. 63, 11. 31–32. See also similar complaints in *V bor'be s proryvom: Itogi rabot obshchezavodskoi proizvodstvenno-tekhnicheskoi konferentsii udarnikov Kolomenskogo mashinostroitel'nogo zavoda* (Moscow, 1933), pp. 41–43.

55. See n. 54.

56. *Soveshchaniia vydvizhentsev*, 1. 33.

57. "Doklad A. A. Gofmana," 1. 52.

58. "Stenogramma doklada B. Iu. Mirskogo: 'Ratsional'noe ispolzovanie oborudovaniia i rabochei sily v metallopromyshlennosti,' " 27,XI.1930. TsGAOR 5286, op. 1, d. 16, 1. 11.

59. Vishniak, during the discussion session following Mirskii's report. Ibid., 1. 19.

60. See "Organizatsiia truda i sistema zarabotnoi platy" in *Industrializatsiia SSSR, 1929–1932* (Moscow, 1970), pp. 263–64.

61. "Polozhenie o pravakh i obiazannosti mastera proizvodstv, tsekha" in *Istoriia zavoda 'Krasnyi Proletarii'*, TsGAOR 7952, op. 3, d. 84, 11. 22–25.

62. Ibid., 1. 23.

63. "Memuary Gorbunkova" in *Istoriia zavoda 'Krasnyi Proletarii'*, TsGAOR 7952, op. 3, d. 94, 1. 130.

64. See app. 15, "O perestroike apparata khoziaistvenno-tekhnicheskogo rukovodstva zavodom," in *V bor'be s proryvom*, pp. 138–52.

65. Shkundin, "Voprosy upravleniia," p. 86.

66. This decree is listed in *Industrializatsiia SSSR, 1933–1937* (Moscow, 1972), p. 615. For a discussion of it, see Shkundin, "Voprosy upravleniia," p. 84.

67. As head of VSNKh and later of the Commissariat of Heavy Industry, Ordzhonikidze led the campaign against functionalism. He had been a critic of functional methods of management since he investigated economic waste and inefficiency as head of the Workers' and Peasants' Inspectorate in the 1920s.

68. Shkundin, "Voprosy upravleniia," p. 84.

69. Avdakov, *Proizvodstvennye ob"edineniia*, p. 300.

70. Ibid.

71. *Industrializatsiia SSSR, 1929–1932*, p. 267. Many engineers and proponents of systematic management opposed the piece-rate system. They argued that piece rates, especially in conjunction with the use of shock work groups, disrupted orderly production tempos and work rhythms. See, for example, the discussion of piece rates and shock work at the series of public debates held in Moscow by the group Organizatsiia Rabotnikov NOTa in 1930 and 1931. "Stenogramma disputa o voprosakh normirovanii i khronometrazha," 4.XII.1930. TsGAOR 5286, op. 1, d. 11; "Stenogramma disputa o normirovanii truda v epokhu sotsialisticheskoi rekonstruktsii," 17.XII.1930. TsGAOR 5286, op. 1, d. 14. "Stenogramma doklada B. G. Iashchenko, 'Normirovanie truda v periode sotsialisticheskoi rekonstruksii,' " 23.III.1931. TsGAOR 5286, op. 1, d. 18.

72. *Trud v SSSR* (Moscow, 1936), p. 156.

73. Ibid. For a discussion of worker response to piece rates through collective work organization, see Lewis Siegelbaum, "Production Collectives and Communes and the 'Imperatives' of Soviet Industrialization, 1921–1931." *Slavic Review* (spring, 1986): pp. 65–84.

74. "Stenogramma proizvodstvenno-tekhnicheskoi konferentsii rabotnikov zavoda i stroitel'stva, 11.X.1934." *Istoriia zavoda 'Kuznetskii Metallicheskii Kombinat'.* TsGAOR 7952, op. 5, d. 69, 1. 10.

75. Quote from M. Kaganovich, 1932, reported in Shkundin, "Voprosy upravleniia," p. 84.

76. Shkundin, "Voprosy upravleniia," pp. 84–85.

77. During one particularly heated exchange at a factory production meeting in October 1934, the head of the Kuznetsstroi trade union committee berated the unnamed head of one shop for the "disreputable" condition of worker's barracks. When the shop head demanded to know why the trade union had not bothered to become involved in the workers' welfare, the union official replied, apparently without irony, "that is the responsibility of the shop head." TsGAOR 7952, op. 5., d. 69, 1. 63.

78. One shop *nachal'nik*, Kaminskii, complained that because of poor housing maintenance, his workers had nowhere else to shower but in the shop. His facilities were inadequate to handle the load, and some of his workers had not been able to shower for a week. Kaminskii drew a direct connection between cleanliness and productivity by noting wryly that "if the director wants us to keep our machines clean and productive, then he should first give us the facilities to keep ourselves clean." TsGAOR 7952, op. 5, d. 69. 1.54.

79. TsGAOR 7952, op. 5, d. 69, 1. 22.

80. "Razve! Vy eta razreshali?" Ibid.

81. Director Butenko of the Kuznetsstroi works to the production meeting in October 1934. TsGAOR 7952, op. 5, d. 69, 1. 17.

82. This was an oft-used phrase of the period to refer to the lack of systematic engineering and managerial control.

83. TsGAOR 7952, op. 5, d. 69, 1. 2.

84. TsGAOR 7952, op. 5, d. 69, 11. 46–47.

85. Ia. Ia. Ossovskii, "K voprosu ob organizatsii rabochei sily kak faktora pro-izvodstva," *Metall*, nos. 10–12 (1930), p. 23.

86. According to the 1932 equipment census, 38 percent of metal-cutting machinery in machine-building factories was being used consistently without attachments to hold the piece being machined, or pieces were being held with jerry-rigged attachments *(sluchaininaia dlia dannoi mashiny)* not specified in the technical "passport" documents of the machine. *Perepis' oborudovaniia* (1935), table 11, p. 34. The census did not distinguish which machines were being used with jerry-rigged fixtures and which were being operated without attachments. According to the census takers, operation of equipment in both cases was "disruptive of a proper technical regimen." *Perepis' oborudovaniia* (1935), p. 19.

87. Shkundin, "Voprosy upravleniia," p. 85.

88. "Doklad B. Iu. Mirskogo," TsGAOR 5286, op. 1, d. 16, 1. 24.

X

CRIMINAL JUSTICE AND THE INDUSTRIAL FRONT

Peter Solomon, Jr.

During the industrialization drive of 1929–35 Soviet leaders used the criminal sanction against persons they held responsible for industrial accidents, production of defective goods, broken machines, shortages and spoilage of food, even delays in paying workers. These problems, all of which resulted from the breakneck pace of industrial development promoted by Stalin, had reached epidemic proportions by the early 1930s. The regime reacted by issuing a barrage of new directives and laws targeting shortcomings in production for special attention by justice officials. However, justice officials failed to implement these directives consistently. Prosecutions were haphazard and poorly prepared, and judges shied away from harsh sanctions whenever possible.

This essay seeks to explain the use of criminal justice in the industrialization drive. I shall argue that despite the belief of some leaders that criminal repression could address the social consequences of rapid industrialization, its main function turned out to be explanatory or symbolic in character. Further, in contrast to campaign justice on the rural front, which, as I have argued elsewhere, had disastrous effects upon the administration of justice overall, the industrial prosecutions had little effect upon the rest of Soviet justice.

I shall begin by considering how Soviet leaders tried to use the criminal law in industry and what obstacles stood in the way of the implementation of their policies. Then I shall examine the practice of justice in three areas: the response to accidents, the attack on low-quality food, and the campaign against defective goods. Finally, I shall introduce comparative material: the use of the criminal sanction by the British government in managing industrialization in the nineteenth century and the mass prosecution of rural officials in the USSR during the 1930s.

Criminal Policy and Industrialization

In most countries the process of industrialization has produced social problems that called for public regulation. This pattern has prevailed in countries where industrialization occurred slowly and was spurred by private rather than public initiative. Thus in nineteenth-century England issues such as the employment of minors, the safety of the work force at large, and the quality of food and drugs brought government into the regulation of industry. That task entailed employment of criminal sanction, albeit in modest ways.[1]

Soviet industrialization in the 1930s differed from earlier Western industrial development. The pressure to build new industry and expand production in old was so intense that the usual social consequences of industrialization assumed extreme forms. Furthermore, the interest of public authorities in responding to these problems extended beyond their responsibility for the public weal. In the USSR political leaders also represented the owners and managers of production. As a result, they had an interest not only in protecting the public but also in maximizing quantity and quality of production. The production of defective goods took on an importance for the Soviets government equal with protecting the work force from accidents. Violations of labor safety belonged to both categories. Not only did they harm workers but they also interrupted the flow of production.

Wherever public authorities own and manage industry, they have at their disposal an arsenal of measures for dealing with their employees that extend beyond those available to private owners. In addition to sanctions associated with the private sphere, such as docking of pay or firing, public employers can apply regulatory (or administrative) sanctions, criminal sanctions, and in extreme cases political sanctions. The availability of the criminal sanction does not mean that public authorities will use it at will. But there is a tendency for governments to adopt extreme responses at times of weakness or crisis, when other, milder responses prove to be ineffective or inappropriate.

Stalin and his colleagues started to promote criminal prosecution as a means of confronting problems in industry in the second half of 1929, less than a year after the start of the First Five-Year Plan and the all-out industrialization drive.[2] Sometimes they issued new criminal laws. More often they directed legal officials to use old, existing laws for new purposes. Sometimes politicians indicated new targets of prosecution explicitly. Other times alert officials in the central legal agencies responded to new priorities of the government at large and directed their subordinates to contribute to the larger goals.

The old laws that were given new uses fell into two categories: official and political crimes. Official crimes, that is, offenses by persons holding office in the public sector, existed as a category in the 1922 and 1926 Criminal Codes. During the 1920s prosecutions for such traditional official crimes as bribery and embezzlement had been commonplace. Hardly used at all during NEP were the provisions associated with the execution of official duties, including the misuse of position (article 109 in the 1926 version) and failure to fulfill one's obligations or negligence (article 111). During NEP the concept of an official was limited to state employees with administrative responsibilities. The frequency of prosecutions was also checked by the availability (until 1928) of disciplinary courts to deal with minor infractions by public employees. However, during the collectivization and industrialization drives articles 109 and 111 became the favored weapons of politicians and legal officials alike for attributing responsibility or blame for a wide variety of mishaps.[3]

When misuse of office or negligence was committed by a person of "alien social origin" in order to harm the Soviet government, these acts, especially wrecking (article 58.7), could be qualified as political offenses. While political qualifications were available throughout NEP, the courts usually required a showing both of intent to harm the state and actual harmful consequences of the act. Charges of wrecking became easier to prosecute when in 1928 the USSR Supreme Court ruled that a showing of counter-revolutionary intent was no longer required, only intent to commit the act.[4] Moreover, after 1928 the atmosphere of political emergency, akin to a civil war, made it easier to escalate official charges into political. Often journalists and sometimes even jurists described cases involving ordinary charges in political terms. Thus spoiling machines through ignorance of how to operate them became "petty wrecking" and those who inadvertently harmed their machines "the helpers of wreckers."[5]

Between 1929 and 1934 Soviet leaders identified a wide range of targets for criminal prosecution. These included:

1. Persons responsible for accidents. The responses ranged from articles 111 or 112 (an upgraded version of 109 and 111), as promoted in a circular of Narkomiust, to article 58. These charges were also brought against persons held responsible for "spoiling machines" and disorganizing production.[6]
2. Persons responsible for the production of defective goods. A law of December 1929, as interpreted by a Narkomiust circular, called for the use of articles 111 and 109 against factory employees. In December 1933 a new law drastically increased the punishments and called for more prosecution of management.[7]
3. Persons responsible for the "lowering of the standard of living," especially for shortages of food and poor quality of goods in public cafeterias. Early circulars called for articles 111 and 58. In 1934 a new

law raised the criminal responsibility of sales clerks who cheated the public through weights and measures.[8]

4. Persons responsible for certain breaches of labor laws. Article 111 was used for officials who failed to apply the rules of labor discipline, article 59.3 (involvement in illegal disorders) against workers who violated disciplinary rules on railroads.[9]

5. Any or all persons or officials who failed to perform a duty or obey a directive. A dizzying number of circulars instructed justice officials to prosecute wayward officials in the construction industry, finance, fishing, rural education. Failure to observe the rules of accounting, disregarding passport regulations by hiring employees without proper documents, delaying the unloading of railroad cars, failing to remove snow from railroad tracks, not providing textbooks for rural schools, losing the fight against fieldmice—any of these "errors" could result in a prosecution for negligence.[10]

This broad construction of the possible cases of official crimes, and the criminal sanction in general, had an intimate connection with the prevailing conception of procuracy supervision. Under NEP general supervision, the central function of the procuracy meant keeping tabs on the ordinances of local and provincial governments and insisting that sooner or later they conform with central laws.[11] During the collectivization and industrialization drives, however, the focus of procuracy supervision shifted from overseeing the consistency of laws to promoting the implementation of regime policy. Like officials from Rabkrin and the OGPU, procurators were mobilized to inspect factories and assure that they operated properly. RSFSR Commissar of Justice Nikolai Krylenko told procurators at the fourth conference of leading justice officials in 1930 that they must do more than "follow the flow of cases." They were to take an active stance, and this meant establishing relationships with particular factories, especially in the key branches of metallurgy, capital construction, chemicals, and transport. Procuracy officials were to visit plants, check for irregularities or omissions in their work, and help factory officials "with timely interventions" when there were signs of breaks in production, low-quality output, accidents, spoiled machines, or problems of labor discipline. Factory visits could bring procurators directly into the productive process. Thus supervising railroad transport in the North Caucasus meant checking on the quality of the repair of cars, delays in operation, inefficient use of stock, diversion of cars, and the proper movement of grain cargo.[12] On their initial visits to factories, procurators were supposed to organize assistance groups among the workers, whose members would signal procurators about times of trouble. Members of assistance groups were also given the right to confront violators directly and protection of threat of political prosecution should the violators wreak vengeance upon them.[13]

Obstacles to Implementation

The policy of using criminal prosecutions for "production crimes" encountered two major obstacles in practice: the policy of protecting specialists and the shortage of legal officials to patrol industry.

From the Shakhty trial in spring 1928 well through 1930, Stalin had encouraged the persecution of engineers and other technical specialists who lacked party credentials or the required class origins. As a result, during the first two years of the industrialization drive engineers and technicians in industry were vulnerable to both criminal and political charges. However, Ordzhonikidze and other leaders managing industry began resisting the scapegoating of their important human resources as soon as feasible, fighting behind the scenes during 1930 to relieve specialists from persecution. By the spring of 1931 they had won the battle.[14] In May Narkomiust issued a new detailed directive cautioning procurators and judges to avoid unjustified prosecutions of managers and specialists and laying down new procedures for vetting such cases. In June Stalin himself gave his blessing to the new line, explaining that the remaining specialists had become loyal to the Soviet regime and had to be treated with respect.[15]

In the months that followed, the legal agencies issued the usual follow-up directives, but they were hardly necessary to achieve the desired effect. The word of Stalin was decisive.[16] In most parts of the USSR the number of prosecutions against specialists declined precipitously. Thus in Moscow oblast, instead of the cases tried against 2,500 accused persons in the third quarter of 1931 (the indictments dating in the main from before Stalin's speech), only fifty-six specialists appeared in the courts of Moscow in the fourth quarter. Similar declines were observed in the Urals and the Central Black Earth region; only in Leningrad oblast was there some stability. By spring 1932 the chairman of the Moscow oblast complained that specialists were getting too much protection. For the rape of a fourteen-year-old maid, one specialist had received a year's corrective work "so as to avoid a break from production," as the judge put it.[17]

Historians cite the policy of protecting specialists for its curtailment of *spets* baiting, but it had another important consequence. At least until the Great Purge, the policy undermined the attempts by some Soviet leaders and law-enforcement officials to focus criminal prosecutions upon management. Even without this policy local justice officials had shown reluctance in prosecuting factory directors and engineers, for this entailed tangling with persons who had protection (either by local politicians or central commissariats). Thus in 1930, before the adoption of the new line on protecting specialists—i.e., when specialist baiting was still legitimate—few prosecutions for production of defective goods involved the bosses of factories. With the new line endorsed by Stalin, the situation became all but hopeless. Prosecutions of those held responsible for this or that mishap or omission came to focus upon middle- and lower-level "officials" (shop foremen, supervisors of railway depots), if not also upon ordinary workers. In those years, the concept of "official" was stretched almost beyond recognition.[18]

A second obstacle to widespread prosecutions in industry was the shortage of cadres. Investigators, procurators, and judges had more obligations than they could fulfil, and some of those tasks had greater political significance than rescuing industry. Thus procurators and investigators at the *raion* level concentrated on the collectivization and grain-collection campaigns. The months they spent in the villages on the campaign trail left them barely enough time to catch up with their regular duties, let alone mount fresh initiatives in industry. Among raion procurators only those in large cities paid any attention to industry, but even they were preoccupied with rural campaigns.[19] As a result, the oblast procuracy turned out to be the main legal agency dealing with industry.

In the early 1930s industry did assume special importance in the work of oblast procuracy offices. Soon after the fourth conference of leading justice workers, Narkomiust instructed these agencies to form industrial departments (replacing the earlier labor departments). Typically the industrial departments employed five or six investigators and procurators, so that even oblast procuracy could supervise no more than a fraction of the factories within their purview. To extend their capacity, officials of the oblast procuracy were encouraged to collaborate with colleagues in Rabkrin and the OGPU who supervised industry. The oblast industrial departments also could assign the supervision of some plants to raion procurators. Finally, to address the growing number of accidents on the railroads, in December 1930 the regime established special line courts. Each oblast procuracy office was expected to assign one procurator to supervise the work of its line courts.[20]

Just what the industry department of an oblast procuracy could accomplish in the face of the constraints of understaffing and the policy on specialists is illustrated by the case of Leningrad. Leningrad's experience may not have been typical, for the caliber of its legal officials was higher than that in other industrial regions and some of its industrial enterprises were well established. At the same time, Leningrad had 14.4 percent of industrial workers in the USSR (20 percent of those in heavy industry), and many of its plants underwent major expansion during the industrialization drive.[21]

The Leningrad procuracy established its industrial department in the summer of 1931 and assigned procurators to particular branches of industry. Assuming direct responsibility for twenty-seven factories, the staff began by making sixty visits to these factories, establishing contact with their directors and organizing assistance groups. During these months the rate of criminal prosecutions in industry dropped markedly (from 215 in the second quarter to seventy-eight in the third). According to Leningrad criminologists studying these data, the drop stemmed from a new focus by procuracy officials on prevention. Thus when an official confronted defective goods in a textile factory, he did not rush to prosecute but instead arranged a production conference. When the shop heads in the plant assumed responsibility for quality of production, defective goods dropped from 24 percent of output to 7 percent. Contributing to the drop in prosecutions, one suspects, was the new line on specialists. Prosecuting even heads of shops might have seemed more dangerous than before.[22]

In 1931 the industrial department expanded its activity taking over responsibility for seventy-seven enterprises, including twenty-seven outside the city of Leningrad. Over the year staff made 156 visits to the factories, during which they held conferences with management on a wide variety of issues—defective goods in one factory, inefficiency in another, inadequate prevention of theft in a third. They conducted some of the visits jointly with the oblast Rabkrin and members of sections of the Leningrad soviet. Still, two visits per factory per year did not amount to regular supervision, even with the aid of assistance groups. Often the groups themselves existed mainly on paper, for factory authorities (including trade union officials) disliked them and would not release their members from other duties or listen to their reports. When procuracy officials did come to the factories, their visits took the form of "mass checkups and raids," suggesting that the relationship of procurators to particular factories had an episodic character.[23] The raiding style prevailed despite instructions from Narkomiust to eliminate "survey methods" in favor of more regular forms of supervision.[24]

No doubt some of these raids had beneficial effects. For one thing, the best procurators took a constructive approach to problems at the factories. Thus at one enterprise the procurator intervened to help its administration obtain key raw materials. In another the procurator held a meeting to force its director (in this case of Electrosila) address issues of safety and sanitation. As a result, new ventilation was installed in some shops. Procurator officials gave talks at many factories and placed articles in factory newspapers.

The raids on the factories also resulted in criminal prosecutions. Between April 1932 and March 1933 the procuracy of Leningrad oblast launched 1,501 cases in industry that sent 1,581 persons to trial. While the defendants were mainly lower officials (593) and workers, they included 100 top enterprise officials and nearly 100 technical staff (ITR).

Nonetheless, the effect of these prosecutions on production and life in the factories was limited. To begin, not all of the cases involved production issues; more than a quarter brought charges of theft. Moreover, the quality of case preparation was so low that the majority of indictments did not stand up in court. Some charges were dropped by judges even before trial

(35 percent of those relating to machine building), 15–25 percent of trials ended in acquittals, and more verdicts were reversed on appeal. Finally, punishments in the "real production cases"—i.e., accidents, defective goods, failures in workers supply—rarely exceeded a fine or corrective work. This finding was confirmed by a special study of the justice agencies in two raiony of the city of Leningrad in the first quarter of 1933. Most production cases in these raiony, including accidents, resulted in noncustodial sanctions. Only in a handful of cases involving drunken workers destroying machines or major failures in the supply of food did judges resort to terms of imprisonment.[25]

These incomplete data suggest that even the Leningrad procuracy, one of the most capable in the USSR, did not meet the demands of Narkomiust for supervising industry. The best this procuracy could do was supply occasional troubleshooters for industry and start enough prosecutions against factory officials to make them wary about visits by its representatives.

To appreciate the meaning of criminal prosecutions in industry during Soviet industrialization drive, it is necessary to examine the practice of industrial justice for the country as a whole. Let us consider first the number one focus of industrial prosecutions, accidents.

The Practice of Industrial Justice: Accidents

Between 1931 and 1935, when procurators in the USSR paid special attention to industry, the most common basis for starting criminal cases was accidents. Whether in the enterprise or on transport, accidents occurred with alarming frequency, harming both the production process and the welfare of workers. Moreover, accidents represented crises that could attract the notice of law-enforcement officials at any time, outside of special investigations or surveys. There was also a tradition in Soviet law of holding citizens responsible for serious accidents that involved loss of life or limb.

Accidents produced a large share of criminal cases relating to industrial production, but according to the available data, only a small proportion of industrial accidents resulted in criminal prosecutions. To be sure, major accidents in industry usually did produce prosecutions. The popular press and legal journals contain scattered reports of such trials. Often they took the form of demonstration trials, and for this reason often resulted in sentences of imprisonment.[26] In many districts lesser accidents in industry also produced a stream of cases, directed as a rule against lesser officials and resulting in noncustodial sanctions. But the number of accidents far exceeded the frequency of criminal prosecutions. Accidents of varying degree occurred regularly in most plants; one factory counted 1,423 accidents in six months.[27] Enforcement levels may have intensified in response to campaign directives (as exemplified by the struggle against mining accidents in 1934).[28] But apart from the most serious accidents, the policing of accidents in industry appears to have been sporadic and inconsistent.

Prosecutions for accidents as well as for the related charge of interrupting or disorganizing production (due to the drunkenness) were far from thorough. A Leningrad criminologist reported that such investigations lacked "objectivity." Either the investigator questioned a few people, made an inference, and drew conclusions without analysis or checking of documents or, having heard the accused, "fully ignored their explanations and sent the cases to court." In more than half the cases of disrupting production, "persons were sent to court for the simple fact of a break without establishing their concrete negligence or wrongdoing."[29] Small wonder that many of these cases ended in acquittal.

The number of criminal cases involving accidents on transport far exceeded those related to industrial accidents. One reason was greater degree of access for the police; police officials, far more numerous than procuracy investigators, generated most criminal cases resulting from transport accidents. Another reason was that more accidents on transport affected life or limb.[30]

Urban public transportation produced its share of the accident cases. Accidents on trams occurred at rates that appalled contemporary observers. In Moscow in 1935 fifty persons a month suffered from accidents on trams. In Leningrad in 1933 accidents led to more than thirty criminal cases per month, most involving careless or drunken drivers and poorly maintained vehicles.[31]

Railroads and water transport produced an even larger number of accident cases.[32] To cope with accidents on the railroads, special line courts were established at the end of 1930. In its first few months of operation the Moscow line court dealt with some 100 crashes and convicted 292 persons, mainly for negligence (article 111) but also a few for wrecking (article 58[7]). Thirty percent of the guilty received terms of imprisonment. In Leningrad oblast the line court (in the first five months of 1931) dealt with 172 accidents, 217 violations of the plan, and 13 cases of poor repairs. The accused in these cases included 473 workers, 409 administrative personnel, and 149 clients. Punishments featured 24 instances of long-term imprisonment, 167 of short-term, 819 corrective work, and 50 other.[33] Sharing the burden of investigation of railroad accidents with procuracy officials were OGPU officers, but many cases handled by the OGPU were treated as nonpolitical and sent for hearing at the line courts. The OGPU prepared cases no better than procuracy officials; whichever agency investigated charges, screening by the railroad procurators stopped 11–12 percent of cases before court, and judges returned 4–5 percent of cases for supplementary investigation.[34]

There was no evidence that criminal prosecutions reduced the incidence of accidents on railroads. But how could they, when the accidents stemmed from the poor quality of drivers and other workers, their lack of training, their lack of culture, and the pressures under which they worked? Some leading politicians seemed disappointed that coercion did not solve the problem of accidents. Addressing railroad procurators in 1935, Kaganovich observed "with classic clarity" that "procurators accuse, judges judge, and the number of crashes rises." Kaganovich criticized judges for giving prison terms to a mere quarter of the guilty, but at the same time warned against mass repression. In the end he seemed resigned to the limitations of the criminal sanction. His only serious advice to the prosecutors was that they adopt a more skeptical attitude toward transport officials who accused their colleagues. Too often the former, he noted, had engaged in "self-insurance." To cover their own failings they tried to transfer blame to others. "We have seen cases where one part of the commissariat complains to the transport procuracy about another part of the same agency."[35]

In addition to the railroads, the rivers and harbors supplied their share of accidents, enough that in 1934 the waterways were given their own special line courts and procurators. This reorganization may have increased the number of prosecutions, but it did not lower the number of accidents. To be sure, in 1935 some 20 percent of accidents on rivers and in harbors led to criminal charges (up from 10 percent in 1932–33), but fully half of these prosecutions failed to end in a conviction that was sustained (18 percent were returned to supplementary investigation before court and 32.4 percent were quashed in preliminary hearings, acquitted at trial, or reversed on appeal). Of those unfortunates who were convicted (perhaps because of a show trial), 38 percent received terms of imprisonment.[36]

Neither on the waterways nor on the railroads did the procuracy devote much effort to preventive work. In the absence of a calamity, prosecutions for violations of safety rules hardly ever occurred.[37]

Criminal prosecutions, especially as conducted by police and procuracy investigators in the mid-1930s, did not reduce the frequency of accidents in industry or on transport. The prosecutions did, however, place the blame for accidents on the shoulders of human beings—workers and officials, those who implemented the policy of rapid industrialization—rather than on the policy itself. No doubt in some cases drivers and other persons did deserve some of the blame, a fact that made the portrayal of human responsibility for the chaos credible. The real significance of criminal prosecutions, however, lay in the drama that they presented to the Soviet public.

The Symbolic Dimension: Food and Workers Supply

The root cause of the rash of accidents, production breaks, and defective goods lay in the reckless pace of the industrialization drive. But Stalin and his colleagues remained committed to achieving industrial modernization quickly. The negative byproducts of their policy called for a separate response that did not disturb the basic strategy. Holding officials and workers criminally responsible for the shortcomings fulfilled this need. In so doing, it had the potential, at least in the fanciful view of some leaders, of frightening members of the public into heroic efforts that might offset the costs of the industrial strategy. More important, criminal repression might help explain the problems, by showing that accidents and poor production stemmed not from the policy of industrialization but from failures of persons implementing it. The failures included the carelessness of toilers and, even worse, machinations by enemies of the Soviet regime.

The explanatory function of the criminalization of production problems was not merely latent; nor did it emerge late in the day. Even the first production trials of 1929 received an extraordinary degree of publicity. Leading officials encouraged procurators and judges to organize show or demonstration trials for production and transport cases.[38] As I have shown elsewhere, demonstration trials held in factories or close to the scene of the crime had figured prominently in Soviet justice during the 1920s. An outgrowth of circuit travel by trial judges, the demonstration trials brought the educational messages of the criminal repression to parts of the public that did not read newspapers.[39] In the 1930s the overall number of production cases did not match the scope of the problems they addressed, but many of their trials were held in the factories or railway yards and attended by large numbers of workers.

The trials resulting from accidents and production failures also received wide coverage in the newspapers. Reading *Pravda* for 1930, one encounters a steady stream of accounts of accident cases. At a time when the main legal journals offered little coverage of industrial justice (because Narkomiust focused its attention on the rural front), the content of *Pravda* suggests (erroneously) that accident cases dominated the work of the courts. Still, until the Great Terror *Pravda* and other national newspapers continued to give special coverage to cases relating to industry.[40]

The use of demonstration trials and the broad newspaper coverage facilitated the explanatory function of industrial prosecutions. The actual presentation of trials to the public did the rest. The portraits of the villains of industrialization represented dramaturgy at its best. A good example comes from the trials dealing with food and consumption.

Apart from increased probability of falling victim to an accident at work or in getting there, the consequence of the industrialization and collectivization drives that most affected ordinary persons was the deterioration of the diet. By 1930 shortages of basic products, including meat and dairy products, had produced rationing. To help distribute the short supplies of food to industrial workers, authorities established public cafeterias at many factories during 1930–32. The quality of food offered at these establishments, though, left much to be desired.[41] Newspapers exposed the public to a series of trials relating to food, some against persons working in trade and retailing of food products, others against cooks in the

cafeterias. Prosecutions relating to food started in 1930 and became especially common from 1931 to 1934 after Krylenko and Narkomiust began
promoting them.[42]

Take, for example, the realm of private trade and speculation in produce. In Leningrad during 1930 and early in 1931 no less than four major
trials were held, each focusing on a different ring of food dealers. Charged
in these cases were respectively forty-five, forty-one, thirty-eight, and twenty-six persons. While most faced ordinary criminal charges, some of the
ringleaders met accusations of wrecking, despite the absence of intent.[43]
This political dimension enhanced the drama of such trials. A 1930 trial
prepared by the OGPU revealed that in Moscow a group of traders had
succeeded in destroying food supply for the whole city. The traders included such manifest enemies of the Soviet regime as a former landowner
and an editor from the tsarist Ministry of Finance. According to the
newspaper account, the group had "consciously tried to create hunger and
produce shortages of goods for workers."[44]

The trials dealing with food in cafeterias were no less dramatic. The list
of foreign objects—nails, soap, ants, roaches, boiled mice—discovered on
the plates of the workers would make even cautious readers ready to
believe that wreckers had penetrated the cafeterias. While most of the
villains faced charges of negligence (and some were acquitted), others
found their acts conflated into political charges and accompanied with the
appropriate melodramas. One case that got major coverage in *Pravda* in
summer 1933 involved an escaped convict, a peasant who had set fire to the
home of a *selsoviet* chairman. Arriving in Moscow with an assumed name,
he was hired by his son, the head of research at a motor factory. From this
prime location, the escapee hired other escaped kulaks by fabricating
forms from the research unit. One of them, a peasant implicated in a
murder, he made chef in the cafeteria, and the troubles began. The new
chef encouraged his mates to drink, and the quality of the food deteriorated. Portions got smaller, and workers found in their food "sand,
hair, nails, glass, unwashed potatoes, and other garbage." The connections
with the worlds of kulaks, escapees, and murderers were enough to make
the case a worthy lesson in the unfolding saga of enemy attacks on the food
of the toilers. Twelve persons were charged with wrecking (article 58.7).
Naturally the newspaper amplified the political side of the story as it
unfolded. By the end of the trial the escaped convict had confessed to
being "a convinced Trotskyite," and the "investigation had proved that the
objects were placed in the food intentionally to harm the workers."[45]

The food trials display the role played by fantasy in the making and
presentation of cases. The fantasy centered on the presence in Soviet
industry of alien classes and enemies scheming to harm Soviet workers. In
the scenarios of the food cases Soviet society was divided into good and bad
people locked in a war of survival. The low quality of food stemmed from
desperate acts by the bad guys to save the day for a losing cause.

For the regime, the explanatory or symbolic function of criminal prosecutions had an importance equal to that of deterrence. The relative weight of the two functions might vary from one type of case to another both in the intent of the leaders and the functions served in practice.[46]

However, there is little question that Stalin continued to believe that the threat of prosecution might successfully address a problem. In the area of consumer protection, to continue the same example, Stalin and colleagues promoted prosecutions in two further types of situations. In 1933 justice officials were instructed to hold factory officials responsible for delays in paying workers, despite the issuing of a law in 1932 that had made overspending from the wage fund a criminal offense. A series of cases of this kind was reported in *Pravda* that spring.[47] Then in 1934 the government issued a new law requiring custodial sanctions for salespersons who cheated customers intentionally or accidentally through the use of weights and measures.[48] The new law on weights and measures alerts us to a further obstacle to the achievement of the leadership's objectives through criminal repression. This particular law could have achieved a deterrent effect, for the threat of punishment might well have restrained persons in trade from intentionally diddling their customers. (Obviously it could do little to prevent tradespeople from unwittingly cheating their customers because of faulty scales that they could not get repaired.) The realization of this deterrent effect depended upon full and consistent implementation of the new law. Most judges seem to have believed that custodial sanctions were too harsh to be applied to ordinary salespersons, certainly when their breaches were minor, if not unintentional. As a result, the judges regularly avoided the mandatory term of imprisonment by requalifying the charges in weights and measures cases to articles 111 or 109. In this way the *narsudy* in Moscow, for example, managed to sentence to prison a mere 21.7 percent of persons charged and convicted of cheating customers.[49]

This was not the first time that judges in the USSR had failed to give harsh sentences in cases that the leaders treated as urgent. Judges at the *oblsudy* had done the same thing a few months earlier in executing the new law on defective goods. The judges exercised their legal discretion against the intent of a new law despite signs that the law issued from Stalin himself.

A Stalin Law and Campaign: Defective Goods

In analyzing the use of the criminal sanction in Soviet industrialization, one must not overlook the personal role of the dictator. Stalin had little to do with the everyday administration of criminal justice, but his occasional interventions caused major disruptions. At least five times during his rule, Stalin got sufficiently disturbed about a problem to issue a new law, criminalizing or raising punishments for some particular misdeeds. One of these interventions involved industry in the prepurge 1930s.[50]

On December 8, 1933, the Soviet government announced a new law holding directors of enterprises and other administrative and technical personnel criminally responsible for the production of substandard or incomplete goods and stipulating a minimum punishment of five years' imprisonment. The promulgation of this harsh law came as an act of desperation. It was not the first time that Soviet leaders had invoked the criminal sanction to deal with the production of defective goods. Already in December 1929, after the initial year of the industrialization drive had produced a sharp decline in the quality of goods, the regime had made production of defective goods subject to prosecution under articles 109 and 111.[51] During the early 1930s procurators had produced a few cases in this area, but many did not stand up in court and the bulk of those convicted received noncustodial sanctions. As a rule procurators avoided starting cases for production of defective goods because of difficulty in establishing causes and reluctance to prosecute specialists.[52]

After the Central Committee Plenum of January 1933 focused on the low quality of industrial output, procuracy industrial departments increased their attention on defective goods. In the first eight months of 1933, for example, the procurators in Leningrad launched 201 cases that led to the conviction of 174 persons. Of these, eleven were sentenced to terms of imprisonment. At the same time, the new lay courts in the factories, known as production comrades courts, were also mobilized to confront defective goods and spoiled machines.[53] However, comrades courts had no authority to give criminal sanctions, and their sessions resembled "noisy production conferences" more than courts. A session of the comrades court at one factory included a litany of charges and excuses. A new inexperienced worker claimed to have followed the veterans. Women at the plant, according to one informant, had gossiped so much that they had paid no attention to their work. Everyone blamed defective goods on objective causes, such as lack of training or assistance in their jobs. The court proposed firing the worst offenders.[54]

In the context of this mild routine campaign Stalin introduced the law of December 8. The text of the law reflected Stalin's personal intervention. Not only was the punishment unusually harsh by current standards, but the preamble of the law contained an emotional portrayal of the crisis of quality in industry. The same preamble offered vague and ambiguous language unsuitable for legal purposes.

> In spite of the steady growth of production in state industry and the successes achieved in the assimilation of the technology, until now there remains a criminally negligent attitude toward the quality of production on the part of the leaders of particular enterprises and economic organizations. The output of substandard and incomplete machines, and also of details and materials on the part of factories, brings a real loss to the government. Especially intolerable and criminal is the issuing of substandard and incomplete items from factories working on the needs of the defense of the country.[55]

Among other things, the preamble suggested that the law might apply only to heavy and defense industry. It also blurred the issue of responsibility. Subject to prosecution were directors found "guilty of producing substandard goods." What did this mean? That they had done so intentionally? That their actions had in some way caused the substandard production? Laws that came directly from the mouth of Stalin rarely met standards of legal draftsmanship.

Another indication that the new law on defective goods came from Stalin was the campaign that accompanied it. The ambitious Vyshinsky, deputy procurator-general of the USSR, took personal charge of the campaign. Within a month of promulgation of the law, Vyshinsky had coauthored a lengthy directive on implementation that required completion of investigations within ten days, had spoken about the law at a research institute, had reported on the law to a meeting of the Procuracy's Collegium, and had organized a two-day radio broadcast about the low quality of production featuring top officials from Narkomiust and leading factory directors, in all 100 participants.[56] When these efforts produced a mere ninety prosecutions in the first two months, Vyshinsky raised the stakes. After confirming the dismal results of the initial implementation of the law at a meeting of oblast procurators in late January, he organized a closed circuit radio hookup for industrial procurators and oblast judges around the RSFSR. For the whole day of February 13, these legal officials heard speeches by such luminaries as Procurator-General I. Akulov, USSR Supreme Court Chairman A. Vinokurov, RSFSR Commissar of Justice N. V. Krylenko, and his deputy F. Niurina. Moreover, the procurators and judges on the line had to answer questions. Vyshinsky personally quizzed them about particular cases, among other things complaining about the tendency to lower charges in cases of production of defective goods to negligence (article 111) in order to avoid giving harsh sentences.[57]

The pressure from Vyshinsky had the desired effect. Following the broadcast procurators "in every province and republic" held meetings about defective goods, and in March and April they launched hundreds of new cases. The quality of the investigation in these cases that were concocted on demand fell below the usual low standards.[58] To their credit judges proved unwilling to convict or punish without legal grounds. Both trial judges (at the oblast level) and the RSFSR Supreme Court introduced restrictive interpretations of the law. It applied only to finished goods, not to spare parts or repairs. It required a showing of intent, or at least a causal connection. Its applicability to subordinate employees in a firm was limited.[59] For these and other reasons trial courts threw out or requalified more than a quarter of the cases that they heard with charges according to the law of December 8, 1933. Many other convictions were overruled by the RSFSR Supreme Court. For the whole of 1935 the 747 prosecutions registered in the RSFSR produced only 163 convictions that stood up at trial and on appeal.[60] In making cases, the procurators had found it difficult to focus on heavy industry; only 27 percent of the cases came from this sector, and few of them ended in convictions. Among other things, the Commissariat of Heavy Industry kept petitioning for the dropping of prosecutions against "this or that manager." Nor did the prosecutions focus mainly upon managers. While one-third of the accused comprised top figures in the enterprise (director, deputy director, or chief engineer), the rest of those indicted came from the middle or lower ranks of officialdom.[61]

Like most campaigns of an hysterical variety, this one ran its course quickly. By the fall of 1934 the number of new prosecutions for the production of defective goods had slowed to a trickle. In 1935 it leveled off; only ninety-two prosecutions were started in whole of the RSFSR.[62]

Comparisons: Industry in
Nineteenth-Century England

To sharpen our analysis of the use of the criminal sanction in the Soviet industrialization drive of the 1930s it is worthwhile placing it in comparative perspective. In Western countries industrialization also generated social problems that called for intervention by public authorities, even though industry was privately owned. Those authorities sometimes employed the criminal sanction. Public regulation of industry in nineteenth-century England has received close scrutiny from historians, and their findings provide the basis for a comparison of English and Soviet experience.

Two features characterized the regulation of industry by government in nineteenth-century England. First, the motivation for government involvement was restricted to protecting the public from accidents on transport, impure food and drugs, and overly arduous or unsafe working conditions. It did not extend to helping entrepreneurs discipline workers or improve production. Second, from the start governmental authorities in England preferred measures less drastic than prosecution and gradually moved away from prosecutions in areas where they had been mounted.

Supervision of the railroads in nineteenth-century England did not involve the criminal law. Even when government inquiries into serious accidents held drivers or other railroad workers responsible, they did not normally result in criminal charges; firing of the guilty was deemed sufficient. At the same time, when the inquiries identified potential safety measures, railroad managers usually agreed to implement them voluntarily.[63]

In contrast, violations of regulations on conditions of work in factories did make managers liable to criminal prosecution. During the course of the century, though, the English Factory Inspectorate shifted from laying criminal charges to a strategy of warning and negotiation. According to one view, violations by factory managers were "conventionalized," that is, decriminalized, because elite public opinion in England did not believe that these breaches deserved the stigma of conviction. Another interpretation stressed the inadequacy of the criminal sanction for achieving the goal of factory regulation. Thus factory inspectors abandoned criminal prosecutions when they realized that the combination of small staff for enforcement, difficulties in detecting violations, and weak sanctions undermined the deterrent effect of prosecution. Not prosecution but "negotiation compliance strategies" elicited the cooperation of managers.[64]

This portrait of the inadequacy of the criminal law for regulatory purposes gains support from the struggle of other public officials in London to regulate the production and sale of impure food and drugs. In this realm criminal prosecution remained the dominant approach of English government throughout the nineteenth century, but the impact of this policy was small. For one thing, overall levels of prosecution were never high. For another, judges were leery of convicting an accused without a demonstration of his or her intent to harm the public. (This reluctance continued even after the law had been amended to include strict liability.) And when judges in England rendered convictions, they sentenced the guilty to warnings or fines.[65]

The parallels between English and Soviet experience are striking. In the USSR, as in England, the use of prosecutions in industry was irregular and episodic, especially after the policy of protecting specialists reinforced the traditional reluctance of legal officials to prosecute important persons. Moreover, like their counterparts in England, judges in the USSR were unwilling to treat factory officials as real criminals. Absent the pressure of a campaign, managers charged with production offenses faced the threat of noncustodial sanctions. In neither country did criminal prosecution deter the conduct against which it was directed.

The key difference was that in the USSR there was a substantial minority of cases relating to production in which employees of factories or railroads were convicted and sent to prison. The employment of the sharp edge of the criminal law in the Soviet Union resulted from two factors that were peculiar to that country: a tradition of punishing persons whose negligence led to loss of life and the use of criminal prosecution for symbolic purposes. The comparison with England underscores the significance in the USSR of the explanatory and scapegoating dimensions of law enforcement. Explaining accidents and poor food and laying the blame on the careless or the hostile were important for Soviet leaders because the reckless pace of industrialization in the USSR made them helpless to address these problems. For Soviet leaders the criminal law represented less an instrument of regulation, however weak, than a substitute for it, and a vehicle for deflecting responsibility away from state authority.

Comparison: Soviet Rural Administration

The use of the criminal sanction in rural administration in the USSR of the 1930s stands in sharp contrast with its use in industry. Instead of the stream of cases relating to factories or accidents on transport, the rural front witnessed a torrent of prosecutions against village officials.[66] While central authorities pressed for higher rates of prosecution in industry and transport, they tried to stem the tide of cases pouring in from the countryside. Between 1934 and 1936 the RSFSR Supreme Court, the Procuracy, and Narkomiust issued repeated directives and circulars calling for an end of "mass repressions" of village officials and introducing mechanisms for vetting prosecutions. While these efforts produced a decline in the harassment of kolkhoz chairmen and selsoviet officials, they did not end the practice.[67] A further signal that criminal prosecution was no longer a legitimate way for raion officials to deal with their subordinates in the villages came with two amnesty decrees. The amnesties of 1935 relieved from further punishment the bulk of rural officials who had been convicted up to that time.[68] Yet even in 1936 the prosecutions of rural officials continued.

The practice of mass prosecutions against rural officials originated during the grain procurement and collectivization campaigns of the early 1930s. At that time the criminal sanction was used both to pressure rural officials and blame some of those who failed to fulfill the nearly impossible tasks imposed upon them. Even after collectivization had been completed, the collection of grain usually involved a campaign. And even though after 1933 most justice officials no longer traveled the campaign trail, raion authorities and plenipotentiaries still relied upon the criminal sanction to deal with rural officials.[69] What other method of supervision could they employ to blame rural officials who did not fulfill their tasks? How else could these supervisory personnel demonstrate their bona fides?

During the mid-1930s criminal prosecution became a tool in rural administration and at least until the Great Purge a substitute for regulation and supervision. As a rule, raion officials had no regular contract with the villages. Communication by mail or telephone was unreliable and tardy.[70] The periodic visits by raion personnel (every few months at most) turned into moments for uncovering mistakes and reacting to shortcomings, real or imaginary. Criminal charges were laid on the slightest pretext: discovery of some spoiled potatoes or missing fodder, the presence of sick horse, a shortfall in the harvest. (The latter sometimes brought a charge of "lowering the harvest.") Laying the charges, usually of negligence, were either plenipotentiaries or the police, and as a rule the police performed whatever investigation might be attempted.[71] During 1935 and 1936 procuracy officials had no involvement with these investigations. In fact, by 1935 even raion procurators did more screening of weak cases issuing from the police than conducting investigations of their own.[72] Contemporary observers recognized the role that criminal prosecutions played in rural administration. One of them wrote, "The sword of Damocles hangs over the head of all kolkhoz chairmen." Or, he went on, "a conveyor policy" was in effect, whereby rural officials were charged and prosecuted on a routine basis and often fired or rotated out of positions of authority in the process.[73]

The rash of prosecutions of rural officials contrasts sharply with the situation in industry, where, as we have seen, there were relatively few prosecutions. One possible reason was the shortage of law-enforcement personnel in industry, but this factor was not decisive. In fact, there were probably more potential enforcers of the law in the cities available for dispatch to the factories (ordinary police, political police, Rabkrin officials, even trade union staff) than were ready for raion authorities to dispatch to the villages. Another possibility is that adequate machanisms of administrative supervision developed sooner in industry than in the countryside and made it unnecessary for authorities to resort to criminal prosecutions. There may be some truth in this hypothesis. But the decisive factor, I suspect, was the value of industrial officials as a commodity. Unlike rural officials, who had no qualifications and could be replaced like cogs in a machine, officials in industry had some training and skills and were not easily replaceable. Furthermore, industrial managers had protection. Not only did the policy on protecting specialists deter prosecutions but also managers were employees of commissariats whose higher officials rushed to their defense. Sometimes managers were also tied into the local power structure. Even middle-level factory officials were better off than kolkhoz chairmen, for the former might receive protection from their bosses. At least until 1938 rural officials had no natural defenders.

In confronting the social consequences of industrialization in the 1930s, Soviet authorities used the criminal sanction more often than had their counterparts in most Western countries. They did so for a number of reasons. Public ownership of industry made prosecution readily available; the excessive pace of industrialization made them incapable of coping in other ways; and Stalin had a personal inclination to resort to all forms of repression. Not surprisingly, though, criminal prosecutions failed to achieve their instrumental ends. Prosecutions did not reduce accidents in industry or transport; nor did they improve the quality of food in cafeterias or goods made in factories. In the best of circumstances such results would have been unlikely, but in the USSR in the 1930s the policy of prosecuting factory officials confronted many obstacles: insufficient cadres to police industry, the competing policy of protecting specialists, the absence of interest in prosecutions on the part of local politicians, and an unwillingness of judges to punish management. Accordingly, implementation of the policy was partial and inconsistent.

The most significant dimension of criminal prosecution and trials in industry proved to be the symbolic. Demonstration trials at factories and accounts of them in the press assured the public that the social and economic problems of industry stemmed not from inherent defects in Stalinist policy (as they surely did) but from mere human failings, compounded at times by political antagonisms. Whether through negligence on the part of managers or workers or, worse, intentional harm inflicted by "wreckers" from alien classes, people had failed the regime and people deserved to be held responsible.

In contrast to the conduct of campaign justice in rural areas, the pursuit of industrial cases had no deleterious effects upon the conduct of other kinds of criminal cases. To be sure, investigation and prosecution in the production sphere was of the normal low quality, exacerbated by the intricacy of some cases and political pressures that accompanied campaigns. But industrial prosecutions did not represent a major part of the caseload nor take legal officials away from their other duties.

Paradoxically, the experience of legal officials in dealing with industrial cases may have had a positive effect on the administration of justice. Certain categories relating to industry and trade—production of defective goods and cheating customers—supplied some of the first areas where Soviet judges tried to frustrate a harsh line from Stalin. Except at moments of great political pressure, the judges resisted using the sharp edge of the law in these cases, finding in the law grounds for avoiding punishments that they found too harsh and means of narrowing the definition of the offenses as well. The judges even required standards of evidence that their political colleagues thought irrelevant, in spite their usual carelessness about procedures. The conduct of Soviet judges in industrial cases reflected not only an acknowledgment of the priority of respecting specialists but also the judges' own sense of fair play. Later in Stalin's rule, judges in the USSR would repeat this performance, for example in handling cases relating to labor discipline (in 1940) and theft of socialist property (in 1947).

Finally, if the prosecution of officials presumed responsible for failures in industry in the early and mid-1930s did nothing else, it supplied an ingredient for the Great Terror. Central to the terror was a campaign of vigilance, in which workers were encouraged to unmask those of their bosses whose actions or inactions had harmed production, a sure sign of readiness to wreck the Soviet economy. The campaign of vigilance of 1937–38 had its roots in the tradition of holding industrial officials criminally responsible for failures at the plant. Both the practice of prosecutions against managers and the metaphors for describing their sins had become part of popular culture by 1937.

Needless to say, during the course of the terror judges could not use the law to restrain prosecutions against managers; judges were lucky to survive the period. Yet at the conclusion of the terror and purge, the tendency of protecting management resumed in full force. During 1939 evidentiary standards for prosecutions against managers were raised to new levels.

Pursuant to directives of the USSR Supreme Court, charges of "wrecking" came to require a showing of counterrevolutionary intent, and charges of negligence signs of a causal link between the omissions and their supposed consequences. Not only did it become more difficult to achieve convictions against managers in production cases, but also procuracy officials had less reason to mount such prosecutions.[74] Reorganization of the structure of procuracy offices on the eve of the purge had eliminated the industrial departments and with them the oblast procuracy's special focus upon industry.[75]

As far as legal officials were concerned, the era of harassing industrial officials with criminal prosecutions had ended. But did Stalin agree? In June 1940, for the third time in eleven years, the Soviet government issued a law on defective goods, a law that sounded just like the ones that had preceded it. Once again, it declared, production of substandard goods was "an antigovernment crime equivalent to wrecking," an act for which managers, chief engineers, and heads of technical control departments would be subject to long terms in prison.[76] The struggle was destined to continue.

NOTES

I would like to thank Professor Clifford Shearing for stimulating conversation and Dr. Gennadyi Ozornoi for research assistance par excellence.

1. See, for example, W. G. Carson. "White-Collar Crime and the Enforcement of Factory Legislation," *British Journal of Criminology* 10 (1970), pp. 383–98, and Ingeborn Paulus, *The Search for Pure Food: A Sociology of Legislation in Britain* (London, 1974).

2. According to data in Soviet engineering journals, already in 1928 some technical specialists were subjected to prosecutions associated with production errors and violations of safety regulations. Nicholas Lampert, *The Technical Intelligentsia and the Soviet State* (London, 1979), p. 92. This practice did not attract the attention of central legal officials until late 1929.

3. A. A. Gertsenzon, *Bor'ba s prestupnostiu v RSFSR* (Moscow, 1928); "Iz rezoliutsii Ivanovo-Promyshlennogo oblsuda o sudebnoi praktike po dolzhnostnym prestupleniiam sviazannym s khoziaistvenno-politicheskimi kampaniiami na sele," *Sudebnaia praktika,* 1931, no. 13, pp. 13–14; Peter H. Solomon, Jr., "Soviet Criminal Justice under Stalin" (book manuscript in progress), chap. 3.

4. "O priamom i kosvennom umysle pri kontrrevoliutsionnom prestuplenii," Ras'iasnenie 18 plenuma Verkhovnogo suda SSSR ot 2 ianvaria 1928 g., *Sbornik postanovlenii, raz'asnenii i direktiv Verkhovnogo Suda SSSR deistvuiushchikh na 1 aprelia 1935g.* (Moscow, 1935), p. 100.

5. F. Kamenskii, "Posobniki vreditelei (porcha oborudovaniia na pischebumazhnoi fabrike im. Zinoveva v Leningrade)," *Sud idet,* 1929, no. 7, pp. 357–60; I. Sadovnikov, "Zadachi prokuraturyi i suda v stroitel'nom sezone," *Sovetskaia iustitsiia* (hereafter *SIu*), 1930, no. 13, p. 19; Vs. Luppov, "Kak rabotaiut organy iustitsii promyshlennykh raionov Urala," ibid., 1931, no. 19, pp. 24–26.

6. Although the use of articles 111–112 in accident cases became widespread in 1929, the circulars of Narkomiust regulating the practice came mainly in 1931. See

F. Nakhimson, G. Roginskii, and B. Sakhov (eds.), *Sud i prokuratura na okhrane proizvodstva i truda* (Moscow, 1931), pp. 338–60; and *Sbornik tsirkuliarov Narkomiusta RSFSR destvuiushchikh na 1 iiunia 1931 g.* (Moscow, 1931), pp. 84–88.

7. I. T. Goliakov (ed.), *Sbornik dokumentov po istorii ugolovnogo zakonodatel'stva SSSR i RSFSR 1917–1952 gg.* (Moscow, 1954), pp. 250, 340; *Sbornik tsirkuliarov Narkomiusta,* p. 81.

8. See Ark. Lipkin, "Vnimanie voprosam kachestva produktsiia," *SIu,* 1931, no. 2, pp. 21–22; Goliakov, *Sbornik dokumentov,* p. 345.

9. *Sbornik tsirkuliarov Narkomiusta,* pp. 164–73; Utevskii, *Obshchee uchenie o dolzhnostnykh prestupleniiakh* (Moscow, 1948), p. 281.

10. *Sbornik tsirkuliarov i raz'iasnenii Narkomiusta RSFSR deistvuiushchikh na 1 maia 1934 g.* (Moscow, 1934), pp. 95–216.

11. See Glenn Morgan, *Soviet Administrative Legality: The Role of the Attorney General's Office* (Stanford, 1962), pp. 44–75.

12. "Rol' i zadachi prokuratury po okhrane truda i proizvodstvu (Tesizy k dokladu tov. Krylenko na 4-om soveschchanii rukovodiashchikh rabotnikov organov iustitsii kraev (obl.) (RSFSR)," *SIu,* 1931, no. 2, pp. 5–8. Iu. Elkind, "Severo-Kavkazskaia prokuratura na transporte," *SIu,* 1931, no. 11, pp. 9–16.

13. *Sbornik tsirkuliarov Narkomiusta* (1934), pp. 24–28.

14. Kendall E. Bailes, *Technology and Society under Lenin and Stalin* (Princeton, 1978), chaps. 5 and 6.

15. "O poriadke privlechenii k ugolovnoi otvetstvennosti khoziaistvennikov i spetsialistov," Tsirk. NKIu no. 58 krai (obl prok.) ot 22 maia 1931, *SIu,* 1931, no. 16, p. 15. At the same time, the RSFSR Supreme Court called for holding procurators and judges criminally responsible for unfounded prosecutions of managers. *Sbornik raz'iasnenii Verkhovnogo Suda RSFSR 3* (Moscow, 1931), pp. 238–39. Lampert, *Technical Intelligentsia,* chap. 3 and pp. 99ff.

16. *Sbornik raz'iasnenii Verkhovnogo Suda 3,* pp. 240–41; "Prokuratura obiazana po-bolshevistki vypolnit direktivy NKIu o spetsialistiakh," *SIu,* 1932, no. 1, pp. 192–221.

17. N. Nemtsov, "Sudebnaia praktika Moskovskogo oblastnogo suda po delam, sviazannym s ohkranym prav spetsialistov," *SIu,* 1931, no. 12, pp. 1–6; Ark. Lipkin and P. Kransnopetsev, "Itogi proverki vypolnenii direktiv NKIu o spetsialistiakh," ibid., pp. 6–9.

18. B. Sakhov, "Organy iustitsii v bor'be za kachestvo produktsii i vypolnenie planov kapital'nogo stroitel'stva," *SIu,* 1931, no. 1, pp. 14–16; Utevskii, *Uchenie o dolzhnostnykh,* pp. 386–94.

19. Sakhov, "Organy iustitsiii"; "Bor'ba s iavleniiami, vyzvaiushchimi proryvy v vypolnenii promfinplana mashinostroenii," Postanovlenie Kollegii NKIu ot 1/X 1931 g., *SIu,* 1932, no. 2, pp. 15–16.

20. "O novoi strukture organov prokuraturov," *SIu,* 1931, no. 24, pp. 31–32; *Sbornik tsirkuliarov Narkomiusta* (1931), p. 40; M. V. Kozhevnikov, "Puti razvitiia sovetskoi prokuratury," pt. 2; *Uchenye zapiski MGU,* vyp. 147, Trudy iuridicheskogo fakulteta, 5 (Moscow 1950), pp. 55.

21. M. Alperin, P. Kravtsov, and G. Sheinin, "Perestroika organov iustitsii v bor'be za promfinplan," *Klassovaia bor'ba i prestupnost' na sovremennon etape,* 1 (ed. B. S. Mankovskii and V. S. Undrevich; Leningrad, 1933), pp. 104–41.

22. Ibid.; Albitskii, Alperin, and Matveev, "Kak Leningradskaia prokuratura pererestravaet po-novomu raboty v promyshlennosti, *SIu,* 1932, no. 2, pp. 17–20.

23. Alperin et al., "Perestroika organov."

24. N. Lagovier, "K likvidatsii obsledovatel'skoyo metoda v prokurorskoi praktike," *SIu,* 1931, no. 34, pp. 12–14.

25. Alperin, et al., "Perestroika organov."

26. See, for example, "Vzryv na shakhte 'Mariia' na Donbasse," *Sud idet,* 1930,

no. 17, pp. 17–18; "Sud nad vinovnikam avarii na zavode im. Stalina," *Pravda*, April 6, 1933, p. 4.

27. "Bor'ba s iavleniiami."
28. Lampert, *Technical Intelligentsiia.*
29. Alperin et al., "Nedochety v rassledovanii dolzhnostnykh i khoziaistvennykh prestuplenii v promyshlennosti," *Voprosy sovetskoi kriminalistiki* (Leningrad, 1933), pp. 32–40.
30. I. Gural, "Bor'ba s prestupnostiu na mestnom transporte v Moskve," *Za sotsialisticheskuiu zakonnost* (hereafter *ZaSZ*), 1935, no. 9, pp. 26–28.
31. Ibid.; Ia. Vitbaum, "Na bor'be s avariiami na gorodskom transporte," *SIu*, 1933, no. 23, p. 10.
32. On the structure and responsibilities of the line courts, see M. I. Kozhevnikov, *Istoriia sovetskogo suda* (Moscow, 1957), pp. 346–47.
33. V. Odintsev, "Kak rabotaiut linenye zheleznodorozhnye sudy Moskovskogo oblastnogo suda," *SIu*, 1931, no. 9, pp. 17–20; "Leningradskii oblastnoi sud v borbe za perestroiku zheleznodorozhnogo transporta," ibid., no. 23, pp. 2, 11–13.
34. A. M. Lipkin, "Prokuratura v bor'be s krusheniiami," *Za SZ*, 1934, no. 5, pp. 5–6.
35. G. Segal, "K itogam maiskogo soveshchaniia sudebno-prokurorskikh rabotnikov zheleznodorozhnogo transporta," *Za SZ*, 1935, no. 7, pp. 7–9.
36. "Bor'ba s avariiami no vodnom transporte," *Za SZ*, 1936, no. 7, pp. 105–7; Merin, "Praktika i zadachi vodno-transportnykh sudov, *SIu*, 1936, no. 11, pp. 6–7.
37. Ianskii, "Prokuratura v borbe za usilenie tekhnicheskoi moshchi vodnogo transporta," *SZ*, 1934, no. 4, pp. 5–7.
38. "Rol' i zadachi prokuratury"; *Sbornik tsirkuliarov Narkomiusta* (1931), pp. 81–88. Sometimes trials were held in theaters. See "Sud nad vinovnikam katastrofii na Volge," *Pravda*, July 22–26, 1933.
39. Peter H. Solomon, Jr., "Soviet Criminal Justice under Stalin," chaps. 1 and 2.
40. *Pravda*, 1930–36, passim.
41. Donald Filtzer, *Soviet Workers and Stalinist Industrialization* (New York, 1986), pp. 91–94
42. "Itogi vypolneniia postanovlenii 4 soveshchanii rukovodiashchikh rabotnikov organov iustitsii RSFSR i ocherednye zadachi organov iustitsii," Doklad N. V. Krylenko na 5 soveshchanii rukovodiashchikh organov iustitsii RSFSR 5 iiunia 1931, *SIu*, 1931, no. 22, p. 7; Ark. Lipkin, "Vnimanie voprosam kachestva produktsii," ibid., 1932, no. 2, pp. 21–22.
43. M. Ravich, "Dela rabochego snabzheniia v Leningradskikh sudakh," *SIu*, 1932, no. 22, pp. 13–18.
44. "Raskryta kontrrevoliutsionnaia organizatsiia vreditelei rabochego snabzheniia," *Pravda*, September 22, 1930, pp. 3–4.
45. Lib, "Vrag ne dremlet," *Pravda*, July 9, 1933, p. 4, and July 10, 1933, p. 4; "Proletarskii sud nad vrediteliami obshchestvennogo pitannia," ibid., July 12, 1933, p. 4.
46. The distinction between instrumental and symbolic functions of a criminal law was developed by Joseph Gusfield. See his "Moral Passage: The Symbolic Process in Public Designations of Deviance," *Social Problems* 15 (1967–68), pp. 175–88.
47. Goliakov, *Sbornik dokumentov*, pp. 337; *Pravda*, April 21, June 4, and June 14, 1933.
48. Goliakov, *Sbornik dokumentov*, p. 345.
49. "Postanovlenie prezidiuma Verkhsuda RSFSR ot 8 dek. 1934 po dokladu ob obsledovanii raboty sudov po delam ob omerivanii i obveshvianiiu pokupatelei i narushenii roznichnykh tsen," *SIu*, 1935, no. 1, p. 23; B. Babichev, "Kak boriutsia s obmanom potrebitelei organy iustitsii Novorossiiska," ibid., no. 2, p. 10.

50. Other interventions by Stalin included the laws of August 7, 1932, on theft of socialist property; April 5, 1935, on crimes by minors; June 26, 1940, criminalizing labor violations; and June 4, 1947, on theft of socialist and private property. See Goliakov, *Sbornik dokumentov.*

51. Goliakov, *Sbornik dokumentov,* pp. 250, 340.

52. Sakhov, "Organy iustitsii"; N. Chekalov, "V bor'be za kachestvo produktsii, *SIu,* 1931, no. 30.

53. P. P., "Bor'be za kachestvo produktsii. Opyt Leningradskih organov iustitsii v 1933 g.," *SIu,* 1933, no. 20, pp. 2–3; Brigada predsedatelei PTS Izorskogo zavoda, "PTS Izorskogo zavoda zovut predpriiatiia na prepreklichku o rabote PTS," ibid., no. 21, pp. 14–155.

54. Volodarskii, "Moskovskii reid po bor'be za kachestvo produktsii shirpotreba," *SIu,* 1933, no. 21, pp. 13–14

55. Goliakov, *Sbornik dokumentov,* p. 340.

56. *SIu,* 1934, no. 3, pp. 13f.; "Proizvodstvennyi pokhod organov iustitsii imeni XVII parts'ezda," ibid., no. 1, pp. 110–11.

57. R. Orlov, "Prokuratura v bor'be za provedenie zakona ot 8 dekabria," *SIu,* 1934, no. 9, pp. 16–17; "Kak my boremsia za kachestvo produktsii," *Za SZ,* 1934, no. 19, p. 15.

58. Ibid.; "O rabote organov iustitsii po primeneniiu zakona 8 dekabriia 1933 g.," Postanovlenie 48 Plenuma Verkhovnogo Suda SSSR, *Za SZ,* 1934, no. 10, p. 33.

59. "Kak Leningradskii oblastnoi sud provodit v zhizn zakon 8 dekabria," *Za SZ,* 1934, no. 3, pp. 43–44; "God bor'by Moskovskoi prokuratury za kachestvo produktsii," ibid., no. 12, pp. 7–10; S. Prigov, "Zakon 8 dekabria v praktike prokuratury Saratovskogo kraia," ibid., 1935, no. 12, pp. 7–14: *Sbornik raz'iasnenii Verkhovnogo Suda RSFSR,* 4 (Moscow, 1935), pp. 299–301.

60. R. Orlov, L. Chernov, "God zakona 8 dekabria," *Za SZ,* 1934, no. 11, pp. 15–18; F. Niurina, "Dva goda zakona 8 dekabria," ibid., 1935, no. 12, pp. 5–6.

61. Orlov and Chernov, "God zakona"; G. Roginskii, "Praktika primeneniia zakona 8-go dekabria," *Za SZ,* 1934, no. 6, pp. 11–17.

62. Niurina, "Dva goda."

63. Henry Parris, *Government and the Railways in Nineteenth-Century Britain* (London and Toronto, 1965).

64. Carson, "White-Collar Crime"; P. W. J. Bartrup and P. T. Fenn, "The Evolution of Regulatory Style in the 19th-Century British Factory Inspectorate," *Journal of Law and Society* 10 (Winter 1983), no. 2, pp. 201–22. See also W. G. Carson, "Symbolic and Instrumental Dimensions of Early Factory Legislation: A Case Study in the Social Origins of Criminal Law," *Crime, Criminology and Public Policy* (Ed. Roger Hood; London, 1974), 107–138.

65. Paulus, *The Search for Pure Food.*

66. For the best data, see A. S. Shliapochnikov, "Prestupnost' i repressiia v SSSR (Kratkii obzor)," *Problemy ugolovnoi politiki,* 1 (1935), pp. 75–100. By the first half of 1934 official crimes represented one-third of all court convictions in the USSR (as opposed to 105 in 1929). More than two-thirds of these were for articles 111 and 109 and the same proportion was directed against rural officials (87–91).

67. "O sudebnoi rabote v uborochnykh i khlebzagatovitelnykh kampaniiakh," Direktivnoe pismo no. 21 Verkhovnogo Suda SSSR ot 17 maia 1935, *Za SZ* 1935, no. 8, pp. 55–57; "O subebnoi repressii v otnoshenii dolzhnostnykh lits v sele," Postanovlenie 50ogo plenuma Verkhovnogo Suda SSSR ot 27 marta 1935 g.," *Za SZ* 1935, no. 5, pp. 58–59; "O sudebnoi prakike po delam o dolzhnostnykh prestupleniiakh v kolkhozakh," Postanovlenie prezidiuma Verkhsuda RSFSR ot 17 marta 1935, *SIu,* 1935, no. 13, pp. 30–31.

68. "Postanovlenie TsIK i SNK SSSR o sniatii sudimosti s kolkhoznikov ot 29 iiulia 1935," *Za SZ,* 1935, no. 8, p. 53; "Ob osvobozhdenii ot dalneishego otbyvaniia

nakazaniia, sniatii sudimost i vsekh pravoogranichenii, sviaziannykh so osuzh-deniem riada dolzhnostnykh lits, osuzhdennykh v svoe vremia v sviazi s sabotazhem khlebozagatovki i vypuska trudovykh zaimov i bon i prochikh denezhnykh sur-ragatov," Postanovlenie TSiK SSSR ot 11 avgusta 1935, *Za SZ*, 1935, no. 9, p. 63. The first decree provided for an amnesty for all current members of kolhozy who still had convictions with sanctions up to five years of imprisonment. Many rural officials of 1932–34 were sentenced to noncustodial sanctions and while losing their post were allowed to remain members of their collective farms. As a result they became eligible for amnesty, as long as they had good work records. The second decree covered any former officials—whatever their current status—who have been convicted of specified offenses (especially political ones) during the campaign of 1932–33. Implementation of the first decree was placed in the hands of raion commissions whose members toured the countryside holding ceremonies of purification in the villages. The pardoned kokholzniki were forced to make appear-ances, describe their crimes and punishments, and show appropriate contrition. See D. Kokorev, "Sniatie sudimosti s kolkhoznikov Voronezhskoi oblasti," *SIu*, 1936, no. 3, p. 7.

69. F. Gusev, "Gorkovskaia prokuratura v bor'be s nezakonnym privlecheniiem predsedatelei kolkhozov," *SIu* 1935, no. 4, p. 14; Tseliev, "Nado pokonchit s derganiem kolkhoznogo aktiva," *SIu*, 1936, no. 7, pp. 6–7. On the use of the criminal sanction to pressure rural officials between 1929 and 1933, see Solomon, "Soviet Criminal Justice under Stalin," chap. 3.

70. R. Rausov, "Organy iustitsii—na bor'bu za ulushchenie pochotovotelegrafnoi i telefonnoi sviazi," *SIu*, 1933, no. 9, p. 19.

71. Mitrichev, "Dozhnost'nye prestupleniia v kolkhozakh Venevskogo raiona Moskovskoi oblasti," *SIu*, 1935, no. 2, pp. 4–5; Gusev, "Gorkovskaia prokuratura."

72. E. G. Lependi, "Praktika privlechenii k ugolovnoi otvetsvennosti pre-dsedatelei kolkhozov po Gorkovskomu kraiu i 'vyvikhi' v rabote sledstviia," *SIu*, 1935, no. 21, pp. 14–15; Tseliev, "Nado pokonchit." Gusev, "Gorkovskaia pro-kuratura."

73. Mitrichev, "Dolzhnostnye prestupleniia."

74. Peter H. Solomon, Jr., "Soviet Criminal Justice and the Great Terror," *Slavic Review* 46 (Fall-Winter 1987), nos. 3–4, pp. 391–413.

75. Morgan, *Soviet Administrative Legality.*

76. Goliakov, *Sbornik dokumentov*, p. 406.

XI

ENGINEERS OF HUMAN SOULS IN AN AGE OF INDUSTRIALIZATION

CHANGING CULTURAL MODELS, 1929–41

Katerina Clark

Between 1929 and 1941 the Soviet Union was transformed from an agrarian to a major industrial nation, agriculture was completely restructured, and the country underwent a massive shake-up in personnel—a social and economic revolution. At no point in its history has the transformation been as radical.

And yet in Soviet culture in this period—books, theater, films—works about production or construction are poorly represented. The paucity is most marked in literature. The major exception is works occasioned by the First Five-Year Plan. After about 1934, when the last of the longer works based on a given writer's own *komandirovka* to a collective farm or construction site during the First Five-Year Plan finally straggled into print, the supply of major fiction about construction or production all but dried up. Although the tendency is most marked in literature, it is clear in all areas of culture. Moreover, even some of the works which are ostensibly concerned with a major Soviet economic achievement treat it rather peripherally and in a way scarcely recognizeable as an industrial theme. For instance, in Friedrich Ermler's film *A Great Citizen* (*Velikii grazhdanin*, part 1 1938, part 2 1939), an apologia for the purges which focuses on the murder of Kirov (who is thinly disguised in the film as the Kraikom secretary Shakhov), much of the action is set in a factory called the Red Metal Worker (*Krasnyi metallist*, read the Red Putilov Factory), and yet it is clear that the factory's function is less to turn out tractors than to turn out an army of political actors opposed to the Left (Trotskyite) opposition. Such tractors as do emerge from the factory shops function not as machines for agricultural production but as props for massive propaganda parades. An even more extreme example of the downplay of the industrialization effort is the popular musical film *Volga, Volga* (1938)—reputed to have been Stalin's favorite—which ostensibly celebrates the construction of the Volga-Moscow Canal. It represents the industrialization and modernization of the country without any account of the processes by which they are achieved; the hitherto drab and backward landscape is suddenly superseded by series of shots of technological wonders. The film climaxes in a scene where the protagonists end their Volga journey as they arrive at the newly constructed Moscow River Port, which is represented as a sort of recovered Grad Kitezh.

The lack of works on industrial themes was in no way in spite of official pressures to produce them. On the contrary, in the thirties whenever authoritative voices listed topics appropriate for a particular genre, production themes were low on the list or absent completely. A *Literaturnaia gazeta* editorial of 1938, for instance, recommends four themes for writers: the Battle on the Kalka, Arctic explorers, Alexander Nevsky, and a brigade of border guards.[1]

Of course this list represents the high point of a xenophobic folksiness (also apparent in works like *Volga, Volga*). However, it is striking that throughout the thirties per se (as distinct from the plan years) the overwhelming majority of all cultural production was on retrospective rather than contemporary themes. In these accounts of the past it is difficult to find much material on industry or agriculture, or even on socioeconomic changes, except perhaps in that writers and filmmakers still seemed constrained (as during the cultural revolution of the plan years) to establish a working-class background—or at least sympathies—for their positive heroes.[2]

This overwhelming obsession with the past is, of course, in part a function of the regime's need to establish legitimizing myths in an age of massive purges.[3] However, it is far from the case that the retrospectivist obsessions of thirties culture are purely for purposes of political legitimization and connected with the age's drive to modernize and industrialize.

It is arguably the case that in those years industrialization functioned as an overarching metaphor for a historical event much broader in its implications than the introduction of modern machinery or the construction of giant hydroelectric plants, important as such activities indubitably were. In the Soviet context, industrialization can be regarded, and often was regarded, as *the second phase of revolution*. Moreover, industrialization might usefully be compared with revolution in the sense that although a revolution has political effects, its impact can hardly be confined to politics, important as they are.

In any process of industrialization the chief actors are the work force, the engineers, the materials used, and the final products (goods and industrial plant). These four can happily be used as metaphors in a scenario for revolution (masses, vanguard, political-economic conditions, results). However, in any Soviet scenario of actual industrialization the role "engineer" is highly problematical. The combined aims of radical democratization *and* rapid modernization result in a major paradox, and much of the craziness and excess can be laid at its door: you can't have modern industrialization without engineers, but their status as white-collar professionals puts them in the wrong class category to be prime movers of history.

Since engineers in a sense specialize in materialist *practice,* they are potentially the least objectionable members of the sociological category intellectual. In the thirties, however, they proved to be for the ideologues the most problematical group within that category, probably because they were for them also the most important. The engineer is not merely another worker on a project, albeit one who is better qualified and more privileged. He is also the *mastermind.* Thus the relationship of the political leadership to the engineer involved working out power relations. When industrialization became the icon of revolution, the category engineer became much more problematical both politically and ideologically. Consequently, the thirties were an age obsessed with engineers, and even though actual engineers rarely appeared in books, plays, or films after the early thirties and rarely at any point appeared in a positive light, yet they played an enormous role in culture as a master metaphor which shaped works with not the remotest ostensible thematic connection to industrialization.

In the thirties, the cause of modernization (economic and political) so dominated all others that in official rhetoric most activities seemed perilously close to becoming mere subfunctions of it. Consequently, the two functions "engineer" and "writer" (or some other kind of creative intellectual), which might otherwise seem to represent opposite poles of intellectual activity, lost much of their distinctiveness in the homogenizing myth of industrialization. The interpretation of the role of the writer became much more mechanistic, and the two functions became, though not equated, closely identified. This was thrown into focus when, at the time of the First Writers' Congress in 1934, writers were pronounced to be "engineers of human souls." A *Literaturnaia gazeta* editorial published on the opening day of the congress makes it particularly clear (citing words attributed to Stalin) that the model for the writer is now tied to the model for the engineer.[4]

The engineer was always a major cultural symbol during the years 1929–41, an age of industrialization. However, what was far from uniform was the precise *meaning* of the symbol. During that period Soviet official culture went through at least three self-styled *perestroiki.* Although the country remained committed to industrialization throughout, at three times a major reevaluation occurred of the principal values underwriting industrialization, and consequently of the perception of the role of the engineer and of the creative intellectual as well. These three periods are, approximately, 1929–31, 1931–35, and 1935–41. In the first period, both the engineer and the creative intellectual were treated as subfunctions of production and politically suspect at that; in the second, both were seen as organizers and guardians of established norms; but in the third period, when Soviet culture was dominated by the paradigm of the Stakhanovite, the *true* engineer or writer was the man of the people, the iconoclast who breaks norms, for the meaning of *to industrialize* was to break through to new heights.

Each of these shifts in the dominant cultural models corresponds more or less to a point when a major shift in the policy toward engineers and other professional experts was announced by Stalin himself (for the first shift, Stalin's speech "New Circumstances and New Tasks" of June 1931; for the second, his speech to the Red Army graduates in the spring of 1935, when he launched the slogan "Cadres Are the Answer to Everything," and his speech that December at the First All-Union Meeting of Stakhanovites).

The subperiods in the thirties marked off by these policy shifts are not hermetic, and trends defining one may be seen in another. Moreover, they emerge much less clearly as subperiods when one looks not at official speeches of the time but at Soviet literature itself and its treatment of the themes of industrialization and the role of the engineer. One finds that for much of the thirties the relationship between party doctrine and literary content was not as close as in the somewhat mechanistic model implied in the term *engineers of human souls.* In each of the three subperiods the change in the dominant cultural model reflected in official speeches, *Pravda* editorials, and the like brought about a comparable change in the way industrialization and engineers were represented in literature, but the fit was not complete. Moreover, in literature the disparity increased over the course of the thirties despite the fact that in the second half of the decade the penalties for nonconformity with official doctrine seem to have been rather more dire than in the first. Ironically, as the thirties progressed and a new kind of Soviet writer emerged, one who was by training an engineer—as it were, the true engineer of human souls had been found—writers began to show *greater* independence of spirit.

The cultural model which was dominant during the First Five-Year Plan conceives industrialization in terms of a process whereby thousands of "little men," of eager proletarians, build the industrialized tomorrow with their collective labor. Engineers are not positive contributors. They are seen chiefly as negative characters, ranging in nefariousness from saboteurs to those who are merely ineffectual because they are bourgeois and hence cut off from the "little men." Thus this age was somewhat utopian in that the country was committed to combining a radical democratism with the overriding cult of industrialization. Expertise, that which singles one man out from the other "little men," was thus *both* essential to the cause *and* a threat to democratism.

The thirties start in a sense with the Shakhty and Prompartiia trials

(1928–30)—of engineers. But these trials were harbingers of a period when there was an extraordinary depreciation of intellectual expertise of all kinds. The trend for vilifying engineers spread in a ripple effect to other branches of intellectual activity; before long there were mass arrests of intellectuals working in the humanities and social sciences which were sometimes called by those who orchestrated them "a Shakhtylike trial of the scholarly intelligentsia."[5]

In these years there was a marked tendency to erect the goal of increased production into an absolute value so that everything in society was considered valuable only inasmuch as it was integrated into that effort. Thus, while for much of the twenties high culture had been an undisputed value (as long as débourgeoisé), during the plan it was no longer self-valuable and could be justified only as an instrument of production (or political propaganda, which often amounted to the same thing). The writers' task was defined as one of effecting a rise in the level of production or of advancing collectivization; they were even expected to ensure a successful sowing with their pens![6] At the same time, the processes of industry and industrialization were considered paradigms for the role and work of the writer; the writer was called a "worker of the printed word" and was to be converted from working as an isolated "cottage craftsman" (kustar') into a proper proletarian by being organized into writers' brigades; literature was to have its own "industrial financial plan" (promfinplan), and the individual writer to have his or her own "plan" for literary production. Not only were writers to write about industrial subjects, they were to know the trades of their subjects and could be criticized if their knowledge of the production processes they described was incorrect; few readers were bothered if the writing was of poor quality, for one of the primary functions of writers was to act as a conduit of information from worker to worker.[7] An ineluctable conclusion to be drawn from such tendencies was that the person who was more successful as a producer would be a better writer (or at any rate ultimately so, after tutelage from an established writer in the rudiments of the craft). Consequently, rather than having intellectuals take the masses under their wing, as was common after the Revolution, factories and other industrial organizations were asked to undertake shefstvo over writers.[8] Given the officially sponsored trend for "proletarianization" of intellectual cadres, i.e., replacing those of "bourgeois" origins with true proletarians and party members, there was enormous pressure to replace bourgeois and even established peasant writers by a new cohort of beginning writers, comprising workers from the factory, kolkhoz, and construction site, who were to be trained by the superseded old-style writers. Ultimately the policy was for mass recruitment into literature of the "shock workers" of production (udarniki); these udarniks were declared the "harbingers" (pervye lastochki) of a new literature which would propel the country into ever greater production yields.[9]

This radical democratization can also be seen in a defining feature of culture in these years, the reversal of the valorization of center and periphery. During the early twenties, the intellectual centers (i.e., Moscow and Leningrad) were considered privileged, and new establishments were set up in the provinces so that intellectuals might spread culture more democratically. However, during the plan years this pattern was reversed as the intellectual's only chance of redemption was felt to lie in traveling to some provincial construction site, factory, or kolkhoz where the intellectual's personal reformation might take place.[10] In consequence, writers vied with each other in making claims for the length of time spent at some far-flung economic enterprise.[11]

As this pattern suggests, during the plan years a serious attempt was made at totally restructuring the role of the writer in society and the institutions of literature. The move to "proletarianize" literature was far from being just a matter of rhetoric but translated into a drastic shift of numbers, circulation, and above all royalties out of the established organs and into militant and lowbrow organizations.[12] The call for "shock-worker" writers, for instance, translated into an increase in the membership of RAPP, the most militant proletarian writers' organization, from 1,500 to 10,000, of whom 80 percent were shock workers.[13] As nonproletarian writers found their very livelihood threatened, they began to entertain seriously various proposals for a fundamental change in the organization of the business of writing. Chief among these proposals was the suggestion that writers be permanently employed by enterprises or publishing houses (rather as Hollywood stars were hired by studios in the thirties). Under such a system, they would be assigned work rather than choose their own topics, and they would become complete subfunctions of the industrialization process. They might be "industrialized," but they would at least be paid.[14]

This radical restructuring of the role of the writer never occurred. By 1931 the tide of extremist democratization had begun to abate, and the movement for worker writers died its own death. An article that year in *Literaturnaia gazeta* which was framed in the language of industrialization and titled "Breakdown [*proryv*] in GIKHL [the State Publishing House]," reported that GIKHL was getting too many "faulty literary products" *(literaturnyi brak)* which could not find consumers. The movement for "shock-worker" writers had resulted in 5,000,000 rubles being paid out to writers for manuscripts which were unpublishable; so much paper had been diverted that publishers could not find enough even for their regular mass publications and had had to raise the price of books 40 percent.[15] Most such excesses of the plan years were quickly reversed in 1931. The movement for a "proletarian" literature, and especially the movement for foregrounding "shock-worker" writers, left scarcely a trace in the writing profession. The worker writers recruited in mass numbers at that time were to fade out of literature as quickly as they had entered it.

By 1931 the country was pulling out of its first plan and gearing up for its second. This was a time of general reevaluation. In official culture, the cult of the humble proletarian which had been so defining in the first-plan years was jettisoned as official spokesmen began to call for "bigger" models for the populace to emulate. Literature too was meant to be "bigger"— grander, of better quality—but in an age when the distinction between writers and engineers was blurred, the shift in literature—a shift which was to embrace institutions, organization, genres, styles, thematics, and heroization—was to be integrally part of a shift in cultural models as a whole.

The wave of reaction in 1931 was so strong that one might call the nexus of values which emerged on the public platform an antithesis to the initial thesis of Stalinism. However, not all the values were reversed. For instance, the problematic status of the intellectual was not eradicated when he became an "engineer of human souls."

At the center of the cultural shift of 1931 was a demand that writers not get bogged down with production statistics and technological detail but concentrate on "the essential." The Soviet writer was told ad nauseum that "the first act of creative work is selection."[16] A sign of the new times came in 1933 when one of the most highly praised novels from the plan years, Valentin Kataev's *Time, Forward!* (*Vremia vpered!*, 1932), which describes the successful attempt of a work brigade in Magnitostroi at breaking a record for the amount of concrete produced in one shift, was subjected to un-precedented attacks. Inter alia, Kataev was reproached for the novel's overemphasis on sheer quantity of production, his "concrete hysteria" *(betonnaia isterika),* and his failure to relate the work of the concrete pouring brigade to an overall account of what was being achieved at Magnitostroi.[17]

Thus what was considered relatively "inessential" in these new times was focusing on production itself! Instead, attention was to be focused on the idea of transforming Soviet society into a totally and integrally organized world. This new emphasis refocused attention away from the site of con-struction or production—which would, after all, be just a part of this world—to larger units, and primarily to entire cities, which represented model microcosms for an architectonically integrated whole. The term *engineer-architect*, which had been popular among Constructivists in the late twenties, gained prominence in official rhetoric. However, its meaning had changed. In Constructivist writings the engineer-architect was seen as a builder of "social condensors," that is, as a builder of workers' housing, workers' clubs, and other such structures which would be so organized as to effect a change in the worker's psyche. In the early thirties, the focus for the engineer-architect's work shifted to designing monumental public buildings as an integral part of a totally redesigned city.

Starting in 1931, plans were drawn up for the rebuilding of several major Soviet cities. However, the lion's share of the funds and activity went to the Soviet capital. In this period, the building of Moscow acquired the status of the central historical paradigm. It replaced the building of the hydroelectric plant or tractor factory, the most common topics of cultural production in the plan years, as the paradigm for the triumph of culture over nature, or order over chaos.[18] More importantly, however, it became a paradigm for revolution in the sense of total transformation. Those who described the rebuilding of Moscow were encouraged to represent it as a massive reconstruction involving the obliteration of the old and the ushering in of the new; "All of Moscow is covered in scaffolding" *(Vsia Moskva v lesakh)* became a commonplace of such writing. The second such icon of the age was the building of the new industrial city Magnitogorsk, whose phantom rise on the bleak plains of Kazakhstan was as it were a guarantor that great transformations were in progress, transformations of such a scale that the only possible historical precedent would be the building of Petersburg in the swampy wastelands of the north.

Thus the end of the industrialization effort was seen not as it was during the First Five-Year Plan in terms of turning out more tractors, more kilowatts of electricity, more tons of grain and cement, but rather in terms of producing such products as a means to building a great "city." But the city, in turn, essentially functioned as it does in utopian writing. As Northrop Frye has remarked, "The symbol of conscious design in society is the city, with its abstract pattern of streets and buildings, and with the complex economic cycle of production, distribution and consumption that sets it up. The utopia is primarily a vision of the orderly city and of a city-dominated society." However, as Frye hastens to add, even the building of the city is not the end of a utopia but rather the medium, the environment for prosecuting a theory of education: "That is, education, considered as a unified vision of reality, grasps society by its intelligible rather than by its actual form, and the utopia is a projection of the ability to see society not as an aggregate of buildings and bodies, but as a structure of arts and sciences."[19]

In the building of such a city, the engineer (designer) must obviously play a crucial role. He is both the symbol and the enabler of the "structure of arts and sciences," the organizer of an architectonically integrated, rationalized whole. In the plan period the little man (the humble worker) had been foregrounded in speeches and fiction; now he paled in stature before the engineer.

Despite the engineer's problematical status as a member of the professional classes, he became de facto one of the great emblems of the early thirties. He stood for an ideal age when engineers would help erect great architectural "ensembles" and gigantic industrial structures and man's entire environment would be thereby controlled in a harmoniously integrated environment. Whereas in the plan years the *-stroi* (quality of constructedness) of Magnitostroi and the other gigantic construction projects stood symbolically for something which was made by the collective efforts of hundreds of little men, by mid-1931 its meaning had changed to become the *stroi-* of *stroinost'* (put together sparely and perfectly), something made without the "confusion" of the milling swarm (which had been idealized in fiction of the plan years), without inessential details. This period, then, would see the flowering not just of engineering and such applied sciences but also of a whole complex of arts and other fields that organize the spatial environment and the objects within it. The engineer-architect as designer, as executor of norms, would be king, and experts from other fields would be subordinated to him and to his system of systems.

Thus the engineer-architect became rather more than the person who simply supervises the construction of monumental complexes or factories. Ultimately, he should be the engineer-architect of human souls. His function was political. Indeed, in actual practice, both Stalin and Kaganovich were the final arbiters on the great architectural projects of these years, and could overrule the professionals.

The new emphasis on design and control ensured that the dominant model for the plan years of the relationship between the center and the periphery was reversed. Hence Magnitogorsk yielded its status as privileged site in favor of Moscow. During the plan years, the standard route for regeneration had been via some trip to a construction site on the periphery. Architects scurried to the remote industrial centers to design buildings and preferably entire "socialist towns" as harbingers of the new world. In the early thirties, however, the center of value shifted back to Moscow, as did the focus of architecture. Indeed, even within Moscow the emphasis was on rebuilding the center of town. That is not of course to say that the industrial center on the country's periphery became a negative space. Rather, its aim was to become a "little Moscow," to imitate the "essential image" provided by the capital.

This pattern is particularly apparent in Aleksandr Malyshkin's extremely ambitious novel *People from the Backwoods* (*Liudi iz zakholust'ia*, 1938). The core of the material Malyshkin used was gathered in trips he made to Magnitostroi in 1931 and 1932 together with Valentin Kataev. Inasmuch as material Kataev gathered on these same trips formed the basis of his famous *Time, Forward!*, a comparison of the two novels helps highlight how the values of the early thirties contrast with those of the plan years. *People from the Backwoods,* unlike the earlier novel, which is entirely concerned with concreting on the production site, downplays the *production* aspect of the work at Magnitostroi. Indeed, Malyshkin shifts the focus of the action from Magnitostroi, the construction site, to Magnitogorsk, the town which houses the workers of Magnitostroi. Moreover, he attempts to provide a comprehensive account of the great changes taking place in "the thirties" (its original title). Hence he relates events in Magnitogorsk not just to their local significance but also to the overall situation of the country in agriculture, industry, politics and intellectual life, no less.

Malyshkin manages to integrate all this disparate material by structuring the novel in terms of a hierarchy of place-time. That is to say, he takes three symbolic points in contemporary Russia—Moscow, representing the future; Magnitogorsk or the new industrial city, representing the present emerging into the future; and "the backwoods," represented by a provincial town called Mshansk (as such, it represents the past, but inasmuch as it is being incorporated in a new kolkhoz it also has potential to become the future). These three places are organized in a hierarchy, with Moscow as the apex and the "backwoods" at the bottom, while Magnitogorsk stands closer to Moscow. The three places are also linked because various members of a single family (originally from Mshansk) reside in or visit each of them. Although Mshansk is based on Malyshkin's own hometown (Mokshansk), the places in the novel are more important for their symbolic value than for their actual physical reality. Indeed, Malyshkin explicitly equates the jaded, sybaritic intellectuals of Moscow with "the backwoods."

The plot is played out as a Manichean drama wherein the protagonists oscillate between identifying with "the backwoods" (chaos, ignorance, primitivism, a mercantilist mentality, and an interest in luxury and comfort) and identifying with "Moscow." When a wavering soul is won for the light, however, it is not because he is captivated by the poetry of collective labor or because he gets a thrill as the first tractor comes off the assembly line, as tended to be the case in fiction of the First Five-Year Plan. In fiction of this period such thrills are definitely downgraded inasmuch as they are now relegated to the province of women (such as, in *People from the Backwoods*, the reconstructed erstwhile gadfly whose principle identity is as an errant wife; she is helped to mend her ways in an encounter with the almighty tractor). Male heroes are now, rather, overwhelmed by imposing structures and above all by a vision of the future socialist town. The most crucial conversion in Malyshkin's novel, that of the youngest protagonist, a former farm laborer who hence can be classified as a rural "proletarian," occurs when the party organizer paints for him an enticing picture of the path he could take in life, culminating in his becoming an *engineer*. The Manichean drama comes to a climax as "kulak" plotters decide to burn down Magnitogorsk, believing that that is the only way of destroying the new age. However, the converted prove their faith by organizing themselves into a volunteer fire brigade and saving the "city": order has not been destroyed, chaos cannot triumph.

The novel is typical of fiction and journalism of its time on industrial themes in that it foregrounds the panoramic ensemble formed by the industrial complex and attendant socialist town as an exemplum of the defining values. In both the press and fiction, industrial complexes are frequently referred to as grand "monuments"; they are described as "stately," as transforming a dreary, unkempt, and nondescript surrounding landscape into what is essentially an object of aesthetic appreciation in that the various units of the complex are said to be placed in a consciously designed and pleasing pattern.

One of the best examples of this can be found in another major industrial novel which also appeared in 1938, Vasilii Grossman's *Stepan Kol'chugin*. This novel, set in a prerevolutionary Donbass mining town, chronicles the progress of its hero, Stepan Kolchugin, somewhat along the lines of Gorky's socialist realist paradigm, *Mother* (*Mat'*, 1907), from callow and oppressed working-class lad to conscious Bolshevik revolutionary. A major distinction between the figure of Stepan Kolchugin and that of Gorky's hero from *Mother,* Pavel Vlasov, however, has to do with the fact that while Pavel is propelled onto his path to consciousness through contact with revolutionaries among his fellow workers, for Stepan a major step forward on that path occurs when he is taken under the wing of a chemist who works in his factory's laboratory and who instructs him in the natural sciences. Stepan conceives the progress to communism in terms of building the city, as is particularly apparent in one scene where he returns one evening from his first such lesson and pauses as he contemplates the benighted workers' housing:

> The tiny houses were barely raised above the ground. Straight ahead the black industrial hill rose up before him and on its summit a lantern shone. . . . the cottages were clustered under its slope as if driven here in a disordered [*besporiadochnuiu*] bunch, . . .
> And Stepan wanted to drive these little huts from the earth [against which they huddled], to make them larger, and higher so that they might stand beneath that distant light on the top of the hill, that a mighty people who have dominion over fire and iron might not stoop, might not creep, coughing, into these dark and damp burrows. Vague and dim notions [*predstavleniia*] rose up in his mind, notions which were alarming, daring and audacious.[20]

This passage shows clearly the extent to which the transformation of man was articulated in fiction in terms of the building of a new, rationally organized, and monumentally proportioned town or city. It also shows, however, a certain fuzziness and vagueness (present not only in Stepan's "mind," but in such texts as well), as to how and by whom the "city" will be built. In part it is the workers who will do it, in part the representatives of practical expertise (in this case the chemist), but above all it will be the proletarian Bolshevik leader, with—or most generally without—any specialized technical training.

It is the party organizer among the various characters in a given work who most frequently functions as the "engineer," as the one most directly responsible for producing both the industrial complex and its new man. Indeed, in *People from the Backwoods* there is little evidence that there are any other engineers at the great *stroi* at all. Even when the party organizer promises the young country lad that he can become an engineer in time, we sense that this lad is more likely destined to become a political leader than a designer of factories or machinery (this development would have taken place in part II, which, due to Malyshkin's death in 1938, was never completed).

In several films of this period, the roles of "engineer" and "party organizer" are effectively conflated in the figure of the latter, who is represented as the builder of the new city. Thus in Sergei Iutkevich's *The Miners* (1936), no attempt is made to motivate this conflation in terms of the party head's expertise. Indeed, all attempts at realism are cast aside as the building of the new industrial city is represented as a sort of mass festival orchestrated by its party head. The local miners all participate as if in a *subbotnik,* and under the party head's direction all the buildings of the old miners' settlement are exploded in a scene reminiscent of the dramatic fireworks which normally marked the finale of the mass festival. Such scenes became a cliché of films in the mid-thirties for motivating giant leaps forward. Cherviakov's *The Convicts* (1937), about convicts working on the White Sea Canal, manages to include not just one set of explosions but three, with the final explosions set over water. However, these events were so fundamentally symbolic that they obviated the need to represent the actual building process. In *The Miners,* the new city is to rise phoenixlike from the ashes of the old, but it is never represented. Gestures are, however, made toward indicating that its engineer-architect (the party head) has designed the new city as a harmoniously integrated whole which will embrace not just the industrial plant and workers' housing but also the arts and sciences. Indeed, the film's original title was "The Gardener."

The "engineer," then, essentially functions as an emblem of order, control, and organization, and as the bearer of culture. As such, he—or the "engineer-architect"—does not necessarily have to be shown in an industrial context, or even in a contemporary one. Hence the novels, films, and plays about historical figures which form the bulk of Soviet cultural production in this period are, at some level, also about "industrialization."

By late 1935, when the Stakhanovite movement was launched in the rhetoric of the official platform, the cult of that which was rational and perfectly integrated was reversed. A new paradigm emerged which glorified not achieving harmonious order but rather violation of norms.[21] The new cultural hero was not the engineer but the *bogatyr'* who thrust all constraints aside—technological, administrative, and institutional—as he strode forward to perform extraordinary feats. One such constraint he thrust aside was the engineer, guardian and executor of norms, designer of the city.

Needless to say, in this new cultural model the "city" was not seriously threatened. It would of course be ridiculous to assume that in the *perestroika* of the Stakhanovite movement, order was disappearing from Stalinist Russia as an ideal. The story of the Stakhanovite is really a ritual of status reversal which is in its function status quo affirming. Indeed, the meaning of the Stakhanovite is in a sense that "every cook" can become an engineer, that every coal miner carries an engineering degree in his backpack (albeit in her or his engineering studies she or he will instinctively reject all foreign theories and authority figures).

Nevertheless, in the new culture hero one can see yet another turnabout in Stalinist culture; the previously dominant "antithesis" has been negated to usher in something closer to the original thesis. The "dragon" which, in Soviet political culture after 1935, the Stakhanovite-bogatyr must slay is the engineer or allied bureaucrat who insists that according to his expertise the proposed production schedule is unfeasible. In other words, once again public vilification of engineers coincided with the onset of a purge.

In the second half of the twenties, at the very time when the "engineer" was most deprecated and the account of what industrialization entails was at its most fantastic, one finds more fiction about industrialization than was to be found in the earlier years. However, literature did not adopt the template of the Stakhanovite in its entirety. The official myths which underpinned the Stakhanovite movement informed such marginally literary works as the hoaked-up *noviny*, or new folk epics, commissioned from some of the most famous singers of folk tales, and also ephemeral pamphlets, sketches written for the press and the like. In film, the official account of the Stakhanovite was generally reproduced with greater fidelity, though not with marked conviction. For example, in the case of Iutkevich's *The Miners* (1936), when problems in getting the film's scenario approved dragged on into the Stakhanovite era, Iutkevich was obliged to slot a Stakhanovite incident into it (after all, the film was set in the Donbass mines, cradle of Aleksei Stakhanov himself). However, even Soviet critics have admitted that the Stakhanovite incident comes across as a sheer formality and is unconvincing.[22]

Inevitably, literary works of these years also show the influence of the Stakhanovite cultural model, but in them its imagery and values are deployed with great ambivalence. Indeed, the two novels I have been discussing as examples of fiction in which the dominant metaphor is the building of the new socialist city as an icon of rational organization (i.e., *People from the Backwoods* and *Stepan Kol'chugin*), were in fact both published in 1938, at a time when one might expect them to be suffused with the ethos of the Stakhanovite movement. Yet both were hailed as models of socialist realism when they first appeared. The same disparity holds for another novel published in the same year but which was greeted with even greater acclaim in official quarters, Iurii Krymov's *The Tanker Derbent (Tanker 'Derbent')*; although the novel's topic is the Stakhanovite movement, it celebrates such values as control, discipline, teamwork, and training which are absent from the original Stakhanovite icon.[23]

The official acclaim accorded *The Tanker Derbent* is also significant because Krymov himself represents a new kind of Soviet writer, as does Grossman. If, during the plan years, writers could be berated for being remote from the tasks of industrialization, this could not be said of the new generation of writers entering literature during the thirties, most of whom were trained and also worked in engineering or some other practical field (such as agronomy) or entered literature from an apprenticeship in economic journalism. Indeed, the emergence of this new kind of writer has to be compared with the emergence of a new kind of political elite also with training in engineering and comparable fields in the applied sciences and which entered high politics at about the same time. These new political leaders, like the new wave of writers, came into greatest prominence in the post-Stalin era.

The novels which Grossman and Krymov published in 1938 were based on their own experience as engineers; Grossman was a chemical engineer who worked in mining towns of the Donbass, Krymov a petroleum engineer who worked on the Caspian and in other Southern locations before returning to an academic career at his old Moscow institute. *Stepan Kol'chugin* is about miners and a chemical engineer in the Donbass, while *The Tanker Derbent* is about a Stakhanovite competition between oil tankers on the Caspian. For such writers to represent "engineers" as totally negative characters would be to deny the value of their own expertise. The strategy both adopted is, rather, to distinguish between false engineers who are bourgeois and unworthy and the true engineer who has risen through the proletarian ranks. The ways they deprecate the bourgeois engineer are clichéd and predictable, but in their account of the engineer of proletarian origins they were able to present a more positive account of their own profession than the original Stakhanovite model allowed.

This disparity is most evident in *Stepan Kol'chugin* where Grossman confronts his hero with two rival mentor figures, one the head of the factory's chemical laboratory who tutors him in the natural sciences and the other Miata, a foreman. The figure of Miata is drawn along the lines of the Stakhanovite paradigm. Miata is, for instance, represented as having access to an almost mystical knowledge about blast furnaces, knowledge with which he is endowed as a true proletarian and which enables him to propose the only effective technical solutions every time the blast furnace breaks down. His solutions contradict, and thus ridicule, the methods recommended by the bourgeois (professional) engineers. Miata is also given a hyperbolically heroic depiction—he is even likened to Galileo, no less[24]—while the chemist is depicted as pusillanimous (like the factory director, he is afraid of the blast furnace). Thus on a formal level the proto-Stakhanovite proletarian nonprofessional triumphs, and yet the course of study Stepan passes through at the hands of the chemist is represented as essential to his development. Moreover, the incipient conflict between the two mentors which should force Stepan eventually to choose between them is never resolved because he passes out of the factory as he becomes a professional revolutionary. In that context, however (and this is quite revealing of Grossman's values), his principal mentor is not proletarian but a member of the old revolutionary intelligentsia (and Jewish).[25]

After the Great Purge was over, the official account of the Stakhanovite and the engineer was revised so that the Stakhanovite appeared less as an iconoclast and more as some sort of engineer-*vydvizhenets*. In literature, this reevaluation was taken further. Thus Iurii Krymov's novella *The Engineer* (*Inzhener*, January 1941), a sort of late straggler from the 1940 thaw in literature, contains in its account of a petroleum works in the Caspian area a critique of the Stakhanovite movement (and even to some extent of Soviet economic administration) from the standpoint of an engineer. The book, like most production fiction after 1931, plays on the distinction between "ideal" and "real," between the "essential image" and the ephemeral-seeming "detail," but it reverses the customary valorizations of the two, favoring the "real" over the "ideal." Thus the novella's "ideal" Stakhanovite cannot cope with a "real" emergency at the petroleum works because his knowledge of engineering is so limited. Of course, the novel's villains are certain professional engineers who deliberately neglect to tutor the potential future Galileo and only take glee as he flounders; they are thus in a sense responsible for the resultant and highly costly economic disaster. Nevertheless, we see in this novel no sign of the alternative and virtually mystical knowledge which in previous accounts of the Stakhanovite seemed somehow to emanate from his inner proletarian being and would emerge in an epiphany inspired by representatives of the Stalinist leadership. This novella confounds the conventions of thirties fiction by giving a negligible role to the party organizer and elevating instead the high government official to the status of the inspirational hero.

In such respects, *The Engineer* anticipates patterns of the post-Stalin thaw to be found in works such as V. Dudintsev's *Not by Bread Alone* (*Ne khlebom edinym*, 1956). One could speculate that the kind of new thinking about economic administration and the role of "engineers" in industrialization which, thanks to the repressive and conservative cultural climate of the forties known as Zhdanovism, had to wait for the early fifties to get much airing in literature, was in fact already being formulated by this new cohort of Soviet engineer-writers. Significantly, much of the most outspoken fiction produced in the early years of the post-Stalin thaw (1953–56) was written by writers who were originally trained as engineers, agronomists, or economic journalists and who were also party members (such as G. Trocpolsky and V. Ovechkin). Moreover, Grossman went on to write *For the Just Cause* (*Za pravoe delo*, 1952), a harbinger of the thaw after Stalin's death. Krymov was killed in the war in 1941, thus he was not able to make a contribution to the post-Stalin debates on economic and administrative policics, as one can only assume he would have done. However, his position was in a sense taken by other figures of an analogous background, such as D. Granin, who was like him an engineer by training (in this case an electrical engineer) and a party member, and who, like Grossman, anticipated the ethos of the post-Stalin thaw in his "Second Variant" [*Variant vtoroi*, 1952]). A little later, Granin produced several classics of the Khrushchev thaw, including *Those Who Seek* (*Iskateli*, 1954) and "His Own Opinion" (*Sobstvennoe mnenie*, 1956), which attack Stalinist excesses both in the industrial workplace and in Soviet science. He proved an outspoken figure under Gorbachev as well.[26]

Thus in the Stalinist thirties, industrialization became such an overwhelming imperative in Soviet society that in its political culture the role of the writer (as icon for the creative intellectual) was reformulated radically, and he or she was instructed to become an "engineer of human souls." Since the goal of industrial revolution was ultimately subordinated to the political, what this really meant was that the writer was virtually to become a faceless agent in a highly mechanistic scenario for the dissemination and inculcation of party doctrine. But then, in one of the many ironies of Soviet history, when the two functions engineer and writer began to *truly* merge in a new cohort of engineer-writers, this new breed of writer proved more active critics of party doctrine than most of their colleagues.

NOTES

1. "V poiskakh temy," *Literaturnaia gazeta*, 1938, no. 20, p. 1.

2. Thus, for instance, when G. Serebriakova produced a fictionalized biography of the young Marx (*Iunost' Marksa*, 1933–34) to mark the fiftieth anniversary of his death, she foregrounded a young proletarian, Johann Stock, to whom Marx allegedly felt a great, and reciprocated, closeness.

3. See "The Stalinist Myth of the *'bol'shaia sem'ia*" in Katerina Clark, *The Soviet Novel: History as Ritual* (Chicago: Chicago University Press, 1981).

4. "Segodnia otkryvaetsia vsesoiuznyi s"ezd pisatelei," *Literaturnaia gazeta*, 1934, no. 104 (August 17), p. 1. Actually, this represents a change from the prevailing position during the First Five-Year Plan when in an atmosphere of militant democratism the writer was expected to identify with the proletarian producer rather than with the engineer.

5. See N. P. Antsiferov, "Shakhtinskoe delo nauchnoi intelligentsii," in "Tri glavy iz vospominanii," *Pamiat': istoricheskii sbornik*, no. 4 (Paris: Y.M.C.A. Press, 1981), pp. 85–110; "Chistka apparata Akademii nauk," *Izvestiia*, September 10, 1929.

6. "Knizhnyi pokhod v derevniu," *Literaturnaia gazeta*, 1930, no. 5 (February 3); "Odnim iz osnovnykh kul'turnykh rychagov," *Literaturnaia gazeta*, 1930, no. 33 (August 5); Brigada RAPP, "Nado pisat' " [a poem], *Literaturnaia gazeta*, 1930, no. 48 (October 19); Iv. Batrak, "Pisateli na bol'shevistskii sev," *Literaturnaia gazeta*, 1931, no. 8 (February 9).

7. "Nam predstoit slomat' pisatel'skii individualizm!" *Literaturnaia gazeta*, 1929, no. 16 (August 6); S. Tret'iakov, "Postroimsia v brigady," *Literaturnaia gazeta*, 1930, no. 1; "Pisateli—V boi za promfinplan," *Literaturnaia gazeta*, 1930, no. 40 (September 9); "Pisateli nakanune tret'ego goda piatiletki. Proizvodstvennyi plan pisatelei na 1931 god," *Literaturnaia gazeta*, 1930, no. 61 (December 24); [Panferov's *Bruski* attacked for its agronomy] Agronom S. A. Kenokratov, "Golos chitatelia o 'Bruskakh'. Uchit' pomogat' sovremennoi derevne," *Literaturnaia gazeta*, 1930, no. 33 (August 5).

8. "Za rabochee shefstvo nad pisatel'skimi organizatsiiami," *Pravda*, August 5, 1930.

9. "Prizyv udarnikov v literaturu—vnimanie!" *Literaturnaia gazeta*, 1930, no. 48

(October 21); "Novye kadry literatury," *Literaturnaia gazeta,* 1930, no. 49 (October 24).

10. "Za rabochee shefstvo nad pisatel'skimi organizatsiiami," *Literaturnaia gazeta,* 1930, no. 34 (August 10), p. 1.

11. M. Shaginian, "O piatiletke i pisatel'skoi poshlosti," *Literaturnaia gazeta,* 1929, no. 16 (August 5), p. 2; "Za rabotu!" *Literaturnaia gazeta,* 1929, no. 27 (October 21), p. 1.

12. See the lament of the nonproletarian Union of Writers about this in "Razve my vredny! Pravlenie zasedaet . . .," *Literaturnaia gazeta,* 1929, no. 32 (November 25).

13. V. Kirshon, "Pervye itogi prizyva udarnikov v literaturu" [his speech to the Fourth Plenum of the Board of RAPP], *Literaturnaia gazeta,* 1931, no. 49 (September 10).

14. See, e.g., "Mozhno li priravniat' pisatelei k trudiashchimsia?" *Literaturnaia gazeta,* 1930, no. 6 (February 10); "Za edineniie pisatelia s izdatel'stvom," *Literaturnaia gazeta,* 1930, no. 8 (February 24).

15. "Proryv v GIKHL," *Literaturnaia gazeta,* 1931, no. 13 (March 9).

16. M. Charnyi, "Chto i kak," *Literaturnaia gazeta,*" 1933, no. 21 (May 5).

17. E.g., Iv. Anisimov, "Kniga o pafose novogo stroitel'stva. 'Vremia vpered,' " *Literaturnaia gazeta,* 1933, no. 6 (February 5).

18. See, e.g., Dziga Vertov's film *The Man with a Movie Camera* (*Chelovek s kinoapparatom,* 1929), Marietta Shaginian's *Hydrocentral* (*Gidrotsentral',* 1930–31), and F. Gladkov's *Power* (*Energiia,* 1932).

19. Northrop Frye, "Varieties of Literary Utopia," in Frank E. Manuel (ed.), *Utopias and Utopian Thought* (Boston: Houghton Mifflin, 1966), pp. 27, 37–38.

20. Vasilii Grossman, *Stepan Kol'chugin,* pt. II (Moscow: GIKHL, 1939), pp. 97–98.

21. This paradigm is described in some detail in my book *The Soviet Novel: History as Ritual.*

22. *Istoriia sovetskogo kino, 1917–1967,* vol. II, 1931–41 (Moscow: Iskusstvo, 1973), pp. 188–89.

23. For more on this novel, see my "Utopian Anthropology as a Context for Stalinist Literature," in Robert C. Tucker (ed.), *Stalinism: Essays in Historical Perspective* (New York: Norton, 1977), p. 198.

24. Vasilii Grossman, *Stepan Kol'chugin,* pt. II, *God XXII. al'manakh chetyrnadtsatyi* (Moscow: GIKHL, 1938), p. 97.

25. In Grossman's first published story, "It Happened in Berdichev" (1934, on which *The Commissar,* the recently released film by Askoldov, is based), the Jewish protagonists see in the commissar-protagonist's final quixotic gesture the sort of revolutionary ideal which they have encountered before only in the Bund. (This dimension was replaced in Askoldov's film by a somewhat sentimentalized account of Jewish ethnicity totally absent from the original.)

26. Consider his novel *The Aurochs* (*Zubr*) of 1987 about excessive scientism in Soviet society, or his open letter to *Moscow News* of November 1989 condemning the Soviet invasion of Czechoslovakia in 1968.

XII

SOVIET INDUSTRIALIZATION FROM A EUROPEAN PERSPECTIVE

Geoff Eley

For an outsider, the Soviet social history field has seemed, during the past ten years or so, to be an exceptionally lively and interesting one.[1] This is partly to do with the remarkable proliferation of primary research and associated publication and discussion. For example, if I think back to the late-1960s, when I first learned my Soviet history, or the late-1970s, when I was teaching it to undergraduates in Cambridge, there were the merest handful of major works from which to take one's bearings—Carr, Shanin, and Lewin, Pethybridge's two books, Cohen's biography, Fitzpatrick's book on Lunacharsky, and that was about it. Now, it seems to me, the situation has changed out of all recognition because of the research, monographs, articles, and continuing activity of those who have been involved in the seminar over the years. If the social history of the Soviet Union exists as a fully constituted field of inquiry, then it has really been due to the students inspired by a small number of senior and relatively senior scholars on both sides of the Atlantic: Davies, Lewin, Haimson, Rosenberg, Zelnik, Rabinowitch, and so on. This seems to me to be no mean achievement, and one that has been borne by a level of collective discussion and exchange through conferences, seminars, and symposia that is simply not present in other fields of modern European social history.

What I'd like to do in these brief comments is (1) to outline some of what seem to me to be the main features of social-historical discussion in West European fields, as a way of establishing a context within which to consider some of the features of the Soviet discussion, and (2) to offer a few comments on the specificities of Soviet industrialization itself. I'd like to raise the question of the general comparability of the Soviet industrialization, and to do this along two dimensions—first, the dimension of historiography (the degree to which the literature and the discussion in this conference in particular reflect problems and approaches broached in other European fields), and second, the dimension of comparison more directly (namely, the degree to which the Soviet industrialization experience itself is comparable or not comparable to other national experiences).

Most obviously, social history in West European fields has simply involved a massive expansion of historical inquiry into new empirical terrain—demography, the family, peasant studies, recreation, the social history of the working class, and so on. With respect to the social history of industrialization, the social history of the working class naturally assumes a central place, and I'm going to make a few observations on this major subfield of social history in particular. Here I want to draw attention to three features of the post-1960s developments, each of which is conventionally attached to the influence of E. P. Thompson and *The Making of the English Working Class,* published in 1963.

First, we can mention the shift from an institutionally and biographically centered conception of the labor movement to the analysis of the class "itself" and its conditions of life, with a stress on "consciousness," "culture," and "ways of life." Second, there has been the gravitation of empirical research to a novel territory beyond either politics or work, defined more residually than theoretically in cultural terms, but suggested by all the characteristic themes of the new left critique of everyday life and by late-sixties countercultural discourse—community and self-management; popular recreation, from entertainment to drinking and sport; madness, criminality, and deviance; youth; the family; and eventually, somewhat later in the 1970s, the history of women, sexuality, and gender.

But third, this exuberant conquest of a new agenda *also* entailed a major change of perspective, in which history became simultaneously an act of partisanship, identification, and retrieval. For a large number of British and American practitioners, social history meant writing the history of ordinary people—recovering suppressed alternatives, returning people to a knowledge of their own past, reconstructing the main record "from the bottom up." Shorn of some naiveté and romanticism and recast by intervening political developments, this remains a powerful element in much social historical discussion. In Thompson's familiar words, he wished "to rescue the poor stockinger, the Luddite cropper, the 'obsolete' handloom weaver, the 'utopian' artisan, and even the deluded follower of Joanna Southcott, from the enormous condescension of posterity." Or, in the recent words of a very different social historian, Charles Tilly, social history is about "retrieving European lives."

If we keep these observations in mind for the moment and turn to the Soviet field, I think we'll find that the latter has displayed both the advantages and disadvantages of the latecomer. On one hand, the Soviet field can benefit from the accumulated experience of other national historiographies, methodologically and substantively, and so in a certain sense can potentially enter the discussion at a higher level without having to repeat some of the mistakes, wrong turnings, and unfruitful controversies that marked the progress of developments in other national fields. On the other hand, the Soviet work has had to begin in an empirical sense virtually from scratch—some of the basic building blocks of knowledge have just not been available (although we can certainly exaggerate the extent to which they have been so available elsewhere).

There is a clear sense in which prior social historical discussions in West European fields have had a major formative impact on the first generation of late-imperial and revolutionary research that emerged from the 1970s. For example, discussions at the Berkeley conference on the social history of Russian labor in 1982 were certainly informed very strongly by the existing discussions of working-class formation in British and other West European fields, not to speak of North American social history, which provided some direct input into the conference itself through David Montgomery. During the past ten years we have also seen the familiar pattern of proliferation that has characterized those other national fields—from the history of the working class to the social history of other social groups, and to studies of mass institutions such as schooling, conscription, and the professions—so that Russian social history has already started to encompass the established roster of social history subfields: leisure, recreation, medicine and public health, housing, deviance, criminality and the law, family and de-mographical history, women's history, and so on. But I think this is true only if we consider the late-imperial, revolutionary, and early Soviet peri-ods as a whole. It is much *less* true when we turn to the 1930s more specifically. One of the things that impressed me most strongly in reading the papers for this conference and listening to the discussions has been the degree to which the established preoccupations of the other national fields have been *absent* from the problematic of the 1930s Soviet working class. In particular, there was very little discussion of the whole question of working-class *culture.* This is very important, because culture, however specifically understood, has been absolutely central to the discussion of the formation of the working class elsewhere and has been similarly crucial, I would argue, to the emerging discussion of the problem of working-class forma-tion in Russia between the 1880s and the 1920s.

It is worth dwelling on this issue. The question of culture has been absent from the discussion of the 1930s for a reason, and that reason has much to do with the conditions of flux and dislocation understandably emphasized in all the contributions specifically dealing with the working class and the peasantry. There is a presumption, in other words, that the culturalist type of class analyses and its nostrums (having to do with notions of community and the salience of certain cultural traditions) *don't* apply. Perhaps the best example here is Hiroaki Kuromiya's essay on the coal miners, in which the cultural dimension of miners' experience is completely missing. In one sense, neither of the culturalist nostrums about class formation—the im-portance of artisan traditions or a particular ideal of working-class com-munity—is relevant to the miners' situation; but in another sense, the culture of work and of the miners' occupational traditions has to remain important, despite the massive mobility rates, the impact of mechanization, and so on. In a broader theoretical sense, of course, it would be impossible to bracket culture as such from an informed account. In the case of the mines in the Ruhr and Silesia before 1914 in Germany, for example, where the levels of flux and indeterminacy in the miners' circumstances were also extremely high (in terms of in- and out-migration, job changing, the brutality of living conditions, and the absence of community), the tacit suppression of culture would make absolutely no sense.

So it does seem to me that it must be possible to identify sectors of industry or categories of skilled and semi-skilled workers (whether printers or sections of the textile industry or parts of the historic metalworking sectors) where the structural continuities across the 1928–29 divide were sufficiently substantial to have allowed a definite culture of work to survive. Likewise, in these and other sectors, new cultural formations must have materialized in the course of and by the end of the 1930s, too. For all its fascination, Magnitogorsk must have represented a particular kind of extreme in this sense; and if cultures of resistance and solidarity can take shape in the townships and labor compounds of contemporary South Africa, then they certainly could have done so in the Soviet 1930s. Incidentally, the question of historical memory raised by John Barber during the discussion seems to me to be quite relevant to this question of working-class culture in the context of specific industries and occupations, because it concerns the processes and forms through which particular values and practices are reproduced and transmitted across generations, and for this the more ethnological conception of culture associated with Thompson and his influence seems to be essential.

Next, I want to say a few words about the question of politics, again with reference to the existing historiography of other European fields. One of the most exciting and lasting goods to come out of the earlier founding moment of social history in the late 1960s was an expanded notion of "the political" in social life—that is, a radically de-institutionalized understanding of politics, in which questions of conformity, opposition, and consent, of the potential for cohesion and stability in the social order, of the strength or fragility of the dominant value system, in short, the fundamental conceptual questions of political order, were displaced *out of* the traditional institutional order for studying them (the state, government institutions, and public organizations in the *narrower* sense) and onto a variety of noninstitutional settings previously regarded as "nonpolitical." Those settings were precisely the new areas of study that the post-1960s social history has been associated with opening up—the workplace, the street and the neighbourhood, the criminal or deviant subculture, the recreational domain, and the family and the home. What this also involved, I think—though reaching this realization has by no means been a simple process in other European fields—was an expanded appreciation of how the state is involved in society, outgrowing the boundaries of government in the conventional sense to embrace areas of social administration, public health, the law, schooling, religious belief, the organization of private life in families, sexuality, gender distinctions at work and elsewhere, and the shifting boundary between the public and the private.

Now, when we talk about the importance of "bringing the state back in," in the sense of a specifically constituted field of relations between state and society, *this* is what we should mean; and sorting out this particular question seems to me to be one of the most important questions on the future agenda.

There are two other areas I want to mention, gender and language, in which current discussions among West European social historians don't seem to have made much impression on the Soviet industrialization problematic as that is apparently being addressed, although they are both much more recent developments in the West European discussions than the ones I have so far been suggesting. There was surprisingly little explicit discussion of gender in the conference papers, with the exception of John Barber's and one or two others, and Stephan Merl's fascinating picture of a reconstituted patriarchy in the collectivized countryside, in which a male managerial and clerico-administrative stratum seems to have abandoned productive labor more or less completely to the women. But I was surprised that gender did not function as a category of analysis, even as a very salient conceptual dimension, in many of the papers.

Similarly, the linguistic turn of recent West European social history seems barely to have ruffled the surface of Soviet discussions. We can argue over whether in general this is a good or a bad thing, but for certain purposes at least it seems to me to be very important. I am thinking especially of the extensive discussions of the language of "us/them," through which the various mobilizations and later the terror were organized and expressed, and for which some knowledge of linguistic and discourse-theoretical approaches would be very fruitful from this point of view. What such approaches amount to at one level is an extremely sophisticated way of conceptualizing the problem of ideology. And that returns us to the question of the nature of the "political" that I have been stressing.

Moreover, when the language of "enemies," "corruption," "pollution," and "degeneration" is used, the technicians of the body are usually at work. In this respect, Susan Solomon's remarks were potentially enormously important, in terms of the medicalization of social phenomena and social policies most immediately, but more generally in terms of the construction of the social via state policies in a new and specific way (and not just state policies, but the action on society of technicians of all kinds). In listening to the discussions about technicians and engineers and specialists and buccaneering extrepreneurs, I was reminded of a term that was used in a conference on the Third Reich that I recently attended, namely *Machbarkeitswahn*—a kind of madness of "makability," a euphoria of project making that became possible under the edicts of the centralist Nazi state. Now, I don't want to reintroduce simplicities of the totalitarian mode, but it seems to me there are important correspondences in this respect that deserve to be thought through.

I want to finish with a comment on industrialization. What is the specificity of the Soviet case? I don't really have any startling new insights to offer here, but it is an important general point to get back on the table. The most obvious point, I think, is that the Soviet industrialization was totally without precedent. It is as if every stage of, say, the British experience of industrialization, from the enclosures of the eighteenth century to the rationalization debates of the 1920s, was taken, appropriated, and compressed into a single five-year period. And, of course, this was done by the conscious vision of a centralist and directive state intervention. There were, arguably, already some anticipations of this in the later European industrializations before 1914; the German, Italian, and of course Imperial Russian ones displayed levels of concentration and forms of state intervention much more substantial than hitherto. The necessary initiating role of the state was also enormously more important; and, as we know, in the Italian and Russian cases, this was already dramatically more directive than in the German case that preceded them. Even so, it seems to me there is nothing that could have prepared European consciousness for the vastness and ferocity of the managed, administered upheaval that got under way at the end of the Soviet 1920s. This may be obvious, but I think there is no harm in reiterating it, and it becomes specifically important when we come to the question of comparison and comparability. It is clear that bits and pieces of the Soviet experience are perfectly comparable to the West European ones. One might also mention the question of mobility and industrialization in the north of Italy between the 1890s and 1915, and even more so during the war years of 1915–18.

But the case I want to come back to is that of the coal miners. For I don't find the figures for mobility in the Donbass qualitatively different from those in the Ruhr in the last two decades of the nineteenth century. It is true that we are dealing with five, as opposed to twenty, years, and that is clearly a major difference, though the respective scales of change are both so great that the comparison seems to me to be perfectly viable. What is really different is the overall societal context, in two senses: first, that the entire society in the Soviet case is in febrile motion; and second, that in the Soviet case there is a state-directive center. What I want to say as strongly as possible is that the plan constitutes the irreducible specificity of Soviet industrialization, and the plan not in some idealized sense but in terms of this administered and managed state-initiated process.

So in that case, what would be a sensible comparison in overall societal terms? The other cases of socialist industrialization, particularly China but also Eastern Europe, are the obvious recourse in this respect, and I certainly wouldn't want to imply that some serious work in this area is anything less than a priority. But in terms of the role of the state, the dimensions of the societal upheaval, the mobilization of the countryside into the towns, the massive social problems of the kind itemized by John Barber, and last but not least, mutatis mutandis, the role of terror, certain cases of Third World industrialization such as Brazil in the 1960s and 1970s may provide very interesting bases of comparison. If we are to think of new and illuminating forms of comparison for the Soviet industrialization, then it is perhaps not back into the European precedents but forward into some of the major Third World industrializations of the recent decades that we should look. In retrospect, the Soviet case may emerge as the most tragic and grandiose example of nationally bounded and state-directed industrialization in a global economy which, at the end of the twentieth century, is fast being transformed in quite new (post-Fordist, transnational) directions.

NOTES

1. These thoughts originated as a concluding comment delivered at the Soviet Industrialization Conference in April 1988. Rather than elaborating the argument and providing detailed references, I have kept the text as it was, that is, as a spoken response to the immediate ambience of the conference. In the meantime, gender and language (whose absence I noted in the discussions in April 1988) have announced their arrival in Soviet historical discussions at a subsequent conference on the formation of the Soviet working class at Michigan State University in November 1990, also referred to by Lewis Siegelbaum and Ronald Suny in their essay earlier in this volume. Otherwise, my use of the Ruhr coalfield for comparison with the Donbass can be pursued through David Crew's classic study of German miners and metalworkers, *Town in the Ruhr: A Social History of Bochum 1860–1914* (New York, 1979). My comparative reference to South Africa labor compounds may be followed up in the writings of Charles van Onselen, *Chibaro: African Mine Labour in Southern Rhodesia 1900–1933* (London, 1976) and *Studies in the Social and Economic History of the Witwatersrand, 1886–1914*, 2 vols. (London, 1982). The term *Machbarkeitswahn* was used by the late Detlev Peukert in his unpublished paper, "The Genesis of the 'Final Solution' from the Spirit of Science," presented to the conference on Re-evaluating the Third Reich, University of Pennsylvania, April 1988. My own extended thoughts on the current state of social history may be followed in "Is All the World a Text? From Social History to the History of Society Two Decades Later," in Terrence McDonald (ed.), *The Historic Turn in the Human Sciences* (forthcoming).

XIII

ON SOVIET INDUSTRIALIZATION

Moshe Lewin

"Change is demonic," David Landes maintained in the epigraph to his book on industrialization[1]—and during the years we are studying, change was certainly more demonic than at most other times.[2] The 1930s was a brief period, but it was crammed with shifting, intermingling social processes that moved in a chaotic and intense historical development. These processes produced, simultaneously, the most advanced and most archaic features, which permeated and actually defined the whole period.[3] On the face of it, the period looked as if it had been neatly packaged into five-year installments, planned and executed by a strong, forward-looking state and led by a towering leader. As historical research advanced, the tidiness of this picture began to crack, revealing contradictions and pathologies. What was transitional in this system, and what was bequeathed to its heirs, also began to emerge.

One of the key features of the whole industrialization process was the role of the state and of the will of top Soviet leaders in the country's developmental strategy (although there was also plenty of spontaneity—the obverse side of the coin—which I will deal with later). About 8,000 huge and presumably modern enterprises were built during the twelve "planned" years (1928–41) under state-imposed tempos and the more or less unlimited priority accorded to heavy industry. The special circumstances of the period added stringency and intensity to the process, especially the dwindling performance of agriculture and the menace of a war looming on the horizon. In particular, the fear of having to fight on two fronts—west and east (Japan)—must have played an important role in the "pushing" and pressurizing style that was adopted by the leaders on the economic "front." There were other issues as well, as we will see.

First, however, it is worth a brief flashback to the later 1920s and the period that triggered the "big drive" from 1928 on. The later 1920s were a watershed. Modern anti-Stalinists in the Soviet Union exaggerate the economic achievements of NEP. They fail to see that much of what NEP accomplished consisted in "restoring" unused or poorly used plants to full production. Restoration could be presented as a success—it certainly was one—but it had its pitfalls. The marking point for the restoration effort was the level of 1913, and attempting to reach this point in Russia's past involved particular difficulties. First, industrial equipment, already old, was aging further at a dangerous pace. Second, despite the successes of restoration, the shadows of backwardness were also lengthening.

"Backwardness" is an idea that comes "from abroad." The level of the most developed countries determines who is backward and to what degree. In the late 1920s, the industrially "advanced" countries were moving ahead in science, technology, and the rationalization of management; they crested, actually, just before the big crash of the 1930s; and from this point of view, Soviet Russia was actually crawling backward. In practical terms, this meant that Russia needed more capital to acquire the most advanced technology, not as a whim but as an economic necessity. The same was true for technical and administrative cadres.

Another difficult problem was the so-called goods famine. Industry was not supplying enough goods at sufficiently cheap prices for the population, most notably for the agricultural majority, including what peasants needed to improve their productivity.

On the government's agenda there thus emerged the vital problem of formulating a strategy for industrialization. The need was to improve and accelerate industrial production and to innovate—and it had to be done on some significant scale, not simply "incrementally." It was not just a matter of how to do it but also of where to find the necessary means. By the same token, an industrialization strategy had to devise social policies, attend to relations with the peasants, and reflect upon the role and methods of planning; in actuality, it affected the shape of the regime itself.

If change is demonic, then speedy economic and industrial change is particularly so, as events in Russia would prove. Those who thought that all that was needed was to go slowly, "on the peasant cart," "on the rails of the NEP"—as Bukharin believed around 1925 (but understood better a few years later)—were wrong. NEP, in practice, showed signs of not coping, perhaps even of the beginnings of a crisis. Rethinking its ways was urgent. Whatever the uses to which the general NEP framework could still be put, the NEP economy itself was too weak a base to assure the safe survival of the Soviet state. Its "restoration," important per se, consisted basically in "catching up" with the prerevolutionary past. This was an historical handicap, emphasized, as we have said, by the continuing advances of the West.

Consequently, 1928 was a real, not a contrived, crossroads, which Stalin seized upon and interpreted in his own way. Does this mean that the policies Stalin and his supporters adopted were justified and that NEP should have been discarded? Was Stalin's interpretation and response at this moment the only one possible, or was it even correct at all? Was everything Preobrazhenskii said during "the industrialization debate" necessarily wrong? Or was NEP itself, so to speak, "guilty" of Russia's difficulties?

To point to the difficulties or even the crisis of NEP is not, in itself, to prejudge the problem of its viability; nor do we imply that there was only one way of dealing with the difficulties. Any student of the Stalinist five-year plans knows that the story of Stalin's industrial and agricultural policies offers plenty of arguments to its critics. At least it requires that very serious consideration be accorded to all and any of the protagonists in the debate, before and during the plans. This is so because the history of industrialization in the 1930s is not just a story of what was done but also a long list of things that should not have been done, nor planned. In fact, when studying the economic history of the period, it makes no sense at all to use the plan sequences as markers for periodization. The First Five-Year Plan, which was supposedly fulfilled in four years, landed the country in such chaos that it took at least two years to straighten things out. One of the causes was the constant augmenting of different plan targets by the center. This deprived the plan itself of whatever coherence it might have had and nipped its very essence in the bud. The second plan was certainly a fictitious product, because it was launched two years after it was supposed to have begun. A look at the printed volumes of those plans, notably the third, in comparison with the impressive (on paper) first plan, tells the story. So it is time to put to rest the myth that the economy during the plans was planned. It was at best administered, but this begins to touch on questions that belong to an altogether different book.

The problem at the end of the twenties were very serious indeed, and good leadership would have responded to the complexity of the situation with an appropriately formulated, thoughtful strategy. What the country got instead was industrialization, not as an economic activity or even an administrative-economic one but as an "onslaught," a civil war cavalry charge, a quasi-military operation, in which military terms themselves became the language of the day, used profusely and with good reason. Why did it get this strategy, rather than a different one?

Before we address this question, we should briefly account for the fact that Stalinist policies in the 1930s and later enjoyed considerable support in the party and the population at large. The degree of this support and its social map varied at different times, but there was enough of it to ensure the whole policy a high degree of success. The sources of support for the policies can be sketched out as follows.

First, one should mention the tactical weakness of the opponents of the line adopted by Stalin. This in itself is related to the character and development of the party at the time the fateful decisions were being taken. Its centralized and "depoliticized" features were reinforced in the battles against the oppositions, and this process occurred against the background of a massive influx into the party of ordinary Russians (and other sociological trends to be explained briefly) who almost by definition could not be a factor in these debates. These people mostly just followed the apparat. This is one of the facets of "depoliticization"—the exclusion, in fact, of party members from involvement in politics.

The narrowness of the ruling apex, the other face of the same process, is crucial; it allowed a small number of people to define the historical situation and the strategy to adopt—and it was this small number that decided that NEP should be discarded. More precisely, this narrowness of the apex in a depoliticized party allowed for very crucial decisions to be taken by only a part of the leading group, its majority (in a system where even a strong minority did not have any statutory way of preserving at least the possibility of regaining power once the policy in question failed).

Obviously, chance also had a role to play in these events (the skill of a leader, accidental elements in the making of the majority, and notably, simply the lack of intelligence or stamina in one or two people at the top). But whatever the explanation, a line of action emerged with incalculable consequences. (The same combination of trend and chance occurred in the transformation of the obvious first fiddle into a personal tyrant—which was just a few years ahead, in conditions that were also part of those "incalculable consequences.")

Our inquiry into the "sources of success" must now consider the large social restructuring that took place, notably the massive promotion of millions of people into new, often socially more prestigious jobs. In view of the low social status of most of the population, this was rather easily done. The process was already under way during the big recruitments into the party during the 1920s, notably during the "Lenin enrollment," as well as in later recruitment campaigns. In the 1930s, the policy of advancement acquired a much broader dimension. The phenomenon of the so-called *praktiki* was the epitome of the process. We must pay attention to the feat of massive schooling that industrialization entailed. But schooling could not supply the necessary cadres quickly enough. The answer was found by promoting people from lowly backgrounds into positions of importance— technical, administrative, and political—in most cases without the proper education and professional training. Such cadres constituted the majority in political, administrative, and even engineering jobs. One would expect on the part of these cadres "gratitude" toward the regime, a feeling of insecurity on the job, a dependence on patronage.

A further impetus to success was provided by the powerful appeal of the "backwardness" thesis, and the need to overcome "backwardness" in a single leap. Stalin's "manifesto" of 1931 about Russia being perennially beaten by foreigners and now having to catch up in ten years to what others had taken a century to achieve became the official ethos of the building effort. Identification of this policy and this leadership with the greatest of national and patriotic tasks, and with the only strategy available, dazzling by its daring and range and without precedent in Russian and world history—all of this struck a chord in many hearts. This has to be remembered and understood.

Here one can see some of the sources for the acceptance of Stalin's leadership by the cadres, and probably by many if not most of the people. Even his resoluteness and ruthlessness in pursuing these aims and their supposed enemies made a big impression, providing the appropriate psychological underpinnings for "the cult" and much of what went with it. But this was also notably so because the "big drive" itself was capable of going a long way toward actually industrializing the country and, by the same token, strengthening its defense.

But locating these supports for the policies of industrialization is not in itself an assessment of what it was and, especially, what it produced. What it produced was *a system*—and this is what counts most for our purpose. The achievements of the early stage were of enormous importance, but it was equally important that this system, which developed early on, contained within itself the mechanisms of its own exhaustion or self-destruction.

Once applied, the industrialization and other political strategies of those years caused a massive and multifarious restructuring. The system now had to live with and endure its results, which were many and quite complex. The economic sphere lashed back at the political system by "economizing" it, notably by transforming the party into an economic-administrative agency. In return, the party "exported" its ways of running the economy to all other spheres of its activities.

The social sphere, stirred up by enormous changes and the ensuing social flux, entered into a state of permanent tension and crisis, which the state tried to control and master, most often by hardening its repressive methods and urges. The effects of the forceful collectivization of the peasants added enormous complications, throwing millions of peasants into the cities but supplying quite insufficient amounts of food. The famine of 1932–33 that took millions of lives has to be attributed to the ensemble of policies rather than to vagaries of nature.

As the big drive unfolded, planning and administration became oriented toward quantitative targets and measures of performance. Such an orientation underscores the extensive character of the policies and of the whole endeavor, with its insistence on tons, units, and percentages imposed from above on economic actors, thereby reverting, as it were, to an old historical tradition. Because the ruling agency was the same, a similar tendency prevailed in many other spheres of life.

The period cannot be understood without considering the cost of eliminating NEP. Markets and market categories, considered to be breeders par excellence of capitalism, became of residual economic importance. On the other hand, the scope of economic nationalization by state agencies surpassed by far the statization that occurred during the Civil War. As prices, profits, and costs lost their guiding function, the economy (except for its illicit sectors) no longer worked for profits, but neither did it work for consumers. It worked "for the plan." And this meant, again, that the whole setting built in the primacy of the political-administrative institutions and principles over the economy and economic ones.

It also promoted a partially illusory independence of those institutions (and of the officials who populated them) from economic realities. The bureaucratic grid and methods that grew immensely during those years managed to arrogate for themselves, for a time, a set of shelters guaranteed by the political will—but no shelter from the political will itself, again, just for a certain period.

A very steep concentration of power at the top—already considerable at the end of NEP—was also built in the "planning" of those years. A bureaucracy that is allowed to operate independently of economic criteria and results, and that lacks a concept of cost, looks for criteria and reference points that are, in its view, natural and manageable, i.e., quantitative targets. Unfortunately, the complexity of real processes, and notably the behavior of economic actors and agents, highly skilled in finding a host of evasive subterfuges, made such targets ineffective. Thus instead of saving resources, the factories hoarded them; instead of using labor sparingly and training it well, they overemployed; instead of working well, they tried to look good.

The list of malfunctions is long and well known. They were countered by more targets and even more controllers to watch over their fulfillment. A quantity-oriented management, with its multiple-target planning, requires a bureaucracy oriented toward control and a growing army of officials. Here was an additional stimulus toward the centralization of power in circumstances that showed increasing signs of suffering from "over-centralization."

Grounded in dysfunctions, the command system was a dysfunctional factor itself. The history of the five-year plans was one of deep-seated arrythmia, of "storming" at the end of each quarter, of spasmodic campaigning, of constant jolting of individuals and masses of people, of cascades of emergencies dealt with by "shock methods." No wonder that the system tended to be characterized as "mobilizational" by some, as "a command economy" by others. But obviously it was also a system plagued by perpetual imbalances. Bottlenecks were treated by shock methods, and shock methods created imbalances: production was surging ahead, but transportation was lagging; workers were massed on a building site, but there was no housing for them and not enough engineers; heavy industry was promoted, but agriculture was in terrible shape; labor productivity was demanded, but not enough food, spare parts, or material ever arrived on time, causing endless production stoppages *(prostoi).*

It conforms to the logic of the situation that mastering such a whirlwind pushed the controlling needs and appetites of the center to new heights. And the personal despot who emerged in those years was the incarnation of supercentralization—one could not go farther than that on this road.

Accompanying this situation was a sense of omnipotence that was real in many ways, even if illusory in many others: a power over the fate of many people, but actual powerlessness in regard to the process in general.

Again, the unplanned character of Soviet industrialization has to be emphasized to make the previous remarks more explicit.[4] Actually, economic activity conducted as a set of pressurized waves of investment for growth and at an imposed pace could not be planned. Hence, despite so many controls and controlling agencies, the mastery of the process itself eluded the state. The economic process as a whole was not obeying any commands, although the planners were drowning in endless details. The system was losing its sense of direction, and the much-vaunted tempos, the heart of the strategy, had to be manipulated by the statisticians to look better than they actually were.

No wonder that this latest version of the age-old tradition of "extensive" methods was showing its limits. It suffered from a penchant to destroy (or a failure to create) incentives and mechanisms indispensable for qualitative improvements and technological change.

The deep bureaucratization of the economy, coupled with the special features of the Soviet polity, produced a mix of contradictory driving forces deriving from bureaucratic self-interest on one hand and arbitrary political will on the other. This was one of the main things that prevented the emergence of the right mix of incentives that could assure a normal function of an economic system. As whole branches of industry were built, some entirely new to the country, one certainly could speak of a new industrial power emerging in Europe—a fact that cannot be taken away from those years. But this new power was endowed with disquieting features. We have alluded to a built-in tendency to produce damaging imbalances that, if left unchecked, were an economic time bomb for the longer run. Initial successes therefore had their Achilles' heel—notably their cost, the cost, that is, of not heeding cost, actually, of not being able to heed it.

This peculiarly "uneconomical" quality was actually an important factor that fed growth during "the big drive," but later, not unexpectedly, it turned into a phenomenon of waste. And here again, costs could not be calculated. The system came to be hooked on waste—it could not work without it, and it built up huge constituencies that thrived on it. Much of what was done was actually unneeded! One day the absurdity simply became overwhelming.

All of this followed from the basic premises of the initial action. In the absence of market mechanisms that could supply feedback to correct problems, the emerging system produced elaborate ways to hide them. On the face of it the ubiquitous party, the trade unions, the secret police, the procuracy—this is not the whole list—should have "seen" the problems, should have signaled and mended malfunctions. Instead, the proliferation of such agencies, mostly irrelevant to economic activity, was itself part of the problem.

The waste that was exposed in Gorbachev's USSR with such vehemence and bewilderment was also embedded in the mode of operation introduced in the 1930s. The pride of those years—the big building sites *(stroiki)* of industrial giants—was the heartbeat of the big drive, but it was also an illustration of the waste that came to stay. These sites were the biggest recipients of the investment splurge of the plan era—"splurge," because too many of them were initiated simultaneously, without enough experience, cadres or builders, and all ended up taking much more time to build than planned, cost much more, and went through extremely painful starting periods. Construction began before the design work was ready; machines arrived from abroad but often rusted in the snow because the factory was not ready to house them or nobody knew how to install or operate them. Such stroiki thus became great consumers of capital, tying up for many years badly needed resources and forcing still further efforts and more investment—all to keep the economy moving. Waste was written all over these methods and, curiously but symptomatically, it remained a permanent part of the system in the form of a large *front* of new stroiki, seemingly never finished, and increasingly obsolete, morally or otherwise, well before they could produce anything.

We can also discern in this sketch the relation between quantity and waste. Pressure for quantity as the main criterion of controllable success led toward the overextension of resources, an overextension that could only be overcome by pouring still more investment that had an ever more difficult task overcoming the accumulating mechanisms of slowdown. The Hungarian economist Janos Kornai, who studied the already mature result of the 1930s in the 1970s, defined the system as basically driven by an orientation on investment, but it was still a mechanism plagued by permanent and widespread shortages.[5]

Kornai stated correctly that such a system can and does function, but he did not ask how long it could last. The resources of a huge and rich country could allow some time to pass, and another internal mechanism—the illegitimate but widely practiced hoarding and concealing of reserves inside the plants—helped to cushion production against stringencies of the plans and thereby afford unwittingly some more breathing space for the whole system. But eventually the system had to come to a grinding halt, after years of stagnation or *zastoi,* as Soviet writers call it. A *zatratnyi* system, i.e., one oriented on spending, was inefficient by definition. It produced enormous amounts of *brak* (waste) and useless items, almost deliberately *na sklad* (for the storerooms), that is, for no one in fact. But such production still earned reimbursement by the state, as if it were normally useful output. Enormous numbers of people, workers and officials alike of different standing, were reared on and invested in efficiency, poor workmanship, and, basically, economic parasitism. The lack of interest in technological innovation in these circumstances goes without saying. Technological progress was selectively introduced by pressure from the state, but primary production units had no use for it nor interest in it. It was actually a nuisance to them and even to the planners.

Here was a powerful trap for the not-too-distant future. The constant attempt to motivate people, to provide them with stimuli to exert themselves or to engage in creative initiatives, did not yield results. Working "for the plan" was not the same thing as an activity exercised in conditions of sufficient autonomy that depended on self-interest and results. In the 1930s the system was still dynamic; in the late 1970s, it was barely moving under the impact of sclerotic sediments accumulated over the decades.

It is of interest to the whole question of Soviet industrialization to mention here, briefly, the anticipations of some Bolsheviks in regard to bureaucratization. Trotsky, for example, in the 1923–24 *Pravda* articles that were collected and published as *The New Course,*[6] observed and analyzed the making of a party apparatus, the concomitant loss by the party of its initial political essence, and its transformation into a different type of organization. The party, a supervisor and direct "guide" of the state apparatus, was being contaminated, as it were, by the object of its supervision. In later years Bukharin, once he turned in 1928 against Stalin's policies, warned equally emphatically against the bureaucratic danger. In his "Notes of an Economist," he forecast that the elimination of markets and small-scale private sectors and reliance on an administrative type of planning would lead to the creation of a colossal and costly apparatus.[7]

Together the observations and premonitions of these two very different Bolsheviks anticipated correctly some of the facets of the coming administrative system, and there were many more such insights and reflections in those years. What they could not yet envisage was the virtual engulfing of the party by the state system at some later stage, and its transformation, essentially, into the mouthpiece for the upper layers of the state bureaucracy.

Obviously, industrialization was not the only impetus to bureaucratic state building of the 1930s, but it was a crucial one; and this time the phenomenon surpassed in scope anything tsarist or NEP Russia had seen. Commissariats and other agencies began to proliferate, especially in the later part of the decade, and acquired a momentum of their own. As they were, in many ways, producers themselves of incoherences and, of course, red tape, the practice of the 1930s consisted in dispatching powerful troubleshooters—a Kaganovich, Ordzhonikidze, Postyshev, or Kirov—to make things move, notably by forceful and energetic pressure (*nazhat'*) which sought the solution of problems "by any means" (*vo chto by to ne stalo*). It is symptomatic to hear these powerful bosses complain in the 1930s about the bureaucratism and red tape that by now had become painfully widespread in the system over which they were presiding. They were constantly trying to shake the bureaucracy up—and yet they remained quite impotent, in substance, in the face of the system they had to rely upon.

One term used to characterize the "creature" is *vedomstvennost'*, denoting a way and style of behavior by the *vedomstva*—a collective term for all kinds of bureaucracies, from ministries to other governmental agencies. Expansion of the economy, urbanization, education, and the growth of different spheres of government activities were all predictable sources of bureaucratic employment. But there were other propellants for the growth of officialdom and its power, as well as for the development of skills to defend vested interests. Imbalances and shortcomings that marred the developmental thrust of the 1930s demanded more agencies to deal with the growing waves of spontaneous social reaction to the tensions and strains of the times. Vedomstva were thus becoming the system's entrepreneurs, its controllers, and, for all practical purposes, the owners of the branch that each of them was entrusted with. The vedomstva quickly became power greedy and investment hungry. They learned to fight tooth and nail for resources, and they could get their way, as the main vehicles for economic action.

The efforts to curtail the growth of officialdom by the presumably powerful center is an excellent example of powerlessness before social processes, even if efforts are unleashed "from above." The party and government would almost routinely decree the curtailment of numbers of officials, dictate stringent rules, and create special agencies to supervise this action, but to no avail. The numbers of officials would soon reach new heights. The efforts were hopeless. Who but the vedomstva themselves could be entrusted with the job of cutting their own personnel? Since the ethos of those years was economic construction, the interest of the main driving power had to prevail.

Moreover, the party itself, now deeply involved in economic construction and, as noted, thoroughly "economized," at a later stage became hooked on the bureaucratized system and part and parcel of it. Under Stalin, as we know, a real war was conducted against cadres and against the whole growing administrative class through the process of the purges. This was a key strategy in the making of a despotic personal rule, but it also exposed its inherent weakness in coping with the crisis phenomena of those years. The accumulation of malfunctions, deviance, sluggishness, and social disorders did not abate. Authorities berated the very phenomenon they called *stikhiinost'*—spontaneity—and as the system was not yet really solid and most people could not yet cope with their new jobs, lines of responsibility were blurred and incompetence was rife. Such conditions were propitious for inducing paranoia in leaders, or in some of them, and hence also for a large-scale criminalization of a whole range of usually normal human behaviors. As most people and institutions worked poorly, the outcry against "sabotage" was heard ever more stridently; and although no one in particular was actually responsible, anyone could be declared guilty. The gates of arbitrariness and terror were thus thrust widely open. They had yet another social underpinning, stemming from the same "developmental" rush of the regime that added more ferocity to the repressive bent of the regime.

The stroiki have now to be brought up again. Although much was made of the new machinery imported and installed during the five-year plans, the work was still, to a large extent, done by the shovels and arms of enormous masses of a primitive, mostly rural labor force. The Russian term for "labor force"—*rabochaia sila*—was collapsed in the 1930s into the term *rabsila*, one that became a symbolic counterpart to official claims about proletarian rule and its full negation. Rabsila was plentiful, looked and was rather cheap, and was quite unceremoniously shuffled around, into and out of one stroika to another, its needs being the last on the agenda of managers and other bosses who were hard pressed to meet endless deadlines. The living conditions of workers on these stoiki were appalling, especially at the beginning. Even in the more settled conditions of older cities this was a time of barracks and crammed rooms for the rubsila—which was neither a class nor an assortment of individuals, but simply a mass. Towering over its members was a growing class of "nachalstvo" that tended often to mistreat them, except when there was a labor shortage. Workers were supposed to partake of the much vaunted *chuvstvo khoziaina*—the feeling of ownership—but very soon it was quite clear who the *khoziain* was.[8]

This attitude toward labor as a cheap and formless rabsila is one of the key features of industrialization in the Stalin era—and of Stalinism at large—notably because the crude treatment it represented in the initial stages carried within it the seeds of a further step downward, into the atrocious mistreatment of labor in the camps. Despite the official emphasis on heroics in those stroiki, Gulag was their obverse and their shadow.

The transformation of the rabsila into *zeki* was strengthened by a paradox. The ethos of economic development that dominated the era under consideration took on a perverse direction when the secret police were allowed to become an agency for industrial and other construction. Security agencies usually engage in surveillance, investigation, punishment. But in Stalin's Russia they knew by the 1930s that the road to more prestige and resources led through the economic function of construction, especially of projects to which a normal labor force would not be attracted or would have to be highly paid. Once granted this function, the NKVD would act like other agencies with plans and quotas for "recruitment" of camp inmates in huge numbers. The sprawling Gulag system was produced by a confluence of all these factors.

The whole industrialization story is therefore one of an economy launched and run "from above" that frustrated and undermined initiatives from below—without being able to prevent the self-defensive, informal, or illegal *(levye)* initiatives that proved to be unbeatable, and shadowed the system constantly. An inability to motivate, a low propensity for innovation, the creation of deep systemic imbalances, the low or falling productivity of labor and capital—all were exacting prices that had to be paid for the strategy chosen at the 1928–29 turning point.

State intervention in priority sectors managed to mend things here and there, but overall, most targets imposed by "the planning system" were met by techniques of dodging that in this economy operated almost like a "law." If technological innovation was translated into targets, it met the same fate. The system did better with motivating in emergencies like war, but this is what it actually was—"a permanent emergency" system, even in peace. The hierarchical bureaucratic model lent itself relatively well to this kind of activity—hence the term "command economy." But economic activity, although extremely intense, cannot be permanently mobilized from above. Constant mobilizations—an important and irritating feature of the 1930s—had to end up producing an enormous sluggishness. The economy could not be stimulated in the longer run to efficient use of resources and effective action without some leeway for autonomous activity from below conducted with a sense of self-interest, as understood and clearly perceived by the producers themselves.

Unfortunately for these producers, there were layers of decision makers alongside and above them with different self-interests. Hence yet another paradox of this economic system: although called *khoziaistvenniki,* the economic bureaucrats were an administrative not an economic class, situated not within but above the economy, as far as their interests were concerned. They were also, for all practical purposes, the owners of their respective branches. The well-known fact that they had to spend enormous amounts of time on "coordination" (the notorious and endless *soglasovyvanie*) showed that despite their monopolistic power, their ability to act and solve problems kept dwindling, reflecting the process of growing cumbersomeness and immobility—without the resources to cut through red tape that were still available to an omnipotent despot.

So long as its main features were not yet fully in place, the system still offered some economic growth and, especially after Stalin's death, improvements in standards of living. Some would even say that in the early Brezhnev period, both butter and cannons could be provided.

But once the characteristics emerged, they quickly began to coagulate into a mechanism of self-destruction. There were limits to incoherences the economy could stand, limits to resources that could be wasted, and limits to the credibility of the political institutions that were so tightly seated on this particular way of running the economy (as well as in other spheres of life).

The administrative character of the party—more, its basically economistic character—deprived it of the capacity to function as a political agency, whereas its functions in the economic mechanism made this so-called party just an organic part of an administration that was detaching itself from the reality of economics, just as it was already detaching itself from the reality of politics.

The whole story, therefore, turned out to be one of an economic system without economics and, in a parallel way, a political system without politics. Each component fed on the other and reinforced the mechanisms that kept undercutting its own vitality. The system had in the beginning an enormous thrust for growth, mostly of a quantitative (extensive) kind, and for self-perpetuation. But later, self-perpetuation counted for more than growth, hence a dwindling capacity for revitalization. There was not much planning either, unless a successful self-destruction can be listed under the heading of planning.

As the Soviet economy falls apart, it is easier—and necessary—to dwell on the roots of decline. Thirty years ago these roots could not be so clearly discerned, because the dynamism of Stalinist industrialization was not yet dampened and could even look impressive.

NOTES

1. David S. Landes, *The Unbound Prometheus* (London, 1969), p. 7.

2. This paper was written during a leave that was supported by a grant from the National Endowment for the Humanities.

3. This is really the idea Trotsky expressed in his *History of the Russian Revolution,* chap. 1, entitled "The Peculiarities of Russia's Historical Development," which he clearly developed under the influence of other Russian historians and thinkers. Interestingly, Trotsky did not apply this idea to Stalin's time, probably because he believed a "workers' state" still persisted under Stalin.

4. I argued this in my contribution to the debate on the feasibility of the First Five-Year Plan, initiated by a pioneering piece by Holland Hunter, with comments by Robert Campbell, Stephen F. Cohen, and myself. The title of my contribution was "The Disappearance of Planning in the Plan"—which is the thesis in question. See *Slavic Review,* June 1973, pp. 273–87.

5. Janos Kornai, *Growth, Shortage and Efficiency: A Microdynamic Model of the Socialist Economy* (Berkeley and Los Angeles, 1982).

6. There are numerous editions. See L. Trotsky, *The Challenge of the Left Opposition (1924–1925)* (New York, 1975), a useful compendium of different texts, "The New Course" among them.

7. "Zametki Ekonomista," *Pravda,* September 30, 1928.

8. This meant that workers were supposed to share as members of the "ruling class." It was one of the most damaging red herrings of official propaganda.

GUIDE TO FURTHER READING

Compiled by Steven Coe

1. Industrialization, Labor, Society

A standard, comprehensive overview of the Stalinist period of industrialization is Naum Jasny, *Soviet Industrialization, 1928–1952* (Chicago, 1961). A number of book-length studies concentrating on the social impact of the First and Second Five-Year plans have appeared in recent years: Hiroaki Kuromiya, *Stalin's Industrial Revolution* (Cambridge University Press, 1988); Donald Filtzer, *Soviet Workers and Stalinist Industrialization: The Formation of Modern Soviet Production Relations* (Armonk, 1986); and Vladimir Andrle, *Workers in Stalin's Russia: Industrialization and Social Change in a Planned Economy* (New York, 1988). R. W. Davies, *The Soviet Economy in Turmoil, 1929–1930* (London, 1989), describes the chaos at its height. Several issues arising out of the process and problems of industrialization are treated in papers (some in French, some in English) presented at a French conference in 1981 and published in *L'Industrialisation de l'URSS dans les années trente* (Paris, 1982). The Stakhanovite movement is the focus of Lewis H. Siegelbaum, *Stakhanovism and the Politics of Productivity in the USSR, 1935–41* (Cambridge University Press, 1988), and Robert Maier, *Die Stachanov-Bewegung 1935–38: Der Stachanovismus als tragendes und verschaerfendes Moment der Stalinisierung der Sowjetischen Gesellschafts* (Stuttgart, 1990). Basic Soviet studies are A. I. Vdovin and V. Z. Drobizhev, *Rost rabochego klassa SSSR 1917–40 gg.* (Moscow, 1976), and A. M. Panfilova, *Formirovanie rabochego klassa SSSR v gody pervoi piatiletki (1928–32)* (Moscow, 1964). The three volumes of the series *Industrializatsiia SSSR, dokumenty i materialy (sbornik)* 1929–32 (Moscow, 1970), 1933–37 (1971), and 1938–41 (1973) contain a wealth of primary material. Soviet "Taylorism" (NOT in Russian, "scientific organization of labor") is the subject of Melanie Tatur, *"Wissenschaftliche Arbeitsorganisation"— Arbeitswissenschaften und Arbeitsorganisation in der Sowjetunion 1921–35* (Wiesbaden, 1979) and Samuel Lieberstein, "Technology, Work and Sociology in the USSR: The NOT Movement," *Technology and Culture*, 1975, 16, no. 1.

Several Americans spent time in different Soviet cities as workers and advisers during the 1930s and wrote books about their experience. John Scott, *Behind the Urals* (New York, 1942; reprinted by Indiana University Press, 1973 and 1990), is the most famous. Others are Walter Arnold Ruckeyser, *Working for the Soviets: An American Engineer in Russia* (New York, 1932), and Andrew Smith, *I Was a Soviet Worker* (London, 1937). For more general and wide-ranging descriptions of Soviet society in the 1930s from the perspective of American journalists, see Maurice Hindus, *The Great Offensive* (London, 1933) (the best known of several books he wrote about the Soviet Union in the 1930s and '40s); William Henry Chamberlin, *Soviet Russia* (rev. ed., Boston, 1935), and the recently republished Eugene Lyons, *Assignment in Utopia* (New York, 1937; New Brunswick, 1991), and Louis Fischer, *Soviet Journey* (1935; Greenwood Press, 1970). Fischer's earlier *Machines and Men in Russia* (New York, 1932) includes some famous photographs of workers in Magnitogorsk by Margaret Bourke-White.

Of numerous biographies of Stalin, the best for understanding the general political situation of the country in the late 1920s and early 1930s is Isaac Deutscher, *Stalin: A Political Biography* (2d ed., Oxford University Press, 1966). Other good, comprehensive biographies are by Robert Tucker, *Stalin in Power: Revolution from Above, 1928–41* (New York, 1990) (the second of three projected volumes), and Adam Ulam, *Stalin: The Man and His Era* (New York, 1973), which was recently reprinted.

Other topics involving social changes during these years are treated by Frank J. Miller in *Folklore for Stalin: Russian Folklore and Pseudofolklore of the Stalin Era* (Armonk, 1990) and Ann T. Baum, *Komsomol Participation in the Soviet First Five-Year Plan* (Basingstoke, 1987). Probably the best contemporary fictional account of Soviet industrialization is Valentin P. Kataev, *Time, Forward!* (1933; Bloomington, 1976).

2. Economic Theory and Policy

Excellent accounts of the theoretical economic debates preceding the industrialization drive are in Alexander Erlich, *The Soviet Industrialization Debate, 1924–28* (Cambridge, Mass., 1960); Nicolas Spulber (ed.), *Foundations of Soviet Strategy for Economic Growth* (Bloomington, 1964), and his *Soviet Strategy for Economic Growth* (Bloomington, 1964) chaps. 1–4; and Eugene Zaleski, *Planning for Economic Growth in the Soviet Union, 1918–32* (Chapel Hill, 1971). A brief discussion is available in Alec Nove, *An Economic History of the USSR* (Penguin, 1982), chap. 5. The views of some of the major protagonists in these debates have been collected in Evgenii A. Preobrazhensky, *The Crisis of Soviet Industrialization* (White Plains, 1979); Nikolai Bukharin, *Put' k sotsializmu: Izbrannye proizvedeniia*, with an introduction by Viktor P. Danilov and S. A. Krasilnikov (Novosibirsk, 1990); and Aleksei I. Rykov, *Izbrannye proizvedeniia* (Moscow, 1990). Good, brief accounts of economic issues and problems generated by crash industrialization are in William L. Blackwell (ed.), *Russian Economic Development from Peter the Great to Stalin* (New York, 1974), and chap. 8 in Nove's *Economic History*. Selected papers from the Second World Congress for Soviet and East European Studies appear with responses in *Soviet Investment for Planned Industrialization, 1929–37: Policy and Practice* (Berkeley, 1984), ed. R. W. Davies. A considerably more detailed, more massive study is Eugene Zaleski, *Stalinist Planning for Economic Growth, 1933–52* (Chapel Hill, 1980), parts I and II. Tatjana Kirstein's *Sowjetische Industrialisierung—geplanter oder spontaner Prozess: eine Strukturanalyse der wirtschaftspolitischen Entscheidungsprozesses beim Aufbau der Ural-Kuzneck-Kombinats 1918–30* (Baden-Baden, 1979) is a detailed study of the planning process in a single area. Anne D. Rassweiler's "Soviet Labor Policy in the First Five-Year Plan: The Dneprostroi Experience," *Slavic Review* 42, Summer 1983, no. 2, is a short version of her *Generation of Power* (Oxford, 1989). The period between the first two Five-Year Plans is the focus of R. W. Davies in "The Socialist Market: A Debate in Soviet Industry 1932–33," *Slavic Review* 42, Winter 1983, no. 4.

3. Collectivization and Agriculture

Collectivization was the other side of the coin of industrialization, and several excellent studies of this "assault on the countryside" have appeared in the past few decades. The background to collectivization is discussed in Michal Reiman, *The Birth of Stalinism* (Bloomington, 1987), and in part II of Moshe Lewin's *Making of the Soviet System* (New York, 1985). The process of what led to the decision is examined by Lewin in detail in *Russian Peasants and Soviet Power: A Study of Collectivization* (New York, 1975) and in chaps. 6 and 7 of Nove's *Economic History*. Collectivization as a whole is the focus of R. W. Davies's *Socialist Offensive: The Collectivization of Soviet Agriculture, 1929–30* and *The Soviet Collective Farm, 1929–30* (London, 1980), and Viktor P. Danilov (ed.), *Ocherki istorii kollektivizatsii sel'skogo khoziaistva v soiuznykh respublikakh (sbornik statei)* (Moscow, 1963). Specific aspects of collectivization are the topics of other works: N. A. Ivnitskii, *Klassovaia bor'ba v derevne i likvidatsiia kulachestva kak klassa 1929–32 gg.* (Moscow, 1972); Iurii V. Arutiunian, "Kollektivizatsiia sel'skogo khoziaistva i vysvobozhdenie rabochei sily dlia promyshlennosti," in *Formirovanie i razvitie sovetskogo rabochego klassa, 1917–61 gg.* (Moscow, 1964); and Lynne Viola, *The Best Sons of the Fatherland* (Oxford, 1987). *Dokumenty svidetel'stvuiut: Iz istorii derevni nakanune i v khode kollektivizatsii, 1927–32 gg.* (Moscow, 1989), edited by Danilov and Ivnitskii, is a rich collection of peasants' letters, regional officials' reports, minutes, resolutions of local organizations, and other primary documentary source material. The horrifying results of collectivization in the Soviet Ukraine are presented in Robert Conquest, *Harvest of Sorrow* (London, 1986).

Two well-known debates about the short- and long-term results of collectivization for agriculture and for the economy are James Millar and Alec Nove, "Was Stalin Really Necessary? A Debate on Collectivization," in *Problems of Communism* 25, July–August 1976, no. 4, and more recently, Holland Hunter and Lynne Viola in *Slavic Review* 47, Summer 1988, no. 2. David J. Morrison's "Soviet Peasantry's Real Expenditure in Socialised Trade, 1928–34," *Soviet Studies* 41, 1989, no. 2, is a recent consideration of a contentious issue.

For information on how collective farms worked in the 1930s and the fate of the peasantry up to World War II, see Naum Jasny, *The Socialized Agriculture of the USSR* (Stanford, 1949); Merle Fainsod, *Smolensk under Soviet Rule* (New York, 1963), a work based on Soviet archives from the Smolensk region captured by the Nazis during the war, shipped to Berlin, then confiscated by the Americans; and these Soviet works: *Istoriia sovetskogo krest'ianstva i kolkhoznogo stroitel'stva v SSSR* (Moscow, 1963); V. P. Danilov, M. P. Kim, and N. V. Tropkin (eds.), *Sovetskoe krest'ianstvo: Kratkii ocherk istorii 1917–70 gg.* (2d enl. ed., Moscow, 1973), sec. III; *Sotsial'nyi oblik kolkhoznoi molodezhi: Po materialam sotsiologicheskikh obsledovanii 1938 i 1969 gg.* (Moscow, 1976); M. A. Viltsan, *Sovetskaia derevnia nakanune velikoi otechestvennoi voiny (1938–41)* (Moscow, 1970); and for Western Siberia in particular, Nikolai Ia. Gushchin, E. V. Kosheleva, and V. G. Charushin, *Krest'ianstvo zapadnoi sibiri v dovoennye gody (1935–41)* (Novosibirsk, 1975). Vasily Grossman's novel *Forever Flowing* (New York, 1972), written in the early 1960s, contains the best fictional account of the aftermath of collectivization, while the penultimate chapter of Lev Kopelev's *Education of a True Believer* (Random House) movingly recalls the violence of grain procurement in the Ukraine.

4. Technical Intelligentsia, Management, Mobility

The technical intelligentsia and factory managers in the world's first workers' state—a key component of industrialization—are studied in Kendall Bailes, *Technology and Society under Lenin and Stalin: Origins of the Soviet Technical Intelligentsia, 1917–41* (Princeton, 1978), and in Nicholas Lampert, *The Technical Intelligentsia and the Soviet State* (New York, 1979), which covers the years 1928 to 1935. Managers and management are emphasized in David Granick, *The Red Executive: A Study of the Organization Man in Russian Industry* (Garden City, 1960), and in the more recent book by Walter Suess, *Der Betrieb in der UdSSR: Stellung, Organisation und Management, 1917–32* (Frankfurt-on-Main, 1981). Production associations, standing midway between top industry officialdom and factory managers until they were abolished in 1932, are the subject of Iurii K. Avdakov, *Proizvodstvennye ob'edineniia i ikh rol' v organizatsii upravleniia sovetskoi promyshlennost'iu, 1917–32 gg.* (Moscow, 1973).

A good fictional account of life nearly at the top of Soviet society is Anatoly Rybakov, *Children of the Arbat* (Boston, 1988), which was originally written in the 1960s.

Issues of social mobility, the problems created and opportunities available in conditions of rapid and wholesale advancement from "the bench" or shop floor to various levels of management, were first raised by Sheila Fitzpatrick in *Education and Social Mobility in the Soviet Union 1921–34* (Cambridge University Press, 1979) and are also discussed in her article "The Russian Revolution and Social Mobility: A Re-examination of the Question of Social Support for the Soviet Regime in the 1920s and 1930s," *Politics and Society* 13, 1984, no. 2. These issues are also discussed by firsthand observers such as John Scott in *Behind the Urals.* Technical schools are the subject of Marcel Anstett, *La formation de la main-d'oeuvre qualifiée en Union soviétique de 1917 à 1954* (Paris, 1958). Closely related issues of social mobility and the "Cultural Revolution" of the First Five-Year Plan which made it possible are discussed in Sheila Fitzpatrick (ed.), *Cultural Revolution in Russia, 1928–31* (Bloomington, 1978), and by Paul Josephson in "Physics, Stalinist Politics of Science and the Cultural Revolution," *Soviet Studies* 40, 1988, no. 2 (See also section 7 of this guide for discussions of Soviet science in its relation to the Cultural Revolution.)

5. General Theoretical Works on Stalinism, Totalitarianism, and Its Critics

The "classic texts" delineating what has come to be called the "totalitarian model" include Hannah Arendt, *The Origins of Totalitarianism* (New York, 1951); Carl J. Friedrich and Zbigniew K. Brzezinski, *Totalitarian Dictatorship and Autocracy* (2d ed., New York, 1966); and W. W. Rostow, *The Dynamics of Soviet Society* (New York, 1954). An early and concise summary of different Marxist approaches to study of the Soviet Union can be found in Antonio Carlo, "The Socio-Economic Nature of the USSR," *Telos,* Fall 1974, no. 21. David Lane, in *The Socialist Industrial State: Towards a Political Sociology of State Socialism* (Boulder, 1976), analyzes several different analytical frameworks. An influential set of articles discussing the nature of Stalinism was published in Robert Tucker (ed), *Stalinism: Essays in Historical Interpretation* (New York, 1977). Moshe Lewin has also written insightfully on the problems of Stalinism in part III of his *Making of the Soviet System.* The most coherent and thorough critique of the "totalitarian model" and its adjuncts is developed into a unique version of the nature of Stalinism in Stephen F. Cohen, *Rethinking the Soviet Experience: Politics and History since 1917* (Oxford, 1985). A view of Stalinism by a prominent "revisionist," Sheila Fitzpatrick, is "New Perspectives on Stalinism," *Russian Review* 45, October 1986, no. 4, followed by a lively exchange of opinions by other scholars. More responses to this article appeared in *Russian Review* 46, October 1987, no. 4.

6. Purges, Prison Camps, Forced Labor

This aspect of Soviet life in the 1930s is now becoming clearer with the release of suppressed archival information and data from the secret and unpublished census of 1937 which fueled a great deal of speculation and controversy. Basic surveys include David J. Dallin and Boris I. Nicolaevsky, *Forced Labor in Soviet Russia* (New Haven, 1947); Robert Conquest, *The Great Terror* (rev. ed., Harmondsworth, 1971); and a recently revised and expanded edition of Roy Medvedev's *Let History Judge: The Origins and Consequences of Stalinism* (New York, 1989). The best-known and most comprehensive work, combining personal experience with personal investigation, is Alexander I. Solzhenitsyn's monumental *Gulag Archipelago 1918–56: An Experiment in Literary Investigation* in three volumes (New York, 1973, 1975, 1978); it was condensed by the author into one volume published in 1985. Good memoirs of this period are those by Eugenia S. Ginzburg, *Journey into the Whirlwind* (New York, 1967), and *Within the Whirlwind* (New York, 1981); and by Nadezhda Mandelshtam, *Hope against Hope* (New York, 1970), and *Hope Abandoned* (New York, 1974).

A challenging interpretation of the purges of the 1930s and especially of 1937 (specifically questioning the interpretation of Merle Fainsod's *Smolensk under Soviet Rule* and using the Smolensk Archives as the main source) is in J. Arch Getty, *The Origins of the Great Purges: The Soviet Communist Party Reconsidered* (Cambridge University Press, 1985). A shorter and preliminary version of Getty's controversial interpretation appears in "The Party and the Purge in Smolensk: 1933–37," *Slavic Review* 42, Spring 1983, no. 1, where it is critiqued and challenged in responses from other scholars. A recent consideration of the workings of the judicial process is Peter Solomon, Jr., "Soviet Criminal Justice and the Great Terror," *Slavic Review* 46, Fall-Winter 1987, nos. 3–4. The most recent revelations about mortality rates in the 1930s (touching on the number of victims of the 1933–34 famine, of collectivization, and of the purges and on the prison-camp population) are discussed by Stephen G. Wheatcroft in "More Light on the Scale of Repression and Excess Mortality in the Soviet Union in the 1930s," *Soviet Studies* 42, 1990, no. 2; follow-up notes by Alec Nove appear there and in vol. 42, no. 4. A whole series of articles treating this controversial subject appeared in *Soviet Studies* and *Slavic Review* in the 1980s.

7. Art, Literature, and Science

In addition to articles in *Cultural Revolution* (Sheila Fitzpatrick, ed.) on literature, town planning, scholarship, and related topics, for discussions of "socialist realism" see Katerina Clark, *The Soviet Novel: History as Ritual* (Chicago, 1981); Harriet Borland, *Soviet Literary Theory and Practice during the First Five-Year Plan* (New York, 1950); C. V. James, *Soviet Socialist Realism: Origins and Theory* (London, 1973); and Ronald Hingley, *Russian Writers and Soviet Society, 1917–78* (New York, 1979). For a wide range of examples of socialist realist literature see *From Furmanov to Sholokhov: An Anthology of Classics of Socialist Realims* (Ann Arbor, 1988). Rosalinde Sartori's *Pressefotografie und Industrialisierung in der Sowjetunion: Pravda 1925–33* (Wiesbaden, 1981) is an interesting look at both the subject matter and the layout of photos printed in Pravda and how they were made to reflect socialist realist values. For changes in architectural styles, see Anatole Kopp, *Town and Revolution: Soviet Architecture and City Planning, 1917–35* (New York, 1970). For Stalinist architecture in particular, see Kopp, *L'Architecture de la période stalinienne* (Grenoble, 1978).

There are a number of books dealing with the institutions and practice of science in these years. Two "classics" of the social history of Soviet science are by David Joravsky: *Soviet Marxism and Natural Science, 1917–32* (New York, 1961) and *The Lysenko Affair* (Cambridge, Mass., 1970). Recent articles dealing with the interaction of Stalinism and science are Joravsky's "Stalinist Mentality and the Higher Learning," *Slavic Review* 42, Winter 1983, no. 4, and John Barber's "Establishment of Intellectual Orthodoxy in the USSR, 1928–34," *Past and Present*, 1979, no. 83. Also see Kendall Bailes, *Science and Russian Culture in an Age of Revolutions: V. I. Vernadsky and His Scientific School, 1863–1945* (Bloomington, 1990); Loren Graham (ed.), *Science and the Soviet Social Order* (Cambridge, Mass., 1990); and, for early struggles of environmentalists with industrialism, Douglas R. Weiner, *Models of Nature: Ecology, Conservation and Cultural Revolution* (Bloomington, 1988).

CONTRIBUTORS

Katerina Clark is Associate Professor of Comparative Literature and Slavic Languages and Literatures at Yale University and the author of *The Soviet Novel: History as Ritual* and (with Michael Holquist) *Mikhail Bakhtin.*

R. W. Davies is Emeritus Professor of Soviet Economic Studies in the Centre for Russian and East European Studies, University of Birgmingham, England. He is the author of *Soviet History in the Gorbachev Revolution* and a multivolume history of Soviet industrialization, the latest volume being *The Soviet Economy in Turmoil, 1929–1930.*

Geoff Eley is Professor of History at the University of Michigan. His publications include *Reshaping the German Right: Radical Nationalism and Political Change after Bismarck, The Peculiarities of German History* (with David Blackbourn), and *From Unification to Nazism.* He is finishing a book on the European Left in the nineteenth and twentieth centuries.

Sheila Fitzpatrick is Professor of History at the University of Chicago. Her most recent books are *A Researcher's Guide to Sources on Soviet Social History in the 1930s* (coedited with Lynne Viola) and *The Cultural Front: Power and Culture in Revolutionary Russia.* She is completing a study of the Russian village after collectivization.

Stephen Kotkin is Assistant Professor of History at Princeton University. He is the author of *Magnetic Mountain: Stalinism as a Civilization.*

Hiroaki Kuromiya is Assistant Professor of History at Indiana University, Bloomington. He is the author of *Stalin's Industrial Revolution: Politics and Workers, 1928–1932* and is completing a historical study of the Donbass.

Moshe Lewin is Professor of History at the University of Pennsylvania and the author of *Russian Peasants and Soviet Power, Lenin's Last Struggle, Political Undercurrents in Soviet Economic Debates, The Making of the Soviet System,* and *The Gorbachev Phenomenon.*

Stephan Merl is Professor of History at the University of Bielefeld, Germany. He is the author of *Der Agrarmarkt und die Neue Ökonomische Politik, Die Anfänge der Kollektivierung in der Sowjetunion, Sozialer Aufstieg im sowjetischen Kolchossystem der 30er Jahre,* and *Bauern unter Stalin.*

William G. Rosenberg is Professor of History at the University of Michigan. He is coauthor (with Diane P. Koenker) of *Strikes and Revolution in*

Russia, 1917, author of *Liberals in the Russian Revolution* and (with Marylyn B. Young) *Transforming Russia and China,* and editor of *Bolshevik Visions: First Phase of the Cultural Revolution in Soviet Russia.*

Don K. Rowney is Professor of History at Bowling Green State University. His publications include *Transition to Technocracy: The Structural Origins of the Soviet Administrative State.* He is completing a study of industrial administration in Russia.

David R. Shearer is Assistant Professor of History at the University of Delaware. He is completing a social study of the Soviet industrial system, 1926–34.

Lewis H. Siegelbaum is Professor of History at Michigan State University and the author of *The Politics of Industrial Mobilization in Russia, 1915–1917* and *Stakhanovism and the Politics of Productivity in the USSR, 1935–1941.*

Peter H. Solomon, Jr., is Professor of Political Science at the University of Toronto. He is the author of *Soviet Criminologists and Criminal Policy: Specialists in Policy-making* and *Criminal Justice Policy from Research to Reform.* He is completing a study of Soviet criminal justice under Stalin.

Ronald Grigor Suny is the Alex Manoogian Professor of Modern Armenian History at the University of Michigan. He is the author of *The Baku Commune, 1917–1918: Class and Nationality in the Russian Revolution, Armenia in the Twentieth Century, The Making of the Georgian Nation,* and *Looking toward Ararat: Armenia in Modern History.* He is working on a biography of the young Stalin.

INDEX

"Administrative command system," xviii, 105; critiques of, 106–108, 115, 216, 283–84; innovation in, 117–18; markets in, 118–19
AMO automobile plant (Moscow), 208
Artisanal organization of production, 194–95, 203–204; *ad hoc* nature of, 214; effect on industrial organization of, 216; reversion to, 209–211, 213–14
Associations. *See Obedineniia*

Backwardness, 8–9, 257–58, 273, 275
Black markets in documents, 87–88, 90
Bureaucracy: growth of, 135–36, 142–43, 205, 277, 280–81, 283; mobilization of, 64–66. *See also* Employment, rural; Industrial administration; Management

Class background: of foremen, 174, 176 (table); of industrial administration management, 131–32 (table); of industrial administration management in France and U.S., 132–34; of industrial administration personnel, 139–142 (tables)
"Class enemies." *See* Industrialization, Soviet; Sabotage
Coal miners: absenteeism and turnover among, 147–48, 158; "labor aristocracy" among, 150; mechanization and, 150–51; seasonal movements of, 148–49; peasant background of, 148; relations with management, 153–55, 158
Collective farm administration, 48–49; compensation of, 52; party membership of, 47–48, 51 (tables); proliferation of, 52; turnover among, 50, 51 (table); women in, 50–52 (table). *See also* Employment, rural: state employees and
Collective farms: differentiation in prosperity of, 42. *See also* Rural-urban migration; Employment, rural
Collectivization, 18, 22; results of, 33, 41, 47, 276
Commissariat of Heavy Industry (NKTP): creation of (1932), 124; Ordzhonikidze and senior managers at, 138; personnel of, 132–33, 137, 139–42 (tables). *See also* Industrial administration; Management
Commissariat of Justice *(Narkomiust)*, 226, 228

Commissariat of Light Industry (NKLP): creation of (1932), 124; personnel of, 132–133, 137, 139–42 (tables). *See also* Industrial administration; Management
Commissariat of Posts and Telegraphs: senior administrators of, 132–33, 138
Commissariat of the Timber Industry (NKLes): creation of (1932), 124; personnel of, 132–33, 137, 139–42 (tables). *See also* Industrial administration; Management
Communist Party: challenge to Stalin's leadership (1932–33) among, 156–58; changes in fictional role of, 258–59, 262; "depoliticization" of, 274–75; "economization" of, 276, 278–79, 281; local authority of contested, 212; membership among industrial administration management and personnel, 138–42 (tables); membership in countryside, 47–48, 51 (tables); membership among foremen, 176–77 (table); mobilization of, 64–66; resurgence of local activism of, 214–15; transformation into administrative agency, 284. *See also* Employment, rural; Foremen; Industrial administration; *Komsomol;* Management
Convict labor, 17–18, 23–24, 33, 259, 282
The Convicts (film, 1937), 259
Crimes, industrial, 227, 228–29; blamed for causing accidents, 230–32; campaigns in prosecution of, 226, 229, 236–38, 243; large range of, 281–82; prosecution of, 229–30, 237–38, 241; as scapegoating device, 158, 233, 239; symbolic function of, 235, 239, 241–42; types of, 225–26, 235. *See also* Judges; Industrialization, Soviet; Sabotage
Crimes, political, 225
Crimes, rural administrative: prosecution of, 240–41

Dekulakization, 17–18; deportation in, 24, 27, 70–71, 72; and entry into labor force, 23–25; flight as response to, 26–27; imprisonment in, 23–24; legislation on (1930), 22–23
Donbass (Don River Basin) coal mines: setting for film, 260. *See also* Coal miners

292